horse-and-buggy MENNONITES

PENNSYLVANIA GERMAN HISTORY AND CULTURE SERIES,
NUMBER 7

Publications of the Pennsylvania German Society,
Volume 40

EDITOR
Simon J. Bronner
The Pennsylvania State University, Harrisburg

EDITORIAL BOARD
C. Richard Beam, Millersville University
Aaron S. Fogleman, Northern Illinois University
Mark Häberlein, University of Bamberg, Germany
Donald B. Kraybill, Elizabethtown College
Kenneth McLaughlin, University of Waterloo, Canada
A. Gregg Roeber, The Pennsylvania State University, University Park
John D. Roth, Goshen College
Hans Schneider, Philipps University, Marburg, Germany
Denise A. Seachrist, Kent State University, Trumbull
Richard E. Wentz, Arizona State University
Marianne S. Wokeck, Indiana University—Purdue University, Indianapolis
Don Yoder, University of Pennsylvania

horse-and-buggy MENNONITES
hoofbeats of humility in a postmodern world

DONALD B. KRAYBILL *and* JAMES P. HURD

The Pennsylvania State University Press, University Park, Pennsylvania

Library of Congress Cataloging-in-Publication Data

Kraybill, Donald B.
    Horse-and-buggy Mennonites : hoofbeats of humility
    in a postmodern world / Donald B. Kraybill, James P. Hurd.
        p.   cm. — (Publications of the Pennsylvania German Society; v. 40
    Pennsylvania German history and culture series ; no. 7) (Pennsylvania German
    history and culture)
Includes bibliographical references and index.
ISBN 0-271-02865-3 (cloth : alk. paper)
ISBN 0-271-02866-1 (pbk. : alk. paper)
1. Wenger Mennonites.
2. Groffdale Conference Mennonite Church.
I. Hurd, James P., 1941– .
II. Title.
III. Publications of the Pennsylvania German Society (2001) ; v. 40.
IV. Publications of the Pennsylvania German Society (2001). Pennsylvania
    German history and culture series ; no. 7.

GR110.P4 A372 vol. 40
[BX8129.O43]
974.8'00431 s—dc22
[305.6/89]
2005036337

Second printing, 2006

The Pennsylvania State University Press is a member of the Association of American University Presses.

It is the policy of The Pennsylvania State University Press to use acid-free paper. This book is printed on Natures Natural, containing 50% post-consumer waste, and meets the minimum requirements of American National Standard for Information Sciences—Permanence of Paper for Printed Library Material, ANSI z39.48–1992.

❖ contents

❖ tables and diagrams

❖ preface

Automobile enthusiasts in San Francisco taunted Horatio Nelson Jackson with a $50 wager in May 1903. Did he have the courage to drive a car from San Francisco to New York in three months, over thousands of miles of treacherous roads? A physician from Vermont, Jackson was up to the challenge. With bicycle mechanic Sewall K. Crocker and a bulldog named Bud, he set off in a 1903 Winton touring car for a harrowing journey, hampered by endless repairs and scores of bumps and bruises. Despite the disruptions, the trio arrived in New York just in time to claim the title: America's first cross-continental drivers.[1]

Jackson's cross-country drive opened America's love affair with the car. Millions of Americans soon were driving the horseless carriages that Henry Ford and other automakers had begun cranking out of their assembly lines.[2] The advent of high-performance cars and the interstate highway system in the last half of the twentieth century soon turned the coast-to-coast trek into a three-day trip. In 2003, a century after Jackson's trip, U.S. households claimed more vehicles than drivers—some 204 million household vehicles for only 191 million drivers.[3] Americans had fallen in love with the car. Indeed, there remained nothing more American than driving one. It had become the symbol of technological achievement, progress, mobility, and independence—the chief icon of American identity.

Not all Americans, however, embraced the car. On a Sunday morning in 1927, the love affair came to a screeching halt in a Mennonite church in eastern Pennsylvania, when half of the congregation refused the communion wine offered by Bishop Moses Horning. The boycott of this holiest of Mennonite moments was, in fact, a boycott of the car, which Bishop Horning had finally sanctioned after years of debate. The controversy over the car led to the formation of the Wenger Mennonites, named for their first leader and bishop, Joseph O. Wenger.

This book tells the story of the Wenger Mennonites, Americans whose cultural habits sometimes appear un-American and who stand on the margins of mainstream culture. They speak a German dialect, shun cars and computers, wear distinctive dress, and finish their formal education at the eighth grade. Yet they have made selective accommodations to modernity over the years: though they forbid owning cars, for example, they do ride in them at times. We might expect a horse-driving group to be on the wane in the twenty-first century.[4] Instead, the Wengers are thriving. The initial cluster of two hundred Wenger families in 1927 has grown to nearly 18,000 people living in nine different states. This rapid growth continues to dispel doomsayers' predictions of the demise of Old Order societies.

These horse-and-buggy pilgrims are strangers in a postmodern world. In some ways they are premodern folks—rejecting the car, the ultimate symbol of modernity, as well as the World Wide Web, the wily symbol of postmodernity. Clinging to rural traditions, appealing to ancient authorities, promoting humility rather than individualism, and spurning mass media and high school, these religious pilgrims have not acquiesced to many of the pressures of the modern world. But, as we will discover, they have selectively modernized some facets of their society.

The Wenger story has rarely been told, partly because the Amish, who are more populous and picturesque in their distinctive dress and beards, often eclipse the Wengers in the public eye. The Wengers represent a small portion of all Mennonites in the United States, but they are the largest of several Old Order Mennonite groups. And, apart from the Amish, they are the largest body of Pennsylvania German speakers in North America. Given their strong commitment to the dialect, the Wengers will likely play an essential role in preserving it.

The Wenger story is important not only because of their success on the margins of the modern world but also because they have preserved many religious rituals—rituals abandoned by droves of other Mennonites, who have absorbed much of the larger American culture. The Wengers have retained age-old rituals rooted in Swiss–South German Anabaptist life as well as eighteenth- and nineteenth-century American Mennonite practices. In this sense, the Wengers offer a significant cultural site for studying the preservation of religious ritual in the face of modernity. Despite conserving many religious traditions, the Wengers do change their socioeconomic practices, albeit with caution.

Our story employs the tools of cultural analysis to capture the Wengers' worldview and values. Cultural codes embedded in the structure and meaning of a language—in this case, Pennsylvania German—shape the way members of a society see and experience the world around them. The values and dispositions ensconced in a culture's worldview guide its perception and response to the larger society.[5] We are particularly interested in the web of meanings spun by Wenger culture over time, a web that enables its members to make sense of the world and their place in it. Thus, we have peppered the text with quotations from our interviews to allow the Wengers to tell their own story in their own voice.

We have not written a systematic history of the Wenger people, even though we have used historical materials whenever possible to show the historical context of current debates. We have focused on values, identity, ritual, and technology—overlooking many topics that would beg for coverage in a more comprehensive study. Moreover, rather than imposing one conceptual scheme on the Wenger story, we have used a variety of interpretive perspectives to understand the Wenger saga.

We have sought to tell the Wenger tale with a spirit of empathetic understanding, trying to see things from their perspective within their world. Two key questions have guided our investigation. How is this car-rejecting group able not only to survive but also to thrive in a postmodern world? And what, if anything, can those of us immersed in the mainstream of contemporary culture learn from these pilgrims on the margins?

We have organized the text into nine chapters. In the first chapter, we provide a sweeping overview of the Wenger community and its place in the larger world of Anabaptist groups. We explore the values, beliefs, and symbols of Wenger culture in Chapter 2 and then the historical roots of Wenger identity in Chapter 3. The social architecture of the community is the subject of Chapter 4, and Chapter 5 describes religious rituals. We focus on life passages in Chapter 6 and on work in Chapter 7. Chapter 8 highlights the role of technology and social change. In the concluding chapter, we explore the Wengers' relationships with other religious groups as well as their engagement with the postmodern world.

Although the official name of the group is the Groffdale Conference Mennonite Church, we refer to them as Wengers, because this is what they call themselves and how they are known among their neighbors. Following Wenger usage, the term *church* refers to the community of believers, not to a building. A church *district* entails the congregation of people who meet for services at a particular *churchhouse*. We use the terms *district* and *congregation* interchangeably throughout the text. The terms *ministers* and *ministry* refer to all three ordained leadership roles (bishop, preacher, deacon). *Boy* and *girl*, according to Wenger usage, refer to both children and adolescents. Wenger consistently use counsel meeting, not council meeting, in their English translation of *Rot*. We use a variety of words—non-Wengers, outsiders, moderns—to refer to people outside of Wenger society, terms that should be clear as they appear in the text. Beyond two standard German words (*Gelassenheit* and *Ordnung*), we occasionally use Pennsylvania German words in the text as reminders that daily discourse in Wenger life is in a German dialect. Although some dictionaries of Pennsylvania German have been compiled, the dialect is primarily an oral language; its words, sounds, and spellings vary considerably among cultural groups. Pennsylvania German dictionaries do not include all of the unique Wenger usages, so we consulted several Wengers for the proper spelling and translation of dialect words that appear in the text. (See Appendix F for a listing.)[6]

Social scientists and philosophers engage in lively debates about the distinction between modern and postmodern societies—debates that this book does not seek to unpack. In any event, the beginning of the Wenger story in 1927 is rooted in a rejection of some aspects of the modern era; however, now, in the twenty-first century, the Wengers find themselves living in an increasingly postmodern world. *Modernity* is, of course, a slippery term that we use in two ways in the text: to describe the historic changes produced by the Age of Enlightenment, and to describe contemporary society. We sometimes use the term *moderns* as a broad label for members of contemporary society and use the word *modern* to designate contemporary forms of social organization in American society. *Postmodern*, in our usage, refers to the emergent forms of culture and social organization in the twenty-first century.

In order to protect the anonymity of those who talked with us about their lives and community, we have, with a few exceptions, not identified them. We have occasionally used pseudonyms. Within the context of Wenger culture, members are admonished neither to take credit for achievements nor to seek publicity, lest it lead to pride. We have sought to respect their requests for anonymity by not identifying them by name unless their story is already public knowledge.

❖ acknowledgments

We owe our greatest debt to the Wenger people who graciously opened their homes, schools, and churches to us and granted us interviews during the ten-year period of our fieldwork. Eight Wenger readers provided comments and corrections on an early draft of the manuscript. Several members gathered historical information and provided in-depth descriptions of cultural activities. We are deeply grateful for the generosity and hospitality of the dozens of Wengers who assisted us. Without their help, the study would not have been possible.

We also benefited immensely from the support and helpful criticism of many colleagues. Florence Horning conducted numerous interviews and gathered key historical documents. Old Order historian Amos B. Hoover provided pertinent advice at various stages of the project and offered suggestions on a working draft of the manuscript. Allen N. Hoover was instrumental in collecting the population information on the various settlements as well as other historical data. Steven M. Nolt assisted us on various aspects of the project. Non-Wengers who reviewed early versions of several chapters or the entire manuscript include Lawrence and Mary Jane Eby, Merle Nolt, John Peters, Judson Reid, Theron Schlabach, and Stephen Scott. Two anonymous peer reviewers of the manuscript contributed valuable criticism and suggestions. Editor Simon Bronner offered many helpful suggestions for improving the manuscript at numerous places. Courtney Fellows, Barbara Hurd, Rachel Laustsen, Sandy Metzler, Abigail Miller, and Valerie Reed provided important clerical and editorial help. We also thank Chelsea DeArmond, who transcribed over fifty hours of taped interviews, as well as Myron Sauder, who assisted us during a summer internship.

We enjoyed the excellent support of the Young Center for Anabaptist and Pietist Studies at Elizabethtown College throughout the duration of the project. James Hurd spent five months in residence as a Center Fellow during the first phase of the fieldwork. Stephen Scott gathered membership statistics on the various Anabaptist groups in Lancaster County and Conrad Kanagy provided data on land use and farm ownership of Old Order groups. We especially thank Cynthia Nolt for her superb work in editing and supervising the preparation of the manuscript. The generous assistance of our colleagues in the Young Center contributed to the project in innumerable ways.

We thank Linda Eberly for designing the graphics throughout the book and the photographers who provided many illustrations for the story. The editorial skills of Laura Reed-Morrisson helped polish our sometimes rough prose. Finally, we acknowledge the enthusiastic interest of Simon Bronner, editor of the Pennsylvania German Society publications, and Peter Potter, editor-in-chief of The Pennsylvania State University Press. Their unwavering support motivated us to bring the project to completion. To all of these generous colleagues, we offer our sincere thanks.

Who Are the Wenger Mennonites?

The more Old Order you are, the more you stick
to the old ways.

— WENGER FARMER

✥ A HORSE-AND-BUGGY PEOPLE

Martha Shirk, the mother of seven school-age children,
lives on a small produce farm in Lancaster County, Pennsylvania, where her family raises vegetables to sell at their
roadside stand and at a public produce auction. Shirk's
kitchen is equipped with electricity but not with an air conditioner, microwave, or television. The Shirk family travels
by horse and carriage to a simple Mennonite churchhouse
for Sunday services conducted in Pennsylvania German.

In the Finger Lakes region of New York, Janet Zimmerman teaches in a one-room private school. Her
twenty-five pupils come from eight families in her local
community. She knows their parents well because all of
them are members of her church. Although she never attended high school, Janet teaches all eight grades. When the

pupils "graduate" from eighth grade, they will work in apprenticeships in homes, farms, and businesses operated by their parents or other church members.

Eli Hoover is a farmer in Morgan County, Missouri, where he raises corn and other crops for his herd of dairy cows. Eli farms with steel-wheeled tractors, but he uses mechanical milkers as well as other modern farm equipment. In addition to operating their dairy, his family raises strawberries and asparagus for a local produce market. Eli's son Reuben operates a small bicycle repair shop that caters to many of the youth in his church who use bicycles instead of cars.

Martha, Janet, and Eli are members of an Old Order Mennonite group known as Wenger Mennonites—named for their first leader, Joseph O. Wenger.[1] The group's official name is the Groffdale Conference Mennonite Church, because Wenger was a preacher at the Groffdale churchhouse in Lancaster County where the group held its first services. The Wengers are sometimes called "horse-and-buggy Mennonites" or "team Mennonites" because their horse and carriage form a team that provides daily transportation.[2] Although the horse and buggy are widely used for local travel, the Wengers also hire vans driven by outsiders for long-distance trips and business activities.

Not only are the multiple labels—Wengers, horse-and-buggy Mennonites, team Mennonites, Old Order Mennonites, Groffdale Conference Mennonites—somewhat confusing, the Wengers are also often mistaken by outsiders for Amish or other Old Order Mennonite groups who also use horse-drawn carriages.[3]

When the Wenger Church formed in 1927 in Lancaster County, Pennsylvania, it numbered about five hundred members.[4] Today, the Wengers claim some eight thousand members (baptized adults) and forty-nine congregations in nine states. When children are included in the count, the number swells to nearly eighteen thousand. Sizable families and strong retention have produced robust growth in the twentieth century. Indeed, the Wenger population, growing at about 3.7 percent a year, doubles every nineteen years. Lancaster County, the parent Wenger community, claims one-third of the members, but migration to other areas has increased steadily since 1949.

The growth of the Wenger Church, along with the cost and scarcity of farmland in eastern Pennsylvania, has prodded many families to move to other states. Between 1968 and 1998, for example, 45 percent of the families in one Lancaster County congregation migrated to other states.[5] Slightly over half of the Wengers live in five Pennsylvania settlements, but new settlements in other states are booming, as shown in Table 1. A member living

✣ TABLE 1 Estimated Wenger membership and population by state

	Adult members	Percentage of adult membership	Total population
Pennsylvania			
Lancaster County	2,840	33.3	4,950
Non–Lancaster County	1,895	22.2	3,935
New York	930	10.9	2,500
Missouri	540	6.3	1,270
Wisconsin	795	9.3	1,760
Indiana	500	5.8	970
Ohio	480	5.6	1,025
Kentucky	320	3.8	725
Iowa	200	2.3	520
Michigan	42	0.5	120
Total	8,542	100	17,775

SOURCE: *Directory* 2002 and informants in various settlements. The total population figures include children and baptized adults.

in Lancaster County explained, "Almost every family has children who have moved to other areas; there is a lot of excitement about moving."

Despite the spread of the Wengers to other states, their practices are remarkably similar across the country. Their cultural template, replicated in new settlements, produces fairly uniform practices from New York to Missouri. Ordained leaders from all the communities gather in Lancaster County twice a year for a ministers' conference. These semiannual meetings harmonize regulations and maintain fellowship among the forty-nine congregations, which are tied together by culture, custom, and the decisions of the ministers' conferences.

Unlike the Amish, who worship in their homes, the Wengers hold worship services in churchhouses—starkly plain buildings devoid of electricity, carpeting, pulpits, musical instruments, stained-glass windows, and steeples. Although the Wengers have electricity and telephones in their homes, they shun radios, televisions, video players, and computers. Farmers use steel-wheeled tractors to pull modern machinery on their small family farms.

Wenger clothing, plain and simple, is not as distinctive as that of the Amish. Wenger men do not wear beards, for example. Both Amish and Wenger women wear capes (an extra layer of fabric over the upper torso), prayer coverings, and bonnets, but clothing styles differ: Amish women

Two couples and their children travel in an open carriage.

wear plain-colored fabrics, while Wenger women wear dresses with modest prints. The color of their horse-drawn buggy, the core symbol of Wenger identity, also separates them from the Amish. The Wengers drive black carriages, while their Amish neighbors, at least in Lancaster County, drive gray ones.[6] Like the Amish, the Wengers operate private schools and speak Pennsylvania German, commonly known as *Pennsilvaanisch Deitsch* (Pennsylvania Dutch).

⁜ ANABAPTIST ROOTS

The Wengers trace their lineage back to the Anabaptist movement, which emerged in southern Germany and Switzerland in the wake of the Protestant Reformation in 1517.[7] The early Anabaptists were young radicals who

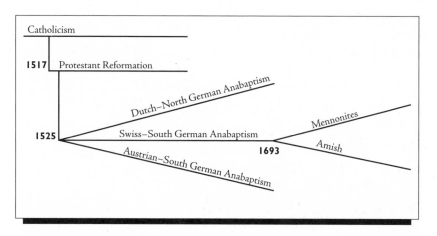

DIAGRAM I   European Anabaptist roots of the Lancaster (Pa.) Mennonites and Amish

were chafing at the pace of the Reformation. They pleaded for religious re-
forms to move faster and to break more sharply with established Catholic
patterns. Impatient for change, some of the reformers baptized each other as
adults in 1525 in Zurich, Switzerland. This defiant act of civil disobedience
laid the foundation for an independent church, free of state control.

Already baptized as infants in the Catholic Church, these free-church
advocates were called "Anabaptists" (rebaptizers), because their adult baptism was a second baptism. Adult baptism was a capital offense in sixteenth-
century Europe, because it threatened to dissolve the marriage of civil and
religious authority that had developed over the centuries. Infant baptism
not only conferred membership in both Catholic and Protestant churches
but also granted automatic citizenship, which gave authorities the power to
tax and conscript. The age of baptism symbolized a central issue of authority
in church-state relations. Who held ultimate authority over religious matters—the church or the state?

In the Anabaptists' view, the authority of the Scriptures towered above
civil edicts. Turning their backs on traditional Catholic teaching, evolving
Protestant doctrine, and the laws of the Zurich city council, the young up-
starts developed their own interpretation of Scripture based on the teachings and life of Jesus in the New Testament.

Known as radical reformers, many Anabaptists paid dearly for tearing
asunder the church-state fabric that had been woven together over the centuries. Thousands of them were tortured and killed by religious and civil

The *Martyrs Mirror* (on left desk) is found in some schools and homes.

authorities—burned at the stake, drowned in lakes and rivers, starved in prisons, or beheaded by the sword. Many Anabaptists fled to remote areas for safety. Stories of the bloody persecution are recorded in the *Martyrs Mirror*, a 1,200-page book first compiled by Anabaptists in Holland in 1660.

Memories of the persecution linger in Wenger minds today and temper their relationships with the larger society. The *Martyrs Mirror* is found in many Wenger homes. Indeed, an Old Order historian says, "The *Martyrs Mirror* stands next to the Bible" in their community.[8] Preachers often cite martyr stories in their sermons, and lay members recount them as well. A favorite one is the saga of Hans Haslibacher, a Swiss Anabaptist martyr beheaded in 1571 in Bern. A poem by an Anabaptist prisoner describing the execution says that, after hours of torture, Haslibacher dreamed that three divine signs would accompany his beheading: his head would jump into his hat and laugh, the sun would turn crimson like blood, and the town well would fill with blood. All three predictions came true, according to the poet. The poem was later sung as a hymn in numerous Anabaptist communities, and even today the tale of Haslibacher keeps the memories of persecution alive across the generations.[9]

Many Anabaptist groups eventually became known as Mennonites through the influence of Menno Simons, a former Catholic priest who became a Dutch Anabaptist leader in the mid-1500s. A few Mennonites arrived in the Americas as early as 1683, but most of the Swiss–South German immigrants came ashore in the eighteenth century. Because of William Penn's warm welcome, Pennsylvania became a favorite haven for Mennonites and other persecuted religious minorities. Eventually, Mennonites fanned southward into Maryland and Virginia, as well as westward into Ohio, Indiana, Illinois, and beyond.

The Amish also trace their lineage to the Anabaptist movement of 1525. They were part of the Swiss stream of Anabaptism until 1693, when they formed their own group under the leadership of Jakob Ammann, a Swiss Anabaptist leader who moved to the Alsace region of present-day France. Sharing common theological roots, the Amish and Mennonites branched into separate bodies in 1693 before embarking to the New World. There, Mennonite and Amish immigrants often settled near each other as they searched for fertile soil for establishing new communities.

⁜ MENNONITES IN THE GARDEN SPOT

Lancaster County, with its limestone soil, fertile farmland, and favorable climate, is often called the "garden spot" of the world. The skills and hard work of Mennonite farmers have helped rank the county first in the nation in agricultural production among non-irrigated counties. In the early 1700s, Mennonites from various areas of Germany and Switzerland settled in the area that would eventually become Lancaster County. Seeking religious freedom, political stability, and fertile soil, Mennonites founded settlements east and south of the future city of Lancaster. By 1717, some seventy-five families with more than five hundred adults and children had purchased hundreds of acres of land along the Pequea Creek. About fifteen miles to the northeast, immigrant communities also sprouted in the Groffdale area and the adjacent Weaverland Valley.[10]

In 1717, Hans Groff, a Swiss-German Mennonite, bought approximately 1,300 acres and settled his family near a large spring a few miles west of the present-day town of New Holland in Lancaster County. This area eventually became known as Groffdale.[11] About three years later, Hans Weber purchased five hundred acres for his sons along the Conestoga Creek, a few miles east of Groffdale, in a valley that soon became known as *Weberthal* or Weaver's Valley and, eventually, Weaverland. The Mennonite communities that sprouted in the Pequea, Groffdale, and Weaverland areas gradually expanded into other areas of Lancaster County during the eighteenth century.

Mennonite churches in the Lancaster area were linked together through the Lancaster Mennonite Conference. The word "conference" carried two meanings: first, a loose network of congregations in common fellowship, and second, a fall and spring ministers' conference for leaders from all the congregations. The ministers' conference established common understandings, expectations, and regulations for the ministers and congregations of the Lancaster Conference.

Expectations for how leaders in the Lancaster Conference should "keep house"—i.e., maintain order—in their congregations were not written down until 1881. Nevertheless, many common Mennonite practices during the nineteenth century included the following:[12]

+ *Plain and simple churchhouses.* For Mennonites, the body of believers, not a building, constituted the church. Reflecting their rejection of Catholic cathedrals and ornate Protestant sanctuaries in Europe, Mennonites gathered for worship in unadorned churchhouses, without pulpits, steeples, stained-glass windows, or organs.[13]
+ *Lay leadership.* Mennonite leaders were called from within their own ranks through a process known as "casting the lot." Leaders were selected from a pool of candidates nominated by the congregation. Ministers received no theological training and served for life without formal remuneration.
+ *Nonresistance to evil.* Following the teachings of Jesus, Mennonites rejected the use of force and violence. They called this lifestyle "nonresistance," meaning that they would not use force to resist evil. Not only did they typically boycott military service, but they rejected retaliation in daily social relationships as well. Even filing a lawsuit was forbidden because it used the force of law.
+ *Nonconformity to the world.* Shaped by religious persecution in Europe, Mennonites taught that the church should not conform to the larger society, which used force and glorified the power of the state. Mennonites prayed for and respected government leaders, but they shied away from participating in politics beyond the local level. They believed that God had called them to live as strangers and pilgrims in the world.

+ *Submission and humility.* Members were taught to submit to the church's authority and to conduct their lives with modesty and humility. These virtues of Mennonite life underscored the power of the church over the individual. The church held the highest authority, followed by the family and then the individual. Although dress standards were not typically codified in writing, eighteenth- and nineteenth-century Mennonites usually wore plain, simple clothing after they joined the church.

In addition to these practices, mid-nineteenth-century Mennonites in Lancaster County continued to speak the Pennsylvania German dialect of their ancestors. Their use of technology was similar to that of their neighbors and, like other rural people, they had little access to education. Nonresistance and nonconformity were the twin distinctions that set them apart from many of their Protestant neighbors. Although they participated in the local economy and had many relationships with non-Mennonites, they were for the most part a rural people ensconced in an ethnic world of family and church. Most of these hardworking German-speaking immigrants were successful farmers, but some became involved in other occupations as well.

Throughout the nineteenth century, the fall and spring ministers' conference provided a network of fellowship that promoted common practices and a sense of unity among Lancaster-area Mennonites. On several occasions, revivalist movements attracted members who had become discontented with the quiet, sober rhythms of Mennonite life. Those who left often joined more expressive and revivalist religious groups. Twice, however, small clusters of Mennonites left the Lancaster Conference to protest changes and preserve more traditional practices.

In 1812, a breakaway group formed the Reformed Mennonite Church.[14] This conservative, exclusive group declined rapidly in the twentieth century. A second division occurred in 1845, when a dispute in the Groffdale congregation led to the formation of the Stauffer Mennonites (nicknamed "Pikers" because they worshiped in a churchhouse along an old turnpike in eastern Lancaster County). The Stauffer Mennonites drew sharp lines of separation from the world that they thought were more consistent with historic Anabaptist teachings.[15] The Stauffer Church persists today, and many of its Lancaster County members live near Wenger families.

Although the divisions of 1812 and 1845 troubled the waters of the Lancaster Conference, a bigger tempest shook the church in the last quarter of the century. Controversies, some of them simmering quietly for many years, erupted into a major division in 1893.

Two women take flowers to a produce auction in Lancaster County.

✤ STICKING TO THE OLD WAYS

Under the cover of darkness on 26 September 1889, twenty-two-year-old Eli Zimmerman, accompanied by a brother and sister, slipped into the newly built Lichty churchhouse in eastern Lancaster County. Scheduled for its inaugural opening in two days, the new building sported a small pulpit elevated a few inches off the floor. A progressive building committee had, without congregational consent, placed the new pulpit at the spot where a small, traditional preacher's table typically stood.[16] This daring act, akin to installing a statue of the Virgin Mary in a Baptist church, offended many people. The simple preacher's tables standing on the floors of Mennonite churchhouses had, for many decades, stood for all things Anabaptist: humility, simplicity, equality, and the selection of lay preachers from the congregation. The sudden appearance of the pulpit, which opponents feared would surely lead to bigger Protestant-like pulpits, outraged the conservative flank of the community.

Taking the matter in their own hands, the Zimmerman family had decided to challenge the forces of change. Finding their way in the darkness, the youth removed the worldly pulpit and replaced it with a traditional preacher's table that their father, Martin W. Zimmerman, had quickly crafted for the occasion.

The Lichty churchhouse was the site of the 1889 pulpit controversy.

The progressives were incensed by the mischief, but the conservatives contended that it was only fair that what was installed without consent could be removed the same way. The local bishop, Jonas Martin—who was privately pleased to see the pulpit go—soon faced a churning controversy between the pro-pulpit and anti-pulpit factions of his community. Despite numerous investigations and several excommunications, the answer to "who tore out the pulpit" remained a mystery for nineteen years. Finally, Anna Zimmerman confessed the secret to Bishop Martin in 1908, ten years after the death of her husband, Martin W. Zimmerman.

The mischief at Lichty's in 1889 fanned the flames of discontent that four years later would divide conservative and progressive-leaning Mennonites in eastern Lancaster County. Although the pulpit issue created a public ruckus, it was only one of many factors that drove a permanent wedge into the community. Disagreements over religious innovations and ritual—not technology—splintered the Mennonite community in 1893 into two streams.

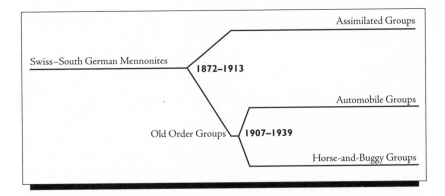

DIAGRAM 2   Formation of Old Order Mennonite groups in North America, 1872–1939

The 1893 breach among Lancaster Mennonites was only one of the schisms that divided Mennonite communities in several states into Old Order and progressive branches between 1872 and 1913.[17] The national Old Order movement budded in the 1860s, when conservative-minded members challenged changes that were creeping into churches near Elkhart, Indiana.[18] When the issues were not resolved, Old Order groups emerged in Indiana and Ohio in 1872 and then spread to Ontario, Canada, in 1889, to Lancaster in 1893, and eventually to Harrisonburg, Virginia, in 1901. Although never formally organized, the Old Order movement was well entrenched by the turn of the century and grew alongside the more progressive Mennonite groups.

❖ FLASH POINTS OF CONTENTION

What social forces propelled this movement of religious renewal and resistance? Clearly, Mennonite churches struggled with popular religious currents sweeping across the emerging American nation. Great evangelists preached in revival crusades; other leaders started Sunday schools in thousands of churches; religious publishers produced books and articles calling for greater personal piety and holiness. These new trends stirred the imagination of some Mennonite leaders and inspired them to try religious innovations in their own congregations. Others resisted, holding firmly to traditional Mennonite practices.[19]

After the Civil War, industrialization began transforming American society from farm to factory. The progressive mind-set that drove the development of industry quickened the tempo of church life as well. As some Mennonite leaders began borrowing practices from other Protestant churches, those with a more conservative bent, soon known as Old Orders, protested a number of innovations that were changing Mennonite life, including the acceptance of Sunday school, evening church services, revival meetings, the use of English in worship, foreign missions, and higher education. For Old Orders, the springs of spiritual renewal were found in new affirmations of older ways, not in innovations borrowed from outsiders. More than mere reactionaries, the Old Orders sought to renew the church by reclaiming and revitalizing precious patterns from the past.

A Wenger farmer, reflecting on the Old Order movement, described it this way: "The Old Orders stayed put and held onto the old things, while the progressives went after new things." He added, "The more Old Order you are, the more you think of yourself as sticking to the old ways. You're on the bottom rung of the ladder. The others are moving up." The Old Order movement was an alternative renewal movement that reaffirmed traditional Mennonite cultural and religious practices in the face of incipient social change.[20] Its primary focus was preserving religious ritual, not shunning technology. The flash points included language, Sunday school, revival meetings, individualism, and Protestant styles of worship. These issues sparked controversies that spurred Old Order groups to form in several states.

Language

Mennonites of Swiss and German descent who settled in Penn's Woods spoke a German dialect eventually known as Pennsylvania German. The dialect separated them from non-German groups, preserved their traditional identity, and symbolized their lowly way of life. English was the currency of the larger society—the world of power, prestige, and politics—and this higher, sophisticated language opened doors to the dominant society. As interaction with outsiders increased in the mid-nineteenth century, Mennonites began speaking more English. With more youth learning English in public schools, some progressive church leaders began conducting worship services in English, the language of the rising generation. Conservatives protested. They did not want the sounds of a worldly language intruding into the very heart of sacred ritual.

Sunday School

Protestant-style Sunday schools caused even greater consternation among tradition-minded Mennonites. Progressive Mennonite leaders welcomed the Sunday school as an important means of Christian education. But to cautious conservatives, the Sunday school was an institution carelessly borrowed from worldly churches that did not espouse the twin distinctives of Mennonite faith—nonresistance and nonconformity. Many Sunday schools were also "union" ventures, conducted jointly by cooperating denominations. Separatists to the core, the conservers shied away from ecumenical cooperation. Moreover, the Old Orders feared that Sunday schools would undercut the role of the family in religious education. In their eyes, the Scriptures taught that parents, not church leaders, held the responsibility of teaching children religious values, mainly by example.

What could be more right, more desirable, or more Christian than Sunday school? The tradition-leaning Mennonites were troubled as much by the practices accompanying Sunday school as they were by its content. Song leaders, in individualistic fashion, stood instead of sat, and they taught children songs in English. Small groups sang special music and women took leadership roles. People feared that Sunday school would encourage parents to shirk their responsibility to instruct their children in the faith. Furthermore, Sunday school was taught by progressive-thinking, non-ordained persons, which not only encouraged pride but also elevated the power of lay leaders. Moreover, Sunday school's national connections threatened to pull loyalty away from the local congregation and encourage evangelism and foreign mission work. Sunday school, in the final analysis, was a Protestant institution that clashed with the traditional Mennonite values of humility, communalism, separatism, and nonresistance.

On a deeper level, Sunday schools introduced a specialized and rationalized model of religious education. The conservatives worried that faith would become a cognitive exercise—something to study, memorize, and debate. Mennonites had always emphasized the *practice* of faith, not the study of abstract doctrines. Besides, Sunday school teachers typically taught their classes in English and often displayed a self-confident spirit that eclipsed the traditional habits of Mennonite humility. Sunday school, conservatives argued, would instill pride in young people. Indeed, teachers often expressed "bold, self-assured attitudes" that hardly reflected a meek and quiet spirit.[21] Moreover, if women taught Sunday school, they would disturb traditional gender roles and usurp the authority of men, the interpreters of faith in public settings.[22]

In all of these ways, Sunday schools threatened the time-tested patterns that had preserved Mennonite faith by immersing children in the waters of family and community life without any formal instruction.

Revival Meetings

Conservatives also objected to holding Protestant-style evening services. These emotion-filled meetings were often called "protracted meetings," because they stretched over a two-week period of time. Patterned after those in outside denominations, the revival-style meetings featured visiting evangelists who emphasized personal experience and stirred emotions. Revivalist preachers often mounted pulpits in a flamboyant style that clashed with the quiet virtues of simplicity, equality, and humility. Protracted meetings challenged the entrenched patterns of authority as well as long-held understandings of salvation. They reflected the values of an expressive and emotional individualism that, conservatives worried, would in time erode the communal foundations of Mennonite faith and life.

Individualism

In all of these squabbles, tradition-minded Mennonites were not quarreling with basic Mennonite beliefs or doctrines, nor were they simply resisting a tide of innovation that might sweep them into the mainstream. Rather, they tried to preserve and renew what they considered the core of Mennonite faith—submission, humility, nonconformity, and nonresistance. Beneath the rhetoric swirling around the use of English, Sunday schools, and revival meetings was a clash of moral orders. Old Order sentiments ran against the progressive embrace of individualism, rationalization, and specialization that accompanied the rising tide of industrialization.

The introduction of English, Sunday schools, and revival meetings embodied a confident individualism that mocked the lowly ways of humility. The resisters of change feared that these innovations would eventually wear away the spiritual and social foundations of their redemptive community. Bucking trends that might pull them into a whirlpool of worldliness, tradition-embracing Mennonites in several states, including Pennsylvania, clutched older customs as large numbers of their fellow Mennonites drifted toward the Protestant mainstream.

✣ JONAS MARTIN: PROMISES ON MY KNEES

Lancaster-area Mennonites were not exempt from the cultural changes spreading across the country after the Civil War. It became typical for Mennonite young people to dabble with worldly practices before joining the church. Wedding pictures from the era show Mennonite couples dressed in fancy fashions. Women wore trendy hats and jewelry, and men wore tailored suits, all of which they would abandon in a few years when they joined the church.

Despite these changes, some Mennonite leaders worried more about borrowing religious innovations—Sunday schools, revival meetings, and "inspirational" singing, to name but a few—from Protestant churches. Some Lancaster Conference congregations began embracing these practices, as well as more formal preaching, singing in English, and using public law to settle church affairs. By 1883, twelve congregations were operating Sunday schools.[23] Disagreements over these "Protestant innovations" threatened church unity more than other cultural challenges from American society did.

Jonas H. Martin feared such innovations. A successful farmer who lived near Goodville in eastern Lancaster County, Martin was ordained bishop in 1881 at the age of forty-two. He agonized over creeping changes that he worried would bring worldliness into the church. Martin, soon the leader of Lancaster's Old Order movement, wrote to a friend, "I never thought it would happen in my lifetime. Dear Brother, I am of a mind to remain steadfast to those principles I promised on my knees, which I believe will hold out in that everlasting day."[24] With his oft-quoted phrase, "Once to live, and once to die, and then to appear before an Almighty God," he urged members to be faithful to the principles of the past.[25]

Martin feared that using English in church services would open the gate to other innovations. He was dismayed that the Groffdale congregation sang, without his approval, an English hymn after church one Sunday in 1884. He also grieved over two other issues: bishops marrying unbaptized couples and the growing acceptance of Sunday schools.[26]

Jonas Martin had been baptized before he was married, and he believed that the church should marry only those who had been baptized. To do otherwise, he feared, would encourage young people to seek non-Mennonite mates. One of his fellow bishops had begun marrying unbaptized couples, hoping that they would later join the church. To conservative leaders like Martin, these marriages violated the biblical command, "Be ye not unequally yoked together with unbelievers" (II Cor. 6:14), and they also violated a historic Anabaptist confession of faith that restricted marriage to members of the same faith.[27] In 1892, against his own conscience, Jonas Martin reluctantly agreed to allow other bishops to marry nonmembers, although he never conducted such a marriage.[28] Nevertheless, he was busy. During his ordained ministry, he conducted 332 weddings and attended 1,136 funerals—preaching at 717 of them.[29]

According to some members, Bishop Martin preached "very hard against pride."[30] Pride could pop up in many places, but the place that especially troubled him was Sunday school. Worried that some young people were drifting toward the world, change-minded leaders hoped that Sunday school would keep children in the church, give them Bible training, and protect them from non-Christian ideas. To tradition-minded Mennonites such as Bishop Martin, however, Sunday school itself was a worldly, Protestant innovation that would only promote pride among pupils and teachers.

On 7 June 1891, the Sunday school "disease" reached one of Bishop Martin's congregations. Samuel Musselman, a New Holland businessman, opened a Sunday school in the Weaverland school building adjacent to the churchhouse. So many children arrived that Musselman decided to use the churchhouse instead, but Deacon Daniel Burkholder told the sexton to keep the church doors shut. Bishop Martin sought support from other bishops to close the Sunday school, but to no avail. Eventually, the Weaverland congregation voted 154 to 37 to close the Sunday school, but the issue continued to churn.[31]

❖ SATISFIED WITH THE OLD GROUND: THE DIVISION OF 1893

In 1893, the tensions smoldering over Sunday school, the marriage of unbaptized people, the use of English, and the pulpit scandal at the Lichty Church burst into flame. Mennonite leaders agreed on one thing—that something had to be done. But what? At the October ministers' conference at the Mellinger Churchhouse, the "Jonas Martin issue" eclipsed everything else. Martin declared that he would take a stand on the issues that troubled him and other tradition-minded people. "I am one with the old ground and council," he said, "but not with the new things that have been introduced. I have for a long time already agreed to these things against my conscience and I want to continue no longer in this, or keep house this way."[32]

During the meeting, the five bishops of the conference retired to a small "counsel room" in the churchhouse. They urged Martin to moderate his objections to the proposed changes. Tension hung heavy in the room. Moderator Jacob Brubacher pulled out his watch and said, "Jonas, we will give you ten minutes to confess your error." Martin replied, "I want to be understood correctly. I would be satisfied with the old ground [the old way of doing things], but not with the [Sunday] school and not with the giving into marriage of such that are not members."[33] The die was cast. In a few minutes, the other bishops revoked Martin's ministry and suspended his membership in the conference. Martin and a few supporters went outside, met under a tree to discuss the turn of events, and then mounted their horses and went home.[34] From that day on, Old Order leaders followed a separate, more traditional path from the Lancaster Conference. There are no exact records, but several hundred Old Order people followed Jonas Martin's departure from the Lancaster Conference, which numbered about 6,500 members before the division.

Lancaster Conference leaders determined that the churchhouses in Jonas Martin's Weaverland District belonged to their conference. On some occasions after the division, Martin's people arrived at the Weaverland churchhouse only to find the doors locked. The same thing happened at the Groffdale and Metzlers churchhouses. Bitterness laced memories of the lockout even a hundred years later, when a Wenger bishop said, "They chased us out of all their churches, except Martindale." Because most of the Martindale congregation followed Jonas Martin, Lancaster Conference leaders let his people use the Martindale churchhouse every fourth Sunday.[35]

If the division hurt, the lockouts hurt even more. The Old Orders responded not by mounting a lawsuit, but by building new churchhouses near the old ones.[36] Feelings ran so high in the Groffdale congregation that seven bodies were removed from the Lancaster Conference cemetery and reburied in the new cemetery adjacent to the newly constructed Old Order churchhouse. Today, in several locations, Old Order stone or wood-frame churchhouses stand within sight of church buildings owned by the Lancaster Conference. These structures serve as symbolic monuments and reminders of the painful division of 1893.

Because Jonas Martin had been a preacher and bishop in the Weaverland district, the newly formed Old Order church was formally known as the Weaverland Conference. The Pennsylvania Dutch name for Jonas is *Yonie*; hence his followers were often nicknamed "Yonies" or "Martinites."[37] By the time Bishop Martin died in 1925, eleven Old Order congregations had been established. After the division of 1893, the Weaverland Conference and the larger Lancaster Conference, like two lanes of a forked highway, gradually drifted apart.[38]

Few people then could envision the long-term consequences for Lancaster's Mennonite community. At the time, differences primarily focused on religious programs such as Sunday school, but on other practices, the two conferences were similar for some time. Gradually, however, differences emerged in virtually all areas of life.[39] A Wenger man observed, "You couldn't tell Lancaster Conference people apart from the Yonie Martin people for years, but then they [Lancaster Conference] began to change." And change

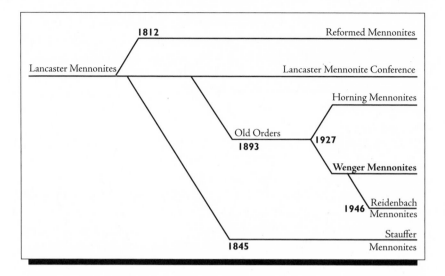

DIAGRAM 3   Major Mennonite branches in Lancaster County (Pa.), 1812–1946

they did. Lancaster Conference practices, from personal dress to worship practices and technology, began to move far away from the older traditions.

A century after the bitter breach of 1893, Lancaster Conference leaders extended a hand of conciliation to the Old Order churches. In a 2004 letter to Old Order leaders, the Lancaster Conference board of bishops acknowledged the pain of the division and "the lack of grace and the bad attitudes of some of our forebears. We ask for your forgiveness for the wrongs done to your people by the leaders of our church at that time and to the present day." The bishops of the Weaverland Conference responded by accepting "the hand of peace . . . extending to you forgiveness for any wrongdoings on your part. We in turn ask forgiveness for the wrong attitudes and responses that we and our forebears . . . may have had over the years." The great-grandchildren who inherited the memories of the old division could finally reach across the chasm and shake hands.[40]

✛ THE DIVISION OF 1927

The conflicts of 1893, which split the Lancaster Conference and the Old Order community, had focused on traditional church practices. The Old

Orders, however, soon faced some technological challenges of their own. Public telephones, installed in some towns in the 1890s, were used at first by the Yonies with little objection from the church.[41] But when some church members began buying stock in telephone companies and installing telephones in their homes, the issue became contentious.

At the Weaverland ministers' conference in April 1907, Bishop Martin, in an effort to avert another division, tried to settle the unrest with a delicate compromise. Although the church opposed the phone, it would "bear in love with those who had it," according to the resolution adopted by the ordained leaders. The wording of the ruling placed the moral burden on the offenders: "If the phone is wrong, they themselves shall bear the guilt." Moreover, those who used public phones in town were forbidden to "go into hotels to do so." And most important, no minister could install a phone and prospective ministers had to remove their phones before ordination. This compromise, while frowning on phones, permitted lay members to have them. It pleased Deacon Daniel Burkholder, who had declared, "One division in a lifetime is enough."[42]

Hardly had Jonas Martin averted a division over the phone when another technological toy—the car—arrived. Indeed, the first marketable car in America was built by Frank Duryea in 1893, the year Martin was expelled from the Lancaster Conference.[43] For the final fifteen years of Martin's ministry (until his death in 1925), the car disturbed the peace of the Old Order church. And although Bishop Martin compromised on the telephone, he opposed the car until he died.

Martin often said that an automobile reflected a "high and haughty" spirit that was out of step with Old Order life.[44] He cited a Bible verse (Luke 16:15) when preaching against the auto: "That which is highly esteemed among men is an abomination in the sight of God." The first abomination arrived in the village of Martindale in 1910, when Eli Zimmerman rigged up a homemade horseless carriage by mounting a one-cylinder engine on a spring wagon originally built to be pulled by a horse. Soon tempted to buy a real car, Eli yielded. He was promptly excommunicated, abomination and all.[45]

Within a few years, bishops of the Lancaster Conference, along with other Americans, were buying cars. And by the late teens, some members of Yonie Martin's Old Order congregations were buying cars, too. On any Sunday, more and more cars arrived at churchyards designed to accommodate horses and buggies. Moses G. Horning, ordained to assist Bishop Martin in 1914, had a more positive view of the car than the old bishop did. Although the car-driving faction had patiently and courteously awaited Martin's death, it boldly pressed for change after he died in 1925.

The car controversy eventually tore the fabric of love in Lancaster's Old Order community in 1927. Those who opted for the "machine" became known as the Horning Church, named after Bishop Moses Horning, who had taken charge after the death of Yonie Martin. Those who kept the horse and carriage—about half of the Old Order community—were led by Joseph O. Wenger, who was ordained bishop after the division. The horse-and-buggy people were soon called the Wenger Mennonites.

The Wenger-Horning division was less painful than the breach of 1893. Indeed, the 1927 division became known as "the peaceful split" because it avoided the bitter property disputes of the earlier one.[46] Even some seventy-five years after the schism, the Horning Church and the Wenger Church continue to share five churchhouses every other Sunday. The Wengers drive their buggies to the churchhouse on one Sunday, and the Horning people park their cars in the same horse sheds the following Sunday. This cooperative practice led one tourist to conclude that the congregation had miraculously converted from carriages to cars in one week!

Since 1927, only minor divisions have troubled the Wenger Church. In 1946, some families left because they thought that the church should not permit young men to serve in Civilian Public Service camps as an alternative to military service. Some of the dissenting families returned to the Wenger Church, but others eventually formed a small church known as the Reidenbachs, named for the area of their origin. This group was nicknamed the "Thirty-fivers" because about thirty-five people were in the first wave of those who refused to take communion as a protest against participation in Civilian Public Service camps. The Reidenbach people eventually divided into small family clans and followed more traditional practices than the Wengers.[47] In the United States, the Wengers are the largest and most robust horse-and-buggy group under the traditional Mennonite banner. There are several smaller horse-driving Mennonite groups, but for the most part, they have not flourished like the Wengers.

⁘ THE WENGER WORLD TODAY

The social sea of the Wenger world is filled with many other Anabaptist ships, providing continuous points for comparison. Church practices ranging from the size of women's head coverings to the acceptance of divorce and remarriage are often contrasted with Wenger views. These religious reference groups enable the Wengers to assess their position as they navigate

An Amishman (left) sells melons to a Wenger couple. His hat style, beard, and use of horse and steel-wheeled wagon distinguish him from the Wengers.

the waters of modernity. Members can quickly identify the location of the Wenger ship regarding the use of computers, the behavior of youth, women's ordination, and the use of horses. The comparisons and distinctions sharpen Wenger identity, purpose, and solidarity.

Some of the religious communities on the mind of the Wengers living in Lancaster County appear in Table 2. Subgroups within some of the churches add even more complication to the cultural mosaic. Because the points of reference depend on which groups live nearby, the comparisons vary somewhat for Wengers living outside Lancaster County.

Wengers in Lancaster County communicate frequently with Wengers who live elsewhere in Pennsylvania and in eight other states. A continual exchange of telephone calls, letters, and visits reinforces the bonds of solidarity across the communities. This lively communication also pinpoints small differences between settlements: Lancaster Wengers are quick to note that churchhouses in Indiana have clocks, for example.

Beyond their own people, the Wengers see themselves in a larger Old Order world of several dozen groups.[48] Those with the closest ties are the Old Order Mennonites of Virginia and Ontario. These horse-and-buggy groups

✤ TABLE 2 Religious reference groups for Wengers living in Lancaster
County (Pa.)

Wengers outside Lancaster	Sixteen settlements in nine states
Horse-and-buggy groups	Old Order Mennonites in Ontario and Virginia
	Old Order Stauffer and Reidenbach Mennonites
	Old Order Amish
Car-driving groups	Horning (Black Bumper) Old Order Mennonites
	Beachy Amish
	Plain-dressing Mennonite groups
	Lancaster Mennonite Conference
	Other Anabaptist-related groups
	Non-Anabaptist churches

share many practices with the Wengers and maintain warm fraternal bonds
even though they are not formally affiliated with the Groffdale Conference.
Old Order ministers from the Virginia, Ontario, and Groffdale conferences
preach in each other's congregations, despite differences among their groups.
Virginia Old Order Mennonites use English in their worship services, for
example; Canadian Old Order Mennonites permit rubber tires on tractors.
Such dissimilarities reinforce the distinctives of Wenger identity.

The Stauffers ("Pikers") and the Reidenbachs ("Thirty-fivers") provide
the Wengers with a more conservative Mennonite point of reference within
the horse-and-buggy groups. These ultra-traditional neighbors, who farm
with horses and shun electricity, enable the Wengers to see themselves as
more progressive. Lancaster-area Wengers also frequently compare their
practices with their Amish neighbors. Ironically, sometimes it is easier for
the Wengers to cooperate with their Amish neighbors than with some other
Mennonites, because the Amish represent a different stream of Anabaptist
heritage. The Amish and the Wengers collaborate in areas such as schools
and publications. Although they reflect two different Anabaptist traditions
and have many different practices, the Wengers and the Amish share a common Old Order identity.

When they compare themselves to the automobile-driving groups, the
Wengers first look at the Horning Church, the group from whom they
separated in 1927. Many Wengers have family members in the Horning
Church, and in Lancaster County the two groups share some churchhouses.

Ex-Wengers often join the Horning Church, and thus its practices offer a frequent point of comparison for Wengers. Other plain-dressing Anabaptist groups whose members drive cars provide additional examples of "plain" worldliness that tempt wayward Wengers.[49] The Beachy Amish, the Eastern Pennsylvania Mennonite Church, and various Amish-Mennonite hybrids illustrate, for the Wengers, the erosion of Old Order practices when groups float toward the outside world. The women's head coverings shrink, covering strings disappear, traces of lace appear on dresses, more technology is used, businesses expand—all of which, in Wenger eyes, signal a capitulation to worldly culture. (The differences among the Wengers and other Old Order groups are explored in greater detail in Chapter 9.)

When the Old Order movement began in Indiana in 1872, John Funk was an influential leader and publisher who championed some of the changes in church life that the Old Orders protested. His name was associated with the more assimilated Mennonites who became further involved in American society. Old Orders continue to use the term *Funkeleit* (Funk people) as a broad label for various assimilated Mennonite groups.[50] For the Wengers, one of the best examples of *Funkeleit*—of creeping worldliness in the Anabaptist world—is the Lancaster Conference. Since the division of 1893, their parent body has changed in many ways that Wengers consider not mere worldliness, but outright sin: accepting divorced and remarried people as members, giving women leadership roles in the church, and no longer requiring women to wear head coverings. To Wenger thinking, the worldly practices that creep into the Lancaster Conference underscore the critical importance of standing firm on the old ground to protect traditional practices from erosion.

The Wengers also hear reports of other *Funkeleit* Mennonites who permit divorce and remarriage, military service, the ordination of women, homosexual unions, and other cultural practices that the Wengers believe the Bible calls sin. Although they share a common theological heritage, Old Order and assimilated Mennonites live in different cultural worlds. It would be wrong, however, to assume that the Wengers are a static, change-resistant group. The Wenger people *are* changing, only at a slower pace and in different ways than their *Funkeleit* cousins who have moved toward mainstream American culture.

Finally, there are the "worldly" non-Anabaptist churches— Presbyterians, Methodists, Lutherans, and Catholics, as well as independent fundamentalist and evangelical groups. These churches still symbolize, in the Wenger mind, the vain, High Church religion that persecuted Wenger forebears in sixteenth-century Europe. Wengers hold no personal animosity toward these churches or their members. In fact, they may work and trade with

✤ TABLE 3 Estimated adult membership of Lancaster County (Pa.)
Anabaptist-related groups

	Number of groups	Number of congregations	Adult members
Amish[1]	2	137	10,415
Brethren[2]	5	33	9,625
Brethren in Christ	3	25	4,595
Mennonites			
Assimilated	8	102	15,910
Conservative (Plain)[3]	16	41	4,100
Old Order (Groffdale/Wenger)	1	10	2,840
Old Order (Weaverland/Horning)	1	13	2,815
Old Order (others)[4]	9	15	700
Total	**45**	**376**	**51,000**

SOURCE: Directories of various groups and informants. Data gathered by Stephen Scott.

NOTE: If children were counted, the population size for some groups would more than double. The Lancaster Mennonite Conference is the largest body (11,717 members) among the assimilated Mennonites. Conservative Mennonite groups wear plain clothing, own automobiles, and use electricity but generally forbid television.

[1]Does not include Amish in Chester and York counties.
[2]Besides Church of the Brethren, includes several groups originating from
  Schwarzenau, Germany.
[3]Includes Beachy Amish and Amish-Mennonite groups.
[4]Includes the various Stauffer and Reidenbach groups.

them in friendly ways on a daily basis. However, the beliefs and practices of churches with ornate facilities, professional pastors, and tolerance for all things American provide negative reference points that symbolize exactly what the Wengers hope to avoid.

In Lancaster County, the Wengers represent 5.6 percent of the total constellation of Anabaptist-related groups, as shown in Table 3. Yet among Old Order Mennonites, the Wengers hold 45 percent of the membership. Lancaster County has some forty-five different Anabaptist-related groups in 376 congregations. The three largest groups (Lancaster Mennonite Conference, 11,717; Amish, 10,415; Church of the Brethren, 8,060) claim about 60 percent of the total Anabaptist-related membership of 51,000 adults in Lancaster County. These religious lights provide critical points of reference on the cultural waters as the Wengers navigate their way in the postmodern world. The Wengers' cultural radar tracks these other churches—most of which they see drifting toward the larger sea of worldliness—to chart a course that avoids both the worldly currents that, in their mind, have shipwrecked some other groups, and the rigidity of the ultraconservatives.

❖ FOUR CONCEPTUAL WINDOWS

We use four analytical perspectives to interpret the Wenger story. These conceptual windows enable us to see the coherence of Wenger practices that otherwise might appear discrete or even disjointed. Viewing Wenger culture through these windows provides interpretive power for understanding the deep sentiments that lie beneath surface-level descriptions. The four concepts are redemptive community, *Gelassenheit*, redemptive rituals, and selective modernization.

Redemptive Community

The Wengers fit the definition of a religious group that sociologists typically call "sectarian"—a group that draws sharp boundaries between itself and the larger society. Although Wengers separate themselves from mainstream American culture, that is not their primary mission. Rather, they are propelled by the vision of building and maintaining a redemptive community—*Gemeinde* in German, *Gmay* in their dialect—that Wengers typically translate as "church."

For Wengers, the *Gmay* encompasses much more than the word "community" does for most Americans. It is not equivalent to "neighborhood," nor to the people of a particular region. It is not a cultural enclave based on an upscale lifestyle and it is certainly not a virtual community! In the Wenger mind, the *Gmay*, the redemptive community, includes all the members of their local congregation, which typically includes some extended family and many neighbors. It is impossible to overstate the importance of the local orientation of the *Gmay*. It is rooted in place—in a specific place—where members engage each other daily in face-to-face interactions that build bonds of trust and reinforce Wenger views of the world. The *Gmay* is not a virtual community of fleeting digital images. In short, *Gmay* refers to the people and practices that constitute the entire Wenger way of life. Distinctive symbols clarify who is in the redemptive community and who is not.

Membership in the *Gmay* is a religious citizenship, because the members live under a sacred canopy. It is a redemptive community because salvation is not only an individualistic experience; salvation is also mediated through participation in the life of the community. In the *Gmay*, members feel and commune with the divine presence. A redemptive community ideally experiences wholeness and oneness. It is a unified, pure, and peaceful community living under the blessing of God. This understanding of *Gmay* is rooted in the early Anabaptist view that the spirit of Christ in the gathered body transforms it into a holy body, the body of Christ.[51]

The redemptive community merges religion and life, faith and culture, and the sacred and the mundane. In the *Gmay*, all of life—dress, technology, worship, education—assumes religious significance and consequence. In the words of one Old Order writer,"It is difficult to separate the culture from the beliefs of Old Order Mennonites because the two are so interwoven."[52] Clearly, in the redemptive community, religious meanings penetrate many crevices of daily life.[53]

Gelassenheit

The German word *Gelassenheit* captures the deepest root value of Old Order life. The concept of *Gelassenheit* carries multiple meanings—yieldedness, surrender, submission, humility, calmness. It is a deep and broad disposition that undergirds the entire Wenger worldview. *Gelassenheit* stands in sharp contrast to the individualism of American culture, which nurtures a bold, assertive self that clamors for individual freedom and choice. Those who embody the virtues of *Gelassenheit* surrender themselves to God, yield to the authority of the church, and defer to others in authority over them. They exhibit a meek and mild personality, one that is willing to suffer rather than defend itself.

For sixteenth-century European Anabaptists burning at the martyrs' stake, *Gelassenheit* meant the literal abandonment of the self into the hands of God. Over the centuries, this meaning has been translated into cultural forms of communal values and simple living. *Gelassenheit* is the crucial bridge between the individual and the redemptive community; members who are filled with this virtue are willing to deny self, to surrender self, for the welfare of the community. An abstract concept, *Gelassenheit* has diverse expressions and applications. Although Wengers rarely use the word *Gelassenheit*, they frequently extol one of its virtues—humility—and contrast it with the vice of pride, or with haughty individualism.

Gelassenheit, however, is more than just an attitude or a personality trait. As a deep cultural disposition, *Gelassenheit* expresses itself in both values and behaviors, attitudes and practices—not only in individuals but also in the architecture of church buildings, the rituals of congregational life, dress practices, and other aspects of the simple life. One Old Order writer summed up the significance of this keystone of Wenger life in these words:"The Old Order Mennonite community and the Anabaptist ethos of

Gelassenheit are synonymous."[54] In the words of another Old Order leader, "Two old German words, *Gelassenheit* and *Demut*, capture for us the special beauty of community better than any English word. . . . *Gelassenheit* means submission. . . . *Demut* suggests humility. The opposite of these two words is arrogance and self-assertion. That in a nutshell is how beauty is expressed in an Old Order community."[55]

Redemptive Rituals

Certain rituals periodically reenergize the redemptive community and reaffirm its worldview.[56] These ceremonial moments, filled with divine presence and blessing, rejuvenate and legitimate the *Gmay*. They are redemptive rituals because, when they function properly, they bring wholeness, unity, and divine blessing to the community. Not all ritual activities, however, carry the same degree of sacred intensity. The ordination of a new minister is filled with greater collective emotion and intensity than a silent prayer before a meal or the wearing of plain garb on a trip to town. Following the pathbreaking work of Sandra Cronk in her study of Old Order ritual, we apply ritual analysis to a broad spectrum of activities in Wenger society.[57]

The ritual life of the redemptive community can be roughly sorted into formal and informal rites. Although both types carry religious significance, the formal ones are typically performed when the community gathers in the churchhouse and include ceremonies such as Sunday worship, singing, baptism, communion, ordination, and the spring and fall days of fasting. Examples of informal rituals include wearing Wenger garb, working together, participating in mutual aid activities such as a barn raising, offering a silent prayer before a meal, and participating in school activities. In general, the formal rites are filled with greater religious intensity than the informal ones.

Regardless of when or where they are performed, Wenger rituals share several features. They are filled with religious meaning; they are owned and regulated by the community; they are public performances offered to an audience—typically to other members, or in the case of dress, to outsiders. Participation in these redemptive rituals reminds Wengers who they are and to whom they belong, reaffirms their basic values, declares their citizenship in the redemptive community, and recharges their spiritual batteries.

Selective Modernization

Many of the values cherished by the redemptive community—self-denial, humility, simplicity, tradition—stand in sharp opposition to the values of mainstream American culture. In order to keep some semblance of order and

A large, self-propelled combine on steel wheels illustrates the Wenger process of selective modernization—accepting technology with some restrictions.

purity in their redemptive community, Wengers are cautious about how and when they interact with the outside world. Many facets of the larger society, including immodesty, abortion, vanity, divorce, and violence—sin, in their eyes—threaten their community's well-being. The Wengers have created symbols and practices of separation to buffer themselves from such wanton worldly influences. Separation from the world does not mean social isolation. Rather, it signifies selective interaction with the surrounding society.

Social scientists often use the concepts of acculturation and assimilation to describe the process of small groups merging with larger ones. Acculturation focuses on a small group's acceptance of the cultural values of a dominant group, whereas assimilation involves greater participation by members of a smaller group in mainstream organizations.[58] The term "selective modernization" refers to the rational decisions a group makes about the degree to which it absorbs outside values and participates in external organizations.[59] Selective modernization focuses on which external values, practices, and organizations are acceptable and which ones are rejected because of their perceived threat to the group. Throughout their history, the Wengers have engaged in selective modernization, accepting some aspects of modern life while rejecting others.

Modernization and modernity are slippery terms.[60] While its roots reach back to the European Enlightenment, the modern period of history can loosely be equated with the rise of industrialization, although the scope and depth of modernity is both broader and deeper than the process of industrialization. The modernizing process has involved transformations of worldviews and values as well as changes in social and economic structures in the transition from a rural agrarian society to an urban industrial one. Greater application of technology to all aspects of social life also permeates the march of modernization.

The Old Order movement that emerged in the late nineteenth century rejected many of the values and structures that were embedded in American society by the early twentieth century. With their roots in the Old Order movement and their own origins in 1927, the Wenger story emerged in the context of major twentieth-century transformations in American society. But given their separatist impulses, the Wengers remained rather aloof from these changes, even though they were influenced by them.

Occupational specialization, a chief characteristic of the modern era, separates many activities that were once integrated in traditional societies. In the transformations propelled by modernity, work moves from home to factory, education is separated from family, religion recedes from daily life, self-identity detaches from ethnic identity, leisure activities leave the local community, and so on. The modernizing process, in short, pulls apart the social bonds of local, geographically based communities.

In order to separate themselves from modernity—itself the "great separator"—Wengers have engaged in selective modernization, accepting some elements of modernity while rejecting others. They accepted electricity, but not higher education, for instance; tractors, but not cars; washing machines, but not television; alarm clocks, but not wristwatches; fax machines, but not computers. By engaging in selective modernization, they have harvested the fruits of progress that enable them to thrive as a community, while keeping a discreet distance from those they consider toxic.

We turn next to an exploration of Wenger faith and culture. Peering through our four conceptual windows, we explore how the Wengers create and perpetuate a redemptive community. Wenger culture provides a grid of values that guide these "strangers and pilgrims," to use their words, in the contemporary world. What elements of Wenger culture infuse their world with meaning and guide them on their journey in a postmodern society? We examine that question in Chapter 2.

2 The Fabric of Faith and Culture

If cattle have no fences, they get to wandering, and forget where home is.

—WENGER MINISTER

✤ A PRACTICAL FAITH

The fabric of Wenger culture consists of distinctive beliefs, practices, and symbols. These strands of faith, woven together over the generations, constitute the cloth of Wenger life. Although these distinctive threads can be unraveled into analytical parts, in reality they blend into a coherent cultural ethos. Religious beliefs about humility, for example, are expressed by using horse-and-buggy transportation, which also serves as a symbol of Wenger identity.

The ministers in the Wenger Church write no books on theology. They make no formal defense of their beliefs and do not order them into a doctrinal system. Wenger beliefs, rooted in biblical teaching and historic Mennonite confessions of faith, are passed on to new generations through sermon, story, and song. The Wengers focus on practice rather than doctrine. "We live what we believe, but don't talk about what we believe," said one member. "We let our light shine by our actions." Religious convictions, translated into daily practice, become the embodiment of faith. "It's not that religion plays a larger role in our life," said a member. "Our religion is our life."

The Wengers base their beliefs on the Bible as interpreted by the eighteen articles of the 1632 Dordrecht Confession. This old Anabaptist confession of faith covers topics such as God, sin, Christ, the church, nonresistance, swearing of oaths, footwashing, excommunication, and the resurrection of the dead. Most households have a copy of the confession, reproduced in the centuries-old booklet *Conversation on Saving Faith*, which members are encouraged to read.[1] Candidates for baptism are instructed in the Dordrecht Confession's articles of faith.

Salvation lies at the heart of Wenger belief. The fourth article of the Dordrecht Confession describes Jesus as "the son of the living God, in whom consists all our hope, comfort, redemption, and salvation." One member says, "Although salvation is not in a church, a church setting and a church group are very important." Wenger people believe not only in personal redemption but also that the fruits of salvation must be expressed in daily life—that is, in personal practice and in community life.

One leader tells the story of a young man working in a public setting who said, "No one noticed that I'm a Christian." The preacher concluded that "if no one noticed a difference in his life, then he wasn't a Christian." Translating their religious faith into daily life can have economic consequences. A young man who operated a successful small-engine shop in Lancaster County decided to move to Michigan to work as a farmer, explaining that he was "afraid for his salvation." He worried that unless he moved, his business success and growing contacts with the world would pull his heart away from God.

Because the Wengers emphasize distinctive practices, some people accuse them of legalism. Visitors to the home of a bishop asked, "Why do you trust in horses, buggies, and plain clothing for salvation?" The leader explained that Wengers do not "trust" in these things for salvation but see them as expressions of their faith in Christ: "We want our people to be conscientious, and not just submit outwardly. We don't want to build our salvation on the way we dress, or farm, or the way we drive on the road. But still those things help us to lead more common lives."[2]

Moreover, the Wengers do not claim to be the only group on the road to heaven. One member explained, "I don't think it [salvation] has to do with any one certain group because it says in Revelation that they will come from the four corners of the world." Wenger people typically do not claim "assurance of salvation." Indeed, some members have left the Wengers for churches that emphasize greater assurance of salvation. An elderly Wenger woman questioned a neighbor's bold claim of salvation, asking, "How can anyone know that? There's always a chance you will turn away during your life."

A bishop explained the Wenger view: "I have assurance of salvation, but I must continue faithful to the end. Anyone is capable of falling away." Wenger cautions about claims of eternal salvation were summarized by a lay member this way: "I might think that, well, now I'm saved and I can sit down and I don't need to do anything anymore. That's not the way we should feel. We strongly believe that if you sin, you're out of the grace of God, you know. If I commit adultery, I'm out of the grace of God, but I can repent and come into that grace again." In the words of a Wenger woman, "We strive for the high goal. Personally, I think we must just live so close to the Lord, or as John Bunyan [*Pilgrim's Progress*] says, walk so closely in his path that we can see the drops of blood. . . . I don't think we should say we're sure of our salvation. We can easily fall. We just try to stay close with the Lord. That's our trust. Our hope is that we can stay close enough and not err." For Wengers, redemption relates to repentance and daily practice. According to one leader, "Satan can't lead us to death unless we let him . . . we have a lively hope because we're under grace . . . this doesn't mean that we can never lose our salvation. We can, but God has provided a way for us to repent and receive his grace so we can endure to the end."

From their origins in 1893, Old Order Mennonites have been reluctant to declare their assurance of salvation, seeing claims of assurance as a sign of arrogance and pride. After all, only God can know and judge such weighty eternal matters. Many ministers emphasize a born-again experience—a genuine change of heart—before young people seek baptism and church membership. But despite their use of such words, the Wengers are not garden-variety evangelicals. In fact, most of them discourage missionary and evangelistic efforts.

Rather than trying to convert the world, Wengers seek to "let their light shine" by their manner of living. They have several reservations about overt evangelizing activities. First, they believe that members should live their faith, not talk about it. Second, they fear that evangelistic efforts might fracture church unity by attracting converts from diverse backgrounds. Third, they worry that witnessing about their faith will lead to pride. One member says, "I want to share [my witness], you know. I just don't want to share it in a boastful sense." Finally, Wengers see the Lancaster Conference as "an example of exactly where we don't want to go." As it developed a large mission program, the Lancaster Conference dropped plain dress, permitted women in leadership, and accepted divorced and remarried members.

✣ THE CHURCH AS REDEMPTIVE COMMUNITY

Wengers distinguish between the *Gmayhaus* and the *Gmay*, the building and the people. In their mind, church and community are inseparable. In the modern world, a religious affiliation may be one of an individual's many communities, but in the Wenger world, the *Gmay* is *the* community. Wengers do not shop around for a church that caters to personal needs or one that claims outstanding preachers, excellent music, or recreational programs. Church membership is voluntary. Wenger parents encourage young people to make a personal decision to follow Christ before they join the church, but try not to coerce them. Nevertheless, childhood socialization, peer pressure, parental encouragement, and other social forces funnel youth toward church membership.

Church membership is not a casual consideration. The decision to request baptism and join the church is a monumental one. Those who take the big step covenant to support the rules of the church and come under its discipline. A member says, "There has to be conviction; if there's no conviction, it will not stand. We believe that there is no salvation except out of a personal conviction." Typically, when young people who want to join the church are seventeen to nineteen years of age, they attend classes based on the Dordrecht Confession.

At her baptism, a young woman confesses her faith and covenants with the church community. She promises not only to submit to its discipline but also to help fellow members who may face disaster from fire, illness, or other catastrophes. New members willingly surrender some personal freedoms and agree to abide by the regulations of the church; in return, they receive the security of lifelong material and emotional support from their redemptive community. Such a posture diverges radically from the core American values of individualism and independence.

Wenger people believe that the church—the body of Christ—should strive for purity. The early Anabaptists rejected the Catholic notion that the "real presence" of Christ appears in the sacraments of bread and wine. There was only one sacrament for the Anabaptists, only one place where the presence of Christ appeared—in the gathered body of believers.[3] Following this understanding, Wengers think the body of Christ should strive for purity by practicing the beatitudes of Christ's kingdom described in Chapters 5 through 7 of Matthew's Gospel. Disciples of Christ should seek a pure heart, an inner communion with God, and a spirit of forgiveness and mercy. The redemptive community becomes a visible sacrament as it practices the spirit of Jesus in daily life. Purity of heart, in Wenger eyes, translates into humility, plain clothing, restricted use of technology, and modest recreational activities. Above all, the cardinal sign of purity is unity within the church, the body of Christ.

The redemptive community, in the Wenger view, is a disciplined and disciplining body. Ordained leaders hold the authority to excommunicate people who stray from church beliefs or standards. An expelled person may attend services but not partake of the communion bread and wine. Members hope that such discipline will lead the wayward to repent and amend their actions. And indeed, with proper confession, ex-members can be received back into the church.

Excommunicated people are shunned from the Lord's Table, the communion service, but they are not formally ostracized or avoided.[4] Indeed, ex-members are free to attend services and members may interact with them in daily living. If someone leaves and buys a car, "some members may refuse to ride with them as a matter of principle," explained a member. "We are advised not to have companionship with them," said another member, "especially not in the things that they were excommunicated for," which often involves riding in their cars. The ostracism of excommunicated members is mostly a private matter. Regardless of the circumstances, excommunication brings anger, pain, shame, and disappointment for the offenders and their families.

⊹ ORDNUNG: RULES FOR LIVING

Wengers do not simply believe their faith; they practice it. In fact, practice, more than belief, distinguishes them from mainstream Christians. Wengers are more concerned about proper practice than correct doctrine. Because God speaks through the redemptive community, its expectations loom large in their understanding of faith and salvation. Moral authority in Old Order communities emerges from traditional practice, rests on collective wisdom, and covers a broad scope of behavior.[5]

The regulations of the church are known as the *Ordnung*, a German word that roughly means "rules and order." Although a written version of the *Ordnung* is available to the leaders, the *Ordnung* is primarily transmitted orally.[6] Leaders read it to the congregation twice a year at a preparatory service prior to communion. One mother says, "The church rules are like a screen door . . . they keep the bad out, but let the good things in."

An expression of the collective moral order, the *Ordnung* serves a variety of functions: it (1) anchors the church to its heritage, (2) confesses its Christian faith, (3) marks the boundaries of the community, (4) affirms the authority of church leaders, (5) articulates basic Wenger values, (6) regulates the use of technology, (7) expresses the essence of Wenger identity, and (8) promotes order and unity across the various settlements. This religious blueprint also defines the roles of bishops, ministers, and deacons as well as the threefold responsibility of lay members: "to be obedient to the word of God . . . to keep the rules and ordinances of the church and to support the ministers of the congregation." In short, the *Ordnung* is a guide for daily living that specifies both the pathways and the prohibitions of Wenger life.

The *Ordnung* helps keep order in the household of God. It is the broom, so to speak, of the ordained officials, whose task it is to interpret and enforce the *Ordnung* guidelines. As stewards of the household of God, Wenger leaders often talk of "keeping house," keeping order in the church. In the words of the *Ordnung*, "We want to add nothing nor subtract anything from the Gospel but simply keep house with the whole Gospel of Jesus Christ and with the evangelical counsel of the church." Although the *Ordnung* spells out taboos and expected behaviors, it acknowledges that "external ceremonies alone cannot save anyone." True faith involves being "born anew of water and the spirit."[7] A bishop explained, "We want our young people to not just be bridled by the *Ordnung*; we want them to be conscientious. Otherwise, if there's an opportunity, they'll throw off the bit and bridle and run wild."

The moral order of Wenger culture is stratified into six levels of behavior: widely accepted, frowned upon, counseled against, forbidden by the church, forbidden by the Bible, forbidden for ministers.

Widely Accepted

On the first level are acceptable behaviors—the hundreds of things that one is permitted to do without question, such as lick an ice cream cone, wear shoes, play softball, kiss one's spouse, and read the daily newspaper. Unless the church for some reason addresses these issues, they by and large do not require moral guidance. Some Wenger practices simply follow tradition and

✣ TABLE 4 Social and cultural restrictions

Discouraged: Not a test of membership (counsels)

Alcoholic drinks*[1]	Playing cards
Amusement places	Pleasure trips
Belts for men	Pool rooms
Bowling alleys	Pornographic books*
Buying on Sunday*	Posing for photographs
Coed swimming*	Powwow and quack doctors
Festivals and fairs*	Short dresses*
Fishing trips	Showy, "proud" clothing
Fortune tellers*	Skating rinks (public)
Games of chance	Social Security
Golfing	Stylish furniture
Hunting trips (overnight)	Tobacco (raising and using)
Large tractors	Untied covering strings
Modern appliances	Yoga, meditation, and Oriental mysticism

Forbidden: A test of membership (rules)

Baseball uniforms	Marijuana/cocaine
Buying lottery tickets	Military service
Cameras**	Motor vehicle ownership
Computers**	Police duty
Electioneering (political campaigning)	Political meetings (attendance)
Hiring lawyers (for legal defense)	Radio/cassette/CD players**
Horse racing (public)	Secret society membership
Labor union membership	Serving on a jury for a capital offense
Life insurance	Televisions/VCRS**
Manufacturing weapons	Theater (drama and movies)

SOURCE: Groffdale Conference *Ordnung* 1976. Recent revisions provided by various informants.

NOTE: Items marked with an asterisk (*) are very strongly discouraged; owning or borrowing items marked with two asterisks (**) is forbidden.

[1]Wine is acceptable for medicinal purposes, weddings, and communions.

need no explicit rules. The *Ordnung* rarely prescribes expected behaviors for dress. For example, despite an array of distinctive garb worn by Wengers, the church only explicitly discourages belts and baseball uniforms for men and short dresses and untied covering strings for women. Wenger dress practices are largely driven by custom, oral tradition, and informal social pressure.

Frowned Upon

The second level consists of mild taboos that Wengers simply take for granted but rarely discuss. Behaviors such as riding in a hot air balloon, wearing a necktie or a bikini, or using nail polish or cosmetics of any type are not explicitly discouraged. These are understood as off limits for upright members of the community. Someone who engages in these behaviors will stir commotion in the community and face rebuke.

Counseled Against

Third-order behaviors and activities such as the counsels shown in Table 4 are discouraged ("counseled against") by the church, but they are not tests of membership, and violations will not bring excommunication. Items that are "strongly counseled against" include stylish furniture, modern appliances, large tractors, card games, pool halls, bowling alleys, fishing and hunting trips, games of chance, yoga, meditation, powwow "doctors," and pornography.[8] Members are discouraged from purchasing disability and retirement insurance and accepting food stamps, Social Security payments, and welfare benefits. Other borderline activities discouraged by the church include attending festivals, going on pleasure trips, purchasing goods on Sunday, drinking alcohol, playing golf, and listening to worldly music.

In the words of one bishop, "good members just don't do these things," yet they are not strictly taboo. Because members may be tempted to indulge in these activities, the church needs to "counsel against them." Those who engage in them may be admonished to stop but will not likely be expelled from the church. A member may persist with a habit such as smoking for years, for example, without risking expulsion from the church.

Forbidden by the Church

Forbidden behaviors specified by the rules of the *Ordnung* include owning automobiles, computers, and televisions and serving in the military. Those who cross these lines face excommunication if they fail to confess their behavior and change their ways. These fourth-order behaviors, strictly forbidden by the *Ordnung, are* a test of membership. Someone who enters military service, races horses, or joins a labor union will, if not penitent, be excommunicated from the church. Other tests of membership include owning pistols and cordless telephones, playing the lottery, and wearing wristwatches, cowboy outfits, sideburns, moustaches, and form-fitting dresses. Members may not accept police duty. They may not serve on a jury if a death penalty is possible. They may not hire a lawyer for defense in court or bring a lawsuit against anyone. Members who indulge in any of these behaviors will jeopardize their membership.

Forbidden by the Bible

Fifth-order activities that Wengers believe are forbidden by biblical teaching include drunkenness, fornication, sexual abuse, divorce, and swearing oaths. Because these are "already covered by Scripture," the church sees no need to speak of them in the *Ordnung*. The *Ordnung* specifically addresses third-level activities that are discouraged ("counsels") and fourth-level behaviors that are forbidden (rules)—and, by implication, fifth-level behaviors forbidden by biblical teaching. In one sermon, a bishop reminded the congregation not to "be drunk with wine." The Wengers are not teetotalers; some drink wine in moderation, and it is served at weddings. Habitual drunkenness, however, provides sufficient reason for expulsion from the church.

Forbidden for Ministers

Ordained leaders are expected to model higher ideals of behavior than other members. Borderline behaviors such as farming tobacco are strongly discouraged for ordained leaders. Ministers were not permitted to install electricity in their homes until the mid-1990s, long after most members had installed it. Standards of dress are also stiffer for ministers and their wives. Ordained men are expected to wear a special overcoat in the winter, for example. All of the higher expectations for ministerial conduct are informal except for a prohibition on signing political petitions, the only ministerial taboo referenced in the *Ordnung*.

⁜ DRAWING LINES

The lines drawn by the *Ordnung* symbolically separate the church from the world. Mennonite leaders admit that "not everything is evil about the forbidden things." In the words of the *Ordnung*, "If we owned all these worldly things, we would not be separate from the world and its worldly symbols. So we believe it is pleasing to God that we do not have these things and do not set our hearts on them, but rather believe in the Lord Jesus Christ."[9] In other words, not everything proscribed by the *Ordnung* is sinful. Many things are just worldly practices that, while not necessarily immoral, would inch the church closer to the world.

The *Ordnung* has few restrictions on home furnishings, but tradition and humility encourage simplicity in most homes.

The rules of the *Ordnung* focus on behaviors that threaten the welfare of the church. Wengers evaluate and monitor new technologies and reject those, such as television and computers, that might undermine the well-being of their community. As new technological "gadgets" arrive on the market, leaders tend to make the *Ordnung* more specific. One member noted, "When I was a boy, the *Ordnung* was short." Yet at a recent preparatory service, it took fifteen minutes to read the actual *Ordnung* and another fifteen minutes to read the list of items "earnestly counseled against."

By classifying a threat as "forbidden" or simply "counseled against," leaders can moderate and manage social change. Rather than being rigid and inflexible, the *Ordnung* is an organic, pliable set of guidelines that slowly changes over time—a product of countless discussions in the community. The final collective understandings that emerge typically reflect several years of discussion as the redemptive community seeks to discern a wise direction in the process of selective modernization.

Disobedience to the *Ordnung* means defying the authority of the body of Christ and the servant leaders who were selected by divine providence to guide the church. Such defiance brings shame and embarrassment to the culprits and their families. Pressure to comply with the *Ordnung* arises from sincere motivations to obey the will of God as well as to avoid the shame of stigma among friends, family, and leaders.

In the final analysis, the *Ordnung* reflects the sacred authority of the church over the individual. What matters most is one's attitude toward the church's authority and one's willingness to obey. The *Ordnung*, in Wenger eyes, details the expectations of a godly lifestyle and promotes uniformity and unity in the church. A common set of practices across all the settlements clarifies expectations, harnesses social change, and produces a single public identity.

❖ CROWDING THE FENCE

A subcultural group that hopes to avoid being engulfed by the dominant culture must specify standards of distinction. The *Ordnung* provides a cultural fence that marks the boundaries between Wenger society and the larger world. Leaders urge members to stay well within the Wenger pasture so that they can live plain and simple lives. Deviants and innovators in the community are often described as "crowding the fence." One minister explains, "If cattle have no fences, they get to wandering, and forget where home is. They need fences. We don't want [our young people] to find out too much about the outside world. The eye is never satisfied; they'll always want more."

Another asks, "How can a person say he's spiritual or interested in spiritual things, yet not become plainer in his life?" Spirituality and simple living flow together, in Wenger thinking, because God wants Christians to live a simple, plain life. A minister who tries to live more simply than the *Ordnung* explains, "I don't crowd the fence. I need to be a good example. It's easy to let things slip. One generation's luxury becomes the next generation's necessity. Our children get used to things and then think they can't do without them."

Still another member describes how youth sometimes push against the boundaries: "Yeah, they always want to crowd the fence. The grass always looks greener on the other side. . . . We just heard of one young guy from our church who didn't listen to his parents and went out and got a car. I believe he was using drugs lately. He was out [in the world] for I don't know how many years. Just lately he's come back and confessed to his parents that he wants to live like we wanted him to in the beginning." The member concluded, "This 'being out there,' there's nothing to it. It's nothing compared to being steadfast and living conservatively. There's nothing out there, regardless of how far you go, whatever you try. You won't have a satisfied feeling."

✢ CHANGING THE *ORDNUNG*

The *Ordnung* can only be changed at the semiannual ministers' conference. Prior to the fall and spring communions, each congregation holds a "counsel meeting" to discuss issues of concern. These meetings offer members a chance to voice concerns about the *Ordnung* and members who are crowding the fence. The ministers carry these local concerns to the ministers' conference, where the ordained leaders try to resolve the issues and, if necessary, revise the *Ordnung*. Then, in the preparatory service held the day before communion, the bishop reads the *Ordnung*, including any revisions, to each congregation.

In one congregation's counsel meeting, several concerns were voiced. Some boys had cotton dice hanging in their buggies. Some of the adolescent girls had curled their hair so it would puff out in front of their prayer coverings. One minister explained,

> We often discuss women's dress and hairstyles. This will always be a problem in our environment. We're surrounded with all this stuff; we are influenced. . . . It's that rebellious mood in young people that brings these things in. You go in town and see boys with bill caps on backwards and pants twice as big as needed; that's just orneriness . . . and they [pants] were tight ten to twenty years ago, so tight, how did they ever get in 'em?

Concerns like these are aired in the counsel meeting and then reported to the ministers' conference. If a consensus emerges, it may lead to a revision in the *Ordnung*.

All congregations and ministers must abide by the *Ordnung* approved at the ministers' conference. A minister outside Pennsylvania who wanted a more conservative *Ordnung* tried to institute his own by making dancing, smoking tobacco, and using tractors a test of membership.[10] One member asked, "How can he have his own *Ordnung* if he's alone, and no one's working with him?" A leader concluded, "He can be more conservative if he wants to, but he shouldn't keep talking to others about it." When a minister or bishop does not support the *Ordnung*, it creates a difficult situation for the local members as well as for the church-wide leaders.

⚜ HUMILITY AND SELF-DENIAL

Unlike modern culture, which values personal achievement and acclaim, Wenger life lifts up the virtue of humility. In the words of one member, "Humility is the greatest virtue." Leaders frequently cite James 4:6: "God resisteth the proud, but giveth grace unto the humble." *Demut* (humility) and *Hochmut* (pride) are the key oppositional values in the Wenger moral order. "Low" and "lowliness" are contrasted with "high" and "haughty" in their moral grid.[11] These deep values articulate the subordination of the self to communal priorities. Behaviors considered high and prideful reflect individualistic impulses that spurn the counsel of the church and threaten the well-being of the community. Humility is an attitudinal characteristic of *Gelassenheit*, a characteristic that denotes a meek, obedient, and yielded personality. Although Wengers rarely use the word *Gelassenheit*, their frequent references to humility signal their deference to the deep disposition of yieldedness.[12]

Hochmut carries two meanings in Wenger culture—a haughty attitude and pride in possessions. Members may be asked to "take the *Hochmut* off their carriage," meaning unneeded adornments or decorations. Preachers often remind members from the pulpit that "pride has been thrown out of heaven and can never return again." To guard against pride, Wenger leaders are even reluctant to count individual members, preferring instead to count households and congregations—collective units rather than individual people. When asked the meaning of humility, one minister said nothing about attitude, but instead told the story of a member who had a bicycle stolen and a few days later saw it parked in town, but did not report it to the police or try to contact the thief. Clearly, for this bishop, humility is related to behavior, not merely to attitude.

Members are admonished "not to think after high things, but rather to keep [themselves] lowly, and live in humility as pilgrims and strangers in this world."[13] They are called to humble themselves in the sight of the Lord and urged not to boast or do things that call attention to themselves or mock the virtue of meekness. The *Ordnung* calls members to self-denial and obedience: "Let us be plain and humble in our homes, clothing, carriages, and everything we own."[14] Ministers also warn members not to be proud of being plain and humble!

The humility theme is underscored in several Wenger hymns. One of them describes the posture of humility this way:

Help me with all my heart to feel small,
To exercise humility and meekness,
So that I, pure from all love of the world,
May continually grow in Jesus' love.[15]

Another hymn, with eight verses devoted to humility, reminds members that

Humility is the most beautiful virtue,
The glory and honor of all Christians . . .
He who is devoted to humility is loved by everyone;
He who doesn't desire to be great and learned,
He it is to whom God gives honor:
Humility has always pleased God.
Humility brings great blessings and finds favor with God . . .
For he who has this virtue [humility],
Is adorned in his soul,
And blessed in his doings,
He is blissful (happy) in this time,
And saved (blessed) in eternity.[16]

The Wenger embrace of humility and rejection of individualism reflects their culture's deepest and most fundamental cleavage from modern life. Viewed as expressions of pride, all forms of jewelry and makeup are taboo. Even wristwatches are forbidden because watches are "objects of pride and decoration." Many men and women carry pocket watches instead. Women are urged to keep their pocket watches "under their capes" and not use them "for adornment." Cameras are off-limits and members are counseled not to pose for personal photographs and portraits because they highlight the individual and might encourage pride. Photographs of an individual are sometimes compared to the graven images prohibited by the second commandment in Exodus 20:4. Colorful decorations on buggies, carriages, and harnesses are also discouraged, along with "stylish" furniture. "You don't have to have a car to have pride," remarked one minister. Pride expresses itself in any splashy display of clothing as well as in speech and posture. Any expressions of vanity in voice, body language, or lifestyle that call undue attention to the self violate the ethos of *Gelassenheit*.

Harmonicas and accordions are generally accepted, but guitars, pianos, and other instruments are forbidden in home and church.

Musical instruments are discouraged in homes and forbidden in church services. The *Ordnung* is very specific in identifying pianos, organs, violins, and guitars. These instruments are not only symbols of worldly culture but also tools of self-expression that might cultivate pride if individuals were to show off their musical skills. One Wenger teen explained, "If we are permitted the guitar, it would make a hole in the fence and might lead to bigger things." Accordions, although "counseled against" are often used at youth singings and gatherings. Harmonicas, small and unpretentious, are acceptable.

Commercialized forms of entertainment are considered self-gratifying activities that lead to mischief, worldliness, and sin. Thus, members are counseled to "stay away from" amusements—shows, movies, festivals, card games, poolrooms, golf courses, bowling alleys, "and all worldly music and pleasure places." The list of "counseled against" activities also includes horse races, pleasure trips, fishing and hunting excursions, trips to the beach, and professional sporting events.[17] Such amusements are considered a waste of time that encourages self-indulgence and intermingling with the world in ways that might lead to sloth and pride.

Coupled with pleas to live a plain and humble life are admonitions for self-denial, repentance, and confession. A member explains, "We try to teach our children to live with humility—this should be our aim. We are to have a meek and quiet spirit, because God resists the proud, but gives grace to the humble. We should forgive as God forgives—salvation is in forgiving, you know. If we would not have that forgiving from God, we would be lost. If somebody sins and falls, if they show true repentance and want to start over, yes, we can forgive them one hundred percent and they can have a fresh start."

The emphasis on *Gelassenheit* underscores the primacy of the community over the individual. With its inverted value structure (as compared with American individualism), Wenger priorities are church, family, and self, in that order. The values of Wenger culture accent communal patterns. They stand in sharp contrast to the triumphal individualism of postmodern culture, which heralds self-acclaim and personal achievement. Two practical expressions of *Gelassenheit*—nonconformity to the world and nonresistance to evil—are twin distinctives of Wenger faith.

✤ NONCONFORMITY TO THE WORLD

The social boundaries of religious groups can be ordered along a spectrum from bounded to open. Those groups that emphasize boundaries, like the Wenger Church, specify lifestyle expectations that set the church apart from the world. Members are disciplined when they fall short of the prescribed guidelines. Churches with more porous external boundaries, by contrast, emphasize core beliefs and pay scant attention to practices that set them off from the larger society. Churches concerned about purity may fall into provincialism and legalism; those without boundary markers may diminish their identity.

The Wengers strive to maintain a pure church, one separated from the surrounding world.[18] Worried about outside contaminants, the Wengers resist both acculturation (absorption of outside values) and assimilation (social interaction) into American society.[19] In support of their views, leaders point to Romans 12:2, "Be not conformed to this world," and also note that Jesus taught his followers to be in the world, but not of it (John 17:15–16).

Moreover, in 1 John 2:15, the apostle says, "Love not the world, neither the things that are in the world. If any man love the world, the love of the Father is not in him." The world, says John, is full of lust and pride, leading Wengers to avoid it as much as possible. Yet the world, in Wenger thought, is not identical with sin; it is simply a place of temptation, a place where sin is hard to avoid and where people easily go astray.

In Wenger minds, the church always stands in opposition to the world. Historically, the world, according to one member, "was in the *Schtadt* [town]." For a rural separatist people, the city is a cauldron of worldly activities—the place of wrong dressing, wrong entertainment, and wrong use of money. In the city, Satan hovers in the shadows. Spiritual dangers lurk in bars, massage parlors, and movie theaters. The city embodies the lust for material things, the fast-paced life, and the worship of progress, technology, and money. City life poses special dangers for the young. When Wengers lived in secluded rural areas, the ways of the *Schtedler* (town people) influenced them very little. Now suburbanization, tourism, electronic media, and high-speed transportation bring the city closer and closer to Wenger homes. Population growth and soaring land prices have so transformed the character of rural Lancaster County that one member lamented, "Today we have almost as much of the world in the country as in the city."[20]

Wengers usually refer to people who do not wear plain clothing as *Outsidas* (outsiders). "We don't mean it in a bad way, no bad feelings," explained one woman. "They are just outside our group, our faith." When Wenger people refer to the *Schtedler,* they mean those who dress in a worldly manner, partake in questionable entertainment, and drive costly automobiles. "[We use *Schtedler*] for people from big cities, tourists, non-local people who dress extreme, wear jewelry to the max and all the latest fashion," explained one member. When referring to a member of another Plain group, Wengers simply say, "a Horning," "a Piker," "a Thirty-fiver," and so on. Some Wengers also use the term "English" to refer to outsiders who speak English, but this term is much more common among the Amish.

In recent years, Wengers have also used the term *Weltleit* (people of the world) to refer to those who do not wear plain clothing. Members of more assimilated Anabaptist groups, such as the Lancaster Conference and the Weaverland Conference, are often called "higher Mennonites," or *Funkeleit,* rather than *Weltleit.* Thus, while the label of "worldly" historically focused on the city, it is now applied to all who wear worldly clothing—reflecting urbanism's pervasive influence even in rural hamlets. Worldliness, in short, means striving to look and live like the masses in mainstream society. Wear-

Carriages remain the most prominent symbol of separation from the world. The back of the small carriage shown here opens to form a wheelchair ramp.

ing a watch, curling one's hair, adorning carriages, installing drapes, buying an air-conditioned tractor, and advertising products on television are all examples of worldly behavior in the Wenger mind.

Separation starts with childrearing. Knowing they cannot fully insulate their children from the world, parents try to influence them by word and example. Attending school with other plainly dressed children reinforces Wenger culture and values. Parents sponsor wholesome recreational activities to keep adolescents from seeking worldly entertainment. Young people grow up in a subcultural world that minimizes contact with outsiders, an ethnic world of distinctive symbols—clothing, technology, entertainment, language, worship—underscoring separation from the larger society. This symbolic code shapes and filters a young person's view of the outside worldly society.

Despite their convictions about separation, Wengers do not live in a cocoon. They do not dislike outsiders; many members have formed lasting friendships with them. Church members interact with their neighbors on a daily basis. Although youth are discouraged from friendships that may lead to romance or business partnerships, many adults have numerous outside friends.

A retired Wenger minister and his wife, for example, have frequent contact with their non-Wenger neighbors. The husband assisted one neighbor, a sixty-year-old disabled by Parkinson's disease who was living alone, by helping him take his medications and checking up on him three or four times a day. Another non-Wenger neighbor stops in at the retired couple's home every Saturday morning just to talk. The outsider raises raspberries and gives some to the Wenger couple in exchange for homemade pies. When another outsider's father (described as "a hell of a reprobate") died, the retired minister and his son rented a van to attend the funeral to support their neighbor. These gestures of neighborliness illustrate the friendly patterns of interaction that often occur between Wengers and their outside neighbors.

Members also buy and sell products in the larger marketplace. Those who operate farms or businesses are in frequent contact with salespeople and customers. Some members volunteer with local fire companies and ambulance crews, and others volunteer with Mennonite Disaster Service or with Christian Aid Ministries, an international relief organization representing numerous Plain groups. Outside service clubs, civic organizations, professional groups, and political parties, however, are off-limits for Wengers.

Unhappy moments sometimes remind Wengers that they are indeed pilgrims and strangers in this world. In one community, two non-Wenger teens went on a two-day spree "shooting Mennonites," in their words. Both were charged with using pellet guns and slingshots to shoot Wenger youth riding bicycles on backcountry roads.[21] A professional who serves the Wenger community also describes some harassment: "English people treat Plain people like they are a lower class. Outsiders get aggravated sometimes because of the buggies and bikes on the road. They harass them, throw things at them and yell at them." Such incidents hardly compare with the severe persecution of their European forebears, but they do remind Wengers that they are strangers in a foreign land.

According to Wenger ministers, separation and nonconformity should flow from an inner spiritual transformation of the heart. One leader says, "Some of our people stop with the first part of Romans 12:2, which says, 'Be not conformed to this world.' They need to follow the second part of the verse: 'Be ye transformed by the renewing of your mind.'" An oft-repeated Wenger saying ties the inward and outward together: "One step closer to the world is one step farther away from God."

A second distinctive of Wenger faith is nonresistance—the traditional Anabaptist belief that followers of Christ should not use violent means to resist evil. One Wenger historian sees nonresistance and nonconformity as pillars of Wenger faith and practice.[22] Both of these distinctive beliefs stand on the foundation of *Gelassenheit*.

Practically, this means that Wenger Mennonites will not participate in the military, take people to court, or fight for their own rights. Conscientious objectors to war, they believe that Christ calls them to love, not kill, their enemies. This nonresistant teaching challenges a core value of American culture: that one should stand up and fight for one's rights or defend one's claims. Wengers refuse to do this, believing that God will defend them and avenge any wrong against them, if necessary, in this world.[23] The use of force, in Wenger eyes, belongs to the secular, worldly system.

Wenger convictions about nonresistance were challenged and clarified during World War II. In an unusual move, Wenger leaders produced a one-page broadside likely intended for distribution to outside neighbors, draft boards, and government officials—all of whom found their refusal to help purge Europe from the evil of Hitler incredible and unpatriotic.[24] Signed by the twelve ordained leaders, the statement reprinted Article xiv from the Dordrecht Confession, "Defense by Force," and summarized Wenger nonresistant beliefs. The writers reviewed brief portions of Scripture and noted that "many similar passages, as well as the whole tenor of the Gospel," supported nonresistance and nonparticipation in war. The statement included salient passages such as "the weapons of our warfare are not carnal," "love your enemies," "do good to them that hate you," "resist not evil," and "not rendering evil for evil, or railing for railing." It invoked other biblical directives as well: "Put up thy sword into its place: for all they that take the sword shall perish with the sword"; "Dearly beloved avenge not yourselves"; "If thine enemy hunger feed him; if he thirst give him to drink; for in so doing thou shall heap coals of fire upon his head"; "Be not overcome of evil, but overcome evil with good"; "The servant of the Lord must not strive, but be gentle to all men"; and "My kingdom is not of this world: if my kingdom were of this world, then would my servants fight."

The nonresistant stance of the Wengers was severely tested during World War II, when more than a dozen of them were arrested and imprisoned for refusing to serve in the armed forces or to enter Civilian Public Service (cps) camps operated by *Funkeleit* Mennonite groups. Many draft-eligible

Wenger men received farm deferments during World War II, as did farmers in other religious groups. Those who were not eligible for a farm deferment faced a stark choice: CPS camps or prison. The Wengers were reluctant to enter CPS camps operated by *Funkeleit* Mennonites, because Wenger leaders feared that their young men would fall under the negative influences of peers from assimilated Anabaptist groups. Wengers who refused to enter CPS were arrested and imprisoned. Fourteen were jailed at the Lewisburg (Pa.) Penitentiary.[25] Ironically, the Wengers feared associating with assimilated Mennonites more than with common prisoners.[26]

One Wenger youth, Leroy Martin, decided to go to an Amish-operated CPS camp in 1942, where according to his account, he did not need to transgress any church rules. Bishop Joseph O. Wenger thought this was a reasonable accommodation and decided not to excommunicate Martin. A sizable number of conservatively inclined members objected so strenuously that they refused to participate in communion. The dissension over entering the CPS camps was one of the factors that prompted some members to leave and form the Reidenbach group in 1946.[27]

Confrontations with the draft did not end with World War II. During the Korean War, several Wengers were arrested and briefly imprisoned for refusing to enter alternative service programs. One man was arrested twice. In 1952, prior to his marriage, he was arrested and taken to a prison in Philadelphia until his employer provided $2,500 bail for his release. Four years later, he was arrested again for refusing to perform hospital work "because of convictions against public works." A "merciful judge," in his words, "released me on bail and gave me a two-year probation as a farm worker."[28] Several others were also arrested during this time. Clearly, nonresistance is a deeply held conviction in the Wenger faith.

Although they hope that their lives and their community will be "light and salt" in the world, the Wengers generally do not evangelize or proselytize. While at first glance nonresistance and non-evangelism may seem like separate issues, Marc Gopin, in an analysis of Mennonite peacemaking, argues that they are in fact closely related: "all efforts to convert others involve a degree of assertiveness, which easily spills over into aggression."[29] The deep commitment to nonresistance—the rejection of force as a response to evil—also leads Wengers to avoid imposing their faith on others through typical methods of evangelism. Old Order Mennonite Donald Martin agrees: "Our emphasis on humility limits any form of aggressive evangelism."[30]

Old Order Mennonites refuse to take anyone to a court of law—filing a lawsuit would lead to excommunication—and they will not sit on a jury for a capital offense, because they reject capital punishment. When involved with the court system, Wengers affirm that they are telling the truth rather than swear an oath. Holding public office (except on a local township committee) is a test of membership. "We do not hold political offices," said one member, "because we would have to be sworn in and be willing to take someone to court."

Voting is discouraged, but it is not a test of membership. One member expressed the prevailing view toward voting in these words: "We feel that prayer is more important [than voting], that God can accomplish more than we can. We pray and let God decide. How can we know the best person and vote for them, if we don't know the person personally?" Nevertheless, a few members do vote, and the number of Wenger voters likely increased in the presidential election of 2004. Wenger sentiments strongly favored the reelection of President Bush because of his opposition to abortion and gay rights. In 2004, 10 percent of the Wengers in Lancaster County were listed as registered voters, and 92 percent of those were registered as Republicans. Only 53 percent of those registered actually voted—about 5.3 percent of the eligible Lancaster Wengers. But that rate was slightly higher than the 3 percent of Lancaster Wengers who voted in the 2000 presidential election. The Wenger rate of voting (5.3 percent) in the 2004 election was slightly lower than that of the Hornings (6.4 percent) and of the Old Order Amish (13 percent) in Lancaster County.[31]

Wengers generally avoid entanglements with government, even refusing government subsidies, but they pay all taxes according to the biblical injunction to pray for and respect elected leaders, and they seek to be law-respecting and law-abiding citizens.[32] They object to Social Security because they believe that the church should care for its own members. Along with the Amish and other Old Order Anabaptist groups, they were exempted from Social Security by the United States Congress in 1965.[33] Although participation in Social Security is strongly discouraged, it is not a test of membership. One knowledgeable member estimates that 5 percent of the Wengers participate and that none of the farmers do. When Wengers work for English employers, both employers and employees must pay Social Security taxes, but members usually do not receive benefits.

❖ THE DIALECT OF HUMILITY

The Pennsylvania German dialect undergirds Wenger identity and reinforces cultural boundaries. Language serves as the most important vehicle for passing on a worldview to future generations. The Wengers speak two languages: the Pennsylvania German dialect and English. They also learn to read, to some extent, the old Gothic German script. Some of their religious writings and songs appear in this sixteenth-century form of Old German. Although some Wengers can read the Old German script, very few can speak standard High German fluently.[34]

Children learn the Pennsylvania German dialect at home. All Wenger people, regardless of where they live, speak this dialect fluently. It is the mother tongue for home and community. Church services are conducted in the dialect. The bishop reads the *Ordnung* twice a year in the dialect, sometimes interjecting English words (e.g., "television," "computer," "modem") because Pennsylvania German lacks such contemporary terms. Pennsylvania German is the voice of *Gelassenheit*, the voice of lowliness, humility, yieldedness, and identity. The dialect carries the wisdom of the oral tradition of the redemptive community; it stands in sharp contrast to the high-class, technical, professional English of mainstream culture. "It is a continual reminder," said one member, "of who we are."

Children learn English when they attend Wenger private schools. English is the worldly language of commerce and high culture that Wengers use when speaking with outsiders. Many Wengers speak English with a German accent, and they occasionally interject German vocabulary and grammatical forms. The phrase "available farmland," for example, may become "awhaleable farmland."

The prayers, hymns, and Bible readings written in Old German script provide a deep, enduring connection to the past. In church services, ministers preach primarily in the Pennsylvania German dialect, spiced with some English and some Old German when they quote Scripture. Out of courtesy to English-speaking visitors, preachers will often speak some sentences in English and even read a few verses from an English Bible. A bishop explained, "We're interested in getting our points across, but we're not interested in speaking English just for the sake of being like the English people." The amount of English used in sermons for weddings, funerals, and Sunday services depends on the number of English visitors. Explained one member, "If half of those attending a funeral only understand English, a lot of the sermon will be in English, but never the whole sermon."

One bishop expressed concern about a preacher who tries to preach in standard German rather than the dialect. "He's going against a stone wall because the young people are not going to learn that. We don't feel that one language is more preferred by God than another. Some preach in High German to be a little more impressive, but I'd rather preach in *Deitsch* [Pennsylvania German] so the people understand." The leader concluded, "Some people avoid English because it's the language of outsiders, but I like to use a little to help the young people understand better. The important thing is that people understand."

Children learn to read Old German in Wenger private schools, but the quality of instruction largely depends on the German proficiency of the teacher. Occasionally, Wengers hold a German school to teach adults Old German. The curriculum runs for three years with seven three-hour sessions each winter.[35] Some of the students are from the Horning Church. The German school demonstrates the high value Wengers place on the dialect and their desire to pass it on to the next generation.

In the mind of one member, the dialect and the use of horse-drawn carriages are the two most important parts of their identity. "*Everything* else," in his mind, "is window dressing."[36] Nevertheless, distinctive dress is another important symbol of solidarity and separation, a marker that many others in his community would be loath to call just "window dressing."

✣ MARKING BOUNDARIES WITH MEN'S CLOTHING

Distinctive dress is an informal redemptive ritual that articulates the ethos of *Gelassenheit*. It is a redemptive ritual because it is a daily, collective rite that declares membership in the redemptive community and separation from the world. For Wengers, wearing worldly fashions betrays a heart attuned to the world. Common dress marks the boundaries of the community; it preaches a continuous sermon about identity, belonging, and separation. Those who wear the customary garb forgo their right to self-expression in dress and signal their compliance with the church's moral order. Members who scorn dress regulations evince, in Mennonite eyes, a proud and unrepentant heart.[37] Distinctive dress symbolizes a humble heart, one submissive to the church and wary of worldly fashions.

For formal occasions, adult men wear black high-top shoes, dark pants, dark socks, a light-colored shirt, suspenders, and broadfall pants (i.e., without a zipper).[38] Various seamstresses in the community sew the trousers using old-style tailoring, with a flap (broadfall) across the front fastened by buttons. Men wear a black vest and/or a black plain coat with a standing collar and a white or blue long-sleeved shirt to church. Unmarried boys may wear white shirts with fine blue stripes, pants with a zipper, and suspenders. For casual wear, many men and boys wear solid-colored, figured, or plaid shirts. They also wear homemade or brand-name jeans, suspenders, and nylon or straw hats, depending on the weather.[39]

The man's black plain suit has a coat with a standing collar. Typically sewn by a Wenger seamstress, the coat is tailored to fit and is buttoned in the front. Boys may wear a lapel coat until they marry, but then they don a standing-collar plain coat. In cold weather, ministers wear a heavy overcoat with a cape for church. Men wear dark coats, jackets, or windbreakers. Although the *Ordnung* discourages only certain clothing, social pressure encourages conformity. For example, on one Sunday, a man wore a suit with a greenish tint. He felt the stigma of sanction so he never wore the suit again.

Wenger men typically wear a hat outdoors. Most of the bishops wear black felt hats with three-inch brims. Some older men also wear black felt hats with a wide brim, but most men wear black nylon hats. Many of the boys wear a similarly styled black or navy blue nylon hat with a narrower brim and a crease in the crown. Several Lancaster County Amish hat makers supply most of the felt hats. For everyday work, men typically wear store-bought blue or dark-colored pants and jackets. Their distinctive hats and their suspenders set Wenger men apart from outsiders. Belts, neckties, cowboy clothing, billed caps, colored hats, brightly colored coats, and stylish clothing or shoes are discouraged for men. The *Ordnung* also advises men not to go shirtless. Baseball players may not wear uniforms, but small game and deer hunters are urged to wear orange safety jackets.

Almost all Wenger men are clean shaven, although beards are not prohibited. One leader worries about the length of the sideburns that some youth like to grow. "Right now, we mention [discourage] sideburns. I notice those things because I know they just came in with Elvis Presley." Men are advised not to sport fashionable hairstyles, especially not moustaches, which are associated with pride and military officers. Men's hairstyles, in general, reflect simplicity, custom, and avoidance of worldly fashions.

✢ A MODEST WARDROBE FOR WOMEN

Women typically wear plain bonnets and shawls when they travel to church services or other meetings. For religious services, a Wenger woman wears a cape and a half-apron over her dress (made of the same material) and a large head covering with strings that tie under the chin. Her hair is not cut or worn loosely but is pulled tightly into a bun under the head covering. Short dresses, slacks, form-fitting dresses, and fabrics that are sheer or have large prints are discouraged for women. Unlike those of their Amish neighbors, Wenger dresses and shirts may have small print designs, but large, bold, or brightly colored ones are discouraged. Moreover, women are counseled not to have collars, lace, or wide cuffs on their dresses, nor to wear fashionable clothing. Women never wear jewelry or makeup. Above all, they are counseled to dress modestly.

Most women's dresses hang five to ten inches off the ground. Some older women wear their dresses even longer, but young girls wear theirs midway between the knee and ankle. Women wear black calf-length stockings and black shoes to church and formal events such as funerals and weddings. During the week, many women wear dark-colored sneakers and girls wear colored athletic shoes. Older women typically wear plain-colored shawls. Young women sometimes wear woolen "border shawls" (black shawls with a lighter border), but many of them wear black casual coats, especially when riding bicycles, because the coats are warmer and safer than shawls.

According to one woman, "We can wear any color dresses we want to. However, the older women in the church usually wear darker dresses instead of pink or yellow. Females start wearing shawls when they get married. Some older girls do wear them, though." Women wear lightweight solid black shawls in the spring and fall, but in the winter they wear heavier ones with a white border stripe. "A married woman would never wear a jacket to church or to a formal event like a wedding or a funeral. But they might wear a black sweater instead of a shawl if it is not real cold outside," said a young mother. The apron a woman wears to church is always the same color as her dress. Her everyday apron may be a full apron or just a waist apron. Properly dressed women also wear a cape of matching color that fits over the shoulders and attaches at the waist in front and back.

Mothers dress their babies in a variety of outfits—boys in white or light-colored homemade "suits" and girls in white or light-colored homemade dresses. For everyday dress in most families, the boys wear suspenders, dark pants, and plaid shirts. Yet children's attire varies somewhat by family. The church admonishes parents not to "adorn their children" and becomes more concerned about dress as their youth approach adolescence.

Girls begin wearing capes over their dresses when they are "about fifteen or when necessary for modesty," said a mother.[40] Another mother added, "It makes them appear more grown up. My [fourteen-year-old] daughter wants to wear a cape and a covering now." Older women wear capes with a point in the back. One older woman says, "We have to be more 'pointy' than the younger girls," but it is not required and not all older women wear more

The young women (front row) illustrate the variety of prints in Wenger dresses. Some of the men are not Wengers.

pointed capes. A younger girl wears her cape more squared-off in the back with the end sewn on a fabric belt at the waist. Girls wear white prayer coverings with white strings, which are tied when attending church.

Women wear black dresses on several occasions: the preparatory service, Communion Sunday (a black dress signifies that one is "ready for communion"), funerals, and ordinations. They also wear black after the death of a close relative. Formerly, women wore black for the entire year after the death of an immediate family member, but now they wear it for only about six months. Following the death of an aunt, uncle, or grandparent, they typically wear black for several weeks. The black garb supports the grieving process by reminding everyone of the pain of death and facilitating conversation and other forms of caring.

Women buy or sew their head coverings out of white mesh fabric (cotton, polyester, or nylon). The head covering conceals the top of the head and comes down over the ears, although the coverings of teenage girls hide just the upper edges of their ears. All females, even tiny babies, have their heads covered when they go to church. When they reach two or three years of age, little girls begin wearing a covering with light-colored tie strings and a bonnet to church. After they are baptized, girls wear their coverings throughout the day at home. Women start wearing black tie strings on their coverings after they have been married about three years, or, if unmarried, when they reach their early thirties. Wenger women never cut their hair, nor do they wave or style it. Younger girls typically wear braids, but older girls and women wear their hair up, pinned under their head coverings.

Girls wear customary Wenger clothing at school. They do not wear head coverings, but the eighth graders wear their hair rolled up in a bun and fastened with barrettes. Their dresses (without aprons) have small flowered patterns and hang midway between the knee and ankle. They wear calf-length socks, black leather shoes or sneakers, and wear sweaters over their fitted dresses if the schoolroom is cool.

Girls start pinning up their hair at about age thirteen. In one home, a fourteen-year-old eighth grader wears her hair twisted up in back and held in place by several shiny metal barrettes, but she does not yet wear a head covering. She wears calf-length socks and a pink dress (the same color as her mother's) with a full, matching pink apron. The younger girls in the family all have aprons and wear their hair in two braids, except for the two-year-old, who has two short ponytails.

Wenger women typically wear black bonnets over their coverings when they go to church and to formal events such as weddings and funerals. Some wear bonnets whenever they go out in public, but others do not. A new black bonnet costs about $22 and is sewn by local Wenger women. An older man was disturbed to see a girl riding her bicycle on a cool, damp day without a bonnet. She had a plastic sheet tied over her head instead of a bonnet, leaving her covering strings flying out behind. "She dresses like that," he lamented, "because she wants to be dressed like the world around her. In the past, girls never went outside without their bonnets on."

❖ THE DIALECT OF DRESS

Dress speaks two languages. On the one hand, it speaks the dialect of belonging, the language that builds community, identity, and solidarity. On the other hand, it speaks the dialect of separation, the language that draws boundaries between the community of faith and the larger society. Clothing and hairstyles accomplish these objectives by distinguishing Wengers from the surrounding world and providing a "uniform" that binds the community together. Some members chafe at the requirements, so church leaders often remind their flocks not to stray toward the stylish dress that leads to pride and worldliness. But despite occasional streaks of pride, Wenger attire appears plain and simple alongside the ever-changing designer fashions in shopping malls and boutiques.

Wengers who operate businesses also have concerns about dress. A sign on a fabric shop door in Indiana advises outside customers: "Please dress modestly. Modestly means covered from shoulders to knees. If you cannot cooperate, please go elsewhere." Even more blunt was the message at a Wenger food store in Pennsylvania: "Cover your hide or stay outside!"

Church leaders vigilantly monitor dress practices. A minister noted, "If you don't catch the little changes, they'll continue until there's no difference between the church people and the world." The devil is in the details—and only constant vigilance ensures success. Leaders try to build a firewall against the fashions of the world. One of them noted a worldly trend among Lancaster Conference women: "Their coverings got smaller and smaller. I thought to myself, if they get any smaller they'll disappear altogether. And sure enough, they did, and then some of their women began cutting their hair." One member averred, "People say the bishop won't allow something, but dress should be our personal conviction. We should all be involved in our church discipline."

According to one Wenger, one of the ministers' conferences was "all about women's dress." Both women and men voiced their views on the subject in congregational counsel meetings before the conference. Some members urged the ministers to maintain a strict line, or "things would get out of hand." The leaders requested that women not wear dresses with a slight V-neck, saying, "who knows where that might lead." One man commented, "We have more trouble with the women than with the men." Indeed, men have fewer clothing restrictions, leading one wife to complain to her husband that the dress standards were not fair. He replied that it was nature's way, because some male birds wear more colorful clothing than the females. A woman retorted, "Men may not wear more colorful clothing than women. I've never heard of a woman complaining to her husband about fairness. Women are not more of a problem than men. The 'troubles' are more with our youth, and boys have as much a problem with worldly dressing as girls."[41]

For the most part, both women and men conform to the dress norms without complaint. Nevertheless, Wenger women bear a much heavier burden of ethnic identity, especially in the public domain. "The real issue," according to one man, "is that *Outsida* dress styles for women are immodest, and modesty is more of an issue for women than for men."

✣ PLAIN AND SIMPLE CHURCHHOUSES

As they robe their bodies, so the Wengers wrap their churchhouses—plainly and simply. In many ways, the churchhouse symbolizes the essence of Wenger life and culture. The rectangular buildings dot the landscape, white gems against the dark earth and green fields, structures of beauty and simplicity. Intentionally unadorned, the churchhouse has no altar, platform, pulpit, holy place, steeple, or stained glass. The plain, humble churchhouses are architectural expressions of *Gelassenheit*.

The Wenger people have no sacred places; they do not believe that God resides in a building.[42] Because God dwells within the body of believers, the body, not the building, should be holy. Thus they do not call their place of worship a church, but a *Gmayhaus* (churchhouse). Members constitute the living church that gathers in a house for worship.[43] The familial metaphor calls to mind earlier times, when Mennonites met in their homes for worship. Leaders still talk about "housekeeping" in the church—administering the regulations that keep the body healthy. Members speak of "home" ministers, those who serve the church family in their local area. All of these words and images underscore the familial nature of the redemptive community.

Wengers sometimes contrast themselves with the *Kircheleut*, the church people who have altars, steeples, and finely appointed sanctuaries. Unlike High Church people, Wengers are the meek and lowly who worship in plain churchhouses without convenience or adornment. Typically locked throughout the week, their churchhouses are only used on Sunday morning, or for an occasional midweek daytime meeting. They are only opened when the full body, about seventy-five families, assembles for worship.[44]

The churchhouse provides a graphic reminder of the plain simplicity of Wenger faith.[45] Churchyards have a hand water pump just outside the building, even though members have tap water under pressure in their own homes. The brightly painted water pump in the churchyard is a weekly reminder that the church values the old way of doing things. Nearby stand the outhouses, the rows of tie-rails, and the open sheds for horses.

In the adjacent cemetery, simple stones carry the surnames of departed members: Hoover, Martin, Nolt, Zimmerman. To emphasize their plain-

A family leaves a churchhouse in their carriage after a Sunday morning service.

ness, no flowers adorn the graves. Surrounded by a white wooden fence, the graveyard is a continual reminder that Wengers are pilgrims and strangers in this world, merely passing through for a few years. On a typical Sunday, families wheel their carriages into the churchyard and tie their horses in the sheds or to the tie-rails. Groups of women converse in the churchyard. Men clad in black hats, coats, and vests file into the churchhouse for worship.

Inside the building, stark white walls boast no pictures, symbols, or decorations. The walls are made from plaster, not from contemporary drywall boards.[46] The large meeting room has a clear-finish wooden floor, without carpet, tile, or linoleum. There are no drapes, stained-glass windows, or crosses—not even a pulpit. There is no electricity, running water, restrooms, piano, organ, or other musical instruments. Rows of bare wooden benches on three sides of the room face a singers' table and a preacher's table that stand in the middle of a long side wall. Tall windows let in light and fresh air, while window shades screen the sun's glare. Even the entrances reflect the social structure of Wenger society, with a men's door, a women's door, a ministers' door, an entrance for the boys, and one for the girls.

Churchhouses have cloakrooms for hats and coats, one for women and another for men, usually at opposite ends of the building. Bonnets and hats are hung in the respective cloakrooms, or in the meeting room on wall hooks or hooks attached to boards suspended from the ceiling. Adjacent to the women's cloakroom is a small "counsel room" where the ministers consult before each service. In the meeting room, the ministers' bench sits centered along a side wall that serves as the front of the meeting. In front of the ministers' bench stands the preacher's table—small, flat, and unadorned—and the long rectangular singers' table. Facing the ministers, the adult men sit to the right side of the preacher's table, the adult women to the left side. The young people and older children sit on long benches across the middle and back of the main room, directly facing the preacher.

Alms boxes for contributions hang near the doors. At the semiannual preparatory service, members place contributions in the boxes to help maintain the churchhouse and grounds. The Martindale churchhouse, used by both the Wenger Church and the Horning Church, has a dual-fuel furnace in its basement. When the Wenger people meet (every other Sunday), they heat the building with wood or coal. On the alternate Sunday, the car-driving Horning people heat the building with oil. Even in the use of furnaces, the two churches proclaim both their differences and their tolerance for one another![47]

The starkly angular churchhouse represents more than just a meeting place; it symbolizes the deepest value, the *Gelassenheit* of Wenger life. Its plain simplicity—sparsely furnished space, plain benches, and unadorned walls—speaks of practicality and humility. The churchhouse testifies to an orderly community: benches in parallel rows, a place for each age and gender, separate seats for the ministry, and separate doors for men and women. All of these elements reflect the structure of the *Gmay*. Here the redemptive community gathers to worship. Horse and buggy wait outside. Ancestors lie in the graveyard a few steps away.

A quiet, peaceful elegance graces this space, which embodies the values, faith, and structure of Wenger society. Neither poverty nor asceticism dictates this simplicity; it derives from sincere religious conviction. These plain appointments, constant reminders of the orderliness and humility of Wenger life, provide the setting for the ceremonial rites of redemption. Other aspects of Wenger identity are rooted in their unique history, a story we explore in Chapter 3.

Mobility and Identity

The rule against the car is the first one that is read in church.

—WENGER MEMBER

❖ THE RIDDLE OF TRACTOR WHEELS

Group identity is often shaped by the mythology that re-counts the events leading to the group's formation. The Wengers emerged in the midst of a 1927 controversy over the automobile in Lancaster's Old Order community—a conflict that produced the car-driving Horning Church and the horse-and-buggy-driving Wenger Church. Opposition to car ownership and related issues, such as tractor wheels, continues to shape Wenger identity.

According to many Wengers, a ten-year controversy over rubber belting wheels on tractors has been the most contentious issue in their history. It started in the 1970s, when some farmers began wrapping rubber belts under the steel cleats of their tractor wheels for easier use on rural roads. The use of belting wheels came to a head in 1990 and dominated church discussions for a decade. In the words of a farmer born in 1954, "Tractor wheels have been the most persistent and contentious issue in my lifetime." Many members openly worried that belting wheels would divide the church. A young mother said, "It was a big issue. Every time we had communion, the ministers mentioned belting wheels."

Why would debates over tractor wheels dominate preparations for communion services? At first blush, tractor wheels might seem trivial and mundane to outsiders, certainly not the stuff of sacred worship and religion. Yet the tractor wheel debate reveals three cultural lessons about Wenger society.

First, religion is not just an experience relegated to a Sunday sanctuary or restricted to written creeds; rather, it is a sacred canopy that stretches over daily life. Second, issues of faith are not purely matters of personal choice. Farmers, for example, are not free to make personal decisions about their tractor wheels. Some, but not all, lifestyle questions fall under the umbrella of church authority. Many aspects of tractors—their color and lights, for example—are of no interest to the church. Tractor wheels fall under the church's umbrella because they are linked to Wenger identity, which leads to the third lesson. The identity of the Wenger Church is embedded in its historic opposition to the automobile and the circumstances surrounding the church's origin in 1927. That story provides the key to solving the riddle of tractor wheels and to understanding the core of Wenger identity.

✤ SEARCHING FOR A NEW BISHOP

For the final fifteen years of Bishop Jonas (Yonie) Martin's ministry (1910–25), the car presented a growing threat to the peace of his Old Order community.[1] The bishop staunchly opposed the car until his death in 1925. He considered cars "worldly possessions, dangerous, costly, the ruination of young people, and highly esteemed among men."[2] Martin often said, "The elders used to say when someone proceeds in an unusually high [proud] manner, he shall be given the brotherly address [rebuked], and if an automobile is not proceeding in a haughty manner, then I don't know what would be high and haughty."[3] He cited a Bible verse (Luke 16:15) against the auto: "That which is highly esteemed among men is an abomination in the sight of God." When Eli Zimmerman rigged up his own horseless carriage in Martindale in 1910 and eventually bought a real car, he was promptly excommunicated.[4] His expulsion was widely supported, but sentiments across the Old Order community soon began to favor the car.

In 1914, seventy-five-year-old Jonas Martin requested an assistant bishop. Two years earlier, Martin had ordained forty-one-year-old John Dan Wenger as bishop of the Old Order Mennonites in Virginia. Wenger, a strong opponent of the car, developed a close relationship with old Bishop Martin. "He became Martin's right arm and he did everything he could," in the words of one Mennonite historian, "to keep Minister Moses Horning out" of the pool of candidates to assist and eventually replace the aging bishop.

Typically, any minister who received one vote from a member was eligible for the lot. Wenger argued that Horning should be excluded because he could not preach in English, was not talented enough, and was too favorable toward the car. Persuaded by Wenger's arguments, the elderly Yonie Martin agreed to require three votes for eligibility, an exception that, according to one historian, "never happened before and never again." Four other candidates, including Joseph O. Wenger (future bishop of the Wengers), received three or more votes, but Horning only had two. Worried about a controversy if Horning missed the lot, influential eighty-year-old Deacon Daniel Burkholder told Bishop Martin, "If you don't take him (Horning) along, you'll have trouble." He thus added his own vote, which—to John Dan Wenger's consternation—placed Moses Horning in the final pool of five ministers.[5]

During a service of ordination, each candidate selects a hymnbook on the singers' table in the churchhouse. The number of hymnbooks equals the number of candidates. A small slip of paper that, in God's providence, signals who will be ordained bishop is hidden in one of the books. The books are randomly scrambled twice by two different deacons before the casting of the lots.

At the ordination service in 1914, each of the candidates selected a book—except Moses Horning, who fainted and collapsed, hitting his head on a bench so hard that it bled. After his wife stopped the bleeding, he regained consciousness and sat up again. Bishop Martin then invited Horning to take the remaining book on the table, but he replied, "I can't." Unsure what to do amid the high drama, Bishop Martin began searching for the slip of paper in the books held by the other candidates, but without success. Then he turned to Horning's unclaimed book still on the table and found the fateful paper. Upon this discovery, Martin proceeded to ordain the forty-three-year-old Moses Horning as assistant bishop.[6] Car opponents Bishop John Dan Wenger and Minister Joseph O. Wenger, watching the drama unfold, knew that the outcome would surely accelerate the controversy over the car.

The younger, mild-mannered Horning's openness to cars troubled old Bishop Martin. Indeed, Yonie Martin was so troubled that, according to one historian, he told Virginia bishop John Dan Wenger, "I'm looking to you to help keep the car out, because Moses Horning can't." Sometime after this encouragement, Wenger published a ten-page diatribe against the car. (See Appendix E.) Nevertheless, in direct defiance of their old bishop, members of the church had begun buying cars. On any given Sunday, more and more cars arrived at churchyards designed for horses and buggies. About 1916, one member began counting those who had been expelled for buying cars, and by 1920, his list totaled one hundred members. Most of these eventually joined the Lancaster Conference, which permitted cars. The continuing exodus of so many pro-car members created a crisis.

In 1920, Jonas Martin had a mini-stroke, and after that, Assistant Bishop Horning assumed responsibility for most of the leadership duties. With more members buying cars and with little help from his assistant, the eighty-one-year-old Martin was forced to compromise, and car owners were no longer completely expelled. Still considered members, they were "set back" from participating in communion but not formally excommunicated. Many continued to attend worship services even though they were under the stigma of disobedience—of being what some called "half-expelled."[7] Biding their time, the "half-expelled" car owners undoubtedly hoped that the good Lord would soon call Bishop Martin to his heavenly home so that they could drive their cars with a clean conscience. They only had to wait a few years.

Meanwhile, the car controversy continued to simmer. Worried that under the watch of Bishop Horning, more of his flock would buy the abominable automobiles after his death, Yonie Martin encouraged members to read John Dan Wenger's articulate tract condemning the car.[8] The tract was called "A Confession of Faith," showing that the car, in Bishop Wenger's mind, was not merely a technological innovation but a central matter of faith. Despite the Virginia bishop's persuasive arguments, John Dan Wenger had no direct authority over the Weaverland Conference when Bishop Martin departed for eternity in July 1925.

The debate intensified with Yonie Martin's death. The car advocates lacked the audacity to press the issue at the ministers' conference as long as the venerable founder of the Old Order movement had been living. With Martin's departure, however, the car issue came to a head. Moreover, the declining price of used cars made them more tempting than ever. In addition, the Old Order Wisler group in Ohio and Indiana had recently adopted the car. These factors brought "a dark cloud" over the church, in the words of pro-car minister Frank Hurst.[9]

The old bishop's departure created a vacuum. Pro-car and anti-car factions forcefully argued their views in the face of Horning's weak but conciliatory leadership. The parents of some youthful car owners pled with the new bishop to relax the rules; however, despite statements endorsing the car and Bishop Horning's favorable nod, strong pockets of resistance remained loyal to old Yonie Martin.

Members of the Groffdale congregation heard both sides of the controversy in the sermons of their preachers. Preacher Joseph O. Wenger, one of the nominees for bishop when Horning was ordained, staunchly and thoughtfully opposed the car. Wenger, born in 1868, is considered by some Old Order historians as "the best educated of all Old Order ministers ever."[10] As a young man, he taught school for several years and then married Susanna Nolt. Ordained in 1896, Wenger was the first minister ordained after the 1893 division and thus held seniority among all the ministers ordained in Lancaster County's Old Order churches. He was ordained by his brother-in-law, Bishop Yonie Martin. Wenger and Martin worked closely together as minister and bishop, both ardently promoting the Pennsylvania German dialect and horse-and-buggy transportation.

Sitting beside Wenger on the ministers' bench was Preacher John S. Kurtz, brother-in-law of Moses Horning, who argued for a "plain motor car or truck." Already in 1920, Kurtz had written a letter to Virginia bishop John Dan Wenger, arguing forcibly in favor of a "plain truck." (See Appendix E.) For several years, Kurtz and Wenger presented their opposing views to the Groffdale congregation.

Although members were not allowed to own trucks, some hired them (with drivers) to transport products. Indeed, Kurtz noted that "a great part of the tobacco crop was hauled by truck" and that those set back from communion, or "half-expelled," were using vehicles.[11] Kurtz challenged the argument that the car was a symbol of pride and high-mindedness—an abomination in the eyes of God—developed by worldly people. "Was not all that we have," he retorted, "at one time gotten up [developed] by worldly people and highly esteemed among men?" He noted that when carriages with springs first came into use, "only the puffed-up and high-heads had them. But soon, they were common for our people." He cited other examples: sewing machines, tractors, and even changes in plain clothing, all of which were first condemned as prideful but later were accepted.

In a stinging critique, Kurtz concluded, "This auto decision is the 'shacki-est' I ever saw; when a wind blows or a fox runs against [it], it shatters." "Even the bishops," he charged, "hire autos to get around" when they are away from home; and one bishop even used an auto "because it was warmer than the carriage." He charged that "bishops as well as the members and ministers: when they get in a 'ditch,' then they go for the auto even [the] members that talked so hard against it and want to have put back [expel] such that have [a] truck or even run [drive] a truck. Then they [anti-auto critics] take trips with those very machines and men who[m] they put back [from communion]." Preacher Kurtz concluded, "He that is joined to a har-lot is one body at home or abroad." Invoking the image of a harlot surely did not quiet the debate! Finally, Kurtz argued, if the car is "too stylish," it "must be converted and made common [plain] to suit our confession," rather than remain a cause for expulsion. And if members who have a car "get proud or vain, they should be visited and pointed to humility—that is, to Christ."

The car was not the only issue sowing seeds of discord. Minister Frank Hurst, in a letter penned in January 1927, wrote, "There is much contention in our church on acct [account] of the language and auto." After describing the debate over the car, he repeated, "and the same with language."[12] Those arguing against the car wanted to keep the Pennsylvania German dialect and were disturbed by the growing use of English among some of their more pro-gressive-minded brothers and sisters. Various informants confirmed the cen-trality of language in the division and noted Joseph Wenger's strong opposi-tion to English, even though he could speak it fluently. In fact, when Wenger preached in the Old Order churches in Virginia, he spoke in the German dialect despite the fact that those churches used English in their services.[13]

The discord over the car and language was so debilitating that commu-nion services were canceled in the spring of 1926. They were reinstated in the fall of 1926, leading Frank Hurst to observe, "Brotherly love has not all died out yet."[14]

As the community prepared for the fateful spring ministers' conference in 1927, tensions hung heavy, so heavy that farmer Menno Weaver of Martin-dale lay awake at night. No one wanted to see another division cut through the church and sever families as it had in 1893. Weaver was deeply troubled by the "fighting and disputing [over the car] going on right in the midst of our church."

After several sleepless nights, Weaver scribbled a forty-four-paragraph essay about prior changes among the Mennonites living around the village of Martindale.[15] His conclusion implied that the auto was inevitable. He asked rhetorically: If farmers can mount a power engine on four iron wheels, why is it "any worse to have one mounted on rubber wheels? Some might say that rubber wheels are forbidden. But did not the same God cause the rubber tree to grow that placed iron ore in the hills?"

The Martindale farmer, seeking conciliation on the car, wrote, "Some say you can ride in one all you can, hire one to do your hauling, or whatever else you may have. But to own one is very wrong, to sit right at the wheel, this just cannot be. Some say it is wrong, for some of our forefathers said no. May I ask this, did not our forefathers make use of new inventions in their time?" Menno Weaver concluded his rambling essay with a proposal akin to Preacher Kurtz's idea of a plain car: "We can get some [cars] painted black all over, with no stripes and flowers on, as some have on their carriages, or even as some farm wagons are painted in nice and bright colors with stripes and flowers on."

The idea of a plain car appealed to another member, Martin Zimmerman, as the perfect compromise.[16] It appealed so much, in fact, that he had a car customized to look like a carriage. Bishop Horning, trying to mediate the tensions over the car, likely welcomed the emerging compromise: a plain car, even plainer than decorated carriages and farm wagons. Completely black, chrome and all, a plain car should be acceptable to the plainest of the Plain people under Bishop Horning's care. Yet his hopes, however virtuous, were in vain.

✣ THE CAR DIVIDES THE CHURCH

After seventeen years of debate that impaired Bishop Horning's health, the automobile issue came to a boil at the ministers' conference on 8 April 1927.[17] Both sides felt intense pressure. The atmosphere was so volatile that Bishop Horning, moderator of the conference, was too stressed to attend. Instead, he sent a minister with a message: Horning thought the conference should allow cars. Five days before the meeting, word was circulating on the "Old Order Internet" that "the car will be allowed." Confident of the outcome, some members bought cars that week—so many, in fact, that area car dealers sold out.

At the one-day conference held in the Weaverland churchhouse, fifteen ministers and deacons debated the idea of accepting the car with restrictions. Pro-car preacher John S. Kurtz was absent—silenced by death the month before.[18] Bishop Wenger from Virginia, Preacher Joseph O. Wenger, and other like-minded conservatives doubtlessly argued that a car was a car, regardless of its color.[19] And Bishop Yonie Martin, looking down from on high, surely agreed. Pro-car preacher Frank Hurst argued that "so many members now have cars that it will make more trouble if we say that they are not allowed, than if we allow them," using the situation, in essence, to force the conference to allow cars.

At the close of a typical conference, all the leaders give their reaction to the discussion of the day, and then the moderating bishop discerns if there is enough harmony to proceed with communion in each congregation, because communion celebrates the spiritual unity of the redemptive community. On this fateful day, unity had vanished. Joseph O. Wenger concluded, "We are split." Deacon Hoover, however, argued that the leaders could not divide "without talking to our bishop." So the conservatives climbed into two carriages and went to see the sickly Bishop Horning at his home.

To their surprise, he was out in the barn loading manure. When he saw them, he walked toward the house only to fall over in an apparent faint, as he often did in stressful situations. He was unable to speak with them. Bishop Wenger was not amused that Horning was too sick to moderate the conference but well enough to haul manure. Moreover, Wenger accused Horning of playing a prank by feigning a faint.[20]

The failed ministers' conference plunged the church into a stalemate. The first communion, scheduled for 17 April 1927, Easter Sunday, was postponed because of the crisis, which continued into the next Sunday as well. Finally, after a two-week hiatus, Bishop Horning announced that he had decided "to give communion to those who are at peace" on Sunday, 1 May 1927.[21] At the preparatory service, Horning told the Groffdale congregation that members could commune even if they owned cars. Cars, in other words, would be permitted. Horning dreaded the communion because he knew that the community was divided, but he hoped against hope that the ministers would accept the authority of his office and support his decision to proceed. Communion in Mennonite practice is more than the typical Protestant rite of personal confession and remembrance. The somber service is a collective celebration of the peace of the redemptive community, a celebration that typically follows several weeks of discussion that culminates in a preparatory service where members affirm the church's *Ordnung* and the authority of its leaders. But in May 1927, the Old Order community—torn apart by the car—had no peace to celebrate.

Word spread among those opposing even a plain car that they would not accept the cup and the bread from the bishop's hand at the communion service. The pro-car members, on the other hand, welcomed the day that would free them to buy a car, if they did not already have one. Especially delighted were the stigmatized car owners, the "half-expelled" who still attended regular services despite having been banished from communion.

After two hours of singing and listening to sermons, the Groffdale congregation sat in dramatic silence as Bishop Horning rose to serve communion. As always, Deacon Ben Hoover shadowed him, carrying the bread and wine as the bishop offered it to each person, one by one. They served the preachers' bench first, but only half of the ministers partook. Even Deacon Hoover refrained. The congregation watched in silence as the tragic event unfolded. Horning then turned to serve the congregation, older men first. Surely, he hoped, a sizable majority of members wanted the automobile. Bishop Horning, accompanied by Deacon Hoover, proceeded around the churchhouse and offered each congregant first a piece of bread and then, in a second walk through the churchhouse, a sip of wine from a common cup. Emotions ran high as the seventeen-year struggle with the car came to a climax in the Groffdale churchhouse.

Bishop Horning began his first round with the bread, weeping with every step he took, because many refused to stand and accept the bread from his hand or, later, take a sip from the cup that he offered. The broken bread that May morning signaled more than the crucified body of Christ; it signaled the broken peace of the community, as some stood and others sat when Bishop Horning came to them. In the end, about half of the members refused communion—voting, in essence, against the car.

Henry Ford's car—the charm of American productivity and progress—had wrecked the peace of the Old Order community on a Sunday morning in the holiest of Mennonite moments. Those who had not already declared their views on the car would now need to choose sides. Congregations would divide. Families would be severed for generations to come, some owning cars and others driving horse-and-carriage teams. Some, considered proud and haughty by their brothers, mothers, and cousins, would speed away in worldly abominations. In any event, for at least half of the community, the American wheels of progress came to a screeching halt in 1927 in the Groffdale and Weaverland valleys.

❖ AUTOMOBILITY FRAGMENTS COMMUNITY

At the end of the service, Preacher Joseph O. Wenger announced that the churchhouse would open the next Sunday for those opposed to automo-

Wengers and Hornings share this churchhouse every other Sunday; the cars indicate that this is a Horning Sunday.

biles. About half of the members of the Weaverland Conference followed Joseph Wenger to form what would become the Wenger Church. About four months later, in September 1927, sympathetic Old Order bishops from Indiana, Michigan, and Virginia ordained Wenger bishop of the new group, known as the "Joe Wenger" church.[22] Groffdale Conference Mennonite Church became its formal name, because Wenger was a preacher in the Groffdale congregation. The ministers in the Wenger Church held their semiannual conference in the Groffdale churchhouse for several years.

The controversy over the car divided the Old Order community into three clusters: those anti-car, those pro-car, and those undecided or who, because of family complications, were suspended between the other two groups. The undecideds, perhaps nearly a third of the community, had about two years to cast their lot. Some attended car-driving services one Sunday and horse-and-buggy services the next Sunday for a number of months. For two years after the 1927 division, members could go back and forth between the two groups without making a confession or risking excommunication.

After those two years, they needed to declare their membership, and thereafter a move from one group to the other was considered a transgression.[23]

The exact size of the two new groups is unknown, but Old Order historians generally consider it an even division, with half of the people opting for the horse-and-buggy Wenger Church and the other half affiliating with the car-driving Horning Church. The ordained ministers also divided about evenly between the two groups. By 1929, when the dust had settled, one historian estimates that the Wengers had two hundred families (about five hundred members, or one thousand, counting children) in six church districts.[24]

Old Order members who had been "half-expelled" because they had purchased a car could not automatically join the new Horning Church. Those who had been barred from communion because they owned a car were invited to a preparatory service at the Meadow Valley churchhouse in June 1927 to make a confession *en masse*. Before they were permitted to participate in a communion service in the Horning Church, they had to confess that they were sorry that they had grieved the church by getting a car.[25]

With the car controversy settled by schism, Horning Church members began to buy cars.[26] One member bought Bishop Moses Horning a car. Although the Horning Church permitted "touring cars," considered the cheapest and most modest style with their fold-down tops, the church required all the chrome to be painted black, earning members the nickname "black bumper Mennonites." These restrictions eased somewhat over the years. Today, a member's primary car must be black, but only ministers' cars are required to have black bumpers, chrome, and wheel covers.[27]

The Wenger-Horning division was less painful than the original breach of 1893. Indeed, the 1927 division became known as "the peaceful split," because it avoided the bitter property disputes of the earlier one. Nevertheless, families found themselves fractured over the division, and parents forced some youth to end budding romances that might separate future in-laws.[28] Today, the Hornings share five churchhouses cooperatively with the Wengers. The Wengers drive their buggies to the Martindale churchhouse on one Sunday, for example, and the Horning people park their cars in the churchhouse's horse sheds on the next Sunday.

The automobile, supreme badge of modernity, symbolically and literally articulates the core values of contemporary culture—independence, individualism, mobility, power, status, and speed. The Wenger rejection of this prince of progress keeps them in a different world, a local world anchored in face-to-face conversations, a slower world paced by the speed of a plodding horse, a communal world where neighbors see each other daily, an Old

Order world that boldly spurns the relentless press of progress. To Wenger thinking, a full embrace of the car would fragment their community, pulling it apart by high-speed travel in the larger society, and leading members to the city. The constraints of horse travel keep them closer together, tethered to their local area. Because horse-drawn transportation limits mobility, it enhances the community's social integration. The rejection of motor vehicles has become the key symbol of Wenger identity, marking a sharp separation from modern society, as well as from plain-dressing, car-driving Mennonites.

Although the Wengers voted against the car, the American commitment to mobility was unflinching. About three weeks after the fateful communion service, Henry Ford stopped producing the Model T to make way for more advanced cars. And on 20–21 May 1927, Charles Lindbergh made his famous transatlantic flight. These technological advances opened avenues for mobility that would forever change the character of local communities across North America.[29]

✢ CARS AND TAXIS

Although Wengers prohibit the ownership of motor vehicles, they do ride in them. The church allows members to hire "taxi service" from local neighbors. Many Wenger people hire cars or vans for business purposes and for long-distance travel to visit family and to attend church meetings, weddings, funerals, and ordinations. Some businessmen contract with outside drivers to provide vehicles on a regular basis. This informal taxi service provides mobility, allowing Wengers to visit relatives and friends in far-flung settlements beyond the reach of horse and buggy. As many as twenty-five vans loaded with Wenger passengers may arrive at a funeral in an outlying area. English van drivers, often neighbors or friends, charge about sixty cents per mile, depending somewhat on gas prices.

Church leaders urge members, however, not "to make a habit of driving too much with taxis and using them to go where we could go with the horse."[30] Using the horse and carriage for ordinary local travel reduces mobility and exemplifies humility. Even if people routinely hire vehicles for business during the week, they usually come to Sunday services by horse and buggy. Some people criticize members who only hitch up their "Sunday horses" for church services. One man complains, "These people are abusing the car privilege."

People find many reasons for legitimate travel: weddings, funerals, or-dinations, and illness. Some older people also travel long distances to visit their children in Iowa, Wisconsin, Michigan, or New York. Two Indiana brothers hired a van to take both of their families to a wedding in Lancaster, Pennsylvania. A Wenger group traveled by van to a sister settlement in On-tario, Canada. (While there, some also joined a bus tour to Niagara Falls.) In another case, a family hired a van and driver to take them from Berks County, Pennsylvania, through New York, the New England states, and New Brunswick, visiting Mennonite communities all along the way. "There are many vans going back and forth between Yates County [New York] and Lancaster County all the time," said one member.

The Wenger people view travel and vacations like many American fami-lies of modest income do, but the Wengers rarely travel for pleasure alone. They will, however, travel long distances to visit relatives or friends, because the family connections legitimate the trips. Wengers criticize trips made just for "leisure lust" or for the sake of "seeing the sights." Men, for example, are counseled to avoid long-distance hunting trips.

Unlike many Amish people, the Wengers will hire and pay for taxi ser-vices on Sunday. "There is only one person who refuses to do that that I know of," said one farmer. It is even permissible to hire a taxi to go to church under certain circumstances: if one is hosting too many out-of-state visi-tors to pack into a carriage, for instance, or traveling to a church more than twenty miles away.

There are no specific restrictions on the types of vehicles to hire. Still, "I wouldn't want to be seen in a Corvette or a VW Bug with flames on the side," said one father, "and if I did, I would be ducking as I went by." One grandfather refused to ride in a Jeep Cherokee offered by his granddaughter who left the church because, in the words of a member, "He would be aid-ing and abetting the forbidden thing. Doing such a thing would embarrass our community, even if the church has no rule against it and it's not strictly forbidden."

In addition to cars and trucks, the church prohibits owning motorcy-cles, motorbikes, all-terrain vehicles (ATVs), snowmobiles, and motorboats. "Small rowboats with small motors" are permitted, however. Members are allowed to travel by public transportation on bus, boat, and train, but not on an airplane except in extreme emergencies.

Horse-and-buggy transportation remains central to Wenger identity today. Indeed, explained one member, when the *Ordnung* is read twice a year in each congregation, "the rule against the car is the first one that is read in church." "That is the first line you step over if you leave the church," he concluded.

✥ HORSE AND CARRIAGE

The horses that pull Wenger carriages are usually standardbreds, although a few American saddlebred horses are also used. Horse dealers acquire the standardbreds from racetracks and sell them on public auctions, where they bring $2,000 to $4,000 each. The standardbreds, trained to pull open sulkies in races, are comfortable with carriages, but they need to learn to cope with highway traffic when Wengers first acquire them. Good horses usually drive until they are twenty years old, but most Wengers prefer younger ones for stamina when driving long distances. Wengers prize their driving horses. One elderly man lamented the loss of his horse: "I killed it," he said. "I tied it under an apple tree where the grass had just been sprayed. He ate the spray on the grass and died." A horse in daily use must be reshod every six weeks or so. To improve the grip of the horseshoe on roads, blacksmiths apply a hard, coarse material (boron, Driltek, or Drilltex) on its bottom.

Unlike Amish carriages, which are gray, Wenger buggies are black. They have a small window in the back and in both sides, a large one in each of the sliding doors, and a windshield called a "storm front." Carriage makers carefully design buggies for utility and durability. In recent years, the body of the buggy has been made of fiberglass. Many Wenger buggies have storage batteries, whip sockets, pedal-activated hydraulic brakes, and a reflective slow-moving-vehicle triangle on the back.[31] The typical cost of a carriage is $4,500, depending on its accessories. A well-maintained carriage will last a long time. One man has driven the same one for forty years with only a few repairs.

The Wengers use three types of carriages. Family carriages typically have two bench seats; those built for single people have one. A cab spring wagon, the Wenger version of a pickup truck, has a short cargo bed behind the enclosed cab for carrying produce. The open spring wagon, used for light hauling, has a flat bed and an open seat in front. Spring wagons and carts are not always black. Buggies, however, according to one man, "must be black, period!"

In the past, youth often drove buggies that sported a fold-down top, but now they drive enclosed ones with one bench seat. Young people often choose more colorful and plush interiors and small pinstripes on their carriages. Some carriage makers add fine hand-drawn pinstripes to the wheels and body of the carriage. Teens are permitted to have pinstripes on their first carriage, but not on those they purchase after they are married.

In recent years, many members have added hard rubber to the wheels to cushion the ride, a change that sparked much discussion in the church. Hard rubber first appeared on carriage wheels around 1970. "The first guy who did it," said one member, "was an outlaw who also had a red interior in his buggy. He pushed and pushed on it until he pushed himself out of the church. The rubber wheel slipped in because the church did not address it directly. If an issue like this emerges we either get over it, rule it out, or formally accept it." The reasons for hard rubber on wheels include better durability and a quieter ride, which, according to one man, encourages members to use the carriage more instead of hiring taxis.[32]

According to a farmer, "Now 75 to 90 percent of the carriages have hard rubber wheels, depending on the congregation. Those who still have steel bands are the non-liberal element. Most ministers do not have rubber. They mostly have steel, but there is no rule." One lay historian explained, "Rubber on carriage wheels made much discussion in our counsel meetings, but conference never ruled against it. Counsel slows it [change] down as it progresses slowly forward. Perhaps in ten to twenty years there will be no steel wheels and all will be rubber." Rubber on carriage wheels, according to one member, "is very different than rubber on the tractor, which could lead to a car. Rubber on the carriage works against using the car, because you want to use your carriage more." Wengers clearly pay attention to wheels. A twelve-year-old girl, with little thought, estimated the number of carriages in each church district in her area that had rubber and quickly ranked five districts from the lowest to the highest percent with rubber.

⁖ BICYCLES

Bicycles were common in the Old Order church before the Wenger group formed in 1927. "Conference never ruled on the bicycle," said one minister. Some families did not permit young people, especially young women, to ride bicycles to church. "Girls did not ride bicycles into the churchyard before the 1960s," said one mother. "Some rode most of the way to church and then parked them at a neighbor's, but not in the churchyard." Since the 1960s, girls have been riding bikes everywhere, including to church. Girls did not ride them much earlier, according to one member, "because of modesty, de-

The bicycle and the carriage are the primary vehicles for local transportation.

cency, and because it's hard to ride them with skirts." Those concerns have declined, for women, even in their skirts, ride bikes for many types of local travel.

Bicycles are widely used by youth and adults. They are faster than a horse and buggy and, of course, easier to manage. Most bicycles have electric lights for nighttime travel. Some parents worry that bicycles give young people too much access to nearby towns. Unlike the Lancaster Amish, who prohibit bicycles, the Wengers use them widely. Young people often ride bicycles to work and social gatherings as well as to worship services. The use of bicycles has, in fact, become a distinguishing flag of Wenger identity in some communities. Two adult men in one settlement have opted for the advanced-style recumbent bike, on which the rider leans back in a low seat.

Despite the bicycle's popularity, accidents are not uncommon. In one case, four boys were spread across both lanes of a highway on their bikes. Another boy, riding in the opposite direction, came over a crest in the road and collided with them, sending some to the hospital. In another incident, a minister riding down a hill on a borrowed bicycle lost control and broke his shoulder when he could not find the bike's brakes. Wenger people recount these accidents to underscore the truth that even acceptable technology must be used wisely.

Some restrictions on agricultural technology related to wheels flow from the car taboo. In general, the Wengers distinguish among four types of wheels: steel wheels, hard rubber tires, air-filled (pneumatic) rubber tires, and customized belting wheels (steel wheels with some type of rubber belting around them). The so-called belting wheels have been a major source of controversy. Tractors and other self-propelled equipment, including garden tractors and riding mowers, must be fitted with steel wheels. The prohibition of rubber tires (hard and air-filled) on self-propelled vehicles developed out of fear that rubber-tired tractors might be used for local errands and eventually lead to pickup trucks and cars.[33] "The line," one member explained, "is if you can ride it, rubber tires are not permitted." A rototiller, silage cart, or walk-behind forklift may roll on rubber because it is not self-propelled and does not carry a driver. The Wenger Church allows pneumatic tires on wagons and other implements that are not self-propelled.

Wengers make several arguments for not permitting pneumatic tires on tractors. Said one farmer, "If we permit rubber-tired tractors, it will lead to big farming operations. Putting steel wheels on the tractors and keeping the horse and buggy help to keep things small." He then noted, "Some of our people who want bigger things join Weaverland Conference," the more progressive Horning Mennonites. Steel wheels help, in the mind of many members, to keep farms labor intensive, providing work for children. "We don't want the wheel used on the road for transportation. We don't want moms going shopping on the tractor," said a welder who makes tractor wheels. The church fears that if members use tractors for transportation on the roads, it will be a short step to cars.

One member explains, "Some groups allow rubber tires, and some of 'em just run to town on the tractor. Steel keeps us on the farm, not running five miles down the road all the time. Steel also helps to keep things small."[34] A bishop notes, "The New Order Amish have rubber tires on their tractors and use them to go to church and then they lose their youth. And some of them go to the Beachy [car-driving] Church.[35] If we had rubber wheels on the tractor, then I would say, 'Why hitch up my horse if I can take my tractor and go faster and the tractor's not even tired when I get there?'" Another member echoed the fear: "We don't want to become like the New Order Amish who openly use tractors for transportation. Just look at them; their tractor is their transportation and some don't even use their buggy." The New Order Amish provide a negative reference group for all the adverse changes that come with pneumatic tractor wheels—adding air-conditioned cabs on tractors, pulling trailers loaded with families, using tractors to run errands, and allowing young boys to drive them to town.

Some Wenger farmers argue that they need tractors to pull wagons laden with vegetables on the road to produce auctions. Steel tractor wheels often damage public roads, which stirs the ire of township officials. Some farmers have been fined for driving on roads with steel wheels. "A handful of Wengers," said one farmer, "don't respect the road, and their use of wheels on it makes it mean for the rest of us." Flexible rubber belting under steel cleats on wheels reduces road damage and also gives tractors better traction in the field. But the conservative sector of the church still worries that rubber belting on tractor wheels will be a small but fateful step toward the car. "The tractor should not be used like a car," said one member, "but if a farmer has two properties, he can use rubber-belting wheels on his tractor on the road and the deacon can't call him on the carpet for it."

A few farmers have made the case for regular, air-filled tractor tires. A county extension agent who works with Wenger farmers said, "The top-end farmers who have dairy, produce, and a shop are pushing for the rubber tires. They argue that it would be better to permit pneumatic rubber tires and restrict the size of tractors like the Old Order Mennonites in Canada." The proponents of pneumatic tires contend that, with proper restrictions, the church could prevent rubber-tired tractors from leading to the car.

Searching for a technological compromise, some ingenious Wenger mechanics developed ways to cushion steel tractor wheels by embedding small rubber blocks in the spokes of the wheels. Other farmers put rubber pads under the wheel cleats. Still others wound several layers of rubber conveyer belt material around the wheel under the steel cleats. Technically, because the steel cleats still contact the road, they comply with the *Ordnung*. One leader noted, "You can't prohibit specific types of tires, because so many different types exist. The people design what they want."

✢ A SHORT HISTORY OF BELTING WHEELS

The early tractors that were manufactured from 1915 to 1935 typically had steel wheels. In the mid-1930s, air-filled tires were manufactured and adopted by progressive American farmers. Rubber tractor tires became widely accepted so fast that it was difficult to buy new tractors with steel wheels by the late 1940s.[36] This shift forced Wengers to buy used steel-wheeled trac-

All self-propelled vehicles and equipment, including riding mowers, must have steel wheels.

tors and to make their own steel wheels to replace worn-out wheels or to convert new rubber-tired tractors to steel.

A farmer-mechanic summarized the history of belting wheels in the Wenger community. "All Wenger tractors had steel wheels until the mid-1970s when the first rubber belting wheels were made in Lancaster County." The belting process developed in different stages and styles in various Wenger settlements. At first, rubber blocks were used in front wheels, and then in the 1980s they were added to rear wheels. This agitated some church members who viewed the change as a step closer to the rubber tire and the car. Recycled flexible tracks from Caterpillar crawlers were used on some wheels in the 1980s. Later, combination wheels, which mixed elements of rubber blocks, belting, and flexible tracks, appeared. Mechanics in different settlements experimented with different designs, "creating at least fifteen different types of belting wheels with some forty finer variations," according to a knowledgeable Wenger mechanic.

All of these ingenious adaptations helped to limit road damage, cushion the ride, and increase the speed of tractors on roads. In addition, belting wheels provided better traction on roads and fields because more wheel sur-

This combination wheel has various types of rubber belting, including rubber blocks midway between the steel cleats and the axle of the wheel.

This wheel conforms to the regulation that limits rubber belting to two inches.

face touched the ground, giving more flexibility than even an air-filled tire. With so many creative applications of rubber, belting wheels became a hot church issue by the mid-1990s. Some Wenger welders refused to make them. Emotions flared because some farmers welcomed the ingenious wheels and others feared they would surely lead to the car. The controversy struck at the heart of Wenger identity, forged as it was in 1927 by the decisive rejection of the car.

One member described the triumph of the belting wheels: "So with bands of rubber we created a steel/rubber combination wheel that functions like a rubber tire but with no flat tires! And it is even better than rubber on wet grass. It costs about $4,000 to put all four combination tires on a trac-tor, but we don't have to rotate the wheels like a car. When we arrived at the pinnacle of the steel wheel, we had defeated its purpose of preventing the tractor from being used as a substitute for the horse and buggy. We need to use the horse and buggy for local driving, but not just in a symbolic way."

This astute farmer continued, "Now outsiders might say that wheels are ridiculous and have nothing to do with salvation, with the soul. We are now at a ridiculous place inside our own rules because tractors with rubber blocking and links of crawler pads make a flexible wheel with a soft touch. It's dynamite and it's just too good. It's a wheel that outperforms a rubber wheel but it's not a rubber wheel! The advanced combination wheels no lon-ger serve the purpose of preventing the use of tractors for transportation. You might say we've trumped the rubber tire."

Tinkering with tractor wheels may seem silly and insignificant to outsid-ers, but the creative "hackers" and their wheels stoked heated debates in the Wenger Church.[37] Belting wheels stirred controversy because they blurred the long-standing rule against rubber on self-propelled vehicles, designed to keep them off public roads. With rubber-padded wheels, tractors could cruise on roads at thirty-five miles per hour, even passing bicycles. Once again, the debate over wheels was so intense, according to one member, "that it almost divided the church."

❖ THE COMPROMISE

Although it frowned on belting wheels for several years, the ministers' con-ference did not make a firm decision until 1999. Finally, the ministers' con-ference forged a compromise with these understandings: (1) a maximum of two inches of rubber belting was permitted under steel cleats, (2) combination wheels that mixed rubber belting, rubber blocks, and track wheels were taboo, and (3) farmers with combination wheels were given five years (until 2004) to remove them. Replacing rear combination wheels costs about $1,900 a pair, on top of the original cost to install them. Thus the total cost might exceed $4,500—an expensive proposition that underscores why out-of-line farmers welcomed a five-year period of grace.

A leader explained that "at the conference, some ministers wanted no belting wheels at all, but others said, 'Let's decide no more than two inches of rubber, and give those with excess rubber five years to take them off because they're so expensive.' We gave them a grace period, in other words. After five years, a violation of the rule will be a test of membership." Despite the church's blessing on two inches of rubber belting, one mechanic estimates that 20 to 30 percent of the farmers will keep regular steel wheels just because some farmers are traditionally inclined.

Not everyone, however, is happy with the compromise. Farmers in some settlements had very few belting wheels, because their ministers had worked hard to stop them.[38] The compromise ruling permits belting wheels in all settlements to the consternation of leaders in more conservative areas. One farmer thinks the compromise won't settle the issue. "The steel wheel with rubber belting is a superb but pricey wheel; it's a waste of resources. We've gone too far; I think we should just go with all rubber. Look at the Old Order Mennonites in Canada and Virginia; they did it [accepted air-filled rubber wheels] and they are OK and not wasting time and money on belting wheels. The new belting rule will just be an ongoing contention." After the conference agreed to tolerate belting wheels, one leader exclaimed happily, "Now the townships are delighted; the roads are protected, farmers can haul produce to the vegetable auctions on the roads, and even have better traction in the fields." A skeptical farmer worried, "I see rubber coming in the next ten years and then the car."

Tractor tires were involved in two schisms prior to the debate on belting wheels. In 1970, Harvey Nolt, a bishop in the church, withdrew from Groffdale Conference. Although Nolt was a proponent of pneumatic tires for tractors, a variety of other issues also surrounded his departure.[39] Another division involving the use of rubber tires occurred in Indiana in 1981. A disagreement over using tires on skid loaders was one reason that Bishop William Weaver withdrew from the Groffdale Conference, which precipitated a division in Indiana's Old Order church.[40] The main body continued to affiliate with the Groffdale Conference under the leadership of a new bishop, Elvin Martin.

This typical tractor complies with the two-inch belting restriction on front and rear wheels.

The use of air-filled tires that are factory-installed on new tractors is a passive acceptance of standard technology. The Wenger use of belted steel wheels is an expensive, labor-intensive, active rejection of standard technology.[41] Outsiders might see an inconsistency between rubber wheels on a carriage and rubber wheels on a tractor. A member explained the difference: "Rubber wheels on the buggy came gradually. The rubber encouraged horse-and-buggy use; it wasn't a change in essence. Rubber on the tractor brings in a new model, a mix of materials and it changes the nature of use. A change on the tractor threatens our transportation."

The debate about rubber is not just limited to buggies and tractors. Wenger concerns about wheels encompass other vehicles as well.

❖ FORKLIFTS AND RECREATIONAL VEHICLES

Shop owners use forklifts to lift heavy products. Farmers use skid loaders for many tasks, from plowing snow to scraping manure in concrete barn-

A walk-behind forklift may have hard rubber tires because it does not carry a rider.

yards, and excavators use them to move ground. Steel wheels on these small tractor-like implements scratch concrete floors and slide easily, making them dangerous on concrete and macadam. But belting wheels are impractical on skid loaders because they turn by pivoting on their wheels. Some owners of forklifts and skid loaders use hard rubber wheels to aid sharp turning. But critics worry that hard rubber wheels will lead to a pneumatic tire. "This hot issue," said one member, "may need to go to conference." The present arrangement is another compromise: a chain of steel cleats is wrapped around hard rubber wheels. Again, the purpose is to prevent these small self-propelled implements from being used for transportation.

In one settlement, a produce auction operated by the Wengers has two forklifts—one on steel wheels and one on hard rubber. The rubber-wheeled forklift is owned by a Horning Mennonite who allows the Wengers to use it. Even so, church leaders worried that youth might gain access to it and go joyriding, so they asked the auction's board of directors to store the rubber-wheeled forklift in a secure area and asked a board member to keep the key at his home. Reflecting on the controversy over forklift wheels, one Wenger said, "Some people will say we are tied up in dead works. Others, like the Horning people, will say that we gave up, and got a rubber-tired forklift."

Walk-behind equipment that does not carry a rider is permitted to have hard rubber tires, but machines that carry a rider are not. There are only two exceptions to this rule. Large mixing carts for silage, steered by a rider, are used to feed cows. These mechanical feeders may have air-filled tires or hard rubber wheels. Rubber wheels on mixing carts never became a church issue because they cannot be used for transportation. Commercial walk-behind gang mowers (thirty-six to seventy-two inches wide) with pneumatic tires avoided church censure for the same reason.

Golf carts and all-terrain vehicles (ATVS) on air-filled tires did cause a stir, however. Some members used these motorized vehicles for work in orchards or on farms, but they became tempting toys for joyriding. So in Spring 2004, according to one member, "The conference forbade all recreational vehicles, even ones with steel wheels. No recreational vehicles period!"

A more complicated issue involves leasing trucks. Wenger carpentry crews often have difficulty finding drivers. So some contractors buy a truck but title it in the name of an English employee, because members are not allowed to own or drive vehicles. One of the drawbacks of this arrangement is that it is possible for the employee to misuse or even steal the truck, which has happened in one case. Others lease vehicles but, according to one member, "You may not park it at home, or use it at home; you can only use it for business purposes. It is not to be serviced at your home or shop." Some leaders worry that boys will sneak out and take a pleasure cruise on a Sunday afternoon if leased vehicles are parked at home. One bishop objects to leasing altogether. "The carpenter crews have a lot of trouble getting dependable drivers. Members can't buy trucks, but some are financing a truck owned by an English person. But we cannot accept leasing because then it would lead to leasing a rubber tire tractor and it just opens the door to wheels." If more members move into construction or other jobs that require daily transportation, leasing vehicles may become a bigger issue for the church.

❖ WHY WHEELS MATTER

The taboo on car ownership and pneumatic rubber tires is a key principle in the Wenger strategy of selective modernization. Wheels matter because they undergird the heart of Wenger identity and mark the path to greater mobility, the path to worldliness. "The auto brings many temptations," explained one bishop. "If we had the car, we would lose the closeness we have, and then we would not need each other as much any more. But the car is not sinful." Nevertheless, the car has religious implications, according to the bishop. "We don't practice shunning. But we don't ride in a former member's vehicle right away when they leave. It's not shunning. We try to accept them. Later, we might take a ride in their car," a practice that perturbs some members.

When asked why Wengers do not drive cars, a young mother said, "The answer is much more complex than you would guess. It's about our whole lifestyle, our community, our culture. As more progressive Mennonites have accepted cars, radios, and TV, they gradually changed some other things as well. Many of them quit having gardens, doing canning, and sewing and are less self-sufficient in general. Not that I think being self-sufficient is more godly, but it's a valuable part of our culture. Divorce and re-marriage are becoming more acceptable. These progressive Mennonite churches are gradually being assimilated into the larger culture, something the Plain [people] are hoping to avoid by rejecting modern technology like the car."

A Wenger carpenter installed a new kitchen for an English neighbor who asked him, "Couldn't you serve God just as well driving a car?" "Possibly so," he reflected, "but we would lose a lot of community. Without a car, it keeps us home more, we're more family oriented." The neighbor retorted, "We stay in touch with our family on the cell phone." The carpenter responded,

> Being home more is the biggest benefit. Our children see Mom and Dad all day. How else can you really learn to know a person, know what they think and feel? Their deep inner core values shine through in their day-to-day work, in their reactions and responses to things. When children are home working with their parents, more is caught than taught. Having no car reinforces this, because it helps to keep us home. If you have a car it's so easy just to jump in it and go town each day. With a horse, you wait a day or so to go to town and it keeps us home more.

A young father declared,

> The car has done more to separate family life than any other single thing in the modern world. TVs and computers have a big impact, but if you don't have a car, Mom and Dad stay home more. The car is nothing, it's just a piece of machinery—but it's what comes along with it that brings the problems. Ministers talk about the car in sermons. They talk regularly and admonish us not to hire drivers

too much for danger of being gone too much from home. If where you are going is close enough to go with a horse, you should hitch up. We are also told to avoid businesses where we need to hire drivers too much.

A lay member reaffirmed the Wenger view in different words: "The car is not a sin. Having one transgresses the ruling for the values that we hold. It's better for the environment not to have one. It is healthier to ride a bike. Not having a car helps the family to stay more together." He explained that rejecting the car is central to separating the church from the world. "If we get the car, it will radically change our life. There are two different cultures, the car culture and the non-car culture. If we run around, we will give up what we are trying to preserve. Our families won't be agrarian. It is easier to be a Christian in this setting. Too much running around is destructive of Christianity and the family. We have to leave some things behind. We cannot have both cultures, the church and the world. For me, I don't want changes that will destroy this culture."

Roger Abrahams argues that mobility is a central value in American culture. "Americans are movers," he says. "We place such a positive value on mobility, tying it to personal and social progress."[42] Americans want to be "on the move," "on the go," "moving on" to bigger and better things. The automobile in American life provides not only the vehicle to express these cultural values but also a multitude of mobility metaphors for descriptions of other facets of social life. Americans speak of "stepping on the gas," "putting on the brakes," and "checking your rearview mirror," and they ask, "Who's behind the wheel?" All of these phrases underscore the virtue of mobility in mainstream culture.

Controlling mobility is a central facet of the Wenger strategy of selective modernization. Accepting rubber wheels that might lead to the car would surely speed the pace of change. Mobility and identity are tied together in the Wenger mind. But the worry about wheels runs deeper than just identity; it is about the future of their community. Excessive mobility, in their view, could wreck their entire way of life. And that explains the riddle of Wenger wheels—explains why the church spent ten years debating rubber belting wheels on tractors and other self-propelled machinery.

Managing identity and mobility across sixteen settlements in nine states is quite a challenge. How do the local settlements relate to the larger Wenger community? What holds the church together? Those are the questions we take up in Chapter 4.

The Architecture of Community

The congregation is the social center, the focal point.

—WENGER FARMER

✢ THE TIES THAT BIND

Human communities display many different patterns of social organization. These diverse styles of social architecture reflect and articulate the cultural values of a society. In this chapter we explore the patterns of social life that have emerged over time in the Wenger community. What are the distinctive features of Wenger society? How do these components fit together? How does the redemptive community reproduce itself and guard against internal and external threats? What forms of social glue—loyalty, good will, camaraderie, cooperation, trust—bond the community together? And how do religious commitments foster this solidarity?

The Wenger Church forms a tightly knit redemptive community on two levels: local and national. Their strong sense of community arises from common religious values, social networks, and affective relationships.[1] Under the canopy of religion, the Wenger community encompasses social activities, family life, education, and economics. The church in Wenger life is not an optional special-interest group. Community and church are *one*—a single redemptive entity that encompasses their whole way of life.

Extended family, church district, settlement, and *conference* constitute the four foundational units of Wenger society. Kinship ties within large extended families, explored in Chapter 6, provide important threads of solidarity across various communities. A church district consists of 15 to 150 families who attend services and take communion at a particular churchhouse. A settlement is a geographic area where Wenger families live in close proximity. A young settlement may have just one churchhouse; older ones have several. The ministers' conference, the semiannual gathering of ordained officials, regulates the *Ordnung* (lifestyle rules) and serves as the ultimate authority for any disputes.

Beyond the family, the church district (congregation) is the basic unit of community life. Each district typically has two preachers, a deacon, and a bishop who gives oversight to several districts. Members of a district gather in their local churchhouse for regular Sunday services, counsel meetings, communions, baptisms, ordinations, and funerals. "The congregation is the social center, the focal point," said a farmer. Horse-and-buggy transportation tethers social life to the local community. Although congregations do not have precise geographic boundaries, members typically participate in the one closest to their home. Said one member, "There's no rule against it, but it's frowned upon if you drive past another churchhouse."

About two-thirds of the Wenger congregations gather for worship every Sunday. A few districts continue the older nineteenth-century practice of meeting every other Sunday. In Lancaster County, five of the ten churchhouses are shared with the Horning Church every other Sunday. Each Wenger settlement has its own schedule of church services.[2] Members of local congregations refer to each other by the name of their respective churchhouse—the "Churchtowners," "Martindalers," "Groffdalers," and so on. They typically refer to their own district as simply *Unsrerleit* (our people).

If members do not have services in their own district on a particular Sunday, they may drive their carriage to an adjacent district where they worship and visit with friends. The Sunday noon meal is an important time for visiting others and entertaining guests. The visiting rituals build social solidarity beyond

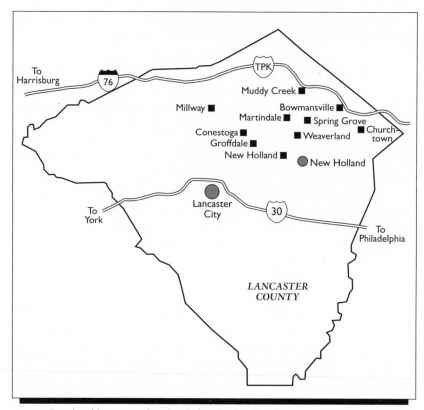

NOTE: Five churchhouses are shared with the Horning Church.

DIAGRAM 4   Wenger churchhouses in Lancaster County (Pa.)

the bounds of the local congregation by weaving together multi-layered relationships, across neighborhood, family, and the larger community. The fabric
of Old Order life is reinforced by local rituals of visitation, as well as by visits to
distant settlements for weddings, funerals, and special church meetings.

The church district forms a matrix of support for young people, wel-
coming them at birth and watching them complete various rites of passage.
Teenagers kneel before the assembled congregation for baptism, and many
of its members will attend their weddings. When illness, tornado, or fire
strikes, the district rallies with support and aid. At the end of life, the congregation gathers to mourn, pray, and lower their loved ones into the grave.
Throughout the life cycle, the church provides a dependable web of care
resting on enduring friendships and deep familial ties.

Wengers in a new settlement are typically lay members who begin holding services in their homes until enough families arrive to build a churchhouse.[3] The small cluster of families sing and read from the Bible but do not have preaching in their worship services. Leaders from other settlements occasionally come to hold more formal services and serve communion. When the new settlement has ten or more families, a bishop from another settlement comes and ordains a preacher for the new district. As new congregations form, they replicate the established practices that define Wenger identity. A member from Pennsylvania visiting a Wisconsin service needs to make few adjustments, because both churchhouses and services are similar. The Wengers do not encourage unique regional patterns; each new district replicates the others in roles, rituals, structure, and the format of Sunday services.[4]

When a new district grows to about fifteen families, members of other settlements help to construct a churchhouse. The social architecture of the new settlement gradually takes shape—Sunday services, ordained leaders, a churchhouse, and a schoolhouse. A deacon, a bishop, and other preachers are ordained as the district expands and the replication is soon complete. The new congregation has the intimacy of an extended family, plus ample guidance from the wider Wenger Church. For the Wengers, religious patterns structure community life; indeed, without the church, the redemptive community would die.

❖ SERVANTS AND SHEPHERDS

In the Anabaptist tradition, servant-ministers humbly submit to the will of God and to the will of their congregation. Indeed, the German word *Diener*, which the Wengers use for ordained leaders, means servant. The ministers are seen as God's servants who nurture the flock and protect it from worldly dangers. Ordained leaders not only uphold the traditions of the community, they create and embody its ethos. They nourish its lifestyle, guard the social order, and protect it from disruptions. If the ministry grows too strict, young people may not join or families may leave. If too lax, the flock may stray into danger. The shepherds of the flock must remain vigilant against worldly practices that may threaten the welfare of the church.

Wenger leadership is organized around three roles: *bishop, minister,* and *deacon.*[5] The terms "ministry" and "ministers" are often used as a blanket term for all ordained leaders. And because all the leaders sit together on the ministers' bench in the churchhouse, they are sometimes simply called "the bench." Among the Wengers, only men can be ordained. Both women and men strongly support this practice as the way things should be, according to their interpretation of the Bible.

Bishops

A bishop typically oversees the ministers and deacons of several districts. As the senior official, the bishop presides over baptisms, weddings, preparatory services, communions, funerals, confessions, and excommunications. He instructs the baptismal candidates, interprets the *Ordnung*, and guides the overall welfare of the community. The average age of bishops is about sixty-two. The senior bishop of the conference, the one who has been ordained the longest, serves as chairman of all the leaders and exercises considerable influence over the entire community.

Among other charges at his ordination, a bishop is admonished "not to be self-willed, not to be given to anger, but to be kind, chaste, just, holy, pure, and to remain so." At the conclusion of the ordination, the congregation is asked to, among other things, "Accept your servant with joy as your shepherd sent from God. . . . Obey your teacher and follow him, for he watches over your souls."[6]

In addition to conducting special services in his districts, a bishop preaches frequently and conducts instruction meetings for baptismal candidates. Every six months he reads the *Ordnung* to the congregation at the preparatory service prior to communion. A bishop can exercise considerable leadership, depending on his personality—a bishop with a dominant personality is more influential than one with a reserved style—but he can only operate effectively with the support of his people.

A bishop does not exercise absolute power; he must cooperate with his fellow bishops at the ministers' conference, which makes major decisions unanimously. With church duties on top of their own vocational work, bishops have a full schedule. In the course of a week, one bishop attended the ministers' conference on Friday, conducted a baptism service on Saturday, a communion service on Sunday, and a funeral on Monday, then officiated at weddings on the following Tuesday and Thursday!

A bishop, with the support of the ministers' conference, can silence or "set back from the bench" a minister who stumbles morally, or defies the authority of the church. Silencing prevents the offender from performing the duties of his office. To resume his duties, he must confess his failure to the church. In protest of some issues, one minister missed several services, including communion. His bishop did not permit him to preach until he confessed his wrongs. When he refused, the bishop silenced him.

Ministers

The ministers (often called preachers because one of their primary tasks is preaching) provide leadership for congregational life and preach at services. In their sermons, they typically exhort members from a chapter in the Bible, rather than on a topical theme as is common in many other Christian denominations. When a minister visits another churchhouse, he anticipates being asked to preach on Sunday morning. Although they have no formal training in homiletics, ministers spend long hours preparing to speak without notes. After a preacher is ordained, he assumes his duties immediately. In one case, a preacher, ordained on a Tuesday, preached his first funeral sermon on Wednesday, followed by a wedding sermon on Thursday. Ministers also visit the sick, counsel errant members, and guide congregational decisions.

A minister preaches most frequently at his home church, but he also preaches in nearby districts. This rotational system reduces the prominence of personalities and the attachment of members to a particular preacher. A member says, "We try to keep everything all mixed together so that it's one whole large church." One bishop explains, "If you would have a favorite minister, you might run after 'em. We don't want people to know where a minister will be on a particular Sunday. We don't want people to have favorites." Said another member, "We feel very strongly about shuffling our ministers around so that no one knows who will preach. This keeps everything tied together." According to one preacher, "Ministers know a year in advance where they will preach, but the people don't."

This unpublicized rotation strengthens the solidarity of ministerial leadership across the conference and helps to prevent people from giving allegiance to one minister in ways that might encourage a division.

Unlike the typical Protestant model where parishioners identify closely with the lead pastor of their congregation, the rotational model weakens ties between members and specific ministers. At the same time, it separates the ministry as a group from the lay members, subtly enhancing the collective authority of the ordained.

Deacons

Deacons aid the work of ministry by reading Scripture during worship. The deacon also assists the bishop at baptism and helps to serve the bread and wine at communion. In some ways, he serves as the eyes and ears of the bishop, reporting problems in the community and violations of church standards. If a deacon becomes aware that a member is violating a church rule, he will visit the member and seek a resolution. If someone misses two communions, the deacon, often accompanied by another ordained leader, will visit the member to seek reconciliation. One deacon says that the most satisfying part of his job is "giving counsel" (spiritual advice) to people.

The deacon is also responsible to manage the alms fund for the poor and oversee mutual aid to members who need assistance with health, fire, storm, or other issues. One member explains, "The deacon takes care of the ones who receive communion here. So, if I'm a member here and we have a high hospital bill, the deacon is responsible to help us."

Ordained leaders receive no remuneration for their work, but they occasionally receive gifts of food or other gestures of goodwill. Without formal theological training, they serve the congregation throughout their active life. With only an eighth-grade education and no compensation for their services, these men support themselves and their families through regular occupations. Members expect them to model godly living for the whole congregation and carefully uphold the regulations of the church. Filled with a spirit of *Gelassenheit*, they are viewed as servants of the congregation and charged with guarding its spiritual welfare and preventing any wayward drift toward the world.

In the wider Protestant world, "consumers" often "shop" for a church based on its style of worship, special services, or the eloquence of its preachers. Search committees scan the marketplace for the best-trained and most articulate preacher they can afford. Although Wenger preachers have considerable influence, the focus of church life is on the gathered congregation, not the ministers. Every baptized male could be ordained, because ministers are chosen from the laity. At baptism, young men promise to serve as a leader for life if the congregation nominates them, and if God so chooses.

Leaders are chosen by the biblical practice of casting lots, a process that puts a check on the powerful and ambitious who might otherwise seek ordination. This method of selecting lay leaders expresses *Gelassenheit* by eliminating individual choice from ministerial calling. It also builds solidarity within the church because members view ministers as servants selected by God, which legitimizes their authority.

Ordained leaders are expected to uphold a simpler lifestyle than other members. Some of them, for example, do not have telephones in their homes. Before 1993, none of the ministers had electricity in their homes. Today, many have electricity, but some still do not. Ministers and their immediate family are expected to demonstrate exemplary practices in their clothing, technology, and home décor, as well as other lifestyle areas.

Parents train their children to respect ordained leaders. A member says, "Children have got to have confidence that there is salvation in the church. They have to have confidence in the ministry . . . you don't downgrade them all the time, you know, or they [children] will find out. . . . We are really taught to reverence our ministers as people." Even wedding customs reflect respect for ministers. The young hostlers who care for the guests' horses customarily expect tips for their service, but not from ministers.

Reflecting the growth of the Wenger community, the number of ordained leaders has almost tripled in the past twenty-five years. In 1978, 41 ministers (4 bishops, 27 preachers, and 10 deacons) served the entire Wenger Church.[7] By 2005, the church had 134 ministers (16 bishops, 73 preachers, and 45 deacons), yielding one bishop for every 207 families.[8] On a typical Sunday, services are held in forty-one churchhouses. With two sermons in each service, about 80 ministers on average preach each Sunday. Thus, with a pool of 89 preachers and bishops, most of them preach each week.

Today, many evangelical churches see change as indispensable, even desirable, as they seek to adapt religious patterns to changes in contemporary culture. By contrast, the Wenger Church honors tradition and resists change. Church organization, leadership roles, and even churchhouse architecture keep continuity with the past. Although church rules, shaped by the ministers' conference, flex with the changing needs of the people, the patterns of church authority and leadership are firm and unwavering.

❖ THE GROFFDALE CONFERENCE

The semiannual ministers' conference is the highest authority in Wenger society. It holds the ordination of leaders and establishes the lifestyle regulations for members. Groffdale Conference Mennonite Church is the official name of the Wenger Church. The conference encompasses nearly 18,000 men, women, and children in its forty-nine congregations in sixteen settlements scattered over nine states. Twice yearly—on the Friday before Good Friday in the spring, and on the first Friday in October—most of the ministers (preachers, deacons, and bishops) from every settlement convene for "conference" at the Lancaster County Martindale churchhouse, about six miles northeast of New Holland, Pennsylvania. Leaders from afar typically travel to the one-day gathering in hired vans with outside drivers.

Ministers from all the settlements greet each other in the churchyard before a fall ministers' conference at the Martindale churchhouse.

The word conference carries several meanings. It refers to the authority of the church, to the semiannual meeting of the ordained leaders, and to the network of local congregations. As the highest authoritative body, the conference has power that supersedes that of individual bishops and congregations. In the words of one member, "We have a conference form of government, not a congregational one." If a major issue is stirring—the use of pagers or computers, for example—the ministers' conference may approve or ban the questionable practice. This twice-yearly gathering reaffirms the authority of the church over leaders and congregations, and regulates social change. If lay members in a district think their bishop is too liberal or too rigid in his interpretation of the *Ordnung*, they can appeal to the conference through their ministers.

Prior to the ministers' conference, counsel meetings are held in local districts. At these meetings, presided over by a bishop, members voice any concerns they have about clothing, entertainment, and technology. The bishop and the ministers of each district then report these concerns to the churchwide ministers' conference at Martindale.

One member recalls the ministers' conference in the early years of the Wenger Church: "My dad was a deacon. First time he went over to the con-

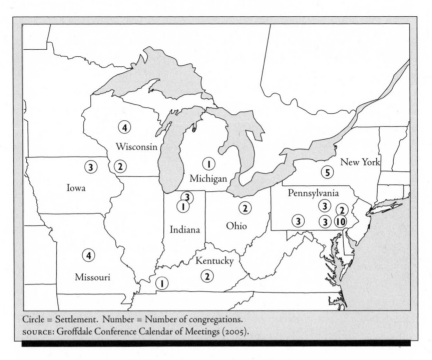

Circle = Settlement. Number = Number of congregations.
SOURCE: Groffdale Conference Calendar of Meetings (2005).

DIAGRAM 5   Location of Wenger congregations in North America

ference meeting at Martindale, they just had it in their little counsel room, just a small group—one bishop, and a few preachers and deacons." Presently, over a hundred leaders from as far away as Indiana, Iowa, and Wisconsin converge in Martindale to discuss issues that are stirring in their local districts. The senior bishop provides leadership for the conference. The gathering unifies leaders and members by standardizing practices across districts hundreds of miles apart. Decisions are made by consensus, not by voting. "*Gelassenheit* is the foremost theme at an Old Order conference. Yielding to the conference body is very important," according to an Old Order writer.[9]

On the Saturdays following conference, known as *Faschtdaag* (fasting day), congregations gather for a preparatory service in anticipation of communion, which is the culmination of the counsel meetings and the ministers' conference.[10] In the fall, the preparatory service often includes baptisms. The *Ordnung*, with any new revisions, is read at the preparatory service. Communion services begin on the next day, Sunday. Communion services continue among the districts over several Sundays because a bishop must preside over each one.

The conference gatherings bond the church together through common values and interpersonal ties rather than bureaucratic structures. Despite the lack of central offices, paid staff, and systematic procedures, the church functions effectively across nine states. Leaders do not use computers or e-mail to keep track of members. Deacons do not use electronic spreadsheets to balance financial accounts. Nevertheless, Wenger leaders maintain a remarkable consistency of practice across all forty-nine districts.

The ministers' conference weaves Wenger communities across the nation into one social fabric. The bishop of a settlement located outside Pennsylvania said, "The conference has been helpful to us. Ten years ago we had some problems. Now we have learned to work together more closely. As a bishop I can fall back on the conference for support. I don't have to carry the full load." The rapid growth of the Wenger faith outside Pennsylvania has prompted some members in outlying states to ask about forming a "western conference" for congregations in Missouri, Iowa, and Wisconsin. One bishop contended, "It would really be hard to keep us all together if we had a western conference. It is easier for the people and the bishops to have one conference." As the church continues to grow, the question of a centralized conference will not likely disappear. Will ministers from all over the country continue to make the pilgrimage to Pennsylvania's Martindale churchhouse every spring and fall? Will a single conference structure fit the needs of local districts as more churches spread across the country?

✢ MUTUAL AID

Wenger society has no bureaucratic organizations, no corporate headquarters, paid officials, or annual conventions—not even retirement homes, publishing houses, mission boards, colleges, or seminaries. One-room schools, organized by local parents, are the only formal type of organization. On this dimension, Wenger society stands far apart from the complex large-scale organizations of American society. Personal ties and obligations are the sinews that bond Wenger communities together.

One of the strongest bonds of solidarity is mutual aid. But even mutual aid in the face of fire, flood, and illness is handled in an informal fashion. A nationwide fund provides financial assistance, but in the moment of need dozens, if not hundreds, of members help clean up rubble or rebuild homes. Reluctant to depend on commercial insurance to bail them out of disaster, the Wengers turn to fellow believers for aid and support. They believe that their faith and confidence should be "in the Lord." Members are admonished, according to Scripture, to trust in the Lord and in the goodwill of their community. Propelled by religious values, an enormous pool of social capital is marshaled to assist needy members in moments of crisis.

The Wenger community has a long tradition of helping each other with material aid. In the first half of the twentieth century, Wenger farmers cooperated in "threshing rings," clusters of farmers who shared a threshing machine and exchanged labor when they harvested grain each summer. Today, most settlements have what the Wengers call a "community wagon" that is maintained by one of the members. This trailer, pulled by a tractor, hired truck, or van, contains a full set of equipment for community functions, especially weddings. Among the items typically found in the trailer are folding chairs, hymnbooks, table service, and a gas stove.

The Wengers have a national fund to cover the major costs of medical service, fire, and storm that cannot be paid by the local district(s). Periodically, voluntary collections are taken in all the districts for these needs. The Old Order Mennonites in Indiana do not contribute to the national fund because they have their own.[11] Money from the fund also helps to build new churchhouses. About five or six times a year, the deacon in each church district appoints several men to go door-to-door to collect a freewill offering to replenish the fund. If too many disasters strike, additional collections are taken. In a recent year, the national church collected $2 million to help members with the cost of healthcare and damage from fire and storm. A commercial insurance agent estimated that commercial coverage for their healthcare needs alone would have cost at least $6 million!

One member explained the Wenger system of mutual aid this way: "We help each other out with hospital bills and that type of thing. When somebody has a hospital bill that they feel they cannot pay, then we hold a collection. Several men go around and stop at each home. They carry a box, a zippered bag, or a drawstring bag, and most people put a check or cash in. We try to avoid knowing how much each person puts in. That's based on Scripture, not letting the left hand know what the right hand does. The deacons organize this work."

Several factors help to undergird the system with integrity. Checks for the fund are written to the church district's fund or to the local volunteer collector, who then writes a single check to the fund. This way the local deacon who disburses the funds to needy members is blind to the family's giving history. Disbursements from the fund are reported publicly by the deacon at a semiannual church meeting so everyone in the district knows how much assistance each family received. The public reporting discourages abuse. "Everyone will know," said one member, "if I just got a brand-new tractor and then say I can't pay for my hospital bill. If you can't trust the church, who can you trust?"

A member explains, "If a barn burns down, we have an inventory taken. Three members appointed by the deacon take an inventory to assess the loss and appraise it. Then the church contributes about 75 percent of the loss and the freewill labor to rebuild." People contribute voluntarily, "as they are able." Members expect wealthier people to give more than others. Property values are not assessed in advance and no one pays a premium. One member summed it up this way: "All mutual aid is freewill, there's no assessment, no one is told how much to contribute." Some members shun any help. An elderly, ailing man said, "I haven't had any help yet, and I'll pay all my own bills until I run out of money."

Wenger people quickly point out that mutual aid is not insurance. Families pay their own medical bills, if they are able. When they cannot, the church will pay 75 percent of amounts over $700. It will pay the entire bill if the person is poor. The costs of child delivery are usually paid by the family unless there are complications with additional costs. Some hospitals extend a discount as high as 30 percent to Old Order people who pay in cash. A hospital administrator said, "It's not a program that's offered to anyone who walks in off the street, but we know that the Mennonites and the Amish are going to pay their bills."

Should the church pay for alternative medical treatment? This issue prompted spirited controversy in the community. One member reported that, after appointing a committee to research the issue, the church decided "it will not cover alternative doctoring. They won't pay for trips to Mexico for cancer cures or for alternative treatments in Nevada. If I think I need to go to Mexico, the local church on a case-by-case basis might help, but they can't use the national fund." The church-wide fund will cover chemotherapy for cancer if it is a standard medical treatment. Something like a liver transplant, according to one member, "would be decided on a case-by-case basis."

❖ MUTUAL LOVE IN ACTION

One member provided a written description of mutual aid. "Look at the spirit of neighborliness among our people. The other year our neighbor's barn burned down. The owner, like most Wenger Mennonites, did not have insurance. Imagine how devastating such a catastrophe could be. A young struggling dairy farmer trying to pay off his farm suddenly is left with no barn, almost no equipment, no money. He has no place to house or milk his cows that were saved. Can you imagine seeing him stand there with his family on that fateful Sunday evening after the fire trucks finally left, looking at the smoldering remains of what had been, just a few hours before, his livelihood, his dairy operation?"

The writer explained how the community organized its social capital to meet the need. "Immediately, that evening the 'system' began kicking in. Neighbors helped herd the remaining cows to a neighboring dairy farm. There, they were fed and milked until a new barn could be rebuilt. Early the next morning (Monday), over two hundred people converged on the site. Two bulldozers were trucked in, neighbors came with their tractors and wagons, a local contractor came with a skid loader and a backhoe. Men and boys swarmed over the rubble, cleaning up the charred remains."

Beyond the volunteer sweat labor, the local deacon "came and talked to the young farmer about his financial situation. The deacon had already appointed three neighboring farmers to assess the damage, because we always assess property values after a catastrophe rather than before. A church member who owned a local sawmill put his other customers on hold so he could saw lumber for the new barn."

Preparations for rebuilding were soon under way. "Early Monday morning, the young man's father had been on the phone calling local carpenters. They needed a head carpenter to engineer all the work that needed to be done in the next few weeks. By 9:00 A.M., the new head carpenter had arrived. A middle-aged contractor, he agreed to drop all his other projects until the project was finished. He began measuring the site immediately, because by evening they would start digging the footers for concrete for the new barn. Throughout Monday morning, the head carpenter ordered lumber, concrete, blocks, metal roofing, nails, and many other supplies. Neighboring women brought bread, bologna, cheese, potato chips, cake, drink, and whatever else it might take to feed an army of hungry workers."

This scene, with some variations, is repeated for several days. "First, the debris is cleared away. Then the backhoe and bulldozers move in to excavate for the new barn. Concrete footers are poured, concrete block walls are laid, and lumber is sawed. About two weeks later, hundreds of hands gather for the barn raising. Then the milking equipment and cow stanchions are installed and calf pens are built."

Barn raisings are one example of mutual aid in the Wenger community.

Within three weeks, a new barn stood on the old site. "Except for the head carpenter and some heavy equipment operators, neighbors reaching out to an unfortunate member have donated hundreds of hours of labor. A collection, announced in church, helps to pay for the new barn and equipment." The church paid $70,000 of the farmer's $100,000 loss. An elderly man from a neighboring church district offered to finance the rest at a low rate of interest.

"What is really amazing about this," concluded the writer, "is the lack of fanfare that accompanies the outpouring of help. There is really nothing unusual about it. It is simply our normal way of doing things. If one member suffers, all members suffer. In our opinion, this is the way that it should be. There is nothing extraordinary about it." This remarkable system of corporate care, based on mutual trust, religious conviction, and spiritual capital, is obviously much more efficient, humane, and inexpensive than commercial, bureaucratized insurance.

✢ POPULATION GROWTH

Large Families

A group can only grow two ways: by converting outsiders or by recruiting insiders. The Wengers are thriving because of large families, not because of evangelism. But large families do not guarantee growth: children must be persuaded to join the community as adults and they must be retained after baptism. The Wengers have grown rapidly in the last half-century because of large families and strong retention. In the fifteen-year period from 1987 to 2002, the number of Wenger households grew from 1,670 to 2,890, an average annual growth rate of 3.7 percent. If this rate of growth continues, they will have 5,780 households and 31,000 people by 2021. Unlike the American population, which bulges with elderly, about 20 percent of the Wenger population is under five years of age, 47 percent under fifteen, and 66 percent under twenty-five.[12] Such large numbers of youth accelerate the rate of growth. Only 4 percent of the population is over sixty-five years of age.

Childbearing rates for Wenger women propel the growth. Because the church rarely has converts from outside, its growth depends on birth and retention rates. The average number of children born to married women is 8.3.[13] This is a high birthrate, even for a rural farm population. Couples, on average, have their first child within a year of their marriage and less than 1 percent are conceived before marriage.[14] Mennonites poke fun at themselves by telling a story of Canadian tourists visiting Lancaster County. The visitors noted many, many mailboxes with the name "Martin." Finally, they saw a mailbox that said "Martin's Hatchery" and exclaimed, "Oh, so that's where they all come from!"

Conversion and Baptism

Young people are baptized and join the church in their late teens, typically at about eighteen years of age.[15] Only a few outside converts have joined the church. Some of these have married Wenger mates and fit in quite well. A bishop notes, though, that "most converts haven't worked out very well." One convert was arrested for disorderly conduct. Others have left the church after a short time. Some leaders tell potential converts that they might be hap-

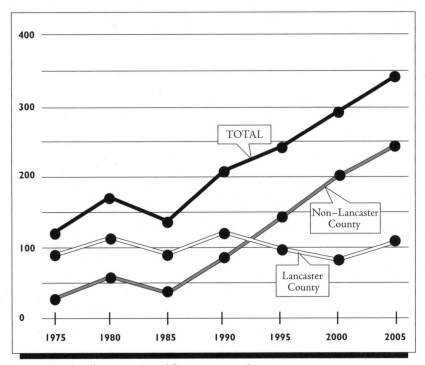

NOTE: Numbers for 2005 estimated from current trends.

DIAGRAM 6 Wenger baptisms in all settlements, 1975–2005

pier in the Horning Church or in the Lancaster Conference because of the challenges of adapting to a traditional way of life.

About 90 percent of Wenger youth join the church.[16] Members claim that more young people are staying in the church now than ever before in their history. In one church district, as shown in Table 5, 95 percent of nearly two hundred children joined the church. Several factors contribute to the high retention rates. Strict lifestyle rules discourage youth from pursuing vocational opportunities outside of the Wenger community. The eighth grade ceiling on education also reduces vocational choices. Some Wenger leaders attribute their strong retention to the ministers' conference, which holds the church together. Others point to the church's flexibility in allowing some farm machinery—silo unloaders and automatic manure cleaners—that benefits young farmers.

One Wenger bishop observes that youth in the more liberal Mennonite churches tend to rebel more. He contends that youth with less freedom in

✦ TABLE 5 Demographic profile of Wengers in the Martindale District

		Number	Percentage
Birth (1953–68)	In Martindale district	199	100
Baptism	In Wenger church	189	95
	In other Mennonite Anabaptist churches	8	4
	Unknown/unbaptized	2	1
Marriage	To a Wenger	162	81
	Unmarried	26	13
	Unknown	11	6
Church membership (1998)	Wenger church	177	89
	Other Mennonite/ Anabaptist churches	22	11
Residence (1998)	Martindale district	41	21
	Other Lancaster districts	37	18
	Other Pennsylvania settlements	20	10
	Outside Pennsylvania	79	40
	Unknown	22	11

SOURCE: Martindale District Study, 1968–1998 (see Appendix A).

more conservative churches are more likely to join the church. But in the words of another Wenger leader, "We're finding that we have the same problems as anybody else. The children will rebel, but because we draw the lines where we do, our children don't go quite as far."

Defection and Loss

Defections from the Wengers occur both before and after baptism.[17] One leader estimates about half of the defections occur before baptism. In some settlements, more couples leave after marriage. The rate of defection in the Martindale Church district before and after baptism was 11 percent over a thirty-year period. Technically, unbaptized youth cannot defect, because they are not members. Some youth become fascinated with other churches through peer friendships. Others might have a boyfriend or girlfriend in

another church, or might drift away because of alcohol or behavioral problems. One man sadly described his grandson who never joined the church:
"He was nineteen when he left the church. But now he wants the [inheri-
tance] money the others are getting. He doesn't bring his paychecks back
either. He endorses them himself and spends the money." In Wenger tradition, obedient sons typically give their earnings to their father until the age
of twenty.[18]

According to one father, "Leaving goes in spurts. Buddies follow each
other. If one or so from a buddy group goes, then others step in unison."
Nevertheless, "The percent of our youth staying with the church now is
higher than ever. I can't think of five who left in the last year," said a farmer
in Yates County, New York. Explaining why, he pointed to "more technology
in our homes and barns that makes it easer and more comfortable now. And
what's going on in the world scares us now more than ever. Things like ram-
pant divorce, venereal disease, AIDS, rap music, tattoos, just plain craziness,
the degeneration of society is just more obvious now." All of these factors,
according to this member, encourage youth to stay with the church. Indeed,
in Yates County, the retention rate is above 90 percent.[19]

Some sheep, of course, do stray from the Wenger flock. Sometimes,
young married couples leave after they have been baptized. A bishop outside of Pennsylvania said, "Very few have left our church in the last five years.
Not more than five left. One went into the world, I'm not sure where. Some
leave after they are married. Five years ago a carpenter came and said, 'I can't
be a hypocrite and hire out a van every day for my work,' and so he left. Two
couples left and joined Charity Fellowship. A majority of those who leave go
to the Horning Church."

Other stories illustrate the patterns of defection. One family had sixteen children. All were baptized in the Wenger Church except the oldest
son and the youngest son. The oldest married a Wenger woman, but soon
grew restless. He moved to Florida and divorced his wife. Later, he became
ill with pancreatic cancer and at the age of forty-four returned, dying, to
his parents' home. He began attending a Lancaster Conference church
and resolved to join it. Unfortunately, he died at midnight on the day before his baptism. The youngest son bought a car and began attending the
Horning Church. When he decided to be baptized, the Horning Church
insisted that at least one of his two cars must be black. His black Chevrolet
Monte Carlo did not pass because it had raised white lettering on its tires.
Some black spray paint made the car acceptable, and he joined the Horning
Church.

Wenger youth are exposed to the larger world when they travel on service projects or other trips. These boys enjoy the Gulf of Mexico from a boardwalk during a break from a service project in Texas. The non-Wenger van driver is fifth from front.

Another Wenger boy courted a Horning girl, but her mother discouraged her from joining the Wengers, telling her, "You could never do without a car!" After they married, the couple joined the Horning Church, but they grew dissatisfied and then affiliated with the conservative Holdeman Mennonite Church.[20] Later, her mother lamented, "If I'd only let her join the Wengers!" Children who defect sadden parents, but if they do leave, parents prefer they join some type of Mennonite church.

In another defection, a man stopped attending communion and grew distant from the church. He contracted cancer, returned to the church, and was reconciled with other members. He was reluctant to shave his moustache, however, which stirred some controversy. One member noted, "He sort of mingled too much with the Seventh Day Adventists." Too much "mingling" with the world, contend the Wengers, may lead one astray.

One Wenger woman had a young daughter who was very ill. A Wenger minister refused to anoint her child with oil. He would not, he said, unless the child was old enough to believe. So she took her daughter to a healing service in a different church where she received an anointing. The mother herself was "converted," and received "assurance of salvation" in that healing service and eventually joined the other church. In another case, a person left and joined the car-driving Horning Church because, in his words, "I felt I couldn't do what I wanted to do for the church if I stayed with the Wengers." He later joined a more liberal Mennonite church and became active in its relief and service agency. Occasionally even Wenger ministers forsake the church. Some leave because of a conflict with other leaders or a desire to form a more conservative group.[21]

One member explained the steps toward the world if someone leaves. He noted two different patterns. First, "If someone joins us from the world and later leaves, they take one big step into the world." On the other hand, "If someone is born Old Order and leaves, most of the time they will take little steps toward the world, perhaps joining the Horning Church, then the Mid-Atlantic group, then Lancaster Conference, and finally out into the world." In any event, he concluded, "It's very rare for someone raised in the Wenger Church to make one big leap out into the world."

✣ SEEDING NEW SETTLEMENTS

Overview

A *settlement* consists of the general geographic area where a cluster of Wenger families resides.[22] A brand-new settlement will have only one church district and about a dozen families; older settlements typically have several districts. Wenger people do not map their world with reference to large cities and interstate highways. On the maps that they design and print, such typical features are often conspicuously missing. In speech, they refer to the names of valleys, townships, and counties where Wenger people live ("Penn Valley" [Berks County, Pa.], "Blair County" [Pa.], or "Marshall County" [Ind.]). When members speak of "Wisconsin," they mean the Wenger settlement in central Wisconsin, not the state as a whole. Their mental map reflects the location of their own communities.

Migration has stretched the Wenger community across nine states, as shown in Table 6.[23] Today, the community comprises sixteen settlements. Lancaster County is the largest and oldest settlement with ten church districts. Outside Pennsylvania, New York has the largest community with five churchhouses, followed by Missouri with four. Since 1990, new settlements have rooted in Montcalm County, Michigan (1992), Marshall County, Indiana

❖ TABLE 6 Profiles of Wenger settlements by state

Settlement	Date of origin	Number of church- houses	Ordained leaders[1]	Households	Population[2]	Members
Pennsylvania		21	57	1,785	8,885	4,735
Berks	1948	2	5	140	875	400
Blair/Bedford	1970	3	9	140	740	340
Cumberland	1967	3	9	230	1,320	630
Lancaster	1927	10	27	1,080	4,950	2,840
Union/Snyder	1960	3	7	195	1,000	525
Indiana[3]		4	11	195	970	500
Elkhart	1872	3	8	150	750	400
Marshall	1992	1	3	45	220	100
Iowa	1992	3	7	90	520	200
Kentucky		3	7	140	725	320
Casey	1975	1	3	70	400	165
Christian	1987	2	4	70	325	155
Michigan	1992	1	3	20	120	42
Missouri	1970	4	10	215	1,270	540
New York	1973	5	16	385	2,500	930
Ohio	1972	2	7	165	1,025	480
Wisconsin		6	16	315	1,760	795
North	1973	4	13	275	1,560	710
South	1996	2	3	40	200	85
Total		49	134	3,310	17,775	8,542

SOURCE: *Schedules* (2004) and informants.

[1]Bishops, ministers, deacons.
[2]Includes children and adults.
[3]The Indiana Old Order Mennonites affiliated with Groffdale Conference in 1973.

(1992), and Grant County, Wisconsin (1996).Because of this migration, many Lancaster County families now have children and grandchildren living in two or three states. One Lancaster man lamented, "Some of our youngest children don't know all of their cousins . . . they wouldn't even know 'em by name."

Why Migrate?

The high price of Lancaster County farmland in the last quarter of the twentieth century prodded many Wengers to search for cheaper land elsewhere. In Lancaster's Martindale district, for example, among the children who were fifteen years and younger in 1968, only 21 percent remain in that district. Eighteen percent moved elsewhere in Lancaster County, 10 percent moved to other counties in Pennsylvania, and nearly half (40 percent) moved to another state.[24] Most of those living in other states are farmers who were seeking cheaper land.

The first exodus out of Lancaster County began in 1948, when a few Wenger people migrated to adjoining Berks County. Others moved to Union County in 1960, but the mass exodus came after 1970, as the Wenger population grew and land prices soared, prodding many newly married couples to migrate out of Pennsylvania. The new settlements beyond Lancaster represent the biggest transformation of Wenger society in the twentieth century. "Now when I come back to my home church in Lancaster County," said one migrant, "it feels like an old people's home because all the young families have left."

High-priced land and suburban congestion are the leading reasons people give for abandoning the mother settlement. "Lancaster was getting too full, it was all built up, and everything got too close together," said one minister who left. A farmer who moved away declared, "Lancaster County is depressing, the population, the mad pace, the high prices. I have no desire to return there." A farmer who fled when he was single and twenty-two-years-old said, "I wanted to get away from Lancaster County. Land was too high priced and life too fast paced. I could never have afforded a farm there. Here in New York, I was able to buy a farm and raise a family on it. The Lord opened up a whole new venue for us here."

In the 1970s when Wengers were seeding new communities in several states, farmland in Lancaster County was selling for $5,000 an acre. In out-of-state areas, they could buy land for $300 to $600 per acre. When asked why he left Pennsylvania in 1975, a retiree said, "the availability of cheap land and there was a lot of it. I wanted to stay with the land and I had four boys in a row and the farm is the best place for young boys."

One farmer explained why he encouraged his boys to leave their Lancaster home: "I wasn't wealthy enough that I could buy farms for my boys in Lancaster County and help them get started in this high-priced farming. The people that buy land here have to have some other business that's doing real good so they can afford to keep farming. I would rather have them [my boys] move to other areas where it's possible to make a living. Even if the boys move, they have to buy the machinery, silos, and whatever, at current prices . . . the same as Lancaster County. But of course, land prices are much lower."

A Pennsylvania farmer explained why he sold his farm and moved to Wisconsin in 1996: "You know, Lancaster County is up against it as far as their youth . . . so some went to New York. And now those in New York don't have nowhere to go either. So their children are starting to look elsewhere, too. . . . I wanted to give my children a chance to grow up on a farm . . . so I decided that if I'm going to do something, then I'd better do it . . . because my son is getting at the age where he wants to be with the youth. To have him with the youth, and then pull him away again, I couldn't do that." Timing is everything. If a farmer moves to a new community too soon, it may be years before a sizable community grows and the family may face loneliness and isolation. If he waits too long, however, rising land prices may make the advantage of moving moot.

The average age of the population varies by settlement, due to the age of the settlement and its rate of growth. Migrants to new settlements are usually younger families looking for cheap farmland. In the newer communities, ministers are typically in their thirties, whereas in the older Lancaster settlement, ministers average sixty years of age.[25] Migrants in outlying settlements compare the conservative or progressive bent of their churches with those back in Lancaster. "We say that Gravel Run is like Bowmansville, Benton is more like Groffdale, and Milo like Weaverland. We have both kinds at both places—conservative and progressive," said one elderly man.

Some new settlements, but not all of them, are more conservative than the mother community in Lancaster for a number of reasons. New communities have a smaller number of older people because young families tend to migrate. With many decisions to make about church life and schools, "young men have to pick up responsibility and it has a sobering effect on them," said one man. There aren't as many old men in the counsel meetings. With all the responsibilities, "the youthful forty-year-olds act more conservative, more like older men." Other settlements may be started by a cluster of families on the more progressive side. "It depends on the bishop," explained one woman. "If the bishop holds back, it might be conservative, but not if the bishop pushes more [for change]."

According to one mother living outside of Pennsylvania, "Lancaster is more liberal in the dress of their young folks. Their youth are more casual, they wear casual clothing at Sunday church gatherings. Shirts are casual.

Some boys wear regular blue jeans and loud sneakers at youth gatherings. Some girls in Lancaster have more of the latest styles, fashionable, big flowers, and bold prints, shorter dresses, fresher, and louder colors. Some even have tube skirts that are form-fitting with slits in them on the side. They go down to the ankle."[26]

A non-Wenger agreed that some outlying settlements are more traditional than Lancaster. "The Yates County [New York] settlement is more socially conservative than Lancaster County. Women are more modest here, they wear less form-fitting dresses and have less ornamentation. The men are also plainer. Bishops are more conservative here. There is more interaction with English neighbors in Lancaster. It is more separated here." A big question facing the Wengers in the future is whether a centralized, Lancaster-centric system will survive regional differences that will likely intensify as settlements expand outside Pennsylvania and as a new generation of leaders comes of age.

Wenger settlements rarely fail. Indeed, among Old Order groups, the success of new Wenger settlements is stellar. A variety of factors may explain why new Wenger settlements thrive when groups like the Old Order Amish have seen dozens of settlements fail.[27] The Amish form of congregational government may make it difficult to seed new communities. Some Amish settlements fail because new families arrive from different churches with different rules. Dissension over the different *Ordnungs* may lead to failure. In contrast, because all Wenger congregations have a common *Ordnung,* new settlements rarely splinter over *Ordnung* disputes. The conference-established *Ordnung* leads to more stability in the new Wenger settlements and increases the chances of success. Technology—especially the use of tractors for fieldwork and electricity in shops and homes—may also contribute to the ease of planting a new settlement. With tractors, the Wengers can more easily farm hilly land with harder soil. Wenger use of electricity also requires fewer alternative forms of power that may not be available in new areas.

❖ LIFE BEYOND LANCASTER

Pennsylvania
A brief sketch of the various settlements illustrates how the Wenger people reproduce their communities in new areas. The first Wengers to leave Lancaster County settled in Penn Valley (Berks County, Pennsylvania) in 1948 and built their first churchhouse in 1952. A few years later (1960), Lancaster

The first churchhouse in Missouri, shown here, was built in 1971. The architectural style of churchhouses is similar in all the settlements.

families moved to Union County, Pennsylvania, and, in eight years, built a churchhouse.[28] Today the community has about two hundred families, but the mountains around this narrow valley restrict further growth. A new community was planted in Cumberland County in 1967. The Blair/Bedford County settlement, begun in 1970, also has mountains that restrict the expansion of its one hundred forty families.

Missouri and Ohio

In 1970, five families moved to Morgan County, Missouri, after receiving the blessing of the senior Wenger bishop, Aaron Z. Sensenig. He promised to help them establish the new settlement if they would support the *Ordnung* of the Groffdale Conference in Lancaster County.[29] Within a year, eight more families arrived. Today they number some two hundred families and have four churchhouses and ten schools. Members are involved in a variety of businesses in addition to farming.

A new settlement sprouted in 2005 in Linn County in northwestern Missouri. The half-dozen families who formed the new community came from the mother settlement in Morgan County. "So Linn County," said one member, "is our first satellite of a satellite because Morgan County was a satellite of Lancaster in 1970." Several Linn County families lived in mobile homes until they built new ones.

Wenger people started moving to Richland County, Ohio, in 1972, and that settlement now claims two churchhouses and about 170 families.

Iowa

Eighty families live in the Iowa settlement located north of Charles City. The first residents arrived in 1992 and built the Cedar Valley churchhouse in 1995. Mostly farmers, they milk dairy cows and raise grain crops and a few hogs. A Lancaster County man says with a smile, "I'm jealous of those Iowa farms. No stones, and pretty flat ground." One Lancaster farmer advises, "If you visit Iowa, take your denims along [because they are constructing new buildings]." Until they ordained their own bishop, the bishop from Wisconsin came down twice a year to confer with the Iowa ministers and serve communion.

In 1999, a Wenger businessman in Lancaster County sold his hardware store and moved his family to Howard County, Iowa, for "a little breathing space," away from the fast pace of Lancaster life. He settled his family on a ten-acre produce plot, where he established a small hardware store, but declares, "I don't want to be a Wal-Mart." Enthused about the promise of the young settlement, he sees "a big opportunity for our group of Mennonites here in Iowa."[30]

Wisconsin

In 1973, twenty-one Wenger families from Lancaster County pioneered a new settlement in Clark County, Wisconsin. Even today, Clark County land sells for under $1,000 per acre compared to $10,000 or more in Lancaster County. Wisconsin farmers plant three times as much seed as those in Lancaster to get the same yield, but the low land prices make farming profitable. Today, the Clark County community has 275 families and four churchhouses.

The newest Wisconsin settlement began in 1996 in Grant County, about 150 miles away from the Clark County settlement. One of the settlers explains, "The average [English] farmer here is sixty-five, and the owners are just waiting for somebody to come in and buy. In two to three years, you're going to see a price increase. There's a guy [Wenger] from Ohio that's interested. In fact, even one guy [Wenger] from New York State was with the agent out here looking at farms. There's been a van of our people going through here [looking for farms] on an average of once a week."

For several months, the first Grant County settlers traveled by hired van to church services in the Wenger settlement near Charles City, Iowa, two-and-one-half hours away. In the spring of 1997, four more Wenger families arrived in Grant County and the community began meeting for worship. Now numbering some forty families, the community has two churchhouses.

✣ THE NEW YORK STORY

The first Wengers moved from Lancaster to New York in 1973. Today, over 380 families live on over forty square miles in the Finger Lakes region of Yates, Ontario, and Schuler counties. As in other new settlements, most of them are farmers. The community is vibrant and thriving. In a matter of three decades, the Mennonites have rehabilitated the agricultural economy of the area. Yates was one of the poorest counties in the northeastern states when the Wengers arrived. Many farms had dilapidated buildings, land that was overrun with brush, and less than fifteen acres of tillable land.

The wife of one of the early settlers said, "Farms were really run down. Things were shabby with a lot of grown-up hedgerows. Fields were filled with goldenrod and had no buildings. Much of the land was in soil bank." Expecting her eleventh child when they moved in March 1974, the immigrant "was leery about the move. We left good English neighbors in Pa., but we found good English ones up here. The storekeepers were helpful." During the first year, "We had church in an empty house at first and then had services back and forth in our own homes. The host would read a Scripture, and then we sang in German and in English and had a silent prayer. Preachers came sometimes from other places to preach."[31]

New settlements typically draw young couples at first. A Lancaster father noted, "When our oldest son moved to New York with five young children, he was the oldest man there." Another Lancaster man said that when his younger brother, who lives in New York, attends church, "He sits on the front bench with the older men. But here at the Martindale Churchhouse [Lancaster County], I sit on the back bench with the young men." As a new settlement grows, the core area gradually has older families as the younger ones settle on the margins.

The first minister in Yates County was ordained in 1975 and the first churchhouse was built in 1976. The community grew slowly, however, for the next six years because of leadership difficulties. The settlement ordained its

This well-kept dairy farm is located in the Yates County settlement in New York.

first bishop in 1986 and by 2004 it had two bishops, five churchhouses and twenty-six one-room schools. One member lamented the loss of unity that has accompanied the growth: "In the early days we were one community, one communion, and we all came together for barn raisings."

The Mennonite presence has transformed the agricultural economy of Yates County. Of some 225 dairy farms in the county, 200 are operated by Wengers. A produce auction organized by Wenger farmers boasted sales of $1.5 million just four years after it began. In the words of a local extension agent, "The Mennonites have been innovative and highly productive. They capitalize on family labor." He continued, "They have more orderly farms, with less clutter and machinery sitting around. Mennonite houses are painted, look prosperous, and stand out as well kept." One of the early settlers described the Wenger impact on the county this way: "Everything now up here is more spruced up and we Mennonites had a lot to do with it. Because we fixed up our farms, the outsiders fixed theirs up too."

One member who bought a vacant house "filled with coons and pigeons" said many of the once rundown properties are now attractive and productive. "Go to the local lumberyard and ask them what the Mennonites have done for the county; the stores do a great lumber business because of all the building that is going on." In the words of another Wenger, "Many people say 'we're glad the Mennonites came because of what it did for Yates County and farming.' Businessmen have benefited, feedmills, hardware stores, lumberyards, all have benefited."

Why does the settlement thrive? Yates County Wengers point to low land prices and the fact that the "native people accepted us very well." The short five-hour distance from Lancaster encourages frequent trips between the two settlements. Yates County is also near other Pennsylvania settlements. Others attribute the Yates County growth to good leadership and strong support from the larger Groffdale Conference.

The success of the Wengers in Yates County has produced a new problem: a shortage of available land. According to one leader, "Most of the farms have been bought. Some people are buying homes now without much land. Some carpenters are just buying homes, or just small plots to raise produce." The options for the Mennonites, in the words of an extension agent, include: "1) more intensive agriculture, 2) division of farms, 3) geographical expansion into adjoining Rushville and Ontario County, 4) more jobs in business and carpentry, and 5) buying new land for a new settlement." Vans loaded with land prospectors have already been searching for new sites in other areas of New York. "Maybe someday soon we will start a daughter settlement," said a bishop.

✣ THE INDIANA CONNECTION

The Old Order Mennonites in Elkhart County, Indiana, had separated from the larger Mennonite Church in 1872, two decades before the Old Order church formed in Pennsylvania. About a century after its birth, Indiana's Old Order church was struggling over the use of electricity and telephones. The Indiana bishop, fearing they would suffer a division, traveled to Pennsylvania to counsel with Aaron Z. Sensenig, the senior Wenger bishop in Lancaster County. Sensenig invited the Indiana group to join the Groffdale Conference, hoping that might fend off a church split. The Indiana church accepted the invitation to join in fellowship with the Wengers in 1973. Today, over one hundred families in Elkhart County are affiliated with the Groffdale Conference.[32]

The Groffdale Conference allows the Indiana congregations to have some different practices because of their long, separate history before joining the

Melons are sold to outside buyers at an Indiana produce auction.

Groffdale Conference. One Lancaster bishop explained, "They're not quite in line with us. We won't make them change, but they're a little different. We don't want communities starting near Indiana that think they can be like Indiana, so we list their ministry separately. It's okay if they have clocks in their churchhouses; maybe we should have clocks too, but we don't." In addition to clocks, the Indiana churchhouses also have low pulpits, which of course are not found in other Wenger churchhouses.

Many of Indiana's Old Order Mennonites raise produce—cantaloupes, watermelons, and vegetables. Some of them operate a produce auction that attracts buyers from as far away as Chicago and Indianapolis. The Indiana community has birthed two settlements: one in Marshall County, Indiana, and the other in Montcalm County, Michigan. Most of the families in these settlements came from Elkhart County.

The Marshall County settlement lies about thirty-five miles southwest of the Elkhart settlement. When the new settlement began, ministers from the Elkhart districts visited at least once a month to hold worship services. If no minister was present, the members gathered to read Scripture, sing, and pray. In 1996, Marshall County built a churchhouse and conducted an ordination, in which six of the twelve eligible men were nominated as candidates for preacher.

Can community flourish with a burgeoning population scattered over nine states? A church directory of nearly one thousand pages helps to connect Wenger families in the various settlements. The directory lists the names of all Wenger members and their children. Several of these directories, spanning a fifteen-year period (1987–2002), provide a rich source of demographic data for members and researchers alike. When the first directory was compiled in 1987, more than a hundred people refused to cooperate because they were afraid of "being numbered." This fear rests on an Old Testament warning about God's anger with King David for "numbering the tribes" (II Sam. 24) and from some of the apocalyptic warnings in Revelation about "the number of the beast" (Rev. 13).[33] The historic Wenger objection to counting individuals also reflects their rejection of individualism and their communal commitment to family units rather than individuals. In recent years, most families have supplied the requested information for updating the directory.

Some Wenger people create maps of local settlements that locate all the Wenger homes, as well as every school and churchhouse. They include a directory of household heads, mailing addresses, and telephone numbers. The mapmakers filter out many features considered irrelevant for the Wenger community: large towns, public attractions, tourist sites, public schools, and non-Wenger churches. The homespun maps and the national directories help to build community solidarity and interpersonal connections across all the settlements.

Letters, phone calls, and visits help families stay connected despite hundreds of miles of separation. One mother said she appreciated having the telephone to keep in touch with her distant children. Indeed, some members credit the rise of new settlements with accelerating the acceptance of telephones in the 1970s. Wenger people often hire a van and driver to travel to far-flung settlements to attend weddings, funerals, ordinations, and baptisms. They rarely travel "just to see the sights"; they visit children, attend church events, or help relatives with construction projects. These periodic visits help to maintain strong ties despite the long miles between the settlements.

The Wengers do not publish any religious periodicals. The bulk of their reading materials, typically written in English, comes from conservative Mennonite or Amish publishers. These materials include historical writings, morality stories, and biographies of people from other separatist churches. One woman said, "When I was a little girl, my mother used to read to us on

Sundays some stories out of the *Martyrs Mirror*. And you know, sometimes it kind of made you nervous the way people had to suffer so." Wenger parents closely monitor their children's reading materials, whether in German or English.

Families use a variety of reading materials. One mother explained, "We read nature and animal stories and books like Nancy Drew and the Hardy Boys. We also have the *Young Companion, Family Life,* and other Amish magazines." Parents use children's reading materials to reinforce godly, community values and the Wenger way of life. The only English Bible that many people own is the King James Bible, or often one with parallel columns of standard German and King James English.

Many Wengers read *Die Botschaft* (The Message), a weekly newspaper published by the Amish. Filled with diary-like reports from Old Order Mennonite and Amish scribes, it circulates widely in both Amish and Mennonite communities. Despite the German title, the text is in English. Correspondents from settlements across the country inform readers of the weather, harvests, visitors, church affairs, social gatherings, and other tidbits of news from their area. The Wengers also read and contribute essays to the newspaper *Plain Interests* and to three magazines (*Blackboard Bulletin, Family Life,* and *Young Companion*) produced by Pathway Publishers, an Amish press located in Ontario, Canada. These media are important means of building community awareness and solidarity across many Old Order Amish and Mennonite communities in the United States.

What bonds the widespread Wenger Church together? In the mind of a bishop living outside of Pennsylvania, "Our [ministers'] conference twice a year helps us maintain a common footing. Also the intermarriage across the different settlements, from New York to Wisconsin, from Iowa to New Holland [Pennsylvania]. The family connections, visiting, funerals, and ordinations tie us all together." The social architecture of the Wenger community is coordinated through the authority of the conference, but the churchly authority is reinforced by a web of friendship and familial ties that crisscross all sixteen settlements. In addition to social ties, common patterns of religious rituals also fuse the community together. We explore some of the key redemptive rituals in Chapter 5.

The Rhythm of Sacred Ritual

The lot is cast into the lap; but the whole disposing thereof is of the Lord.

—PROVERBS 16:33

✤ THE ANNUAL CALENDAR

Ritual practices regulate the rhythms of community life and reinforce group identity. National holidays—Memorial Day, the Fourth of July, Labor Day, Thanksgiving, and Christmas—are ritual enactments of American values that pace the flow of mainstream society. The rituals of seasonal sports that shift from baseball to football and to basketball articulate values of competition, teamwork, and sportsmanship; they also govern the cultural calendar of local communities as well as the nation. As they do in all human communities, collective rituals in Wenger life give voice to deep values, shape collective and individual identity, and moderate the cultural cadence of time.

Wenger communities follow an invariable calendar that stretches back to the early nineteenth century. Except on special occasions, no meetings take place in the churchhouse on weekdays. In addition to Sunday morning, services are also held in most churchhouses on Thanksgiving, Christmas, and Ascension Day. The dates for other special meetings—counsel meetings, preparatory services, communions—vary from congregation to congregation because a bishop presides over them. The rhythm of gatherings across all the settlements follows a predictable sequence that gives meaning and order to Wenger life. The annual ritual sequence begins with congregational counsel meetings in March and closes with church services on Christmas Day.[1]

Spring counsel meeting A counsel meeting is held in each local district at the close of a Sunday morning service in March. At the meeting, members air grievances, discuss concerns related to the *Ordnung*, and indicate their readiness to participate in communion, which follows in several weeks.

Spring conference After the local counsel meetings, ordained leaders from across the country convene in the Martindale (Pennsylvania) churchhouse for a day of deliberation. The ministers' conference always meets after the local counsel meetings are held but before any communion services begin. At the conference, ministers report concerns from their congregations and seek agreement on lifestyle issues, but they rarely debate theological doctrines. Discussions typically center on faithful practice: what should be allowed and what prohibited, how disagreements can be resolved, and how congregations across the country can work together in harmony. The decisions made by the conference may also lead to revisions of the *Ordnung*.

Spring fasting day A special day of fasting and prayer known as *Faschtdaag* (fasting day) prepares the local congregation for communion. This day of self- and community examination culminates in a three-hour preparatory service, when the *Ordnung* is read. The spring cycle of preparatory services begins on Good Friday.

Spring communion This celebration of unity occurs on a Sunday in March, April, or May, depending on the date of Easter. Members commune at their "home" churchhouse. The three-hour service includes lengthy sermons that recount biblical stories from the creation to the crucifixion of Jesus, the sharing of the sacred emblems of bread and wine, and the ritual of footwashing.

Ascension Day This weekday event, which comes forty days after Easter, commemorates Jesus' return to heaven. Following worship

Ascension Day *(cont.)*	services in the morning, families spend the rest of the day socializing and participating in nature-related, educational, and inspirational activities.
Instruction meetings	Baptismal candidates gather for instruction classes on six Sunday afternoons beginning in late July. These continue every two weeks or so until a baptismal service that coincides with the fall preparatory service on the day of fasting.
Fall counsel meeting	In late September, a new round of congregational counsel meetings begins as members and leaders prepare for the fall communion service.
Fall conference	On the first Friday in October, ministers from across the country gather once again in the Martindale churchhouse for their fall conference.
Fall fasting day	Held on a Saturday in October on the day before the cycle of communion services begins, the fall preparatory service often includes a baptismal service.
Fall communion	The fall communion services are held on a Sunday in October or November.
Thanksgiving	Congregations gather for worship on Thanksgiving morning. Following the service, many extended families gather for a Thanksgiving meal. Some weddings are also held on Thanksgiving.
Christmas	A special service is held on Christmas morning in the churchhouse, after which people gather with family and friends for a noontime meal.[2]

Occasionally, other daytime services are held for special events, such as ordinations. Wenger life is regulated by these holy days, rather than by the national holiday calendar. Neither congregations nor schools observe the following American holidays: Martin Luther King Day, President's Day, Independence Day, Memorial Day, and Labor Day.[3] Moreover, Wenger children do not participate in Halloween activities.

✦ SUNDAY CHURCH SERVICE

The foundational ritual that undergirds and integrates all of Wenger life is the Sunday church service.[4] Riding in horse-drawn carriages, pedaling bicycles, and walking, members converge at the churchhouse about 9:00 A.M.

Wengers travel to a Sunday morning service on bicycles and in carriages.

They greet each other with a hearty handshake, and some of them exchange a "holy kiss," an ancient biblical custom in which men greet men and women greet women with a kiss on the lips or cheek. The kiss is exchanged between ministers, between ministers' wives, and between ministers and laymen. The holy kiss, long abandoned in the wider Protestant church, symbolizes spiritual fellowship and follows the biblical injunction in 1 Corinthians 16:20: "Greet one another with a holy kiss."[5]

Reflecting their historical departure from Catholic and Protestant practices, the Wengers have no church school classes, offerings, choirs, musical instruments, ushers, candles, robes, altars, or printed liturgy. The floors and walls of the churchhouses are absolutely bare—without any inscriptions, explicit symbols, or objects of adoration.

The ministers sit on the preachers' bench in order of seniority beginning with the bishop, followed by the ministers and deacon. Facing the ministers' bench, the older men sit on the right side and the older women sit on the left side of the meeting room.[6] Young women and girls sit on the left side and young men and boys sit on the right side on long benches in the back center of the room that also face the ministers' bench, as shown in Diagram 7. In most churchhouses, this long midsection rises toward the rear to afford a better view. About eight men sit at the singers' table near the preacher's table and lead the *a cappella* singing.

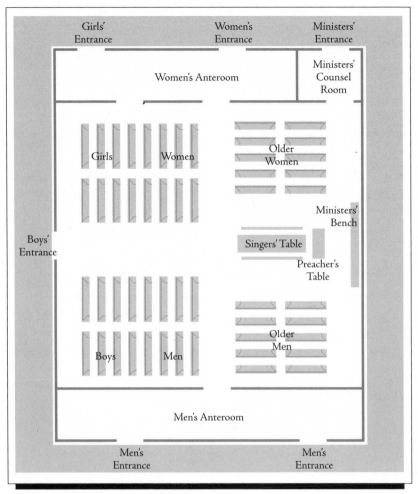

DIAGRAM 7   Typical seating arrangement in a Wenger churchhouse

The congregation uses a German-language hymnbook, commonly called the *Leedabuch* (songbook), which includes words but not music for each hymn.[7] Members sing the tunes from memory at a slow and measured pace, stretching over fifteen minutes. The community values singing and people appreciate good singers. Hymns are sung before and after the worship service, but not during it.[8] Congregations sing in unison, not in harmony. One of the ministers "lines" the second and the last hymn, reading two lines at a time before the hymn is sung. Some people sing without needing to look at their books.[9] There are no solos, small ensembles, or musical instruments.

The two-hour church service is conducted in Pennsylvania German. During the lengthy service, the entire congregation (including toddlers and infants) sits patiently. A mood of lowliness, solemnity, and simplicity engulfs the service as the community yields itself up to the mysteries of divine providence in a spirit of *Gelassenheit*. The order of service varies slightly from community to community but the basic format follows a traditional twelve-step sequence.

Consultation	Ministers meet in counsel room to pray and prepare for the service.
Hymn	A hymn, led by the men at the singers' table, opens the service.
Ministers	Ministers enter the assembly room and sit on the preachers' bench.
Hymn	A minister announces and lines the second hymn.
Opening sermon	A minister preaches a 20- to 25-minute opening sermon.
Silent prayer	The congregation kneels for several minutes of silent prayer.
Scripture text	A deacon reads a New Testament chapter, the text for the main sermon.
Main sermon	A minister preaches a 45- to 50-minute main sermon based on the text.
Testimonies	Several ministers give brief affirmations of the sermon from their seats.
Vocal prayer	The congregation kneels while a minister offers an audible prayer.
Benediction	The minister gives a benediction without raising his hands, as the people stand.
Announcements	The congregation sits for any announcements.
Hymn	The congregation, still seated, joins together in singing a closing hymn.

During the first hymn, the ministers file into the meeting room from their counsel room by rank and tenure: the bishop first, followed by the longest ordained preacher, and finally by the local deacon. Preachers stand behind the small preacher's table and speak in Pennsylvania German without prepared notes. Using stories in their remarks, they often preach with few gestures, but the style varies by preacher. Occasionally a preacher will use some English if outside visitors are present. At the end of the main sermon, the other ministers remain seated on the ministers' bench, while each gives a short affirmation to the sermon which often includes the words, "I can give a hearty yea and amen to the words of our brother."[10] After the closing hymn, people stand and begin talking quietly with others nearby. They gradually file out of the churchhouse and continue visiting in the churchyard, weather permitting, before heading homeward in their carriages.

✢ BAPTISM AND MEMBERSHIP

The rite of baptism symbolizes one's formal entry into Mennonite society. Although it is an individual decision, most of the applicants are eighteen years of age. Each year the church prints a list of all baptismal candidates, listing their church district and their father's name. The Wengers never baptize infants or young children because the church believes that only adults can make informed decisions to follow Christ. The early Anabaptists in Europe rejected infant baptism, contending that a "believer's church" could only be composed of members who had made such an adult decision. This stance provoked severe persecution in the sixteenth century. The Wengers continue to guard this key tenet of Anabaptist faith by insisting on adult baptism.

Baptism carries two meanings: a confession of faith and full-fledged membership in the redemptive community. Each person must decide whether he or she wants to be baptized and join the church. One member says, "You really can't force them . . . they have to do that by choice; they have to make that decision." At baptism, a young person renounces the world and submits to Christ, the ministers, and the church. This rite of passage transforms a person into an adult, with all of adulthood's obligations and commitments. Clothing and entertainment choices change. If the person has been driving a car, he stops. Any behavior that violates the rules of the church must cease. Baptism eliminates any ambiguity—it signifies a decision to live for Christ, to submit to the church and accept its authority.

In early summer, youth who want to join the church present themselves to the ministers in the counsel room prior to a Sunday morning service. The leaders, seated in order of seniority, "emphasize the need of salvation and the seriousness of life," said one bishop. "We ask them if they are willing to be shown a better way—willing to give in if someone sees something out of line in their life." The youth who answer "yes" to these questions then attend six instruction meetings on Sunday afternoons throughout the summer. All the candidates in a settlement attend the instruction classes together. Ministers review three articles of the Dordrecht Confession per session, asking the applicants if they "understand and believe" the article. The first five meet-

Boys walk briskly to the churchhouse for a Sunday service after hearing the first song begin.

ings, held at various churchhouses, are open to members and to other youth who are not yet candidates. Prior to the last instruction meeting, members of the congregation have the opportunity to raise concerns about any of the candidates.

The sixth meeting is special in several ways. It is often held on a Friday, the day before the baptism. Candidates meet in their home churchhouses. Only the candidates and the ministers in that particular congregation may attend. The instruction process comes to a culmination as the bishop clarifies the *Ordnung* and the specific expectations for membership. Young men are asked if they are willing to serve as ordained leaders if the church calls them. This is the last and final chance to turn aside before baptism. The church hopes to see a true change of life in the young person before their baptism. In the words of one bishop, "Those who go to the movies during the instruction classes are dropped from the list." Another member said, "We look for fruits of repentance before baptism, not afterward like some groups do."

Baptisms are typically held on the fall fasting day during the Saturday preparatory service for communion. Wengers baptize by pouring water on the heads of candidates as they kneel on the hard wooden floor of the churchhouse. A bishop explains the procedure: "We first lay hands on their head. Then we speak about the Father, Son, and Holy Ghost. We take a pitcher and pour when we say the three names. The reason we first lay the hands on the head is because, if you read the last chapter of Mark, there it says that they will lay their hands on the sick and they will be better. So we combine laying hands on people and also pouring the water."

Baptisms occur near the end of the preparatory service. In a picture of penitence, the applicants stand before the bishop along a center aisle of the meeting room, where they are literally surrounded by the *Gmay*. The bishop walks from the preacher's table to the candidates and admonishes them directly for five minutes, without notes, as they listen carefully. Then they kneel on the pine floor, hands folded, heads down, as the bishop asks them in the dialect to respond to three questions, which are translated here in an abbreviated form:

1. "Do you believe in the Almighty God, and Father, Lord and creator of heaven and earth ... in Christ Jesus, his only begotten son who is our advocate, redeemer, and Savior ... and in the Holy Spirit, who proceeds from the Father and the Son ...?"

2. "Are you willing to renounce Satan and all his works, the Kingdom of darkness and deceitfulness of this world, as well as your own will, lusts, and desires and promise to be true to God ... and remain faithful in all this unto death?"

3. "Are you willing to submit yourself to the complete scriptural teachings of Jesus Christ ... unto death ... and submit yourself to all the scriptural rules of the Church of Jesus Christ and to be obedient to these unto death?"[11]

The reference to submitting and obeying "the scriptural rules of the Church of Jesus Christ" in the third question refers to the *Ordnung*. It asks, in essence, whether the candidates are willing to accept the moral authority of the church. Agreement means that they will submit to the church's teachings. The candidates must answer *"ya"* (yes) to all three questions before the bishop will baptize them. (See Appendix B for the full text of the vows.)

After the candidates have responded, the bishop kneels with them as the congregation rises for the prayer that he offers. Following the prayer, the applicants remain kneeling as the bishop rises and the congregation is seated. Little children in nearby benches strain to watch the bishop's every move.

Women visit outside a churchhouse following a Sunday service.

A deacon brings a glass or white ceramic pitcher filled with water to the bishop, who begins with the boys, following gender protocol.

The applicants remain on their knees as the deacon pours water into the bishop's hands, which are cupped on top of the first boy's head. A small amount of water drips over his head. The bishop pronounces him baptized in the name of the Father, the Son, and the Holy Ghost, and continues to the next one. After all are baptized and still on their knees, the bishop returns to the first candidate and bids him rise, offers him the "right hand of fellowship," and kisses him. He then places his left hand on the new member's shoulder and offers a few words of encouragement. Before the girls are baptized, some ministers' wives walk up and remove the girls' head coverings. After each girl is baptized, the bishop bids her rise and offers his right hand and words of encouragement. The bishop's wife gives her a holy kiss and a minister's wife replaces her head covering.[12]

Following the baptism, the new members return to their seats and the bishop continues with the remainder of the preparatory service. The new members are now able to participate in communion services and take their place as full members of the congregation. In the fall, the baptismal ceremony is part of the preparatory service that takes place on the Saturday before communion.

✦ THE DAY OF FASTING

One of the most important days in the Wenger ritual calendar is the spring and fall *Faschtdaag*—the special day of fasting and preparation for communion.[13] On the Saturday before communion, members pray and fast before attending a three-hour preparatory service to ready their hearts for the Lord's Supper.[14] At the end of the service, the bishop reads the *Ordnung* with any revisions from the recent ministers' conference and also pronounces excommunications, if any. Members involved in transgressions may also make a public confession and be reconciled with the church at this time. At the conclusion of the preparatory service, the deacon reports recent outlays of money for church expenses and announces an alms offering to maintain the churchhouse and grounds. Small white alms boxes hang near the exit doors. After the *Faschtdaag* service, members contribute toward the expenses— painting, repairs, fuel—of maintaining the churchhouse.

In the morning of a typical day of fasting, dozens of black buggies merge into a caravan along country roads as they flow toward the large, white churchhouse. The buggies wheel into the churchyard and park in the long rows of open sheds that line it. Youth roll in on their bicycles and park them in the churchyard or across the road under a tree.

This "black clothes day" signals somber soul-searching as the community prepares for communion. The married men wear black hats, black coats with standing collars, black pants, and black shoes. The adult women wear black dresses, signifying their contrition and repentance—in short, their readiness for communion. Shortly before the service begins, the women enter by the "women's door" on one end of the churchhouse. The men enter separately by the "men's door" on the other end. The singers' table, in the center of the meeting room, slowly fills with about ten men of various ages. The ministers' wives file in and sit in the front row, facing the singers' table.

The following schedule illustrates a typical fall preparatory service that includes baptism. The ministers go directly to the counsel room and enter the meeting room after the singing begins. The service begins at 9:00 A.M. and concludes about three hours later.

> 9:00 A singer announces a hymn and leads it. The members of the congregation remain seated as they sing. During the fifteen-minute hymn, some older boys walk in and sit in the back rows. The baptismal candidates enter and sit on the center benches facing the ministers' bench (girls on the left and boys on the right). The ministers, led by the presiding bishop, file in from the counsel room.

9:00
(*cont.*) The bishop hangs his hat on a hook above the ministers' bench and sits down. If visiting ministers are present, they take their places on the bench in order of seniority.

9:15 A minister gives the opening sermon on Romans 12, "Give your lives as a sacrifice," and Psalm 51, "Create in me a clean heart." He emphasizes sacrifice and repentance and urges the baptismal candidates to overcome the powers of darkness.

9:30 The congregation kneels for a short silent prayer. Then a visiting deacon reads Matthew 6:1–23, the text for fasting day.

9:35 A second preacher gives the main sermon on the text, standing at the preacher's table, hands clasped in front of him. His singsong delivery sprinkles some English into the German dialect. Some people listen attentively; others doze. He urges members to humble themselves as Jesus humbled himself.

10:30 The local bishop comments on Matthew 6, using some English for the sake of visitors. He says, "Satan can't lead us to death unless we let him. We have a lively hope, because we're under grace. This doesn't mean that we can never lose our salvation. We can, but God has provided a way for us to repent and receive his grace so we can endure to the end." He stresses the importance of following Jesus.

11:00 The bishop walks to the candidates who stand near the center of the meeting room and performs the baptisms.

11:10 When the baptisms are completed, several ministers give brief words of affirmation from their seats on the preachers' bench. They endorse what the preachers have said and admonish the new members to be faithful.

11:15 A deacon stands and reads, without comment, Isaiah 58, which emphasizes fasting.

11:21 The congregation kneels while the bishop leads in a spoken prayer, after which he pronounces the benediction, which ends the service.

11:24 One of the ministers lines a hymn and the congregation sings in unison.

11:35 In preparation for communion the next day, the local bishop reads the *Ordnung* from his seat.[15] During the thirty-minute presentation, he clarifies recent changes in the regulations.

Noon After the reading of the *Ordnung,* the deacon reports some hospital bills of members and the need for contributions. He also announces the time and location of a funeral service.

12:10 The preparatory/baptismal service ends three hours after it started. The men stand, reach for their hats, and begin conversing as the women move toward the anteroom for their bonnets. Slowly people file out, women and men by their respective doors. People linger in conversation in the churchyard for a while on this sunny, cool October day.

The themes of sacrifice, repentance, humility, and obedience are repeated frequently in the fasting-day sermons. Members are urged to allow God to "create a clean heart within them" (Psalms 51) and to "walk in the light so we have fellowship together" (1 John). One preacher explains, "Jesus came to destroy the works of darkness and to bring repentance and amendment of life." He continues, "We should not draw attention to ourselves; that is pride and because of that Satan was cast out of heaven. Rather we should humble ourselves in the sight of God and before our fellow men, as Jesus humbled himself."

In his sermon, the bishop says, "We are to be obedient to our heavenly father. . . . Temptation and evil are all around us but if we fill our mind with good we won't stumble." The congregation should be "like a city on a hill so our light shines forth, the light of the world, the salt of the world. If we all practice the golden rule there will be no war, no police, no hunger, no rich and poor. . . . If we are obedient, we are preaching the Gospel. He that endures to the end shall be saved. Draw nigh to God and he will draw nigh to you. Resist the devil and he will flee from you."

During the three-hour service, which focuses on fasting, baptism, and obedience to the *Ordnung*, members absorb the deep *Gelassenheit* themes—surrender, submission, and yieldedness—on which their redemptive community rests. The mood of fasting and reflection continues as families listen to the clip-clop of horses on their homeward journey. They ready their hearts and quiet their spirits for the next day's communion service.

❖ COMMUNION: THE CELEBRATION OF UNITY AND PURITY

Communion, in many mainline Protestant churches, is an individual transaction of personal faith. By contrast, a Wenger communion is a communal celebration of unity in the body of Christ. All the events leading up to the communion—the local counsel meetings, the conference deliberations, the preparatory service—are designed to prepare and purify the body of Christ for the holy commemoration. These rituals of purification cleanse the body so it can be spotless, without a wrinkle, on the day of communion. Although Wengers do not believe in the real presence of Christ in the bread and wine, they affirm the real presence of Christ's spirit in the disciplined, gathered body.

If baptism is a rite of passage, communion is a rite of intensification.[16] Communion intensifies community solidarity and buttresses core values. It celebrates the unity of the local church body and is closed to nonmembers. Communion is the grand culmination of the counsel meetings, the church-

This singers' table (left) and preacher's table (foreground) reflect the plain simplicity of a churchhouse. Women typically sit to the right of the preacher's table; men, to the left.

wide conference, and the preparatory service. Communion serves as the ritual climax of Wenger life, when the community not only recalls the sufferings of Christ but also clarifies the boundaries of membership, affirms its support of the *Ordnung,* and celebrates the unity of the local district.

Each spring and fall, the communion service is embedded in a lengthy Sunday morning meeting. The two opening sermons underscore Old Testament stories, known as "types and figures," that point to the suffering, death, and resurrection of Jesus. Following a third sermon, the congregation sings hymns that retell Christ's suffering and death while the bishop, assisted by the deacon, administers the communion. The bishop gives a small piece of bread to each member and also offers each one a sip from a common cup of wine. Members then pair off, men and women in different areas, to wash one another's feet by dipping them into a tub of water and drying them with a towel. This rite of humility and service concludes as the partners greet each other with a holy kiss.

Unless they are traveling or ill, members are expected to take communion in their home district. The bishop visits homebound people and conducts a communion service for them. If a member misses communion for unknown reasons, fellow members and the bishop may inquire about the lapse. Two misses will prompt a visit from the deacon and a preacher.

A bishop must be present to conduct the communion service. In Lancaster County, two bishops supervise ten congregations. Thus, in the "communion season," each bishop attends a different churchhouse each Sunday for five weeks to supervise the local communions. If a new settlement does not have a bishop, one from a distance will oversee the communion. One fall, for example, two Lancaster bishops and their spouses traveled to Kentucky to offer the holy meal in two congregations.[17]

Communion Sunday is another black clothes day, a day of perfect compliance with the *Ordnung*. In typical church attire, the men wear black suits, vests, pants, suspenders, and shoes. Some of the older men wear black felt hats with three-inch brims, but younger ones wear navy blue or gray nylon hats with two-inch brims. The boys wear lapel coats. No other styles or colors are visible. The women wear black dresses, capes, and stockings. The strings on their white head coverings are loosely tied. Young children wear a variety of colors. Most girls over two wear head coverings, and the little boys wear suspenders, just like their fathers.

The communion service begins about 8:00 A.M. and, depending on the size of the congregation, continues for about four hours in the following order:

+ The congregation sings a hymn from the German songbook.
+ The ministers enter the meeting room from their counsel room and sit on the ministers' bench.

- One of the preachers gives a 30- to 35-minute opening sermon.[18] During the opening sermon, some tardy teenage boys may enter the churchhouse through the center rear door.
- The congregation kneels for a short silent prayer.
- The deacon reads Matthew 26 and/or Luke 22.
- A second preacher gives an hour-long main sermon.
- The bishop preaches for nearly an hour on the crucifixion story. He urges the members to examine themselves so that they do not "eat damnation unto their souls."
- The congregation stands as the bishop offers a prayer for the bread and then sits as he serves a piece to each member.
- The congregation rises as the bishop offers a spoken prayer for the wine. A minister lines a hymn and the congregation sings as the bishop offers the common cup to each member.
- From his seat on the bench, each minister gives a short affirmation to the sermons.
- The congregation kneels for a spoken prayer by the bishop, then stands while the bishop pronounces the benediction.
- A hymn is lined and sung.
- The bishop reads John 13:1–17 as ministers, their wives, and the janitor leave to pour water into the footwashing tubs.
- The footwashing begins as members pair off in various areas of the churchhouse.
- Singers announce and lead the congregation in singing during the footwashing.[19]
- At the conclusion of the footwashing, the bishop makes some final remarks from his seat and announces the weddings of couples planning to be married.
- People file out, find their carriages, and begin their journey home.

The three sermons address different topics. In the opening sermon, the preacher recounts the stories of Adam and Eve, Cain and Abel, and the great flood. He compares the Old Testament themes with New Testament truths and quotes from Ecclesiastes: "God hath made man upright, but they have sought out many inventions" (Eccl. 7:29).

The second preacher reviews the Old Testament stories of Isaac and Rebecca, Jacob and Esau, Joseph and the pharaoh, Moses and the exodus from Egypt. He names the exodus meal the first communion service in history and reminds members that God instructed the Israelites in Egypt to eat a Passover meal and sprinkle blood on their doorposts for protection from the avenging angel. If time permits, the preacher narrates the story of the Hebrews entering the promised land of Canaan. He mentions the great prophecies pointing to the Messiah, and relates these stories to God's plan of salvation.

The bishop's sermon begins by underscoring the types and figures, the stories in the Old Testament that point to Christ, and then he moves to the New Testament and mentions John the Baptist and Judas the traitor. The bishop admonishes the congregation "not to be contentious, but to seek unity." He urges them to "examine themselves before eating the bread of Jesus' bitter suffering," so they will not "eat damnation unto their soul." The cluster of stories becomes a protracted explanation of God's plan of salvation across the whole sweep of biblical history. The somber mood of the service is punctuated by the noise of cars rushing by on a highway a hundred yards away.[20] Inside the stark and simple churchhouse, the *Gmay* is in a different world, in a different time and mood, in a world where time plods slowly, regulated by the methodical beat of tradition—not the incessant flicker of digital clocks.

The deacon brings out the bread and wine, the sacred elements of communion. The bishop eats a piece of the bread and then serves it to each minister and then to each of the men at the singers' table. He then proceeds around the churchhouse, offering the bread to each member. The deacon follows the bishop, supplying him with strips of white bread. Each member rises slightly to accept the bread from the hand of the bishop. One member explained that while the bishop is passing out the bread, "he usually reminds us that the bread is symbolic of the church. The individual grains of wheat have been ground, mixed, and united into one loaf so no one can say that one grain of wheat is more important than another."

Following the distribution of the bread, the deacon carries the red wine in a corked one-and-a-half-quart glass flask, flared at the bottom and narrow at the top. He pours the wine into a small pewter or stainless steel cup that serves everyone. The bishop drinks first and then serves each minister. Again, moving around the churchhouse, the bishop, one by one, hands the cup to each man, then to each woman. Each person rises in turn to receive and drink from the common cup. As he begins serving the cup, the bishop reminds everyone that all the grapes, big and small, were pressed together into a common wine. In the same way, all members should humble themselves, in the spirit of *Gelassenheit*, into a common body. While the wine is served, a minister "lines" two hymns and the congregation sings.

The ritual distribution of the bread and wine reinforces the gender and authority structure of the community. The elements are distributed in order of seniority: ordained men, older men, younger men, older women, and younger women. The bishop presents the bread and wine to each member personally, acknowledging his or her participation in the holy rite and their accountability to him.[21]

To open the footwashing service, the bishop reads John 13:1–17. Members follow the example and words of Christ, "You also ought to wash one another's feet."[22] The ministers, their wives, and the janitor fetch wooden or plastic tubs from the anteroom and place them around the meeting room. Following the example of Jesus at the last supper, the men remove their coats, exposing their black vests. Pair by pair, people rise, men with men, women with women. Each puts on a white apron and then washes their partner's feet. Some stoop over, others kneel as they wash. After the washing, they exchange a holy kiss and then return to their seats. During this time, the congregation sings a hymn, lined by the bishop. In the stooping or kneeling to wash the feet of others, this ceremony of humility, service, and mutual love articulates in ritual form the deepest sentiments of *Gelassenheit*.

⁜ A PRIVATE SUPPER

The Wengers practice closed communion. Only members in good standing with the church may partake of the Lord's Supper. One minister says, "Some people question why we have closed communion.[23] But it's the only way we can keep our standards for our people." People who refuse to publicly confess their faults risk being "set back" from the ceremony. Closed communion, therefore, serves more to maintain unity among insiders than to eliminate outsiders. This semiannual checkup allows the congregation to settle conflicts and differences before they fester into serious divisions. "This day, of all days," in the words of a member, "is to commemorate love, fellowship, unity, forgiveness, and repentance." The service binds the whole congregation together in harmony and unity. A major rite of intensification, communion reinforces community values, beliefs, and norms; it builds social solidarity through a sacred ceremony, sanctioned both by God and community consensus.

Wengers do not see the bread and wine as sacraments that dispense a special dose of God's grace. "We see the bread as symbolic of Christ's broken body and the wine as his shed blood," said one member. Nonetheless, communion is the summit of ritual solidarity in the body of Christ, which makes the rite a powerful means of social control. By participating in communion, members covenant together to submit to the authority of the church and the expectations of the *Ordnung*. To avoid public humiliation, deviant members typically do not attend the service. Leaders try earnestly through patience and prayer to bring wayward souls back into harmony so all can celebrate the unity of community together.

Occasionally, a member will miss a communion service if he or she feels condemned for attending a movie, installing a computer in his or her business, or otherwise breaking the *Ordnung*. Such a person might stay home on Communion Sunday, but inform the bishop why he or she is absent. If members do not report their absences in advance, the deacon may visit them. In other cases, conflicted members may attend but refrain from partaking. A minister in one congregation declined three times because he disagreed with some aspects of the *Ordnung*. Refraining three times forced the issue.[24] In the words of a bishop, "Now something had to be done—excommunication or something." Abstention from communion proclaims that a member is not at peace with the *Ordnung*, the leaders, or some other aspect of church life.

If a person persists in disobedience, the bishop or deacon will visit the person and ask, "Are things worked out? Are you at peace?" If the member refuses to make amends, the matter comes before the local ministers. In extreme cases, the bishop may decide to excommunicate. Excommunicated people are permitted to attend regular church services but may not participate in the Lord's Supper. If expelled people confess their faults before the church, they can rejoin the fellowship and once again participate in communion. If a spouse is excommunicated, the other spouse can remain a member in good standing as long as he or she attends and abides by the church's teaching. Wengers do not formally shun ex-members by refusing to talk or conduct business with them.[25] Upon confession, a member can be reinstated into fellowship and participate in the supper at the Lord's Table. The communion service is a key redemptive ritual, but its emotional intensity is eclipsed by ordinations.

✣ A HIGH AND HOLY MOMENT

If communion is a rite of intensification that celebrates the unity of the community and the completed work of Christ on the cross, ordination is a rite of divine intervention, a moment when the church experiences God's presence in a special way. Ordination is the holiest of holy moments in the church because Almighty God reaches down from heaven to select a minister in the presence of the gathered community. It is a moment of trembling awe and mystery.

Wengers use the biblical procedure known as the casting of lots when selecting leaders.[26] Ordained officials receive no formal theological training and serve without pay until they retire or die. They typically continue their normal work in farming or related trades. Only men are eligible to serve as bishop, minister, or deacon.

Several events may create the need for an ordination. A church district may have lost a minister due to ill health, death, or defection. A growing church district may require another minister. In rare cases, a minister may have been silenced from preaching because of personal indiscretions or defiance of conference authority. If a new leader is needed, the bishop, in consultation with the congregation, proposes an ordination. Ordination plans must be approved by the church-wide ministers' conference.[27]

The congregation prepares for an ordination by praying for guidance weeks in advance. The Sunday before the ordination, at the close of the regular service, the bishop and deacon enter the counsel room to receive nominations. The congregation prays silently. Any member who wishes may rise and enter the counsel room either to give a word of blessing or to nominate a candidate. Typically, the oldest men submit names; although women may nominate someone, they rarely do. In one instance, a man walked into the counsel room to give his nomination. A few minutes later, his wife walked in to give hers—suggesting to the watching congregation a division of opinion in their home! The ministers themselves may nominate a candidate.[28] A minister records the names of the nominees, and anyone who receives one or more nominations is in the class that will share the casting of the lot. The bishop announces the names of the men in the class at the end of the service. It is typical to have half a dozen or more men in the pool of candidates.[29]

On the Monday following the nominations, the candidates and their wives meet with the "home" ministers, the local bishop, and other bishops who are able to attend. As a minister explained, "The wives also have a large part in the ministry." The leaders explain the duties and expectations for ordained officials and ask the candidates if there is any reason why they should not be ordained. The elders examine the candidates for their suitability for leadership and willingness to adjust their personal attire and behavior to the more exacting standards of the ministry. The most important question facing the candidates is "Are you willing to work with the other ministers?"

This refers not only to interpersonal humility but also to their willingness to yield to the collective wisdom of the conference.

One member compared the examiners to a jury. If members privately raise complaints about a candidate, the ministers may question him about the issue. Because men agree to serve the church prior to their baptism, candidates will rarely beg to be released for personal reasons. Indeed, such a request is considered disobedient to the call of God and the *Gmay*. Church leaders, not candidates, determine who is fit to serve. Leaders rarely disqualify a candidate in the examination meeting. One sixty-year-old minister could not recall a single time when a candidate was disqualified or had withdrawn from an ordination class.

Ordination services, holy moments filled with suspense, typically occur on a Wednesday, just three days after the service of nomination. At one ordination, people begin arriving from many districts about 8:00 A.M. by carriage, bicycle, and hired van.[30] A deacon typically arrives with a small suitcase that contains the special hymnbooks that will be used for the casting of lots. The churchhouse rapidly fills to overflowing with Wengers and non-Wengers from related fellowships hundreds of miles away. For a Lancaster County ordination, ministers come from Wenger settlements in Pennsylvania and as far away as Wisconsin. The host of delegates from far-flung settlements underscores the importance of this emotion-packed ritual.

The service resembles a regular worship service that rises to a dramatic climax in the ordination. The wives of the candidates enter and sit in the front row of the women's side, facing the singers' table. The first row of the men's side, just across the table, is empty. The class of candidates meets with the ministers in the counsel room. The somber churchhouse is packed, silent, and filled with awe, as people await the moment when the divine mystery will be unveiled.

The drama unfolds as the congregation sings the first hymn in a minor, mournful key, which underscores the heaviness of the day.[31] The local deacon escorts the candidates into the meeting room. They walk past their wives to the empty bench on the other side of the singers' table, where they sit according to age, the oldest nearest the ministers' bench. Two dozen or more Wenger ministers file in and hang their hats on hooks on the wall. They sit by rank on the ministers' bench: the presiding bishop, four other bishops, several ministers who will preach, and finally the deacon who will read Scripture. The remaining ministers and deacons find seats in the older men's section, immediately behind the ordination class of candidates.

Divine Selection

The seven men in the class range in age from twenty-one to forty-seven. One is the son of a deceased bishop. The youngest candidate will marry in two days. He looks very sober, wearing his new wedding suit and gazing directly to the women's side where his wife-to-be sits with the other spouses. A minister announces the second hymn and lines it. A preacher from New York reads a Scripture and speaks briefly, after which the congregation kneels in silent prayer. A minister from a related group in Virginia, which does not use German, stands and gives the main sermon in English. He says, in part,

> We stand in fear and trembling and in great weakness.... God has blessed this community with a good heritage.... We are coming in need of another one to preach the never-dying Word.... The Lord needs another worker in this vineyard. The time now draws near when it is to be revealed what God desires. "Not my will but thine be done." May God bless us.

After the sermon, a dozen or so ministers give brief affirmations of the sermon. Among other things, they say, "It seems seven are heavy of heart, but that is how God wants it.... Why did people come? To see who is the new minister? I hope you came to share love with others. ... Accept the new shepherd; pray for him."

A minister from Wisconsin now speaks in English, with his hands folded in front of him. He quotes from John 3:16: "For God so loved the world that he gave his only begotten Son, that whosoever believeth in him should not perish, but have everlasting life." He continues, "Our hearts are pliable, knowing one is chosen, but not yet revealed.... It is God's will he sacrifice. ... He needs the prayers of the congregation.... We might think some are more talented, but this is wrong. ... Search the Word; then apply it. ... Those evil spirits, the powers of darkness, are very present today."

The congregation kneels for prayer, rises, receives the benediction, and sings a hymn. This signals the end of the main service that precedes the actual ordination itself. Out of deference to visitors, the local bishop begins the ordination by speaking briefly in English, but then shifts into the dialect. "I'd like to speak in English so all could understand. But I can express myself better in my own language," he says, as his voice breaks with emotion. He reads the verses in Acts 1:23–26, where lots are cast to choose a new disciple.

When he concludes the reading, the bishop takes the lot, a small piece of paper, out of his pocket. The paper contains the words from Proverbs 16:33:

The counsel room at the end of the meeting room. A solid sliding window separates the rooms.

"The lot is cast into the lap; but the whole disposing thereof is of the Lord." The bishop gives the slip of paper to two deacons. They take it into the counsel room and close the door to the meeting room. One deacon turns his back while the other one inserts the fateful slip of paper randomly into one of the seven hymnals. He shuffles them and then turns his back while the other deacon re-shuffles the hymnals. The hymnals have wire snap-clasps that secure the covers so the small paper cannot slip out. Then the two deacons carry the hymnals into the meeting room and place them on the corner of the preacher's table.

While the deacons prepare the books, the bishop preaches from the book of Acts. When he finishes, the congregation kneels on the wooden floor in silent prayer—yielding themselves to God's will. At the close of the prayer, the singers at the singers' table rise and go to canvas folding chairs in the aisles so that their table can be used to hold the books. Then the bishop says, "Thou Lord, who knowest the hearts of all men, show which of these thou hast chosen." The bishop reshuffles the books a third time as the audience waits in pregnant silence.

Methodically, the bishop takes the hymnbooks and places them on the singers' table, standing them upright in no particular order. Immediately, he invites the seven candidates to stand, come forward, and take a book. Starting with the oldest, each man rises, approaches the table, takes a book of his choice, and returns to his seat. The men may select any book on the table. As the process unfolds, the candidates wait with heads bowed. The congregation waits in dramatic silence for the holy moment—the moment when God will reach down from heaven and select a new servant.

After the books have been selected, the bishop goes down the row, beginning with the oldest candidate. The bishop takes the hymnbook selected by the man, opens the clasp, and riffles through the pages, searching for the lot. He does not find it and returns it to the candidate who sits down. The second candidate presents his book to the bishop who unclasps it and searches through the pages. He finds the lot, takes it out, and puts it in his pocket. The bishop immediately bids the man to rise and takes his right hand. The bishop puts his left hand on the man's right shoulder, and ordains him immediately with these words spoken in German: "I now charge you to preach the Gospel, to exhort the sinner to repentance, to visit the sick, widows, and orphans, and to comfort the discouraged.... Study to show yourself to God, an upright and blameless worker, who then may rightly share in the Word of truth."

The bishop kisses the newly ordained minister, embraces him, and whispers words of encouragement in his ear. The bishop turns and speaks to the congregation, his voice breaking. The singers return to their table and lead the congregation in a hymn, which ends the service. In this highly charged, awesome moment, members feel the miraculous presence of providence as the hand of God selects a new leader in their very midst. Many weep as they witness God's miraculous intervention. Such a divine anointing in the presence of the congregation confers enormous power upon a leader—power that far exceeds academic credentials, a charismatic personality, or a majority vote by a congregation.

Following the service, one by one, all the ministers and the other candidates come up to the new preacher, take his right hand, give him a holy kiss, and speak a word or two of encouragement. The man stands to receive their kiss and blessing. The ministers' wives encourage his spouse as she sobs profusely. Other candidates' wives cry, releasing their pent-up emotions from the last two days. Overcome with the intensity of the moment, the presiding bishop and other ordained men also weep. The tears of release, reflecting the deep emotion of the day, are regulated by restraint.

People quietly leave the churchhouse and return to their homes, knowing that the church has a new shepherd. Some of the ministers and their wives accept an invitation to go to a nearby home for dinner with the newly ordained man and his family.

A Holy Calling

The burden of office falls on the new preacher immediately. He may preach the opening sermon at a special weekday service the day after the ordination. In one case, a minister preached the wedding sermon for another candidate who was in his own ordination class two days before. True lay preachers, new ministers feel a deep sense of God's calling and the blessing of the congregation as they learn their duties. The new responsibilities fall on top of their regular employment. Ministers serve the church without stipend, special education, or formal preparation.

Unlike the individualistic Protestant pattern, in which ministerial candidates follow their own calling and pursue theological studies to prepare for it, Wenger leaders do not select themselves and should not even desire the office. Some men earnestly (albeit secretly) consider the office. According to Wenger belief, however, no one should ever seek ordination. One woman tells of a scandalous incident: "One of the ministers asked another minister, 'What could I do to be bishop?' Something is absolutely wrong if he wants the upper hand, and *even* to say so!" Such aspiration for office is condemned as pride—an abomination in the eyes of God.

Ordination is both an honor and a burden. A new minister appreciates the confidence of the congregation. Because members believe that God truly chooses the minister, the congregation respects him. Those who are unhappy with the outcome can only argue with God, not with a faulty selection process, a biased search committee, or a close popular vote. A member explained, "We are constantly reminded that if we work against God's chosen leaders, we work against God." This powerful divine sanction on leaders not only legitimates leadership but also reduces conflict in the congregation.

The burden of leadership on a newly ordained bishop is especially heavy. When a bishop is ordained, three other bishops lay hands on him and he is instructed to watch over the flock, not as a ruler over them but as one who must give account for their souls. A bishop is sometimes called *Volle Diener* (a full servant) because he is to be the lead servant of the church. If a member commits a major sin, such as initiating divorce, the bishop is required to excommunicate the member. According to one member, "As a servant of the church, the bishop does not have the option to forgive the member without expelling him or her."

Ordained men are never congratulated. Members weep with them in empathy, recognizing their grave responsibility. Ordination is a heavy and solemn obligation; the minister will carry the burdens of office for the rest of his life. He will spend many hours away from his family and occasionally will travel to distant settlements in other states. He must prepare to preach almost every Sunday and attend the spring and fall ministers' conference. In addition, he will confer with ministers or members during difficult decisions, settle disputes between members, and discipline those who violate church rules.

Wengers believe that each congregation needs a full complement of ministers. One bishop explained to his congregation, "God has blessed this community with a good heritage. . . . We are coming in need of another one to preach the never-dying Word." Ordination sermons typically emphasize humility and submission to Christ, observing, "The servant of the Lord must not strive." Ministers must acknowledge their sin and nothingness, but also have courage that God can use them: "If God can make a man, surely he can make a preacher out of a man." Without any special training or preparation, ministers must put their talents in God's hands, because they hold no special wisdom. After all, it is God who chooses them.

Men describe ordination as one of the most poignant events of their lives. Their stories reflect drama, anxiety, pathos, and suspense. In one story, the bishop did not find the lot in any of the books held by the thirteen candidates. Beads of sweat were welling on the forehead of the last and youngest man as the bishop finally came to him. But alas, the lot was not found in his book. The drama continued as the bishop started down the row again, searching each book a second time until he finally found the paper.

One minister, the fourth in age of nine candidates, recalled his experience: "I didn't wish this on anyone, so I thought I had to accept it myself." And indeed, the lot fell on him. "At first, I thought I just couldn't do it, but we just took it one day at a time. The whole family helped out." He has since been nominated twice for bishop. "I felt the same then [that I would have to accept it], but the lot for bishop never fell to me. I am satisfied the lot did not fall to me, but I guess I'd also be satisfied if it had."

One person, nominated for deacon forty years ago, was not selected but remembers the exact names of the other ten candidates. To this day, he can recite their names by order of their birth. He speaks about the event with a great sense of awe. One minister who was nominated for bishop four times but never selected said, "The first time I didn't think it would be me. The second time I just didn't know. You just have to give yourself up," underscoring the spirit of *Gelassenheit*, of yieldedness, required of candidates. One woman explained, "If it [the lot] hits you, you just have to give yourself up [*uffgawwe*] to the Lord."[32]

Some candidates believe their hand was supernaturally guided to a specific book. In one ordination, the youngest candidate took the remaining book, which in this case held the fateful slip of paper. Later, when the young minister asked an older candidate why he passed over the book, the older man replied, "I didn't see it." One Wenger man was nominated for preacher three times but never chosen. He says, "The people wanted me, but God didn't."

A humorous story told by Wenger people recalls an ordination years ago when the presiding bishop forgot his glasses. He found a paper in the book of a candidate, pulled it out, slipped it into his pocket, and immediately ordained the man. After the service, one of the deacons discovered the lot was still inside one of the books. When they showed it to the bishop, he reached into his pocket for the slip of paper from the candidate's book, only to discover it was a jelly recipe! Nevertheless, he did not redo the process, believing that God can work in mysterious ways. Henceforth, however, he was known as the "jelly recipe" bishop.

The service of ordination encompasses mystery, suspense, and a ritual climax. Without a doubt, ordination is the ritual peak of community life. The process embodies the ideals of Wenger faith—congregational equality, lay leadership, submission, and humility before God. For hundreds of years, the mystery of this process has selected servant leaders from rank-and-file members and authorized them to direct, discipline, and defend the church. At ordination, the congregation yields itself to God's choice of its leader for years to come. With patience and forbearance, members simply accept God's providential selection. The chosen leader and his family also submit—surrendering their lives, their time, and their efforts to shepherd the flock with little earthly reward. Ordination is the ultimate moment of *Gelassenheit*, of surrender, for the redemptive community.

Sacred ritual is the last cultural distinctive to fall as a separatist group becomes assimilated into the surrounding society. The Wenger view of moral authority cherishes traditional redemptive rituals because they blend both oldness and orderliness together. More important, they infuse Wenger life with sacred meanings: compliance with community regulations becomes a religious sacrifice; yielding to church authority has eternal consequences.

Religious ritual recalls the wisdom of the past and legitimates the authority structure of the community. Ritual publicly articulates Wenger identity, social structure, and religious values. As it recalls and reenacts the moral order, ritual also reproduces it in the minds of the young. Because formal rituals link *old* and *orderly* together in powerful ways, the Wengers self-consciously devote great efforts to preserve them. Other rituals are found outside the churchhouse. In Chapter 6, we trace the informal rites of passage that mark the Wenger journey from birth to death.

6 Passages from Birth to Death

The lack of TV does not seem to hamper our children's education.

—OLD ORDER HISTORIAN

One of the major consequences of modernity has been the transfer of traditional social functions—childbirth, work, food production, education, recreation, weddings—away from the home. Resisting modernity's pull, the Wengers still perform many social functions in their homes, including childbirth, weddings, and food production, to name but a few. Wenger families, like people everywhere, mark the major events in the life cycle, from birth to death, with rites of passage.

✛ BIRTH AND INFANCY

Newly married couples eagerly welcome children. Couples typically reject artificial methods of birth control unless medically necessary; natural means such as the rhythm method, however, are acceptable.[1] Many Wenger women give birth at home, preferring to use the services of a licensed midwife or family doctor. Families carry no commercial health insurance, and home births help them avoid expensive medical bills. The cost of a home birth is about $1,400, while one at a hospital may escalate to $7,000.

Most of the women who deliver Wenger babies are certified nurse-midwives. Some are English, others belong to other Plain groups, and a few are members of the Wenger Church. One Wenger woman teaches home-birth classes for first-time parents. For some women, their encounter with a midwife is their first examination by a health-care worker. When they begin having children, most families develop a relationship with a family physician. A midwife will typically see a mother about eight times during her pregnancy, including two postpartum visits.

One of the striking features of Wenger culture, noted an outside midwife, is the strong sense of privacy surrounding sexuality, pregnancy, and childbirth. In her words, "They are fairly secretive. They don't speak about their pregnancy. They don't discuss their pregnancy with their children because then they would need to explain where babies come from. They are uncomfortable talking about sex and don't want to have to deal with the questions children might ask." A Wenger mother contends, however, that the secrecy about pregnancy is not true anymore for the majority.

Families typically send their children to a neighbor's or family member's house during the delivery. "They don't want the children to know what is happening," according to the midwife. "They don't want the children to learn that the baby is coming from the mother's body, so they won't have to respond to all those questions." A father explained, "We feel loose or free talk about sex tends to desensitize our sense of morality." Most husbands, according to the midwife, assist with the delivery and "are helpful and supportive, giving back rubs, wiping brows, and following the midwife's instructions."

Typically a hired girl, a mother, or an older sister will come and stay with the family for several weeks and manage the household until the mother can resume her work. With few exceptions, mothers breast-feed their babies. Shortly after the birth, the siblings return, and in the next days dozens of well-wishing visitors flock to see the baby and family.

Traditionally, parents choose biblical names for their babies, especially for the boys: Amos, Daniel, Joseph, Jonas, Moses, Samuel, Reuben, and Isaac. Typical Bible names for girls include Ruth, Rebecca, Martha, and Sarah. The church does not require biblical names, however, and some parents give their children non-biblical names. Middle names and initials are important because many people have the same first and last names and must rely on the middle name or initial for their identity. For example, if Mervin Martin married Laura Zeiset, each of their children would carry the middle initial "Z." Many parents now give a middle name (e.g., Mary Lou, Marlin Ray, Crystal Jane), replacing the older practice of deriving the child's middle initial from the mother's maiden name.

✦ HEALTH AND MEDICINE

Childbirth is an important moment of contact with outside medical practitioners. Most, but not all, Wenger people have a family doctor. Although they use modern medicine, some prefer natural medicine, vitamins, and homeopathic treatments.[2] When one member contracted pneumonia, he chose a doctor who would give him heavy doses of intravenous Vitamin C instead of antibiotics. But most Wengers prefer standard medical treatments. One woman says, "Don't try to heal yourself; that's my theory. Doctors are here for a reason." Chiropractors as well as medical doctors are frequently consulted for medical ailments. According to one father, "Homeopathic treatments and some other practices with 'New Age' connections have caused controversy in the church."[3] The church has a policy that church funds cannot be used for alternative (non-AMA-approved) procedures or medicines.

Moderately high inbreeding increases the Wengers' risk for certain genetic diseases. Two predisposing factors heighten the risk. First, the Wenger population descends from a small European ancestral group and has few outside converts. Second, young people sometimes marry second cousins within the Wenger community. One minister, reflecting on this practice, says, "It's not the best, but we let them choose." These factors allow little opportunity for new genetic material to enter the population.

In 1989, Dr. Holmes Morton founded the Clinic for Special Children, a nonprofit pediatric metabolic disease center near Lancaster, Pennsylvania, to treat Amish and Mennonite children who suffer from various genetic diseases.[4] Thanks to good genealogical records, the clinic has been able to trace the lineage of many children for twelve generations and thus predict families with higher risk.[5] The Old Order Mennonites and Amish strongly support the clinic and often donate items for its annual benefit auctions. The Clinic for Special Children not only provides excellent care for families and children but also makes significant contributions to advances in genetic science through its research on genetic diseases in Old Order groups. A variety of tests developed by the clinic enable early detection and treatment of many diseases that are prevalent among the Wengers.

The clinic has identified fourteen genetic disorders among the Wengers.[6] Three occur so frequently that they are sometimes called "Old Order Mennonite diseases": congenital nephrotic syndrome, Hirschsprung's disease, and maple syrup urine disease. Nephrotic syndrome is a genetic disease of the kidneys located on chromosome nineteen. Hirschsprung's disease is a single-locus recessive genetic defect on chromosome thirteen that hampers the intestines' ability to process food. Most children with Hirschsprung's disease can survive and lead normal lives if they receive surgery in infancy. Maple syrup urine disease, so called because the urine smells like maple syrup, prevents the body from processing certain proteins. If untreated, an infant will die. Early treatment with a special protein diet will enable a child to live an almost normal life. The incidence of this disease among the Wengers is 1 in 378 births, a rate that is roughly equivalent to the incidence of Down Syndrome in the general population.

A restricted genetic pool also has some advantages. No cases of cystic fibrosis have ever been reported among the Wengers. Given typical rates and the size of the Wenger population, about eleven cases would be expected.[7]

✢ CHILDHOOD

Wenger children live in a thick web of extended family, church, and community. Children are typically dressed like their parents. And for the most part, children encounter other children and adults who dress like their own family. Their significant peers have similar values, life experiences, religious faith, and social aspirations. Children are constantly surrounded by role models of Wenger values. They grow up with self-confidence in an environment that reinforces the values of their family and the ethnic identity of their community. This tight social structure makes the Wenger worldview plausible.

Growing up with six, eight, or ten siblings, children have little privacy. They are *always* interacting with siblings—bickering, negotiating, playing, working, eating, waiting for an empty bathroom, and sharing a bedroom. At mealtime, food is carefully divided and shared around the table under many watchful eyes. Pies are carefully cut so that everyone has an appropriately sized piece. On one occasion, eleven children eyed the one remaining deviled egg on the supper table until their mother proposed an equitable way to divide it between two of them. It is impossible to overstate the importance of a large family for learning the virtues of *Gelassenheit*—obedience, cooperation, yielding, and accepting authority. Large families are the incubator of communal values, the perfect setting for learning humility and deference in preparation for a yielded life within the redemptive community.

Religious practices begin in the home, but they vary from family to family. Families pray a silent prayer before meals, and Bible verses hang on the walls of some homes. Although one leader estimates that fewer than half of the households have family devotions together, mothers often read Bible stories to their children in the evenings, and some fathers lead the family in prayer and Bible reading and give a few words of commentary on the text. Some families read a Scripture passage around the table after breakfast. Some adults read and study the Bible on their own. In fact, the ministers urge everyone, especially young people, to read the Bible daily.[8]

Raising children is a serious and sacred task. Nothing is more precious than innocent children. Ministers exhort parents to care for their children and train them in the way they should go (Proverbs 22:6). Parents may occasionally spank their children, but they prefer to discipline with words. One minister in a sermon reminded parents, "We only have our children young once . . . provoke not your children to wrath . . . you must take the main responsibility for raising your children. Parents have not fulfilled their duties if they merely send their children to a Mennonite school because the school is not a reformatory."[9] Parents typically spend Saturday nights at home with their children and interact together through the week in various chores, because much Wenger work occurs around the home.

A young mother shared her view of childrearing in these words: "Wenger parents want their children to be secure, loved, obedient, to enjoy work and stay out of trouble. Plain parents aren't slave drivers but children need boundaries to be secure. Some outside parents let children rule and do their own thing. Children need to know that they are loved and secure. Then parents need to be firm without being harsh. The best method of discipline for older children is to take away privileges. They should only be spanked if there are clear acts of disobedience." Another Wenger mother said, "How children are disciplined varies from family to family."

One health-care professional who has visited hundreds of Wenger homes wonders, "How do they get their kids to behave so well? They spank, but not in public. I have never seen a child spanked. Children are well behaved by age three or four. Obedience is important. Parents compare children by how obedient they are. The discipline is not in public but it is very firm. The kids know that the parents mean business, without yelling at them."

The outside observer continued,

> What impresses me is the tremendous amount of responsibility young children have. At a young age they are responsible for so many tasks and they do them. A six-year-old may be responsible to feed all the calves. He or she knows what to do and no one needs to tell him or her to do a good job of it. He or she may rake the leaves and do the whole yard, without any complaining. If a large family is preparing to go away, each older child may be expected to get a younger child ready. The children learn from each other about things like cleaning the house. Everybody works. They say, "We feel we're no good if we don't do our own work."

One father explained some of the steps of life children anticipate.

> You see, among the Plain people there are many rites of passage. For example, at the age of six or thereabouts, a boy will usually be allowed to sit on the "little boys' bench" in church. Behind this bench there is another bench on which the boys sit that are perhaps a year older. Can you imagine how happy that little boy is on the day that he can walk past the "little boys' bench" and sit on the second bench? Or let's look at a young girl who has always worn her hair in two long braids hanging down the back. One day, at about age thirteen or fourteen, she will come to school with her hair put up in a bun. All the other girls crowd around her with respectful admiration. How grown-up she now looks. From henceforth she will never wear braids again. There are many other rites of passage as a child grows up. And for some, joining church is just another such rite of passage, so we don't always see the fruits of a born-again life.[10]

Because they do not actively seek outside converts, the Wenger future rests on the retention of their young. From an early age, Wenger children are molded in the ways of humility by parents and community members who emphasize obedience and respect for authority. Parents set specific guidelines for behavior, support private schools, and forbid access to electronic media.[11] They exercise firm discipline because they believe that, according to the Bible, it is their God-given responsibility to train children in the path of obedience.

✦ THICK FAMILY NETWORKS

Wenger people pass through the stages of life embedded in a dense web of kinship ties. The stages were memorialized by one family in a friendship quilt. As in other traditional societies, kinship knits the community together. A Pennsylvania bishop's family illustrates this web of kinship. He and his wife have over one hundred grandchildren and many great-grandchildren, some living as far away as Iowa. They visit them as frequently as health allows. Wengers treasure family genealogies. Many people have the Zimmerman or the Wenger genealogy books, which provide encyclopedic listings on hundreds of ancestors of the present-day community. The genealogy books and the church-wide directory of all households are indispensable for tracking family lines. Out of some 3,000 heads of households, for example, 535 are named Zimmerman—4 of them are John Davids, 3 are John Ds, 2 are John Isaacs, and 2 are John Ws. There are 6 Leroy Zimmermans, of which 3 are named Leroy S. Zimmerman.[12]

With Wenger families now scattered in settlements in nine states, long-distance kinship relations are reshaping family life. A Lancaster minister's daughter and one of his sons now live in Wisconsin, and another son lives in Ohio. The father explains, "They're in a line, so we can visit all of them in one trip." One family has six children, but they have not been together for six years. A thirty-two-year-old son, the heir apparent to the farm, lives with his wife and children in the other half of the home farmhouse. The twenty-nine-year-old twin daughters are both married. One lives in Wisconsin, the other in New York. An older, married son lives in Bedford County, Pennsylvania. Despite the dispersion, families maintain frequent contact. Parents appreciate the use of telephones to talk with distant children and grandchildren. Families often hire a van and driver to travel to distant weddings, funerals, births, reunions, ordinations, church meetings, or other gatherings. Because they have more time and resources than the young, older people travel more often to visit children living in other settlements.

Children grow up in the thicket of a large extended family where it is not uncommon to have a hundred first cousins. As shown in Table 7, 52 percent of the families carry four surnames: Martin, Zimmerman, Hoover, and Nolt.[13]

✦ THE BLESSINGS OF "DEPRIVATION"

Mary Ann Horst describes her Old Order Mennonite childhood as a happy time surrounded by family, friends, and numerous pets.[14] Freed of television,

❖ TABLE 7 Wenger household surnames

Name	Number	Percentage
Martin	577	19
Zimmerman	535	18
Hoover	241	8
Nolt	209	7
Burkholder	165	6
Shirk	157	5
Weaver	157	5
Newswanger	95	3
Other names (37)	861	29
Total	2,997	100

SOURCE: *Directory* 2002.

day care, and electronic toys, children learn farm and household chores at an early age. They enjoy homespun play, simple toys, the companionship of animals, and outdoor recreation—softball, fishing, skating, and sledding.

Responding to a charge that Old Order children are deprived, a Canadian Old Order Mennonite quips sarcastically, "Oh, our poor deprived children . . . we deprive them of qualified teachers . . . of education beyond the eighth grade. We even deprive them of that greatest of educators, the television set. They are deprived of the opportunity to watch movies, exhibitions [fairs, shows], baseball, and hockey games . . . to go to the beach, the cottage, or summer camp." Deprived of all these advantages, children are expected to "feed the chickens, sweep the floor, and fill the woodbox after coming home from school. On Saturdays and holidays they help with planting the garden and, later, with picking berries and cherries, peas and beans, corn and potatoes. They drive a tractor or a team of horses for loading hay and cultivating crops. They have very little leisure time."

The Old Order farmer concludes with the playful suggestion that "the lack of TV does not seem to hamper our children's education." Mennonite children are bilingual and, according to him, the trades that they learn through practical apprenticeships "serve them as well as a college degree." In his words, there are "blessings in deprivation." Instead of public entertainment, "our children find enjoyment in nature on the farm: the baby chicks, cuddly kittens, and playful puppies. They learn to know and appreciate the wild animals and birds that abound in woodland and meadow. They swim and fish in ponds and streams. Above all, they enjoy learning by doing."[15]

Children often enjoy playing with animals on the farm.

According to one Wenger mother, "This is a culture that loves, values, and wants children. We don't herd our children off to day care centers so we can search for a more meaningful career. Being at home with our children is the *most* meaningful life, and I can't overemphasize this point."

Squabbles, feuds, and disappointments are also part of Wenger childhood. Indeed, one Wenger parent asked, "What if you are part of a dysfunctional family? What if a husband has fits of temper and verbally or physically abuses his wife? Will the family seek help for him or will they just cover up so they don't appear to be different?" Wenger families have their own share of struggles and problems, and while Wenger children may grow up in an idyllic world of butterflies and baby lambs, not all of them have simple, carefree lives.

A four-part Lancaster newspaper series on domestic abuse among several Plain churches cited some examples from the Wenger community.[16] The series suggested that the patriarchal nature of Old Order communities—governed by male church leaders who may be reluctant to report embarrassing incidents to outside authorities and who emphasize *Gelassenheit*, which encourages yielding rather than asserting one's rights—may make it difficult for women to report abuse. Moreover, the authors pointed out, it may be difficult for members of a separatist subculture to access outside help. One young Wenger woman, annoyed by the four-day series, said, "They made Plain women look too stupid and ignorant to know how to get help. It was insulting because, although we may only have an eighth-grade education and don't watch TV, some of us read a lot and are very intelligent."

✦ NURTURING THE CHILDREN IN SCHOOL

Wenger society does not have kindergarten, day care, or Head Start. Formal education begins with first grade when children are typically six years old. When a new settlement begins, parents think about where they will build a school. More than providing a basic education, parents want to keep their children away from consolidated public schools. Most children attend a private Wenger school through the eighth grade with peers from their community and sometimes from other Old Order groups. Private schools safeguard children from worldly influences and immerse them in Wenger culture. Their formal education ends with the eighth grade. A few families send their children to public schools, and some families homeschool their children, but the overwhelming majority of children attend private schools.[17]

Wenger children attended small, rural public schools prior to 1950. Because the teachers were local women and the ethos was rurally oriented, the Wengers had few complaints. Things changed dramatically with the large-scale consolidation of public schools in the 1950s.[18] One man said, "It seemed there was a different generation of teachers and public officials that came in. They had different ideas about doing things and it just didn't work as smooth anymore." When one-room rural schools were closed and children were bussed to large, consolidated schools, the Mennonites bought some of the abandoned buildings for their own schools. By 1981, there were seventy-four Wenger-operated schools in Pennsylvania. Today there are over one hundred.[19] A three- to five-man board, elected by parents, supervises one to three schools. Each board member serves for four years.

In some schools, the Wengers cooperate with the Amish and other Plain groups. Several schools in Pennsylvania serve both Amish and Mennonite students. Occasionally Mennonite parents will serve on the boards of Amish-run schools, and vice versa. Pennsylvania is divided into several Wenger school districts, and each district appoints a representative to a statewide committee. The identity of a school is determined by the statewide committee, Amish or Mennonite, that supervises it. A school under the Mennonite Committee is considered Mennonite even if the majority of its trustees and students are Amish. For the most part, however, the schools are separate. Indeed, according to one Wenger parent, "they are drifting farther apart," because of differences over required textbooks.

Sometimes a Horning Mennonite parent will serve on the board of a Wenger school, if Horning children attend the school. Wenger children, however, rarely go to Horning schools because, as one member explained, "There are some things we don't like there."[20] A small number of English children attend Wenger schools. A school leader explained, "We don't really turn anybody out if they agree to meet the standards and rules that we have for our schools, but we try to let 'em know what's expected of them."

Wenger parents are involved in educating their children. Each family pays about $2,000 a year to cover the expenses of operating a one- or two-room school. The fee varies from school to school, but families typically pay the same fee regardless of how many children they have in school. Parents also assist with janitorial work, perform needed repairs, and help construct new schools. Fathers serve on the school board, hire teachers, and select the curriculum. The parents help their children with their homework, donate books and materials, and occasionally prepare snacks for special events. At some schools, a few parents bring in lunch on Fridays and eat with the students. Parent-teacher meetings are held once a month. Parents and teachers work together with common purpose and values.

Too much formal education, Wengers worry, will lead youth away from the church and into the secular world. One man expressed typical Wenger concerns: "The higher the education, the more they [youth] begin to get away from farming and the older ways of doing things." The same member worries about his children's safety and shudders at what he reads in the newspapers about school violence. "The paper talked about this nineteen-year-old girl at some school where lots of students were together, and she just started shooting." Bishops warn people against higher education in their sermons. Wenger people distrust education beyond the eighth grade because it may lead to pride and unacceptable ideas and expose youth to worldly people and lifestyles. In short, higher education, because it encourages individualism, critical thinking, and professional occupations, threatens the well-being of the redemptive community.

One mother, commenting on the lively "values" debate in the public schools, thinks that schools "should be teaching values every day of their lives." Although Wenger schools support church values, they do not explicitly teach religion. Schools do not provide religious instruction because the Wengers believe that the parents and the church hold that responsibility.

A teacher is typically responsible for eight grades in a one-room school.

Teachers try to model and teach behavior that builds Christian faith and practice. They read a chapter of the Bible each morning, lead students in singing hymns, and offer a prayer before lunch, but they give no formal instruction in religion.

State law sets the annual number of school days. Many Wenger schools in Pennsylvania open in late August and end in early May. Wenger schools observe Good Friday, Ascension Day (the Thursday forty days after Easter), Thanksgiving, and Christmas. They do *not* close for Memorial Day, Labor Day, Martin Luther King Day, or Presidents Day. There are no extended vacations except for the summer. One grandmother described a school's Christmas program this way: "It don't have a lot of these worldly things you have; just everything that teaches them [students] a lesson. And then of course they each have their recitation to learn and their singing."

Most Wenger schools have only one or two rooms. An exception is the Hillside School in Lancaster County. This two-story brown frame building at the eastern edge of Hinkletown has a first-floor classroom with a high ceiling, a clear varnished wood floor, white walls, fluorescent lights, a telephone, and a clock. This classroom typically accommodates all eight grades. However, if too many students enroll in a given year, one teacher instructs four grades on the first floor and another teacher instructs the remaining grades on the second floor. Hillside School also has a classroom for special-needs students. The cloakroom of the building has indoor bathrooms. Hillside has Wenger and Horning teachers, and its students come from Wenger and Amish families, as well as from other Old Order Mennonite groups: the Stauffers, Reidenbachs, and Hornings.

Sunnyside East, a nearby school, is a white building with green trim and large vertical windows, on a sloping, grassy field. A bell on the roof beckons students from the playground. A rail for tying horses runs along the west side of the property and a hand water pump stands outside one corner of the building. A storage shed as well as the boys' and girls' outhouses stand between the school and the ball field. Five Mennonite students ride their bicycles, two Amish pupils ride push-scooters, and the rest walk to Sunnyside East. The school has seventeen students: six Amish girls, four Amish boys, two Wenger girls, and five Wenger boys. There are four first-graders and four third-graders, five seventh-graders, and one pupil each in second, fourth, fifth, and eighth grades. The boys sit on the left and the girls on the right, although in many Wenger schools, they sit intermixed.

In the vestibule, coats hang in rows and lunchboxes sit in cubbyholes. In the main room, the teacher's desk sits to the front and left of the classroom. Thirty wooden desks with inkwells (which are not used) rest on metal pedestals bolted to the floor. Fluorescent lights hang from the high ceiling. The floor consists of wide tongue-and-groove boards laid in diagonal patterns. The blackboard has both an English alphabet and an Old German alphabet across the top. The numbers from one to one hundred are also printed on a strip of paper along the top of the blackboard. Cream-colored tongue-and-groove wainscoting covers the lower portion of the walls. Poems and sayings—examples of student work—hang on the upper part of the wall. A piece of paper in the shape of a basket with each student's name on it is tacked high on the wall.

An electric clock hangs on the back wall and an oil-burning stove sits in the back left corner. The back right corner holds a bookshelf and a Formica-topped table covered with notebooks. A roll of paper towels hangs on the wall. Pencil sharpeners are mounted on both sides of the room. A terrarium stands in the left back and an electric sandwich oven sits on a side counter. A bench for guests runs along the back wall. Without computers, televisions, science laboratories, and public address systems, Wenger schools have virtually no technology.

"The pupils are all taught by our own people," says a grandmother. "These teachers have just an eighth-grade education but they have the desire to learn what they need so they can teach the eight grades." The teachers are mostly women, and they tend to resign from teaching when they get married. Outsiders rarely teach in Wenger schools. Forty years ago, Wenger schoolteachers earned about six dollars a day; today they earn thirty-eight to fifty-five dollars a day.

Rachel, a typical teacher, is twenty-five years old and unmarried. She has taught at Sunnyside East for six years. She wears a plain-colored dress with a cape. Her white prayer covering extends over her earlobes and is loosely tied with narrow, white strings. She parts her long hair in the center and has it pulled back under her prayer covering. Rachel occasionally speaks snatches of dialect to the younger students to be certain they understand, but she teaches in English, with continuous pleasant affirmations: "That's right; that's good!"

Younger teachers work hard to keep discipline, especially if they have younger siblings in the class. Once, Rachel caught a boy with a cigar in school. Instead of making a big issue of it at the time, she talked to his parents at the monthly parent-teacher meeting. One mother explained, "If they [the students] don't listen too good on the parents, they won't listen too good on the teachers either."

✤ THE SCHOOL DAY

A typical morning at Sunnyside East follows a set pattern.

8:30   The day starts as the teacher reads some verses in English from the King James Bible. Then the teacher and students repeat the Lord's Prayer in unison.

8:40   The students form two rows in front and select some favorite English hymns. One student uses a pitch pipe to set the starting pitch. They sing, in unison, "What can wash away my sins," "Must I go and empty-handed," and "In a lonely graveyard," a song about a departed mother's children who wish to join her in heaven.

8:50   The older students read aloud from their textbooks while the students in the lower grades meet with the teacher at her desk.

8:58   Four third-graders meet in the back. One student quizzes the others with flash cards. Whoever correctly answers gets the flash card and then quizzes the others.

9:02   Middle-grade students study geometry: the circle, diameter, radius, pi, how to find the perimeter, and how to use their protractors.

9:07   First-grade students queue at the front blackboard and practice reading the correct time from the hands on a cardboard clock.

9:10   Each third-grader drills on adding and subtracting. The first grade at the front blackboard practices reading a thermometer and measuring a line in inches.

9:27   The teacher quizzes the seventh- and eighth-grade students at their seats on percents, profit and loss, and finding the area of a figure. Meanwhile, students who have finished their reading begin working on crafts. One boy builds a horse pen out of strips of paper. Another constructs a barn out of cardboard. An older girl helps a younger boy work with an embroidery hoop.

9:40   The third-graders go to the board and practice math: Roman numerals, pounds and ounces, and word problems. The teacher reinforces gender roles by saying, "This question is for the boys" (a question about square feet and acreage). "This one is for the girls" (a question about cookie sheets and the number of pages in a Bible).

9:47   The teacher quizzes a sixth-grade boy on his math. Then she asks first-graders their spelling words: "How do you spell *chip* . . . *shot* . . . *lunch?*"

10:00   Recess. Boys and girls gather separately outside and then mingle to play "hunter." A boy and a girl, the hunters, stand in the middle, while the others form two parallel lines. Children try to cross to the other line without being hit by the two hunters with a tennis ball. Those who are hit stay in the middle and help catch the other runners. The last two caught are the hunters for the next game.

10:15   Classes resume for social studies. The third-graders, who recently studied South America, question a visiting anthropologist about South American people.

11:30   Lunchtime. All bow their heads for a prayer in German. Then, starting with the youngest, they file to the cloakroom, wash their hands, and get their lunchboxes. Cold weather forces everyone to eat inside, and like typical school children, they eat in age- and sex-based clusters: older girls, older boys, younger girls, and younger boys. At the sound of an alarm clock, everyone runs out to play. Older children play softball in an adjoining field while younger boys and girls play another round of "hunter."

The morning is punctuated with two recurring sounds. A small battery-powered alarm clock rings periodically, signifying the end of various tasks. A wall clock chimes each hour, to the tune of "Bells Are Ringing." Similar

Four first-graders listen intently to their teacher. An Amish pupil (second from left) attends this Wenger school.

activities continue into the afternoon. The school day typically ends by 3:00 P.M. Before dismissal, pupils help sweep the floors, wipe the blackboards, and clean up the classroom.

In addition to penmanship, reading, spelling, geography, history, German, and arithmetic, Wenger schools teach social studies, science, health, art, and language skills. Classes are conducted in English, and children chatter in English on the playground. The school uses the *Church and Sunday School Hymnal*, an English hymnal with a few German songs that was published by Mennonites in 1902. Wenger children learn Pennsylvania German as they grow up, but they study the Old German script in school so that they can read the German Bible and German hymns in church. They learn the Old German not to write and speak it, but to understand the written texts.[21]

✤ SCHOOL, CHURCH, AND SOCIETY

Wenger social cohesion is precious and precarious: it can evaporate in one generation if the community fails to socialize its children properly. Like the family, the school inculcates the Wenger worldview. Schools are guarded from undesirable outside interference to ensure the health and survival of the community. The schools perpetuate Wenger values and seek to shield youth from troublesome ideas and outside peer influences.

Wenger schools instill basic religious values as well as fundamental knowledge and practical skills. An example of cultural values appeared as a question on a bulletin board: "What makes a happy s-c-h-o-o-l?" An answer, arranged in acrostic fashion, was <u>S</u>tudy, <u>C</u>o-operation, <u>H</u>onesty, <u>O</u>bedience, <u>O</u>rder, and <u>L</u>ove.[22] Teachers are advised, "Do not tolerate lying, cheating, teasing, and stealing. . . . Keep Christmas plays to a minimum. Discourage competitive ball playing and don't put up Santa or Halloween decorations." School directors urge teachers to emphasize the three Rs of Wenger education, "Respect, Responsibility, and Religion."[23]

Schoolaid, a publishing venture operated by a retired Wenger schoolteacher in Lancaster County, produces many textbooks. Schoolaid publishes a series of English-language books and manuals that introduce Old German to students. Schoolaid also publishes a four-book series on health for grades three through eight: *Healthy Happy Habits*, *Good Growth Guide*, *The Body's Building Blocks*, and *Mankind Marvelously Made*, a title that suggests a creationist view.

The books, averaging three hundred pages each, provide a combined introduction to science, health, and safety. One chapter in *Building Blocks* is devoted to "The Story of the Cell," and others to various body systems—"Muscular," "Nervous," "Immune," and "Endocrine." Additional topics include "Safety on the Farm" and "Mental Health." The eighth-grade text, *Mankind*, contains "The Reproductive System," a two-page chapter on an unusual subject for an Old Order textbook. The chapter emphasizes God's "wonderful and mind-boggling" creation in which "the nucleus of the egg is the blueprint for the body that is to be formed."[24] Regardless of topic, the Schoolaid texts emphasize that all of life is part of God's created order. Science and intellectual knowledge do not challenge religious faith in these texts; they are subsumed under the rubric of God's divine plan.

The authors summarize their purpose for creating the Schoolaid series: "Study, however basic, leaves us in awe of our infinitely great God who has created both the microscopic world and the great universe of stars and space. These orderly and unchangeable laws of nature working together so perfectly reveal a glimpse of the omnipotent nature of the creator. All glory, all credits go to him alone who also made this little piece of work possible and to whom we dedicate the same."[25] A Wenger parent explained, "We feel like true science has been hijacked by naturalistic, evolutionary schemes such as Darwinian, and is dangerous, whether promoted by religious liberals or atheists. True science does not contradict Scripture."

The books in school libraries typically include stories about nature and animals, migration, the settling of the frontier, and some adventure stories such as Nancy Drew or the Hardy Boys. Romance novels are rarely found, but *Uncle Tom's Cabin, Black Beauty*, and biographies of U.S. presidents will likely be on the shelves.

Although federal law requires children to attend school until they are sixteen years old, Wenger children, like other Old Order children, are permitted to stop at eighth grade.[26] Parents believe that children need to learn occupational skills in home, farm, or shop—and do not need high school, let alone higher education. In Pennsylvania, after youth finish eighth grade, they attend a vocational school until their fifteenth birthday.[27] This school meets three hours a day, once a week. Students study practical subjects such as mathematics for farmers and how to write a business letter. They keep diaries of the household, shop, or farming tasks they perform during the week, and they bring the diaries to their weekly meetings for evaluation. "If parents don't live on a farm and they don't have work for 'em at home, they're really eager to have these fourteen-year-olds hired to a neighbor or to someone on a farm to keep 'em busy without bein' out [in the world] somewhere away," according to one father.

Wenger schools are private, parent-operated schools, not parochial schools managed by the church. Church leaders have no direct connection to the schools, except as parents. One minister recalled, "When I was ordained, I no longer served on the school board. We try to keep the ministry neutral on school matters. It works better that way." One parent underscored the sharp separation: "We have a church rule that the church is not involved in the schools in any manner whatsoever." He explained further: "Some of our schools are neighborhood schools with children from different churches." In the words of one member, "School officials should not try to enforce church rules. If the church has no right to have a say in the school, then vice versa: only ordained officials can have a say in the church." School directors are encouraged to "let school be school and church be church."[28] The bifurcation helps separate and clarify the roles and responsibilities of ordained leaders and school directors.

Although Wenger education emphasizes practical skills and their oral-based culture accents conversation rather than literary skills, several Wenger women have written extensively. The textbooks published by Schoolaid have been written primarily by women. Wenger author Carrie Bender published more than fourteen books that have sold some 240,000 copies. The down-to-earth stories are grounded in the author's intimate knowledge of Old Order Amish and Mennonite life. Roseann Zimmerman writes a weekly newspaper column, "Old Order Mennonite Memoirs." Her essays are filled with well-crafted, engaging anecdotes that explain and interpret Wenger life and culture for outsiders. These authors, without the benefit of high school or college, display considerable literary talent shaped by self-instruction and experience.[29]

Public education serves to acculturate youth from diverse backgrounds into mainstream American society. In sharp contrast, Wenger schools not only promote Mennonite values and bolster Wenger identity but also prevent assimilation into the cultural mainstream. In Wenger eyes, the assimilative agenda of public schools threatens the very viability of their redemptive community.

❖ SINGINGS, DANCES, AND CROWDS

As Wenger children grow into adolescence, they enjoy more freedom, but they also face important decisions. After completing their schooling, youth are involved in various forms of work and vocational preparation for several years until they marry. Without the rituals of taking a driver's test, attending the high school prom, and commencement, Wenger youth anticipate four different rites of passage that usher them toward adulthood: running around, baptism, dating, and marriage.

When they turn seventeen, young people enter *Rumspringa*, which literally means "running around."[30] In this greatly anticipated moment, they start "going with the young folks," as Wengers typically say in English. This is the moment when the boys get a carriage, and both boys and girls spend more time with their peers on weekends. Although a few may begin dating before baptism, most romantic ties wait until after baptism. "Indeed," notes one father, "preachers in their sermons often urge youth not to date until they are members of the church." Most are baptized shortly before or after they turn eighteen. Some, but not nearly all of them, begin dating about the same time.

When they begin "running around," young people who live in small settlements frequently travel to other Wenger communities to be with a larger group of peers. For instance, young people from the small settlement in Michigan travel to the larger Old Order community near Elkhart, Indiana.

Two events bring young people together: the singings and the "open crowds." The singings, Saturday evening get-togethers in someone's home, are open to all the young people of a settlement. In Lancaster County, there may be several singings on the same evening. Beginning around 8:00 P.M., they last about one and a half hours. Afterwards, the youth play games till about 11:00 or midnight. In many areas these games are actually a form of square dancing. Parents carefully plan the singings. For example, Wenger parents who live near Martindale might host a singing for 200 to 250 young people. One parent emphasized the importance of including all the young people and treating everybody the same. People appreciate good singers, but poor ones are also treated with respect.

A typical singing begins about 7:45 P.M. when youth start arriving alone or in groups, many by bicycle and a few by horse and buggy. A vanload travels from the Penn Valley settlement some thirty-five miles northeast of Lancaster. A few minutes after 8:00, the girls start singing. Soon the boys file into the room and take their places on one side of a long table set up for the occasion. Some girls sit along the other side. Other girls and boys sit on chairs and benches that have been set up around the room. One of the boys calls out the page number of a song in the *Church and Sunday School Hymnal.* He pulls a pitch pipe out of his pocket, gives the pitch, and leads in soprano. The sounds of "What a Friend We Have in Jesus" fill the room. Some alto, bass, and tenor voices create a four-part harmony. The boys take turns leading as more songs are picked. As the evening wears on, they switch to another songbook, *Favorite Songs and Hymns.* All the singing is in English. Suddenly, loud laughter outside a window disrupts the singing. A group of boisterous boys has slipped outside to tell stories.

At about 9:45, the singing winds down and everyone files into the kitchen for drinks, cookies, and other snacks. Afterward, the tables and chairs are moved out of the singing room so that a dance can begin. The dances are similar to square dancing. Some of the ministers and parents oppose the dances, while others defend them, saying, "The youth could be doing something worse." A forty-year-old says, "Some people have strong convictions against dancing because they touch the girls. But I danced when I was younger and had no problems with it. It's like you're playing a game in a group." Others argue that a true Christian would never be involved in dancing. However, the dancing issue has not surfaced in recent church counsel meetings.

The host family sometimes finds the gatherings challenging. One parent says, "The young people sit around the table and sing but, always, some of

Four girls explore the sand and ocean in Florida during a service trip.

them like to do something different. It's an awful job trying to keep order. There's always some along that don't respect order and orderliness, and they cause a little trouble." When some boys broke some things at one home, the hostess informed their parents. The boys returned with an apology and some money. The hostess was pleased: "It wasn't the money. It was that they showed that they were sorry."

Each summer, three to six "open crowd" events are planned on summer Sunday evenings. Open crowds are large outdoor suppers to which all young people are invited. In Lancaster, several families provide all the food and preparation for this big event. Parents provide volleyball nets, quoits, and other games or perhaps a baseball diamond on their farm.[31] In a smaller settlement, thirty to one hundred youth might go to an open crowd, but in Lancaster County as many as five hundred youth might attend.

The preparations for one open crowd of five hundred youth began six weeks in advance when eleven parent couples met to begin the planning. Several days before the event, a group of girls gathered at the host farm to mulch flowerbeds, weed gardens, and set up twelve volleyball nets and lights. A large enclosed trailer brought dishes, tables, and chairs that are used for various community gatherings. A refrigerated community trailer provided food storage space as well as a freezer and refrigerator. Five flatbed farm wagons were prepared to carry horse feed and provide tie spaces for the horses that would arrive pulling buggies.

Women from the eleven host families prepared the food in advance at their own homes and then brought it to the farmstead a day or so before the gathering. The menu included eight hundred ham and cheese sandwiches, ten large roasters filled with chickenetti (a casserole of chicken, spaghetti, and vegetables), twenty-five pans of layered salad, eight large boxes of chips and pretzels, twenty pails of thickened fruit salad, twenty ice cream cakes, forty gallons of drink, and hundreds of whoopee pies and salty foods for a late-night snack. A special low-protein menu was prepared for six youth who have maple syrup urine disease.

The activities for this particular open crowd began late Sunday afternoon. Supper was served at 5:30 P.M., and a snack followed at 10 P.M. The festivities came to a close by midnight. On Monday, the host families returned to clean and pack up the dishes, tables, and chairs, which were used for a wedding the next day.

Singings and open crowd gatherings encourage youth to associate within the Wenger fold, to stay together and do the same things. Other smaller, impromptu events—Sunday afternoon baseball games, ice skating parties, and volleyball games—also bring young people together. By hosting group events, parents try to keep young people within the community and under the eye of the church so that they are less likely to run around with outside youth. But this effort is particularly challenging in small settlements, where, one member notes, young people relate too much to non-Wenger youth. "There's a ditch on either side of the road," though, he says, explaining that in large settlements groups of youth are prone to form cliques and become rowdy.

One mother described her daughter's Wenger friends as a bit wild: "They never joined our church; they went to those liberal Lancaster Conference churches. ... We have always taught our young people self-denial and the narrow path. We want them to be separated from the world. But things get bad when the boys go into town, go to eating places, and play video games." Many youth, however, are well behaved. Indeed, one member said, "Some people say 'Wenger youth are the cream; others [non-Wengers] are just skim milk,' but that [attitude] is the opposite of what we are taught! Over and over, we are taught, 'This is our way of doing things, but we should not be critical of the way other groups do things.'" A mother added, "We try to prevent the young people from forming cliques; this helps keep them out of trouble." In settlements large and small, parents try to maximize the impact of Wenger peers and minimize contamination from the larger world and its secular values.

✥ JOINING THE CHURCH

During *Rumspringa*, youth are freer from family controls and not yet under church supervision. Because most young people will be baptized within a year or so after they begin *Rumspringa*, there is only a short opportunity to experience some of the outside world. All the social forces of family, school, and church encourage young people to stay in the community, join the church, and adopt Wenger beliefs and practices. Few young people delay joining the church, and very few leave the community. The Wengers' success in drawing young people into the church provides further evidence of the power of community solidarity.

One member contends that baptism does not guarantee that a person has had a true conversion to Christ: "It is said over and over—do not pressure the young people to join the church. That is their own decision; their own heart has to tell them. You shouldn't tell them that they're old enough to join church. We have just a small percentage that doesn't join church. Many join just because all their friends are joining. So they're not coming to the church completely with heart, soul, and mind."

"Heart, soul, and mind" reflects warmheartedness, an inner love for God that finds expression in a commitment to the church community. One member says, "Our younger daughter was just baptized this summer, but our son has not been baptized yet. He's moving toward the church. He's twenty-two. I hope he'll come around." A father noted, "One of our favorite sayings is 'We don't want anyone to be coerced to be a member.'"

While many evangelical groups emphasize dramatic personal conversions, Wengers have a different view. "Salvation is a gradual project," said one member. "We start earlier and work on it longer. It's not so much what's up here," he said, pointing to his head, "it's more a matter of fitting in with our ways."[32] Rather than calling for dramatic, emotion-filled turning points, which one member dubbed "flash conversions," Wengers believe that salvation occurs quietly as young people gradually fit into the ways of their

For youth, table games are a popular winter activity.

people. A younger member insisted, however, that "there does come a time, a moment at the crossroad when a person is born again, but we don't play it up because we fight against pietism." In the final analysis, the ways of salvation, in the Wenger view, are learned by participating in the church, the redemptive community, as individuals find peace with God and show the "fruits of repentance" as they live and work together.

As stalwart Anabaptists, the Wengers believe that young people should be fully aware of the meaning of their decision to be baptized and join the church. This rite of passage shifts accountability from family to church. Typically, when they are seventeen or eighteen, youth attend instruction classes on five successive Sunday afternoons beginning in late July, as explained in Chapter 5. Each meeting covers three of the eighteen articles of faith on topics such as God, Jesus, the church, ordained ministers, and marriage.[33] The last instruction meeting occurs before the fall preparatory service, the day of baptism. The early age of Wenger baptism shortens the window of opportunity for youth to experiment in the world or get lost in it completely.

All of these efforts—careful discipline, Wenger youth gatherings, small-scale social life, and early baptism—funnel young people toward church membership by early adulthood. A young man will eventually take his proper place on the seat of his father's steel-wheeled tractor, at the worktable in his father's carpentry shop, or on the preachers' bench at church. A young woman will almost always marry and become a wife and mother, following in the well-marked steps of her mother.

Although some Wenger leaders emphasize the importance of genuine repentance before baptism, they also recognize the power of social pressure. One leader explained, "Remember, these young people have inherited just as much of the old human nature as any other young people. Some of them are completely sincere, have accepted Jesus as their personal Savior, and want to be part of the body of believers. But peer pressure is as strong among Wenger young people as it is elsewhere. If your friends are all joining church this year, the psychological pressure to also do so is pretty intense."

The more successful the Wengers are in socializing their youth, the more likely young people will choose friends and a mate within their community and reproduce the Wenger way of life. Proper training funnels the Wengers' offspring toward salvation and membership in the life of the church.[34] Their "gradual project" of socialization appears largely successful because about 90 percent of the children join the church. Indeed, in one church district in Pennsylvania, 95 percent of nearly two hundred children joined the church.[35] The exact number fluctuates from community to community, but all things considered, about nine out of ten young people join the church of their birth.[36]

✦ COURTSHIP AND MARRIAGE

Wenger family formation begins with finding a mate. "Dating is not child's play," according to one father, "and casual dating is not acceptable." Having more than one dating partner is not unusual, but more than half of the youth, estimated one member, "only have one dating partner." Young people have ample freedom during courtship to search for a spouse in a local or faraway settlement. For example, a boy who lives in the Martindale district in Lancaster County may have a girlfriend ten miles away in the Groffdale District and travel to her house by horse and buggy. If a girl lives in a distant settlement, her boyfriend may travel with others in a hired van and stay overnight at a friend's or relative's home. Jacob's twenty-one-year-old daughter Susan, for example, has a boyfriend in Bedford County, about 170 miles away. Every two weeks, she either rides in a hired van to Bedford County, or he rides in one to Lancaster County.

Neither the church nor families arrange marriages. Young people are free to select their own dating partners. Dating couples are encouraged to spend time in groups rather than alone. Several couples may go together for nature hikes, for example, or attend singings and open crowds. Some ministers preach against physical contact before marriage to avoid sexual immorality.

Some sexual indiscretions were encouraged by an old practice known as "opening the couch." Most parlors had a couch that opened up as a bed. A dating couple would "open the couch" and lie on the bed fully clothed, according to one member, "hugging, kissing, and petting until about midnight." Indeed, one member dating in the 1920s only knew one girl who refused to open her couch—and "she never got married either." The senior bishop, convinced that the open-couch custom was not conducive to high moral standards, began teaching and preaching against it in the 1950s. The open-couch practice, which "had been prevalent," according to one Wenger historian, "gradually disappeared by 1975."[37]

When two people begin courting seriously, the family assumes that they will soon marry, but their engagement is kept secret. Their congregation learns of their plans about four weeks before the wedding, when the couple is "published" after a church service. A grandmother confided to a visitor in July, "We have a granddaughter getting married in September, but no one knows yet because they aren't published yet; it's one of those strange Wenger customs, you know." After they are published, they begin to act like adults. They no longer attend young people's gatherings and begin acting more like married people.

The modal age of marriage is 21. Indeed, 76 percent marry between 20 and 22 years of age.[38] On the average, men marry at 22.7 years and women at 21.8 years of age. Since the 1920s, the average age of marriage for men has declined about a year, but for women, it has remained stable.[39] Wenger bishops will marry only members of the church. This in-group practice of endogamy strengthens kinship ties across the community and enhances the growth of the church.

❖ A WENGER WEDDING

The Wenger wedding season begins in September and continues through March. During these months, farm work slows and people have more free time. Even the time of weddings helps mark boundaries with the larger

Courtship often involves outdoor activities such as hiking, fishing, or skating.

society. One bishop noted, "You really could have a wedding in any month except June, because we don't like all the worldly fuss about June brides." Weddings usually occur on a Tuesday or Thursday. This avoids Sunday services and gives time for preparation and cleanup. In a dramatic departure from typical American weddings, the ritual formula is determined by the church, not by the bride and groom. Because all Wenger weddings follow the same format, a wedding rehearsal is not necessary. The ritual reflects communal values rather than the idiosyncratic preferences of the couple. The wedding takes place in the home of the bride, never in the churchhouse.[40] No one attends a wedding except by invitation.

The following description traces the events at a typical Wenger wedding. Between 8:00 and 8:30 A.M., guests begin arriving at the bride's home and park their black buggies near the machinery shed. The women gather inside, while the men stand in the yard or inside the barn. Gift receivers accept presents and carry them to an upper bedroom. Four rooms of the house, completely bare of other furniture, overflow with straight-backed chairs packed closely together. Just before the hosts begin seating the guests, two young couples offer all the guests *Kuchen* and *Wei* (cookies and wine). The girls carry cookie-filled trays and their partners carry matching trays with shot glasses filled with wine. The two girls wear white aprons decorated with large white hearts as they serve pastries to each arriving guest. Each female guest receives a small piece of fabric to pin to her dress, cut in the shape of twin hearts, with a rose design.

The hosts begin seating the guests about nine o'clock, announcing each couple and then escorting them to their seats. The living room has two sections of seats facing each other. Younger married couples take their places on one side behind the front row, which is reserved for the wedding party. All the rooms of the house fill with wedding guests—about two hundred adults and children. These include relatives of the bride and groom, neighbors, and members of the local congregation. Several Amish neighbors help prepare and cook the food. English people rarely attend, except by special invitation.

The *Nayva sitzah* (wedding attendants) are the first guests to be seated. While guests are being seated, the ministry meet in a private upstairs room with the bride and groom and both sets of parents. After the guests are all seated, the ministry and parents file in and take their seats. The guests sing a traditional German wedding hymn in unison, which the bishop lines. During this hymn, the bride and groom walk in and sit down in the front row, directly facing the row of ministers in the opposite section. Two ministers begin the service; one preaches a twenty-minute sermon and the other preaches a thirty-minute sermon. The bishop follows with another thirty-minute sermon. All three sermons are in Pennsylvania German.

The bride and groom then stand and take hands as they give assent to the words of the marriage covenant.[41] The bishop puts his hand over theirs and prays. All take their seats, and the ministers each give a brief testimony of affirmation to the bishop's words.

After the ceremony, the guests kneel for prayer and then stand for the benediction. The guests sing a hymn while the bride, groom, wedding party, and other young people go to an upstairs bedroom where the young people offer congratulations and God's blessing to the newly married couple. The remaining guests file out into the yard and visit. About noon, friends of the family call guests into the house by couples and direct them to their seats for the first shift of eating. Later, a second group eats while the first shift converses in the house or yard. The mealtime activities conclude by two o'clock and participants prepare for the singing.

The ministers and the men enter the living room for the singing. Women file in and fill the room behind the men. The bride and groom with their attendants sit directly facing the ministers.[42] Young people are also present.

The bishop lines several hymns and all sing together from the German hymn-book for about twenty minutes. Then the servers bring in more *Kuchen* and *Wei*, and after the refreshment the singing switches to English.[43] They sing in unison with an occasional person slipping into harmony. People select their favorites: "Count Your Blessings," "A Wedding Hymn," "Hand in Hand," "Tread Softly," "Love at Home," or "Just as I Am."

At about three o'clock, married guests begin congratulating the newly-weds and wishing them God's blessing. They shake hands with the bride and groom and prepare to leave. "We used to pass out cigars at weddings," said one minister, "but we don't anymore," reflecting changing Wenger attitudes toward tobacco. As people exit the house, hostlers in jeans and patterned shirts offer to bring buggies for departing guests in return for a tip.

During the wedding, men and women proclaim their gender and age-group identity by the clothes they wear. The groom wears a plain-collar suit (for the first time in his life), black bow tie, newly bought black high-top shoes, and a white shirt. The plain coat is a symbol of marriage. Other men in the bridal party wear pink bow ties. Most male guests wear regular Sunday clothes; unmarried ones wear lapel coats and married men wear plain-collar suits and no ties.

The bride wears a gray dress with a slight V at the neck and three-quarter-length puffed sleeves, low black heels, black stockings, and a prayer covering with the strings loosely tied. Other women in the bridal party wear pink dresses.[44] Older female guests wear dark blue dresses, black oxford shoes, and prayer coverings with black strings snugly tied. Black dresses, a sign of mourning, are never worn at a wedding. Girls wear lighter, brightly colored print dresses, white prayer coverings with the strings loosely tied, and flat or low-heeled shoes. Several of the girls and women wear green brocade dresses. A few younger girls wear long, braided hair hanging down from beneath their coverings. Older girls wear their hair up under their coverings. As they leave the wedding, older women sport sweaters or shawls, and some young women wear down-filled, zippered coats.

✥ GENDER AND KINSHIP

At the wedding ceremony, the ministers explain the proper roles for the bride and groom based on the biblical text of 1 Peter 3:3. The wife should be "subject to her husband . . . that they may be one, just as the church should be subject to Christ." The speaker gives the biblical example of Sarah being subject to her husband, Abraham. In turn, the husband should be willing to sacrifice for his wife and should "nourish and cherish his wife as his own flesh." Women should practice "chaste conversation" [a modest lifestyle], possess a "quiet spirit," and not show outward adornment or "plaiting" [braiding] of the hair. The couple is reminded that "God resisteth the proud and giveth grace to the humble" (1 Pet. 5:5). The presiding bishop reads and explains the words of a hymn to the guests, suggesting that the church is to Christ as the wife is to her husband. All should "prepare for the lamb's wedding feast," that great feast when believers, the bride of Christ, will be united with him in heaven. "Cinderella fairy tales end happily ever after," he tells the audience, "but the reality is not always happy. Therefore, we must 'redeem the time because the days are evil.'"

In responding to the marriage vows, the groom agrees "to love and to care for her . . . to live with her in a Christian and peaceable manner, to take the *heavier* responsibility upon yourself." The bride also agrees to "love and to care for him . . . to live with him in a Christian and peaceable manner, to take the *lighter* responsibility upon yourself, to be *submissive* to him."[45] The subtle differences in the wording of the vows translate into major differences in gender roles. The husband has the "heavier" responsibility and the wife is to be "submissive" to his direction. These power differences are expected to be handled, however, in loving, caring, and peaceable ways.

In the new household, the man will make most of the business decisions. He will be primarily responsible for farming, keeping financial records, buying supplies, paying bills, and supervising male hired hands. The husband-father will take an active role in the education of his children, especially in the religious and vocational education of his sons. The wife will not seek outside employment, especially after she has children. Since she directs the home, her husband will give her the money she needs for purchases and maintenance. With the assistance of her children, she will do the cleaning, cooking, dishwashing, gardening, housework, and laundry.

When couples form a new home, they know what the community requires of them. They in turn will begin reproducing the same social values and process in their own children. They will remain rooted in an extensive kinship system where all speak Pennsylvania German, the dialect of communal wisdom, the voice of the Wenger heart. In the larger American culture, youth create their own future from an astonishing array of choices. They must negotiate marriage, vocation, religion, and a place of residence because neither church, nor family, nor culture dictates a specific path. Such freedom of choice is woven into the fabric of modern culture. The demands of education and vocation pull young adults in dozens of directions—out of the matrix of family, geography, community, and often childhood faith. This independence unshackles the constraints of parents, tradition, and community. But for some people, such abundant choices lead to loneliness, rootlessness, alienation, and a lack of belonging.

❖ DEATH AND DYING

Living in the Wenger world means not only celebrating the happiness of a wedding but also mourning the sadness of a death. The beloved community always mobilizes in times of crisis, especially when death strikes unexpectedly. Farmers often face special risks. One young man was killed when he fell from a silo. Another farmer died when his tractor rolled over on top of him. One father backed a tractor over his two-year-old daughter. In another case, a man was pulled into a feed grinder.[46] Deaths of younger people are especially painful. One grandmother reflecting on three deaths in her family said, "Well, these deaths, they're all a loud call from the Lord, not just for that family but for everybody that hears it and takes it to heart. . . . Many times our hearts are more soft and more open in time of discouragement or sorrow."

Funerals follow a similar ritual sequence across all the settlements.[47] In one community, a man in his seventies collapsed with a heart attack on his kitchen floor in the middle of the night. He was taken to the hospital by ambulance and died shortly after arrival. The following description chronicles the preparation for his funeral.

An English funeral director takes the body from the hospital to the funeral home, embalms it, and dresses it in white clothes. The next day, Thursday, friends and relatives gather at their home to plan for the funeral. On Friday, the family holds a viewing at the home from 2:00 P.M. to 9:00 P.M., where family, friends, and neighbors view the body and console the immediate family.

Late Saturday morning, several relatives join the family for an early lunch at the house. The bishop and local ministers meet with the family at noon at the house for a brief service. Several church members drive their buggies to the home to help transport relatives to the churchhouse. In the midst of rain, the pallbearers take the coffin from the house and load it onto a horse-drawn hearse. The coffin lies on the back of the hearse under a low, flat enclosure with a tarpaulin thrown over the top. The driver sits exposed to the rain on a seat at the front of the wagon as he guides the horse. The widow and her two daughters ride in the first carriage behind the hearse. Fifteen buggies and four vans form a procession behind the hearse. A son, who had previously left the Wenger Church, drives his car in the procession.

The procession arrives at the churchhouse about 12:45. Some thirty vans carrying friends and relatives from other settlements park in the churchyard as buggies fill the sheds. Some of the people greet each other with a holy kiss. Usually the coffin sits in the churchyard for the viewing but, because of heavy rain, it sits on a stand in the horse shed. One member explains, "It has been our custom to never have a coffin inside the churchhouse."[48] A few congregations will place the coffin in the churchhouse if the weather is inclement.

Two long lines form as many people hold umbrellas in the heavy rain. The coffin, made of furniture-quality stained wood, is tapered at both ends and peaked in the center. Women walk by in a line on one side of the coffin; men file by on the other side. Horning people and other non-Wenger neighbors also stand in the viewing line. Widow, daughters, and other relatives stand near the coffin, watching as the people walk by. One daughter sobs. When the viewing ends, the funeral director closes the two narrow lids on the coffin. He gives three bent poles to six young grandsons, who slip them under the coffin. They carry it thirty yards around the back of the stables to the graveyard. The extended family walks just behind the coffin, followed by the rest of the mourners.

A large pile of dirt beside the grave is covered by a blue tarpaulin to keep it dry. A plain pine box serves as a vault at the bottom of the grave.[49] Several two-by-eight planks lie in the mud on both sides of the open grave and three two-by-four boards lie crosswise on top. The pallbearers walk around the grave and rest the coffin on the two-by-fours. The family members stand on the far side of the grave, but the widow is seated. Wenger men typically remove their hats at the graveside.[50] The funeral director places wide fabric straps beneath the coffin and removes the two-by-fours. Then the pallbearers hold the coffin with the fabric straps and lower it into the wooden vault. Under his umbrella, a minister reads a Scripture, a hymn, and/or other words of comfort. After the ten-minute service, two men shovel dirt into the grave. As the grave fills, people begin leaving for the funeral service in the churchhouse.[51]

Family members enter the churchhouse, followed by the other mourners. The women of the extended family sit in the first row of the women's side of the room. The male relatives sit across from them on the first rows of the men's side. More than five hundred people pack the building. The women's cloakroom swells to overflowing. Folding chairs fill all the aisles. Men hang their hats on the many hooks on railings hanging from the ceiling above their seats, but many of the women continue wearing their black bonnets. All the women are clad in black dresses, capes, stockings, and shoes. Most of the men wear plain black suits with black vests and black felt hats. Fifteen men sit at the singers' table, and several ministers seat themselves on the preachers' bench.

The service starts at about 1:30, when a minister reads a hymn from an English hymnbook and the congregation sings it in English to the tune of "Abide with Me." The first two sermons are preached mostly in English, in deference to the English visitors. Among other things, the minister says, "Our brother is called away ... it is appointed unto man once to die. ... Death came through sin. ... This night thy soul shall be required of thee."

The bishop prays in Pennsylvania German as the congregation kneels. Then, in English, he gives the name of the deceased and date of birth and death. He reads all the verses of the English song, "Let Me Go." Then the congregation sings the verses, printed on a sheet in the bookracks on the benches. The service ends with a few words from the bishop.

A death, especially an untimely one, underscores the uncertainty of life. Ministers remind members to "treasure family members, especially the old, to care for one another. God will support us now in our time of grief and also in the future." The funeral service brings the grieving community together in a ritual experience that underscores central Wenger values: humility, simplicity, trust in God, and the enduring importance of the *Gmay*.

The stages of life—birth, childhood, youth, married years, and death—provide many opportunities to reinforce central values of Wenger life. Each rite of passage allows the community to rehearse and remind members of the enduring truths, the basic beliefs and convictions of Wenger culture.

Wenger rites of passage provide clear boundary markers of various stages and roles in the life cycle. The distinctions that mark the steps to adulthood clarify and crystallize identities as young people grow up. Unlike the broad elastic span of adolescence in American society that may stretch over many years, Wenger youth move quickly from their roles as boys and girls into adulthood.

In another departure from American culture, the rituals that govern Wenger rites of passage are not customized by individual preference. Wenger ritual is collective ritual, owned and performed by the church. Thus, the cost of funerals and weddings is very modest compared to that of mainstream ceremonies, where families engage in conspicuous displays of wealth. "The cost of our funerals," said one man who recently buried his father, "is $500 to $1,000, compared to $10,000 or more on the outside."

Old Order ritual evokes and embodies the community's own virtues—not the wealth and wishes of individuals, as it often does in mainstream society. The communal script is similar for weddings and funerals across all settlements. Again, bride and groom do not create their own individualized wedding ceremony and thus have no need for a wedding rehearsal, because all weddings are alike and everyone knows exactly what to expect. Likewise, funerals are not customized. Ritual practice reflects communal values, not individual preferences. The community-owned rituals that govern rites of passage constantly remind Wengers of the core values of their community.

Another rite of passage involves entering an occupation. Work in Wenger society is embedded in family life. In Chapter 7, we explore how Wengers collaborate to make a living.

Making a Living Together

They have a contagious optimism for family farming.

—AGRICULTURAL EXTENSION AGENT

❖ THE CALLING AND CULTURE OF FARMING

Wenger society rests on a foundation of frugal financial practices. A traditional, farm-oriented economy provides manual work, strong ties to the land, and a rural ethos. In Lancaster County, some farms have remained in the same family for generations, anchoring the family and bonding it together in common work and culture. Farming is not merely a family business; it is a way of life, a calling and a culture that is passed from generation to generation. Family farms are not large commercial operations designed to turn a profit for investors. The rural homestead not only provides for the material needs of the family but also nurtures and fertilizes the cultural base of Wenger life.

One Wenger man spoke earnestly about the importance of his children's staying on the farm. It would be much easier financially if his children worked away from home or started their own businesses, but he wants them to begin farming so that they can raise their families on the farm. Farm owners try hard to keep their children involved in farming and seek equitable ways to pass on the family farm to one of them.

Young men sometimes work in shops before marriage, or in the first years of marriage, until they can purchase a farm. One leader estimated that over 75 percent of the men enter farming after they "settle down."[1] Many farmers have a sideline business to supplement their farm income and provide work throughout the winter, and a growing number of people devote all of their time to small shops and various enterprises. Woodworking and machine shops are the most common. It is not unusual for parents and adult children to live on the same homestead where one family operates the farm and others have a small business.[2] Nevertheless, farming remains the primary vocation for the majority of Wengers.

As noted in Chapter 4, when faced with urban sprawl and expensive land in Lancaster County, many Wengers migrate to other states to continue plowing. The Amish in Lancaster County, by contrast, have more readily abandoned their plows and established small businesses.[3] "Staying on the farm for the sake of the family is the 'in' thing," noted one Wenger farmer. "We encourage moving out of the area so we can stay in farming."

Various cottage industries often mingle together on a farm. Wives and children may run sideline operations that sell eggs, honey, baked products, produce, and crafts. Older men may have a specialty business—a harness, welding, or furniture shop. Regardless of the enterprise, children typically work alongside adults in informal apprenticeships. Older unmarried girls may work off the farm, "hiring out" to a neighbor as a housekeeper, while young men may work for a mobile construction crew or in a small shop. Whether they are involved in farming or business, parents believe that children and youth must learn to enjoy work and be kept busy—not only to avoid idleness, "the devil's workshop," but also to learn vocational skills and the basic values of Wenger culture.

A portion of the wages of an unmarried child goes to the parents until the child turns twenty-one. In return, the parents provide for the needs of the child and eventually help him or her get established in farming or another vocation. The *family*, not the individual, forms the unit of production and consumption, an economic unit that often includes extended family members as well. This contribution *to* and dependence *upon* the family increases adolescents' loyalty to their parents: the young person's economic future rides on the family's productivity and wealth.

✣ TABLE 8 Occupational profile of Wenger adults

		Number	Percentage
Employer (N=175)			
	Self-employed[1]	147	84
	Non-Wenger employer	19	11
	Wenger employer	8	4.6
	Unemployed	1	0.6
Occupation			
Males (N=77)	Farming	57	74
	Small business	9	12
	Manual labor	9	12
	Factory	1	1.3
	Other	1	1.3
Females (N=98)	Homemaker[2]	73	74
	Manual labor	7	7
	Other	6	6
	Factory	6	6
	Teacher	4	4
	Small business	1	1
	Unemployed	1	1

SOURCE: Martindale District Study, 1968–98 (see Appendix A). Occupational information was not available for 24 people in the study of 199 subjects.

[1] Includes homemakers.
[2] Some homemakers have small sideline businesses.

Among 175 adults in one church district, 84 percent are self-employed (including homemakers), 4.6 percent work for a Wenger employer, and 11 percent work for a non-Wenger employer, as shown in Table 8.[4] Some younger people work off the farm for non-Wenger employers doing carpentry, masonry, house remodeling, or heavy construction. If they work for someone in the neighborhood, they often drive their teams to the worksite. Others ride to work with a non-Wenger employee in a motor vehicle. Nevertheless, "the bicycle is by far the most widely used vehicle to get to work," said one shop owner.

Despite a steady exodus of Wengers out of Lancaster County, in the mid-1990s they still owned some 400 farms with a total area of 21,878 acres. Wenger farms in Lancaster County average a modest 54 acres, with plots ranging from 25 to 138 acres. No member owns a large tract of land and no one owns more than three farms.[5] Forty percent (386) of 972 Wenger heads of households in Lancaster County own a farm. Many of those who do not own a farm work on one. One congregation in the center of the Lancaster settlement claims 74 percent of its adult men as farmers (see Table 8). In congregations outside Lancaster County, a similar or even higher percentage of families are farming.

Many households, then, are engaged in farming. Even so, Lancaster Wengers increased their ownership of farmland by only 500 acres from 1984 to 2002—a paltry 26 acres a year, despite the fact that the community's population doubled during this period. Most of the new members moved away to other settlements or worked in a business. By contrast, in the same nineteen-year period in Lancaster County, the Amish added 21,000 acres and the Hornings increased their farmland by 2,600 acres. In this period, the Wengers sold eight farms to the Amish but bought none from them.[6]

Dairy Farming

The traditional Wenger farmer is a dairyman. A member described a cow in these humorous words: "She's a mobile, animated machine, housed in unprocessed leather. One end has a mower, a grinder, and other standard equipment including bumpers, headlights, wing-flaps and a foghorn. At the other end is a milk dispenser, a fertilizer spreader, and an insect repeller." This whimsical quip illustrates the down-to-earth humor of Wenger farmers. Many dairymen milk up to fifty cows. The *Ordnung* permits an array of modern equipment: electricity, automatic milkers, milk pipelines, bulk holding tanks, and automatic gutter cleaners to dispose of manure. There are taboos, however, on computerized feeding equipment and rubber tires on tractors and skid loaders, as well as frequent admonitions not to develop large-scale operations.

After his initial investment, a dairy farmer has many ongoing expenses: (1) making mortgage or rental payments, (2) purchasing cattle, fertilizer, seed, pesticides, and any feed beyond what he can raise, and (3) maintaining buildings and equipment. Milk sales provide the primary income for dairy farmers, but profits fluctuate as milk and feed prices rise and fall.

Many of the Wenger barns in Pennsylvania are bank barns, built with an earthen ramp on the back side leading to the second story, which holds some grain and large quantities of baled hay. Cows and calves occupy the first floor. Some farmers collect milk in buckets and then carry them to a large bulk tank in the milkhouse. Others pump the milk directly from the cow to the bulk tank through glass or stainless steel pipelines. Mechanical

Chopped green corn is blown to the top of fifty-foot silos for cattle feed on this dairy farm.

paddles stir the milk as it chills in the large tanks. Large commercial tank trucks collect the milk every other day, including Sundays, and transport it to a processing plant.

Dairymen raise most of their cattle feed on the farm, planting and harvesting both corn and alfalfa. The church allows farmers to use steel-wheeled, self-propelled corn harvesters. Some of the larger harvesters have different cutting heads for various crops. The harvester cuts the stalks of corn, chops the stalks and ears together, and blows this mixture into a wagon trailing behind. At the barn the green mixture is blown into a seventy- or eighty-foot storage silo where it ferments into silage. Corn silage is a primary source of feed in the winter when cows are not grazing.

Alfalfa's high protein and productivity, and its ability to put nitrogen back into the soil, make it an important crop. Farmers cut alfalfa to make hay or haylage about four times each summer. Some farmers bale the alfalfa before it fully dries and roll it into huge round bales that are sealed to make high-moisture haylage.

Besides corn and alfalfa, farmers may raise barley, wheat, oats, other grains, and grasses. These provide feed for farm animals and extra income when sold for cash. To supplement homegrown crops, farmers buy protein or other supplements for cows, chickens, and hogs from commercial vendors.

The migration of Wengers to Yates County, New York, in the 1970s demonstrates how a new settlement can invigorate the local agricultural economy. In 1980 the county had 100 dairy farms but by 2003 it had 225 dairies, 90 percent of which were owned by Wengers. "They brought a contagious optimism for family farming here," said an extension agent, "and their success in farming helps to perpetuate their culture."[7] The Wengers in Yates County typically farm about one hundred acres. They have relatively small herds, 35 to 40 cows, compared with New York's statewide average of 125 cows. Alfalfa and timothy grass mixtures are raised for hay; corn is raised for silage and high moisture ear corn. Some small grains such as wheat and soybeans are raised, but no tobacco.[8] Situated in the largest wine grape county east of the Rockies, a few Wenger farmers in Yates County raise grapes for juice, wine, and table use.

Heifers, Tobacco, and Produce

Wengers also engage in other types of farming. Instead of milking cows, some farmers raise young heifers. One man explains, "I raise heifers until they're about half-grown, to about five hundred pounds.... Then I sell them to guys that raise them on up 'til they're ready to be milk cows. I usually raise twelve to fifteen heifers at a time." Other farmers raise beef cattle, hogs, and chickens for food or egg production.[9]

In the first half of the twentieth century, tobacco was the chief cash crop for most farmers in Lancaster County, regardless of their religious affiliation. A year-round crop whose cultivation and harvesting were never mechanized, tobacco provided a reliable source of cash and plenty of work for large families. Most important, it kept youth at home, away from the temptations of factory work. Tobacco's high per-acre income and year-round employment for the entire family made it an attractive crop. Tobacco was often called "a good mortgage lifter." One father explained that his sons "decided to raise it just to get out of debt." Tobacco is not grown in many settlements outside Lancaster County, however. One man experimented with a few stalks in New York State, but according to an observer, "we didn't have tobacco barns up here or a market for it."

The *Ordnung* counsels against raising and using tobacco, but it has never been a test of church membership. As late as 1975, some 80 to 90 percent of

Wenger farmers raised tobacco in Lancaster County. Yet by 2000, tobacco stalks were drying in less than 10 percent of Wenger barns.[10]

Why did tobacco raising decline? Church teaching against tobacco, poor prices, health concerns, and alternative sources of income for small farmers explain much of its demise. The senior bishop began preaching against growing tobacco in the late 1970s, citing his belief that it was wrong to grow it. Such sermons were a hard sell for some members, especially for young, struggling farmers, because tobacco was such a well-entrenched cash crop. The wise bishop did not threaten members with excommunication; he believed that gentle persuasion would be more effective. Poor prices added credibility to the bishop's advice. Over time, his counsel was heeded as more and more members stopped raising and smoking tobacco. Many farmers gradually began growing vegetables and other produce as an alternative to tobacco.

In settlements across the country, Wengers raise and sell produce such as watermelons, cantaloupes, tomatoes, sweet corn, and other vegetables. Instead of milking cows, one Lancaster farmer now grows spring onions, turnips, cantaloupes, and watermelons. In addition, he operates a small hardware store in his barn. An Indiana farmer hauls cantaloupes, tomatoes, and peppers on his horse-drawn wagon into the city of Elkhart and sells them in a Wal-Mart parking lot. He raises produce in the summer to keep his children busy, and he also fattens heifers, breeds dogs, and builds small wooden chairs for tourists.

Produce farmers often raise six to eight acres of vegetables alongside traditional crops like alfalfa or corn. Home-based greenhouses, in which flowers, vegetable plants, and vegetables—tomatoes, cucumbers, peppers, snap beans, squash—are grown, have sprouted in many settlements. In Yates County, the number of greenhouses more than quadrupled within seven years, increasing from ten to forty-three.[11] "The Mennonites," in the words of a county extension agent, "have been very innovative with their greenhouses. They grow tomatoes, cucumbers, and peppers—bred to be grown in water—in soil. They said, 'Let's try growing them in the soil' and it worked! They put a twelve-foot hoop over them and heat them in a raised bed. They are very successful and now the land grant universities are trying to catch up with the Old Order growers!"

The big story in small-scale farming is the development of some fifty produce auctions in Mennonite and Amish communities in the eastern United States since the mid-1980s. Many of these successful auctions have annual sales of several million dollars. Buyers from roadside markets, local grocery stores, and large chains purchase vegetables, flowers, and other produce

Many families have a roadside stand for supplemental income. Here, tobacco dries in the shed at the end of the lane.

that growers bring to the auctions on wagons, horse-drawn carts, or rented trucks two or three times each week. These new marketing ventures fit perfectly with the values of Wenger culture. The auctions support small labor-intensive farms that help keep large families working together at home.

In Lancaster County, several Wenger families helped start the Leola produce auction in 1984. On auction days, dozens of trucks and wagons arrive with cantaloupes, peppers, tomatoes, potatoes, flowers, and other produce. The Amish pull their loaded wagons with teams of horses; Wengers pull theirs with steel-wheeled tractors. Buyers from Philadelphia and other cities crowd a central platform as several auctioneers sell wagonloads of pumpkins, squash, watermelons, and corn as they slowly pass through the auction barn. A Wenger man whose sons raise cauliflower and sweet corn for the auction says, "A lot of these people quit growing tobacco and are now making a lot of money with produce." The prices fluctuate wildly, however. On one day, a dozen ears of sweet corn may sell for $2.00 and, on the next day, the same amount may sell for only $.50.

Similar auctions have sprung up in other settlements. In Elkhart, Indiana, Old Order Mennonites built a produce auction that operates Wednesdays and Fridays during the growing season. All the stockholders are Mennonites. The auction attracts produce buyers from as far away as Chicago, Indianapolis, and Detroit. A similar success story unfolded in Yates County, New York, where a wholesale auction was organized in 2001 to sell fresh fruits, vegetables, and flowers. The produce from some one hundred local growers attracts buyers from 150 miles away. Within four years, the annual sales of the Yates County auction exceeded $1.5 million.

An extension agent who assists the Yates County auction called it an "excellent marketing mechanism, an incredible achievement by the Mennonites." Moreover, he noted, "What is brilliant about the auction is that it can slowly grow in size as it attracts more and more buyers from roadside stands to supermarket chains." Auctions increase the number of small family farms but do not encourage large-scale farming. In the words of the agent, "The market does great things. It helps the small family farm market its labor without worrying about marketing. In the past, buyers would go from farm to farm searching for the lowest price and pitting the farmers against each other. Now the market pits the buyers against each other and it also raises the prices for farmers." In a glowing accolade, the agent concluded, "Old Order Mennonites and the Amish deserve the credit for creating these auctions across the country and it didn't take a university economist to figure it out!"[12]

Buying and Selling Farms

When a Wenger farmer decides to buy a farm, he faces the greatest financial challenge of his life. He cannot merely buy anywhere he pleases; he must consider his church, his family, land prices, climates, and the various Wenger settlements. For example, Iowa has good farmland, but no Wenger members lived there until a new community formed near Charles City, Iowa, in 1992. This attracted other families from as far away as Lancaster County, including a man who bought a one-hundred-acre farm for $90,000. Wenger lore is replete with stories about buying farms.

A Lancaster father explained how his son-in-law bought additional farmland in Wisconsin. The son-in-law owned a farm in Wisconsin adjacent to a fifty-five-acre farm with a nice barn and livable house. "An old man [who owned the adjacent farm] could hardly get around anymore. He wanted to move closer to his daughter in town and he came over to my son-in-law and asked, 'What would you give me for it?' Some evenings when my son-in-law was milking, the old man would come down and just beg for an offer until finally my son-in-law asked him, 'How much do you want?' He offered the fifty-five acres with buildings for $35,000, and my son-in-law finally bought it for $33,000."

Another farmer noted, "My father-in-law had ten children and they are all on farms. He bought five for his five sons and two for his daughters so he bought seven all together. He either bought the farms or borrowed the money for them. He had the first one [child] started by the time the second one was ready and could use the collateral from the first farm for the next one and so on."

Besides buying land, a new farmer must invest thousands of dollars in machinery. For fieldwork he needs not only tractors and wagons but a harvester, haybine, combine, disk harrow, plow, cultivator, and silage blower as well. A milking operation requires a bulk milk tank, a pipeline system, milking machines, and a barn-cleaning system.

Selling a farm and moving to a new settlement is a major decision that involves not only finances but also family and community ties. A Union County, Pennsylvania, farmer who sold his farm to move to Wisconsin explained, "You need one good buyer to buy your farm privately. But you need at least two if you sell on public auction." He had hoped for $275,000 when he placed his farm on the auction block, but when the bidding stalled at $205,000, he decided not to sell. Later he sold it privately and moved to southern Wisconsin, where he bought another farm.

When Wengers sell a farm, family and relatives usually, but not always, get the first chance to buy. One man who bought the family farm from his brother explained, "He never approached anybody else that I'm aware of. ... He wanted more money than he should have, but finally we talked about it. We decided we'd do it rather than having it sold on public auction. ... It's sort of a tradition that the family gets first chance. Of course, you have a free choice, but it's frowned upon a little if somebody sells it at auction." One woman noted, however, "It keeps the natives happier when we sell on public auction."

Passing on the Farm

Upon retirement, farm owners face a big decision: what to do with the family farm. A couple typically considers several questions. Should they sell the farm before they die or dispose of it in their will? If in their will, how should they divide the farm or its proceeds among their children? If they sell it, should they offer it on public auction or to their children? If one child buys the farm, how should the other children be compensated? The decisions they make carry major economic consequences in a place such as Lancaster County, where farms may sell for a million dollars or more.

Sell while living or place in will? Most farm owners carefully consider the fate of their farm to avoid family disputes after they die. One older man noted, "Some people don't have their plans made on how this should be handled and others say to their children, 'Well, I'll keep it as long as I live and then you do with it what you want.' Different people have different attitudes." One man sold his farm and buildings and divided the money equally between his three children, telling them, "If there's two cents left over, I want them thrown away, so there won't be any arguments!"

If conveyed by will, how should the farm be divided among children? Ideally, bequeathing the farm means dividing it equally, but this is rarely practical. Numerous children may want to farm. Typically, a farmer needs at least forty acres to support a family and, in most cases, dividing the land into several small farms would make each one too small to be a viable farm. For this reason, families usually convey modest-size farms to one child, often to the youngest son.

If sold while living, should the farm be sold at public auction or to children? Some farmers sell the farm at public auction; others sell it privately to their own children. One son explained that his father had sold him the family farm at a "family price," which allowed him to survive financially. "I could never have afforded it on public auction. This also saved my parents capital gains taxes. In a sense, I got more than the other children because I got the farm at a low market value." A teenage son who aspires to farm said, "My father helped my brothers a lot when they got set up [bought farms]. I would like to buy my father's farm some day, and I hope he will sell it to me at a lower price because of the high costs of farming."

One young man begged his father to sell him the farm for a family price of $85,000. The father, not ready to retire, finally sold him the farm but kept three acres to raise llamas, emus, and goats. After the son bought the farm, he left the Wenger Church and eventually quit farming. He offered to sell the farm to one of his brothers for $300,000, a price that grieved his aging father.

In this patriarchal society, land is typically passed on to sons rather than to daughters. One farmer has three young sons at home plus two already farming who live nearby and rent land. All five sons want the farm. In this case, the father will probably sell the farm to one son. He may favor a son who shows special interest in farming, or the youngest, who may be starting a family at the time the parents plan to retire. The parents may consider how much they have already helped other children and how well established they are in farming or business.

How should other children be compensated? If one child receives the farm at a family price, it usually comes with conditions. In a typical case, the parents may enjoy a lifetime right to remain in the farmhouse as long as they live and receive care from their son and his family. One fifty-five-year-old farmer says of his parents, "They had their 'liferight' here, living rent-free for the rest of their life. So, they didn't have to buy another property. Plus, I agreed I wouldn't sell the farm while my parents were living. Dad died seven years ago. After Mother dies, I could sell the farm, but it wouldn't be appreciated by the others [my siblings]." Sometimes, the purchase agreement may prohibit the sale of the farm for ten years or so and/or give siblings the first option to buy.

Parents typically try to find some way to compensate children who do not receive land. Unmarried siblings may have the right to live and work on the farm until they marry, may receive a lump sum cash payment, or may get part of the monthly mortgage payment. Such arrangements aid other siblings in setting up their own homesteads when they marry. In one family, the father owned two farms, and he gave one to each of his sons and gave gifts of money to his daughters to equalize the situation. The children accepted this arrangement, but as the farms increased in value, the sons could have sold them for much more than the daughters ever earned from savings.

Inheritance issues can be complicated by a variety of factors. For instance, a father may not be ready to retire when the first son marries. The father, as he is able, may help the first son buy a local farm or one in another state. Often, when the youngest son marries, the father is nearing retirement—giving the youngest the best opportunity to acquire the family farm. If a rebellious son leaves home and church, the parents might consider excluding him from any inheritance, but not necessarily, because Wengers are taught not to coerce children into membership. Married daughters are typically the beneficiaries of land or financial gifts from their husband's parents. Through these inheritance practices, Wengers seek, whenever possible, to pass land on to their children.

✠ COTTAGE INDUSTRIES

Despite the fact that virtually all Wengers will attest to how farming binds families together, it is only part of the occupational story. Some Wenger farmers supplement their income with woodworking or machinery repair. Others work full time in a shop or small business. Although many Wengers have abandoned farming, their commercial involvements are less extensive than those of the Amish. Typical Wenger businesses include roadside stands, cottage industries at home, manufacturing shops (machine and wood), mobile carpentry crews, and retail stores.[13] A network of small businesses and

Wenger retail stores sell hardware, books, fabrics, and household supplies.

stores keep many transactions within the Wenger world. These informal economic webs emerge naturally in a cohesive, small-scale society.

Some woodworkers make components for other manufacturers who complete the assembly. One furniture shop makes chair parts and ships them elsewhere for final assembly and finishing. A carpenter fabricates parts for carriages and supplies a Wenger carriage maker. Another Wenger man employs two other men in a woodworking shop that produces table legs and pedestals for Amish furniture companies. Wenger entrepreneurs have a sophisticated knowledge of the market. One shop owner, who describes his business as a "niche business," said, "When my niche disappears, I change niches." A woodshop owner garners a full income making traditional-style wooden rakes and pitchforks for the tourist market.

One entrepreneur buys and reconditions used woodworking machines. He also adapts electrical equipment for the Amish, who cannot use 110-volt electricity. For his Amish customers, he buys new electric-powered wood-

✣ TABLE 9 Types of small businesses

Auctioneer	Dry goods store	Painting
Bent and dent groceries	Electric supply	Produce auction
Bike shop	Farm supply	Sandblasting
Bookstore	Feed store	Sawmill
Bulk food store	Garden and farm supply	Sewing machine sales and repair
Buggy shop	Gift shop	Silo construction
Cabinet-making shop	Greenhouse	Small engine repair
Construction	Harness shop	Sign-making shop
Custom butchering	Machine shop	Tractor repair
Custom poultry dressing	Metal roofing	Woodworking

SOURCE: Horning et al. (2004) and J. B. Shirk (1998).

NOTE: Examples of Wenger businesses from a total of 108 in two settlements. There are often several businesses of the same type in a settlement. For example, there are eight greenhouses in these two settlements.

working machines, removes the electric motors, and modifies them for belt-driven or hydraulic power. In another service to the Amish, a Wenger shop uses $400,000 computer-operated machines to fabricate high-precision metal parts for Amish shops, which are not permitted to use programmable computer-controlled machines.[14] This state-of-the-art milling operation also provides services to many non-Amish customers. Wenger employees learn to operate the equipment through hands-on apprenticeships.

Another Wenger man has a woodworking factory with twelve employees. He started small but built up his business over thirty years. He had made buggy wheels, but he now specializes in bent and embossed wood parts, such as chair backs and buggy frames. He also produces special wood wingtip bows for Piper aircraft using hickory, ash, cherry, oak, and other woods. In addition to two sons in partnership, the factory employs eight Wengers and two Hornings. It operates assembly-line style at high volume.

In Kentucky, a Lancaster-born Wenger man operates a furniture shop that crafts fine products ranging from intricate bedroom furniture to jewelry boxes. The products from this shop can be found in Germany and St. Louis. The shop specializes in solid wood bedroom furniture. Practicing the Wenger ethic of integrity, the owner can only recall two customers over eleven years who were dissatisfied with the custom furniture they had ordered.[15]

Some Wenger people sell vegetables, breads, eggs, or honey at roadside stands. Some semi-retired men repair harnesses, build furniture, or sell veterinary supplies. One enterprising man in Indiana had an egg route. He bought eggs in the country near his farm home and sold them house-to-house in the town of Elkhart. In addition, he dressed chickens and sold them to grocery stores. These entrepreneurial activities sometimes grow into substantial businesses with several employees.

Cottage industries provide many social advantages. Some of the work can be done in seasons when farming slows down. Cottage industries allow family members to work in or near their home; children and youth often help in shops and stores. Other types of businesses offer less flexibility. Retail stores, for example, require a standard schedule of hours and greater interaction with the outside world. Manufacturing firms can get locked into production schedules that make it easy for business to eclipse family life and community involvements. The work of carpentry crews takes them away from home to non-Wenger environments, and the need to travel requires the daily use of vehicles.

The legal organization of businesses includes sole proprietorships, partnerships, and corporations. In some cases, depending on the type of work, "employees" are actually independent contractors. Many business owners do not provide employees with health insurance or a pension because the church and extended family cover those needs. In Pennsylvania, shop owners are exempt from paying Social Security or workers' compensation for Old Order employees.[16] Some shops have one or more outside employees who sometimes provide a vehicle or a cell phone for business use. Carpentry crews that travel to construction sites often have a non-Wenger crew member who drives them to and from the work sites each day.

The Wenger *Ordnung* places some restrictions on businesses. It counsels against involvements with Social Security, liability and fire insurance, unemployment, disability, retirement and accident insurance, and also against receiving workers' compensation, welfare payments, and food stamps. Although the *Ordnung* does not make these practices a test of membership, community social pressures discourage members from accepting government handouts and commercial insurance, which undercut the church's role in mutual aid and make members dependent on the outside world. These restrictions help keep shops on a smaller scale, one more in harmony with Wenger community values.

Domestic production at home and commercial production at other sites have different social consequences. Working on the family farm builds family-centered solidarity. Operating a retail business, by contrast, increases

Some farmers have a welding or woodworking shop on the farm for supplemental income.

interaction with the broader world; in fact, it requires contact for the survival of the business. One observer noted that the "Come In, We're Open" sign on the door of an Old Order business is a graphic denial of economic separation from the world.[17] When individuals conduct business outside the Wenger community, they become more entangled in the cultural values and social networks of the larger society.

This potential threat motivates many of the *Ordnung's* restrictions on business. For instance, in the 1970s, the church discouraged members from owning shops that bought and resold finished products for a profit without adding any value. The church did not want members simply buying and selling products to turn a profit without investing their own labor. The *Ordnung* specifically speaks against "buying and selling as daily business." This caution developed because cattle traders who could make a profit with little physical labor were often tempted to cheat. Explained one member, "Sin sticks harder in trading deals than a nail in a stone wall." More recently, the church has been more flexible with members in such occupations.

Some small cottage industries eventually grow larger. An Indiana couple started a dry goods shop in their home in 1976 with a $5,000 investment. By reinvesting their profits, they were able to build a large 2,500-square-foot store adjacent to their farmhouse. An entrepreneur in Union County, Pennsylvania, began building and repairing buggies for the Wenger community. Eventually his operation required five employees and now he not only serves Wengers but also builds and repairs fancy buggies for outside people.

One Wenger farmer started a business selling Bernina sewing machines. His son eventually took over the growing business, which now has outlets in several settlements. Dozens of new sewing machines fill the stores and others wait for repair for the customers, including many outsiders, who patronize the store. The owner of a woolen mill business buys raw, cleaned wool, cuts it into pieces, runs it through a machine to make it into batting, and then wraps it on a large roll. His son and daughter-in-law, who now operate the mill, supply customers seeking natural, organic wool from all over the United States.

❖ WOMEN AND BUSINESS

A few businesses are owned by women, but these shops tend to follow traditional gender lines. "Typical enterprises operated by women are roadside produce stands, dry goods and clothing stores, and some sewing shops," according to one woman. Other women have quilt or upholstery shops. In one case, a husband and wife own a store that sells shoes, dry goods, dishes, and kitchen items. Some women have produce or handicraft stands at public farmers' markets.

One of the largest enterprises operated by a Wenger woman and her family is the Amish Country Store near Penn Yan, New York. Operated by Weaver-View Farms, the shop, according to its promotional brochure, sells "useful old-fashioned wares and one-of-a-kind country gifts," quilts, jams, jellies, and small handicrafts. Trading on the Amish name, the shop promotes quilts made by Amish and Mennonite women as well as Amish-made furniture. This enterprise targets the tourist market in upstate New York with a Web site and an attractive brochure that proclaim its location as "minutes away from major hotels, resorts and wineries, and a scenic drive along Seneca Lake." The Web site, developed and hosted by a third party, promotes the venture but notes that the shop does not accept online orders because "we spend our time making quilts." The Web site text also explains that the products are "made by Amish and Mennonite families in the eastern USA, many at kitchen tables or in old wood shops. Your purchase helps many families work together in an uplifting, nurturing environment. . . . And yes, your order faithfully rides to the post office in our horse-drawn buggy."[18]

Most enterprises owned by Wenger women are small, local operations. The percent of Wenger women who operate businesses is much lower than in Amish society, where as many as 20 percent of the businesses are owned and operated by women.[19] The reason for the difference, in the mind of one leader, is that "so many more Wengers than Amish are engaged in farming and the whole family needs to help with the farm work." A young Wenger woman explains,

Amish women are more aggressive. They go to market stands more. They go out of their homes and make money more. Amish women are raised that way. Wengers focus more on raising our children and raising them right. That is more important than getting into business because getting into business can detract from family. The Amish do more things away from home. They go to the beach more, to cabins in mountains, run here, run there, and work outside home more. Wenger women stay at home more.

For whatever reason, the bulk of Wenger businesses are operated by men.

These two women operate a small quilt shop.

✦ WAGE LABOR

For Wengers, working at home on the farm is typically the most desirable occupation. Working on another Wenger farm ranks next, followed by working for wages in a Wenger-owned business. Working for wages in an outside business is least attractive. Because of high land prices, however, more Wengers, especially in Lancaster County, are turning to wage labor to support their families.

Day labor employment can take various forms. One farmer who formerly raised tobacco, for example, stopped doing so after the church counseled against it. He still farms thirty acres of land, in addition to working almost full time on an outside carpentry crew. He does most of his farming in the evenings and on Saturdays, taking an occasional day off from carpentry when farm work is urgent. In order to continue his farming, he declined an offer to supervise the carpentry crew. In another case, a father and two sons run a dairy operation on their farm, but the sons also work for an outside construction contractor who transports them to work each day.

Because they have only an eighth-grade education, Wengers, especially women, lack opportunities for high-paying work outside the community. One Wenger woman has been employed in a shirt factory for fifteen years. Her daughter worked there for eighteen years, interspersed with teaching in a Wenger school. Employees of the factory get a ten-minute break in the morning and afternoon, and a half hour for lunch. They work from 7:00 A.M. to 3:30 P.M. and are paid by their rate of productivity rather than an hourly wage.

Wage labor is the most capitalistic type of labor, because an individual's labor becomes a commodity exchanged for money and shrinks to one dimension, the economic value of his or her work. Most Wenger people would probably agree with an Amishman who said, "The lunch box is the greatest threat to our community." When a farmer packs a lunch each day and leaves his family for a wage-labor job, his family life suffers. The modern wage system and consumption patterns, which focus on the individual as the primary economic unit, threaten traditional Wenger values. Individually produced income undermines the collective economic role of the extended family. For this reason, Wenger people actively promote a collective, family-based economy. For example, families, not corporations, own and operate most businesses and farms. A wage-based economy *individualizes* the worker, transforms marriage roles and child-rearing patterns, and undermines community solidarity. Working on a Wenger farm in the thick web of extended family provides the best preparation for community life.

Young people are increasingly being pulled from farm work and cottage industries that directly contribute to the family economy to work for outsiders who pay an individual hourly wage. Wage labor from English employers also poses other dangers. Outside employment, in Wenger eyes, may lead youth away from their birthright community. Daily work that immerses Wengers in a "worldly" peer group outside the community is dangerous because it cultivates relationships that may dilute the influence of the church.

✛ STAYING SMALL AND FAMILY-CENTERED

Wenger culture favors small-scale operations and fears large ones.[20] The church urges members to limit the size of their businesses and to resist entanglements with outside corporations and the government. Business owners are encouraged to hire Plain people and to keep their enterprises modest. The *Ordnung* counsels against "luxuries" of any type, thus stifling incentives

A family transplants onion seedlings. Labor-intensive produce farms fit the value system of Wenger society.

for expansion just to display wealth conspicuously or hoard it beyond the needs of subsistence.

One father in Indiana chided his son for trying to build his business too big and too quickly: "He lost money because he had too many people working for him, and too many accidents." The father also noted that when children take over a business they often try to build it too big. Many church members criticize larger businesses as too "factory-like," and as anti-family, because they threaten traditional community values—simplicity, humility, and small-scale living. Church leaders and members, by and large, want small-scale social units, which means human-scale, face-to-face interactions with others who live in networks of faith, economics, and kinship. Unlike the virtual reality of mass media and the Internet, these deep relationships form the rich interpersonal weavings in the tapestry of Wenger social life.

Limits on technology help curb the size of farming operations. The church fears that large operations would place too much wealth and influence in the hands of one person and might weaken the viability of small family-centered farms. Moreover, large-scale technology would take jobs from Mennonite youth and push them into outside occupations. Large tractors and self-propelled harvesters are "testified against" by leaders but are not a test of membership. Farmers, in the words of one leader, are urged to "be satisfied to remain more ordinary and to use their horses more," despite the fact that few of them own draft horses for farming anymore.

Small-scale farming operations are affirmed by the *Ordnung*, which restricts the size and nature of dairy equipment. A dairy farmer may not use electronic feeding systems or computers for dairy operations. The *Ordnung* forbids automatic feeders specifically, in its words, "to control the size of herds." One farmer explains, "We try to stay with the smaller equipment, a little bit less modern. A tractor is the same way. I don't think there is anybody in our area that has a new tractor. In this day and age, we try to stay with the tractors that might be twenty or thirty years old already. They're a lot easier to fix than these modern ones." Even though tractors are permitted in the field, some Wengers still use horses for pulling a garden cultivator or a manure spreader.

One farmer said, "Most of us have fifty- to one-hundred-acre farms. There is no church rule on a specific limit, but admonitions and other factors limit the size of farms. If they were three hundred acres, you couldn't buy one for each of your four sons!" In addition, he explained,

> The other factors that help to keep the farm small are your expectations. You grow up expecting to have a small farm. You look around and hope to have an eighty-acre well-managed farm. You don't expect to have a big farm. Anyone trying to buy a three-hundred-acre farm would be strongly advised against it. Also, the cost of it is a restriction. Further, with small farms we have more flexibility to go to barn raisings, to weddings, to auctions, funerals, and so forth.

For most Wenger people, farming is not primarily a commercial venture; it is a total way of life that serves social as well as economic ends, an enshrined way of life sacralized by religious belief and tradition. "Using the tractor in the field has helped us start new settlements," according to one farmer.

> Our farm technology helps young people to want to farm. You need to have a middle ground so that young people will want to farm. If my son has to pull weeds by hand all day in the hot sun, he will hate it. If he can work the land in a small tractor he will like it. The child needs to like to farm. We need a sufficient level of technology

so that it is satisfying to farm but not so much that it ruins our small-farm way of life.

Above all else, the Wenger community wants to preserve the small-farm way of life. A small-farm way of life means a rural setting, somewhat isolated from the intrusions of contemporary society. It is a family- and community-centered way of life, one that supports a communal economy where family members work together for the common good. Small businesses, especially home-based ones, are acceptable as long as they do not dominate the Wenger economy, but the small family farm remains the occupation of choice. Wengers believe that the rural, small-farm setting is the best nursery for their children, the best way to preserve their religious values, and the best assurance of the future success of their community in a postmodern world. Indeed, that is why hundreds of Wenger families, at considerable inconvenience and cost, fled their homeland in eastern Pennsylvania for refuge in the hinterlands of eight other states.

Although Wengers prize rural, small-farm living, they are not a social museum. Technological advancements and the tentacles of modernity have touched their sectarian enclaves. In Chapter 8, we describe the dynamics of change in Wenger society.

Technology and Social Change

The Internet just doesn't fit our Plain way of life—it's too hard to control.

—WENGER SHOP OWNER

The Wengers may be the guardians of old Mennonite traditions, but they are not a static, fossilized culture. They are constantly changing in response to external and internal forces. Ever cautious about change, any change, the Wengers try to brake its speed. They constantly struggle with what to accept and what to reject. As one leader explained, "As things change, we must be realistic and change too." There are many pressures to adopt new technology as well as other cultural and religious practices. Despite their cautions, the Wengers have made many changes in the twentieth century—including how they set their clocks.

Time, the mother metaphor of cultural change, slows down in Old Order communities. Perceptions of time tick more slowly in Old Order life: their world is regulated by the seasons and the weather as well as the slow pace of singing in Sunday services.

When the United States adopted daylight saving time, the Wengers did not adjust their clocks, preferring the traditional rhythms of "God's order." Tampering with time—especially speeding it up—seemed out of character for a slow-moving Old Order community. Indeed, keeping time by "God's clock," as they always had done, was a convenient way for Wengers to separate themselves from the fast-paced, hyperactive outside world. As more Wengers became involved in business and other outside activities, however, it became increasingly difficult to juggle their lives in two time zones. One member confessed, "It became a big, confusing mess." Since the 1970s, objections to daylight saving time were gradually dropped by all but a handful of families. Illustrating the resistance of religious ritual to change, the fall ministers' conference and the October communions still begin on eastern standard time.[1] This resistance suggests that conference and communion are some of the most sacred moments of Wenger religion.

Many new forms of technology have challenged Wenger sensibilities and induced change in recent decades. Despite their aversion to some forms of technology, the Wengers are not Luddites.[2] They do not categorically dismiss technology or consider it inherently immoral. They view it as a neutral force that can, depending on its use, impair their community or strengthen it. Rather than condemning all technology, the Wengers adopt and use it selectively, ever cautious about its long-term impact on their community. One shop owner said, "Technical things are not wrong; we just choose not to have them. We watch out for items that would change our way of life and culture in a revolutionary way. We have an identity and if we blunder it will be the end of our culture as we know it. We now have a blending of old family values and some conveniences that are helpful to our way of life." According to one shop owner, "The two things that help us make decisions are the abuse of new technology by some people and foresight about where it will lead."

The question of how a new form of technology will enhance or hurt the welfare of the community hovers over many debates about change. Where will it lead? Will it take us a step closer to the world? Will it lead our young people astray? These and related questions guide how the Wengers screen technology. Looking out for the welfare of the community sometimes means shifting into reverse. "Sometimes a thing is accepted by the church and then we see a problem on the horizon and we just have to cut it off," said a carpenter.

Many technological distinctions drawn by the Wengers may appear silly or trivial to outsiders. Some practices seem like a time warp that stretches across a century of social change. A leader with an eighth-grade education drives a horse and carriage but scans the small screen of a handheld language translator for the English equivalent of a German word. An atomic clock with a large digital screen keeps microscopic time in a home without a radio, television, computer, or air conditioner. A businessman drives his horse-drawn carriage to his machine shop, where computerized equipment spins out high-tech valves and fittings. Such leapfrogging across technological worlds appears baffling at first glance, but beneath the surface, within the context of Wenger history, a coherent cultural logic clarifies why a handheld translator is acceptable and a computer is not, or why a digital atomic clock is welcomed but not a car.

The process of social change involves the delicate work of moving cultural fences without tearing them down. These adjustable fences have both practical and symbolic consequences. A taboo on automatic feeders limits the size of dairy herds, but it also sets Wengers apart from outside farmers. Many of the cultural fences, especially clothing, distinguish Wengers from outsiders as well as from other groups of Mennonites and Amish. As one bishop explained, "Not everything is wrong with these forbidden things, but we can't distinguish ourselves from the world without them." In other words, the cultural restrictions have moral and practical consequences in Wenger life, and they also fortify the lines of separation from mainstream culture.

The Wengers accepted many changes in the course of the twentieth century. Farmers began milking their cows with automatic milkers and plowing their fields with tractors. A band of rubber appeared on carriage wheels—a transition that one bishop called a "very hot issue." Electrical appliances became common in most homes. Despite the numerous changes in recent decades, the Wengers have drawn a firm line of resistance in the cultural sand on certain issues.

✣ TELEPHONES AND ELECTRICITY

In 1907, Bishop Jonas Martin reluctantly agreed to permit members to have telephones in order to avoid another church split on the heels of the traumatic division of 1893. The acceptance of phones did not extend to ministers, however. Thus, when the Wengers formed in 1927, the telephone was not a contentious issue because the church had spoken to it twenty years earlier, and some families already had telephones. Yet the issue resurfaced when Indiana bishop John W. Martin came to Lancaster County to ordain Joseph O. Wenger bishop in September 1927. As noted in Chapter 3, Martin did not permit telephones and electricity in the Old Order churches in Indiana, and he urged the newly formed Wenger Church to disallow both items for ministers and to counsel lay members strongly against them. According to one historian, "The telephone and electric were already here in Lancaster, but our church leaders decided to restrict them for ministers out of courtesy to the Indiana people." According to one older minister, "They [the telephone and electricity] were talked against a lot in counsel meetings." Several members, in fact, remember lay people who, out of courtesy and conviction, removed their telephones and/or cut their electric lines after 1927.[3]

Thus, in the first half of the twentieth century, in deference to the counsels of the church, many families did not tap electricity from public utility lines or install telephones. Installing public electricity or a telephone violated the principle of separation from the world and increased dependence on the larger society. The telephone provided easy access to the outside world. One historian recalled that "the debates over telephones were more heated" than those over electricity because the telephones provided more connection with the outside world.[4] Some leaders worried that electricity would open the door to a multitude of unnecessary conveniences—not to mention radio and, later, television. These factors stifled the acceptance of electricity and telephones, although they were never a litmus test of membership.

Both telephone and public utility electricity were gradually adopted in the 1960s and later. A few members had tapped into electricity earlier, in the 1930s and 1940s, but often just for lights in the house or in the barn. One farmer remembers that some families used electricity in the barn but not in the house or vice versa, "depending on the husband's or wife's thinking." Migrations to other states in the 1970s accelerated the acceptance of the telephone. In the words of a bishop, "Groffdale Conference adopted the telephone as an evil necessity because so many of us have families in other states." One parent said, "There's one thing we like with the telephone. We keep in contact with our children [in other states] once a week or so to find out how they're doing." By 2002, most families had telephones in their houses and were using electricity from public utility lines.

A few elderly Wengers still have not electrified their homes. One minister remembers that his parents had a gas refrigerator with an icebox when he was young, but no electricity. When they began using electricity for lights and a refrigerator, their electric bill was $5 per month. Today, a son living in

Wenger kitchens are not ultramodern, but they do have some electrical appliances. This family processes grape juice together.

the same home pays $200 per month for electricity for his dairy operation. One older couple still uses the same propane lamps that they bought forty-six years ago when they first married. Another member illuminates his home with hanging Coleman lanterns, and rather than using an electric water pump, he has a small water wheel in a nearby stream to propel levers and cables that power a manual pump. Water runs slowly out of the kitchen sink spigot into a pitcher. One Wenger minister has no electricity in his home, but he uses an electric generator in his shop to power his woodworking tools. These traditional practices are rare residues from a bygone age in Wenger life.

The most intense discussions over telephones and electricity focused on ministers. For years the church said that lay members could have electricity, but it expected ministers to uphold the old taboos. In midcentury, as electricity was coming into more homes, ministers were still expected to shun it—and even to tear it out of their homes when they were ordained. Some exceptions to the electricity rule were allowed. One minister's wife could not breathe well without air conditioning, so the bishop allowed the family to run an electric line into her bedroom. The church made another exception for a newly ordained minister when his bank required an electrical system until his mortgage was paid. In the early 1990s, two young ministers were asked to remove their electrical connections and refit their barns when they were ordained. As a consequence, one of them had to build a gigantic loft above his barn to hold fifty batteries to power his electric milking equipment. Another, at great expense, converted all the tools in his workshop from electric to hydraulic power. These cases and others added pressure to relax the long-standing taboo on electricity for ministers.

Finally, in the fall of 1993, a newly ordained minister refused to take the electrical service out of his home because, in his words, "I never promised not to use it." Some ordained leaders wanted to force him to either take it out or resign. Another newly ordained leader was a farmer with electric milking equipment in his barn. These new ministers did not remove their public electricity, and the church took no action against them. Delicately sidestepping the issue, conference leaders did not bring it to a vote, which permitted the newly ordained to keep electricity by default and opened the door for other ministers.[5] Deacon John M. Martin was so upset by this decision that he left the Groffdale Conference in 1993 and formed his own group (see Diagram 8).

Many of the younger ministers across the church soon installed phones and public utility electricity, but not some of the older ones. A few bishops installed phones but did not list their numbers in the local church directory, out of respect for tradition. By 1995, 87 percent of all Lancaster County Wenger households had a telephone, and by 2003 most ministers and bishops did as well.[6]

CHANGE AT HOME

The interior and exterior of Wenger homes have also undergone cultural renovations in the twentieth century. Because their culture changed slowly, many middle-aged Wengers have memories of more traditional household technology in their homes than their non-Wenger contemporaries. One woman recalled, "My mother had a wood cookstove, a dumbwaiter to lower food into the cellar to keep it cool, and an icebox." Although this older household technology was typical of many American homes in the first decades of the twentieth century, it lingered much longer in Wenger homes.

Although they span a spectrum from traditional farmhouses to modern-looking ranch houses, Wenger homes today share some distinctions. One of those is practicality. Said one mother, "There are really no specific [church]

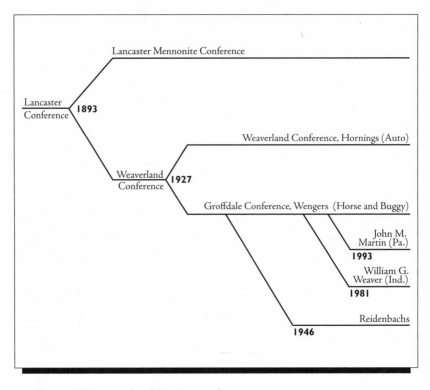

Lancaster Mennonite Conference

Lancaster
Conference **1893**

Weaverland Conference, Hornings (Auto)

Weaverland
Conference **1927**

Groffdale Conference, Wengers (Horse and Buggy)

John M.
Martin (Pa.)
1993

William G.
Weaver (Ind.)
1981

Reidenbachs
1946

DIAGRAM 8   Wenger-related Mennonite divisions, 1893–1993

restrictions on stoves, freezers, refrigerators. No restrictions on wall-to-wall carpeting. Practicality has the upper hand. We need linoleum on floors to keep them clean because of our large families." Some families have modest wall-to-wall carpeting in living rooms and bedrooms, but floors in the large kitchens and living areas typically have washable coverings.

Many homes do not have the latest appliances, even though they are not officially restricted. Very few homes, for example, have automatic dishwashers or air conditioners. "Ministers admonish us not to get newer, modern kitchen gadgets," said one homemaker. Nevertheless, many families have purchased automatic washers and electric dryers partly, said one woman, because "it's hard to find wringer washers anymore." The automatic washers "came in over the last twenty years," said one mother. "The ministers used to admonish against them, but they don't mention them anymore."

By 1960, outhouses had yielded to simple but modern indoor bathrooms in most Wenger homes. Electric stoves and refrigerators are common to-

Young men share a meal after a service project. A non-Wenger visitor is on the left.

day, as are appliances such as blenders and state-of-the-art KitchenAid mixers. One mother with eleven children under nineteen years of age sings the praises of her KitchenAid mixer because, as she says, "I can make bread dough with it. We used to have an old electric mixer with two beaters, but that was nothing compared to these new ones." More and more families are also installing microwave ovens.

Despite the adoption of some newer appliances, many Wenger women have reservations about them (or at least use them sparingly). With an ample number of children to help with dishwashing, many families see such an appliance not only as extravagant but as stealing work from children. Moreover, said one grandmother, "A dishwasher takes too much time to stack, wash, and rinse the dishes, and then unstack them again. It's faster just to wash them in the sink." Women who have electric dryers often hang their clothes outside in the fresh air when the weather permits. Some homemakers use old-fashioned wringer washers alongside automatic ones. They use a wringer washer, according to one mother, because "it's faster, uses much less water, and washes dirty pants much cleaner and better." The automatic washer is then used to spin out the excess water so that the wet clothes dry faster. Although air conditioners are not taboo, "they are frowned upon," said one woman. "Very few people have them and those that do typically have window units for a bedroom."

Wenger homes have a distinctive décor inside and out. Many have wood paneling on the lower half of the walls in the kitchen and living area. Green blinds are typical in most homes. "The ministers," in the words of one woman, "admonish against drapes. No fancy curtains and drapes. We get strong admonitions against these. We are to stay with dark blinds, and dark green ones." But "most people have a few plain curtains," said another mother. Regardless of the specifics, what is most important for the sake of ethnic identity is that Wengers can identify the style of a "Wenger house."

Explaining what is distinctive about the exterior of a Wenger house, a young father said, "Most of us don't have false shutters on the outside because they are expensive and just for looks." His wife added, "Outsiders do not have as many flower beds and gardens. Wenger women and children love flowers and gardens. There is less landscaping on our lawns. Our landscaping is not as extensive, but we do have raised flower beds." Describing a grand old farmhouse that has lovely landscaping and a large A-frame addition for a family room, a member said, "There are a handful of these fancy ones, but that is the only A-frame with a vaulted ceiling in our community."

⊹ FAX MACHINES, PAGERS, AND CELL PHONES

Although telephones have long been accepted by the Wengers, fax machines, pagers, and cell phones have been on various forms of probation. Members pay attention to technology. When asked how many people have fax machines in his settlement, one member, without hesitation, said, "three." In April 2004, the Groffdale Conference approved the use of fax machines after admonishing against them for about fifteen years. Unable to use computers, business owners claimed that fax machines were a necessity for their operations. Caught between the advice of the church and the needs of their business, over the years some shop owners had purchased a fax machine and then "gave it as a gift to an [English] neighbor, with no strings attached except that the shop owner could use it," according to one carpenter.

One member explained the caution of the church: "We had phones and copiers. So the fax is a mix of those, but you could fax pornography. Some worried about the slippery slope. If you allow everything, then you might end up on the bottom. But the world slips faster and makes more technological advances and so we are always on behind." Another member observed, "We held off on this [the fax machine] long enough to see that it won't bring any other things into our home that we don't want." Although the screening process took about fifteen years, church leaders were finally comfortable that the fax was safe. When asked about the decision, one bishop admitted that he could not explain what a fax is, had never seen one, and was "confused about how they work." Nevertheless he was confident that the conference had made a good decision.

In the late 1990s, the use of beepers stirred considerable controversy. Some members had them because they were members of local volunteer fire companies. After first banning all pagers, the conference, in a surprising move, rescinded its action and divided pagers into two categories: digital and voice. Digital ones were acceptable, but voice pagers were not permitted, except that members of local fire companies could have voice pagers to hear the location of fires. The frequency of the pagers, however, could only be set for the local fire company. "They are not allowed on any outside clothing and must be hidden in a pocket so they don't become an object of pride," said one member, "because all the young men want to wear them to show off." [7] Digital voiceless pagers were permitted for members involved in business, enabling their employees or clients to call the pager and wait for a return call. Many Wenger businesspeople carry these digital pagers.

Although standard phones are permitted in houses and shops, the church forbids cordless phones, cell phones, and answering machines. Voice mail provided by the telephone company and caller ID are permitted. One member explained the evolution of the cell phone taboo: "When cordless phones came out, there were many concerns and the church said 'no' to them. Then later when cell phones came, the rule [taboo] was extended to them as well." One member recalled that the cell phone was "restricted in the fall 2003 conference. They [leaders] made the wording more restrictive on the cell phone. No cordless phones, no answering machines, but it's ok to have multiple phone lines. They don't want cordless because we try to limit the phone for business, not pleasure. When it's connected to a line it controls mobility." A shop owner explains that the taboo on cell phones is "because there is computer technology in the cell phone. Mini game boards, radios, and cameras now come in the cell phone." There is additional cultural logic behind the cell phone prohibition, though. "It's the slippery slope principle," said one shop owner. "One thing leads to another and soon you fall into a pit."

Despite the *Ordnung* ruling against cell phones, many businesspeople have access to them through a variety of means. "Some Wengers," said one shop owner, "seem to have one of their customer's cell phones all the time." A conscientious businessman on a trip to New York used his customer's cell phone and "felt very bad about it." Some Wenger contractors have a non-Wenger employee who provides a cell phone on a daily basis with expenses paid by the business owner. To most church leaders, using it and owning it are identical. "The use of cell phones owned by others," thinks one member, "will likely come to a test and conference will have to decide." Although no cell phones are to be owned by members, one person said, "Some games go on, some people have a neighbor own the cell phone." Another member admitted, "A few cell phones may be owned on the sly. We don't have a police force that goes around checking for phones. But word on the street will eventually point to someone."

A minister explained that people "who work away from home in construction, can use one [a cell phone], but not at home for their own purposes. If someone has a cell phone for their own use, it's not allowed." An ordained leader who opposed making the cell phone a test of membership said, "Why not just earnestly testify against it? But the other ministers didn't want it that way." A senior leader, recognizing that more and more communication is wireless, worried, "What will we do when the country takes down all the telephone lines?" A lay member is less worried about the future. "If there are no longer landlines, then we might be in a corner. But never underestimate the speed of technology. If landlines are dead, we'll come up with something!"

✥ TABOOS ON TELEVISION AND VIDEO

The automobile and television are the two most salient symbols of worldliness and modernity in the Wenger mind. Both provide connections to the outside world; both reflect a spirit of individualism; and both represent cultural values that are antithetical to Wenger life. Despite the fact that Wenger beginnings sprang from their rejection of the car, their opposition to television runs even deeper than their objection to the car. Ownership of motor vehicles is forbidden, but not their use. Yet even the use of television in a faraway motel room can induce guilt—but that is getting ahead of our story.

Like many other Old Order groups, the Wengers restrict media technologies that would beam outside values into the minds of members and children. Radio and television are strictly forbidden, as are citizen band radios and monitors, record players, tape players, video cameras, and CD and DVD players. Such devices are viewed as instruments of cultural contamination: they would expose members to foreign values that mock the ways of humility and the bedrock beliefs of Wenger life.

Apart from newspapers, the line of resistance to mass media is firm. For Wengers, radio and television—especially television—would connect their homes to a cultural sewer filled with immorality and violence flowing from Hollywood. Unlike some religious groups who use electronic media to promote their religious views, for the non-proselytizing Wengers, mass media is a one-way channel that would flood their living rooms with alien images, sounds, and values. Radio is less objectionable than television because it does not have images, but radio has always been forbidden—a test of church membership. One Wenger man was annoyed when some Wenger boys, working for an outside contractor, listened to a radio while remodeling the member's farmhouse: "Some of the boys had a radio playing in the house while they worked. I was offended. I decided I had to talk to them about it, and they turned it off."

The cultural content of much media represents many of the things the Wenger Church opposes—pride, vanity, materialism, violence, infidelity, explicit sex, and individualism. To them, it would be foolish to pump such cultural garbage into their homes. The home is a sacred place for rearing and nurturing children in the fear of the Lord. It is the place for family prayer and devotion. It is the incubator of Wenger beliefs and convictions, a refuge from the tempest of the outside world. To open this sacred abode to the forces of modernity transmitted by mass media would be downright foolish in Wenger eyes. A woman explained, "Television isn't wrong in itself, there are some educational programs, but we don't allow it so the children, especially teens, don't drift into the world."

For all these reasons, the Wengers staunchly oppose television and similar media. Beyond having little practical or useful value, mass media present an obvious and real danger to their entire way of life. Video and television are not topics of debate; their danger is obvious and clear. The taboo against such media is so strong that some members feel guilty watching even a few minutes of television.

One member, traveling away from home, stayed overnight in a motel room and turned on the television. After watching for three minutes, he turned it off. Nevertheless, he felt condemned and confessed his guilt to church leaders. Others have had similar experiences. At one preparatory service, a bishop reported that two families had apologized for watching television in a motel while on vacation. On the other hand, a retired minister, attending to the needs of a sick English neighbor, frequently watched the progress of a hurricane on his neighbor's television. Weather reports on television fall into a different moral category, however, than prime-time shows.

Beyond concerns about cultural values and separation from the world, a deeper issue undergirds Wenger opposition to electronic media: television, computer, and video images decontextualize social reality. Virtual reality floats between fabricated sites on television screens and computer monitors. Digital images portray a host of fleeting realities. For Wengers, social reality is anchored in a local geographic community, a community woven together by a web of face-to-face relationships. These authentic, trustworthy relationships reflect different realities than the fleeting virtual images that flicker across the screens of postmodern life.

⚜ COMPUTERS AND THE INTERNET

The taboo on television, in fact, sealed the fate of the computer among the Wengers. Discussions about computers typically point to similarities between computer monitors and television screens and note that the acceptance of computers would likely lead to the acceptance of television. In any event, computers are forbidden—at least those with monitors.

"We couldn't rule out all computers completely," a bishop noted, "because digital clocks and calculators are widely used and they have computers in them. But we don't want the large personal computers with screens." Another bishop explained, "The conference made a decision on computers. We may have them [word processors] for record keeping. This helps the business owners. There are also small computers in watches and in hay balers. So we made a rule now that we can have computers if they do not have three things—a modem, a screen [monitor], or a keyboard. Word processors are OK if they do not have a big screen [monitor] on them," but the leader confided that he had never seen a word processor.[8] Thus, in the bishop's mind, the microchip technology used to operate a calculator or word processor was acceptable—but not computers with a monitor or Internet capacity.

In 1996, the Groffdale Conference forbade personal computers with monitors for fear they would lead to television and video games. Any computer that has a separate monitor or the capacity for Internet hookup is forbidden. "The Internet just doesn't fit our Plain way of life—it's too hard to control," said one leader. "It makes it too easy to let worldly entertainment and pornography come into our homes." The church prohibited computers capable of being hooked up to the Internet based on the biblical command, "Be not unequally yoked together with unbelievers" [11 Cor. 6:14]. One member says, "Some of our people studied the Internet closely, and decided we shouldn't allow it." A member who subscribed to Prodigy, an Internet service, says, "I wouldn't do it again; it doesn't go along with our way of life."

In the mind of a layman, "There is a firm rule: No electronic gimmickry that you can go online with. We cannot have a computer with a monitor or even a laptop if it has a provision to hook up to the Internet. A Palm Pilot would be OK as long as you cannot hook it up to the Internet." Handheld electronic dictionaries and language translators, digital scales, calculators, and word processors are accepted. "The limit," explained one person, "is that things should not have big keyboards." Wenger people question computers because, as one man said, "you can bring in so much with them." The computer brings the world into the home, and for a separated, redemptive community, such a device is a toxic threat to its health.

Many businesses use word processors. One shop owner has a word processor with a software package to track his inventory and a fifteen-inch black-and-white monitor. He would like to have more computer power, but since computers are off-limits, he says, "That's OK; I'm not getting anything else. Computers don't fit in with our way of life." Another business owner observed that "word processors are not really very techy and the church never spoke to them. Most of us are farmers and don't need one."

Computer technology is used selectively in some areas. Small manufacturing shops are permitted to have CNC (computer numerical control) machines for repetitive production tasks.[9] These machines have a computer that can be programmed to repeat high-precision tasks in machine or cabinet shops, dramatically increasing speed and efficiency. Some businesses hire an outside third-party vendor to provide Web site services for advertising and selling products. The use of Web sites is not generally accepted, and one leader thinks that the ministers' conference will eventually rule against it.

Another leader confessed, "It's hard to say something about computers when we're ignorant of them, but computers are everywhere." To illustrate, he pointed to his pocket watch with a quartz movement, a small spelling corrector, and a handheld language translator, all using microchips. Church leaders struggle to understand the new technology. Decisions about computers, explained a member, "evolved over a ten-year period, and came to a head in the mid-1990s. When the Internet came along, it led to a final rejection and we lost some members over it." Confessed one ordained leader, "I would have accepted the computer, but not the modem, because businesspeople need them, but the other leaders said no."

The church prohibited the use of large monitors on computers to prevent the display of objectionable images, but not all members welcomed the decision. One leader said, "Some business owners were upset by our conference decision to rule out the computer. They needed them to order supplies and track their parts. There are much worse things on the telephone. You can call 800 numbers and talk with bad women and all kinds of pornography." Despite such protests, most members fully support the church's firm opposition to standard personal computers. Some members use computers in public libraries for business and educational purposes—a practice the church has not discouraged.

✣ THEOLOGICAL SHIFTS

Assurance of Salvation

Not all the changes in Wenger culture relate to technology. Deeper theological shifts, more difficult to detect, are under also way. The deep disposition of *Gelassenheit* that shapes the Wenger worldview not only tempers individualism but also cautions against making overly confident statements about salvation and eternal life. A simple theology of humility is willing to leave eternal outcomes in the hands of God's providence. Unlike modern evangelicals, Wengers are reluctant to make bold statements about the assurance of salvation. Claims of assurance of salvation are deemed to be downright haughty, cocky, and arrogant—the stuff of pride. Wengers fear highly emotional expressions of faith because subjective declarations shift authority from the church to the individual, who in the worst case becomes his or her own arbiter of truth. For a community that upholds the church as its ultimate source of faith and authority, individual claims, coated with emotional passion, are suspect.

Historically, the Wengers have steered clear not only of revival meetings and evangelistic programs but also of the born-again label of evangelicalism, which to Wenger ears sounds like pride and self-confident individualism. "Twenty years ago," said one member, "'born again' was a dirty word, but now it's become more okay." Other members agree that the phrase has become more widely spoken in recent years. The growing use of the born-again identity reveals a greater openness to heartfelt conversion, but it also signals an incipient and increasing individualism that focuses more on personal experience.

Individual pronouncements of "once saved, always saved" are often dismissed as expressions of pride and arrogance. Nevertheless, one member noted, "Assurance of salvation is not a test of membership." A minister explained that "twice the Bible says, 'He that endureth to the end shall be saved.' We think about salvation in the future tense, not the present." He continued, "'Once saved, always saved' does happen one day, at the Day of Judgment. And if we are truly born again, we are in a humble state."

"Born again" may increasingly be on Wenger lips, but it is not the arrogant, self-confident "born again" of some modern fundamentalists. In the Wenger context, "born again" emphasizes endurance to the end, humility, and ultimate salvation in the future, at the Day of Judgment. Although the term has a different slant than it does in the evangelical mainstream, this new language nevertheless reflects an underlying shift in the Wengers' worldview and their understanding of the role of the individual versus the church. But born-again language is still used very cautiously. A group of adults in the privacy of their home might sing, "I'm saved, I'm saved, I know I'm saved," said one member, "but they'd never do it publicly because it's frowned upon."

Rules or Personal Experience

The changes in Wenger society have focused a dilemma for some members. What is the source of their salvation: faithful practice or a personal faith experience? Surely they would argue for a combination of both, but changes in recent years have pulled these views apart a bit. On the one hand, the church emphasizes the importance of following its rules, reviewed by the conference twice a year and presented to members in the preparatory services. The rules matter because they define the moral order of Wenger society, the path of Christian discipleship. Yet increasingly, some Wengers are using born-again language and speaking more about the importance of a personal faith experience, which elevates individual experience. The sentiments of *Gelassenheit* are loath to make bold claims of salvation based on individual experience.

While the rules of the *Ordnung* are a test of membership, one member said, "The rules don't save us. We have a saying from Isaiah [64:6] that 'our own righteousness [just following the rules] is like a soiled garment.'" Nevertheless, Wengers emphasize the "fruits of repentance," meaning that a conversion experience should produce behavioral changes that conform to the *Ordnung*. Moreover, members are taught to "live by the Sermon on the Mount, Matthew 5, 6, 7 and do no evil to anyone."[10] Yet, when explaining why the *Ordnung* is not printed and distributed to members, a leader said, "We don't want people to be picky about the *Ordnung*. We don't want them to think

Wenger boys, serving with Mennonite Disaster Service, repair the roof of a hurricane-damaged home in Texas.

they are saved by it. Our salvation is not in the rules; they are safeguards only." The *Ordnung* explicitly says, "External ceremonies *alone* cannot save anyone." External ceremonies include the church's regulations for daily living. Saying that external ceremonies *alone* cannot save implies, however, that they do save at least partially—but that in and of themselves they are not enough.

Some members worry that young people join the church because of social pressure rather than because they have made a clear personal choice. "It's their own decision," said one parent, "but many get baptized at seventeen when they begin going with the young folks." If youth are making a sincere, heartfelt adult decision to join the church, why do they make the same decision at the same time? In addition to peer pressure, the church adds its own incentive for church membership—romance. By strongly encouraging youth to be baptized before they begin dating, church leaders are also encouraging same-age baptism. Early baptism in many ways serves as a mode of social control to bring youth into the church before they begin dating or exploring the outside world. Once they are inside the fold, the church is better able to control youth by reminding them of their vows, made on their knees, to follow the teachings of the church.

The tension between practicing the rules of the *Ordnung* and seeing salvation as a gift of God is a real one in Wenger life. To demean the rules or consider them unnecessary undercuts the entire web of practices that distinguishes Wenger life and marks its boundaries with other groups. Leaders want members to experience a heartfelt conversion, but they worry that too much emphasis on personal experience will speed the drift toward more assimilated Mennonite groups that use typical evangelical language and emotional expressions of religious experience.

One woman explained, "Salvation is a gift from God and we don't need the *Ordnung* to assist God in saving us. However, the *Ordnung* is a boundary, a fence that protects us from doing and having things that would hurt us spiritually." Said another member, "We believe that God offers assurance of salvation, but we don't accept the Calvinist idea of once saved, always saved, unconditional eternal security. We don't deny the importance of faith as opposed to works, but we believe that faith produces works as it says in Matthew 7:20; 'by their fruit you shall know them.'"

⁜ OUTREACH

The new religious language also underlies a growing interest in outreach and service activities. Mission work is not encouraged, but many members support the distribution of material aid for international relief and service agencies such as Christian Aid Ministries (CAM) and the Mennonite Central Committee (MCC). One farmer said, "We think we should help poor people, but we should do it from here, not go to Africa to do it. The MCC meat canner came here [Penn Yan, New York] this spring for the first time in the renovated produce auction building.[11] It was here for two days and operated from 5:00 A.M. to 10:00 P.M. and we had forty people helping in each shift, including some Amish and Hornings." Underscoring the same trend, another member said, "Our people contribute much more to CAM then they used to, much more in recent years. We contribute to CAM and are unified on it, none are against it. We help MCC and CAM much more than we did twenty years ago."

Many Wengers also serve in short-term (one-week to two-week) volunteer assignments with Mennonite Disaster Service (MDS), an inter-Mennonite agency which coordinates cleanup and rebuilding efforts in communities devastated by natural disasters. Typically traveling in large vans, they clean up debris after fires, floods, hurricanes, and tornadoes, repair damaged homes, and build new ones. Over a twelve-month span in 2004 and 2005, dozens of Wenger volunteers worked on cleanup projects in Alabama, California, Florida, Louisiana, Mississippi, Tennessee, and Texas. One MDS co-ordinator said that interest in volunteering "has really increased since 1995. I used to have to make a lot of calls to get volunteers. Now as soon as a hurricane hits, people call me asking when they can go. This year [2005] I could only send a third of those who wanted to go." Most of the volunteers are eighteen to twenty-four years old, and for many it is an opportunity not only to serve the larger society but also to see some of it for the first time.

The new interest in outreach and service as well as the cautious use of born-again language discloses a shifting worldview that is more open to individual expression, personal religious experience, and the needs of the larger world. The confidence expressed by this new language reflects a slight erosion of *Gelassenheit*—slight at this moment, at least.

The Big Question

At stake is the very future and identity of Wenger society. A shift toward a more individualistic, experiential language of faith may move authority from the church to subjective feelings and erode commitments to distinctive Wenger practices of dress, technology, and lifestyle.[12] Yet leaders want members to make a sincere personal commitment of faith that expresses itself in daily fruits of righteousness, not "works of righteousness that merely comply in robotic fashion to the *Ordnung*." The underlying issue is one of authority. Does it reside in the collective decisions of the redemptive community or in the personal, subjective experience of an individual?

For the time being, the Wengers have resolved this dilemma by emphasizing "the fruits of repentance." The fruits, in the context of the Wenger community, mean following the rules of the *Ordnung* and steering clear of things that are earnestly "testified against." Humility, the age-old Mennonite virtue, mediates the tension. As one bishop explained, "When we are born again, we are in a humble state, like a little child." Individuals can be born again and talk about personal salvation as long as they remain humble, expressing a humility of spirit that is open to guidance from the church and is willing to practice the fruits of repentance prescribed by the *Ordnung*. But it is a delicate tension. If humility is lost amid the babble of born-again personal experience, the enthusiasts will demean the rules as simply human-made regulations unnecessary for eternal salvation, thus undermining Wenger commitments to church loyalty and conference authority. On the other hand, if Wenger leaders downplay personal experience with heavy-handed dictates, members may leave and join other nearby churches that enthusiastically champion personal experience, have fewer rules, and also offer the incentive of a car. The traditional threads of humility maintain the delicate balance, but the strands are somewhat fragile.

⚜ PRESSURE FOR CHANGE

A variety of forces prod changes in Wenger society. Economic interests propel some of the changes. Farmers want to expand herds, automate feeding operations, and buy bigger equipment to increase production and spike profits in a tight farm economy. Business owners hanker after computers and Internet service to order parts and supplies as well as to sell their products. They sometimes press the limits on cell phones and other technology to enhance productivity and compete with outside businesses. Homemakers want larger, more efficient mixers for making many loaves of bread.

In addition to productivity, sheer convenience also propels social change. In the words of one bishop, "Whenever you deal with these new things, you are dealing with human nature." Despite their commitments to humility and simplicity, the Wengers appreciate the convenience of a copy machine, a vacuum sweeper, and an air conditioner.

Government regulations also induce change. Sanitation requirements for dairies and child labor restrictions in shops alter traditional social habits. Statewide environmental regulations impact farming practices as well as safety standards in shops. Even views toward raising and using tobacco are prodded by outside forces. One minister asked, "Now that the government is making such a fuss against tobacco, how can we be a beacon of light on a hill?" In the mind of this leader, public health concerns and low market prices were as persuasive as religious convictions in reducing the longtime tradition of farming tobacco. External forces, then—political, economic, and cultural—are significant sources of social change.

The availability of new technology in retail stores—from roller blades to atomic clocks—also invites change. The Wengers adopt some new technology without hesitation as long as it does not compromise separation from the world or rupture their community. Greater involvement in outside organizations also induces change. Serving in local volunteer fire companies, for example, created a need for voice beepers, which prompted controversy and eventually a small change in the *Ordnung*.

As noted earlier, many members credit the proliferation of new settlements as a reason for the rapid adoption of the telephone. The expansion of

Wenger churches into other states also challenges the authority of a centralized church structure that for many years found uniform regulations easy to enforce with a small number of churches in Lancaster County under the tutelage of one bishop. Different conditions in each community will make it more difficult to achieve uniformity across some two dozen settlements. Fire company beepers, an issue in one area, were a nonissue in other settlements where Wengers were not serving as volunteer firefighters.

Senior leaders play an influential role in initiating, permitting, or obstructing change. One longtime leader is credited with reducing tobacco raising, permitting ministers to use electricity, and hindering the use of computers. Personality factors and interpersonal relationships among the leaders also influence the process of revising the *Ordnung* that governs community life.

Church leaders worry that rapid change will ruin the church. One bishop compared social change to a hole in a dike: "If a small hole develops in it, the water will eventually flood everything." The leader went on to explain that regulating social change is difficult when it comes to things like computers, because "you can make a dummy out of yourself if you don't know what you're talking about." The Wengers make intentional choices about technology, judging the latest gadgets not merely by the yardstick of efficiency but also by their potential to strengthen or threaten the redemptive community.[13]

✣ BLENDING RULES AND COUNSELS

The formal regulations of the church fall into two categories: *rules* and *counsels*. The distinction is crucial to understanding the process of social change. The *Ordnung* consists of the rules of the church, which specify what is firmly forbidden—a test of membership. The counsels focus on the objects and activities that church leaders discourage and counsel against, but violations of the counsels will not commence the process of excommunication. Serving in the military and owning a snowmobile, for example, are violations of the *Ordnung*, and if unconfessed, they could trigger excommunication. Going to a bowling alley or having an accordion, though earnestly counseled against, is not a test of membership.

Objects and activities that church leaders want to ban completely are placed in the rules; those that they want to discourage, but are willing to tolerate, fall under the counsels. Reflecting the counsel of their people, leaders can regulate the process of social change across the church by addressing an issue with a rule or a counsel. Cell phones, at first counseled against, eventually became forbidden. Raising and using tobacco, a longtime custom in the Wenger community, was counseled against in the 1980s and 1990s by leaders. But it was never forbidden, said one leader, "because the senior bishop was afraid that making it a rule would split the church." Judiciously determining if something should be forbidden or just frowned upon enables leaders to manage social change. "Lay members give counsel to the ministry," explained one person, "and then the ministers' conference reflects the main themes back to the districts as formal counsels. We don't have a dictatorial ministry running things."

The process of social change may begin in several ways. A new practice may gradually enter Wenger life with little fanfare, if it appears harmless to the well-being of the community. Other practices may stir discussion but never reach the agenda of the ministers' conference. Practices that threaten Wenger values, however, will likely be discussed at local counsel meetings and again at conference. At this point, leaders may decide not to act, thus permitting the practice to slip into place by default. Alternatively, they may decide to testify against it or to forbid the practice outright.

If an item is counseled against, leaders put the practice on probation, in essence. Some items stay on probation for many years and some are eventually forbidden. Sometimes, but rarely, a taboo, such as the one on fax machines, is dropped completely. "Making a rule is much easier than changing one," said a member. "It is very rare to have one changed. The fax machine rule is the only one in my lifetime that was changed." When the *Ordnung* is read in the preparatory service, the list of forbidden practices is always read first, followed by the list of activities counseled against. "Everyone listens very carefully," said one member, "when the bishop reads the *Ordnung*."

The rate of social change is regulated by the "understandings" of the *Ordnung* as well as by the example of ordained leaders who cling to old traditions. By complying with the old ways for a long time, the ministers keep traditional practices visible as a moral virtue, which helps slow the rate of change. Some lay members, more conservative than the ministers, also contribute to this conserving influence. By keeping the older traditions in full sight, the leaders discourage lay members from quickly adopting new technology. Due to the leadership lag, a change that might otherwise have occurred rapidly may instead be stretched over several decades. For example, lay members gradually began placing rubber tires on their buggies in the mid-1970s, and one person estimated that by the mid-1990s, 80 to 90 percent of the lay members—but hardly any of the ministers—had rubber-wheeled carriages.

Rubber is not forbidden by the *Ordnung*, "it's just understood that the ministry should not have it," said one bishop.

⁜ WHO DRAWS THE LINE?

The ordained leaders, meeting in conference, largely shape the moral order of Wenger society. Although decisions may come to closure in conference, the discernment process occurs constantly as lay members discuss issues informally throughout the year. Percolating issues are discussed during family visits, barn raisings, auctions, and quilting parties. At the fall and spring counsel meetings, lay members voice their concerns to the ministers in their local churchhouse. One member noted, "This is your opportunity to speak up or forever hold your peace. If you don't say anything about an issue at this point, you have no right to say anything later." Another member explained, "Our bishop says, 'Today is your day to express yourself and share your counsel.'"

After gathering the concerns of their people, the ordained leaders from all the settlements gather for the one-day ministers' conference. This national meeting provides a forum for deciding how the church should respond to any issues that are brewing. Sometimes there are no pressing issues; at other times, several may surface at once.

The process of discerning a direction on an issue leans heavily on seniority, based not on age but on the length of time a leader has held a particular office. One leader explained, "When we gather, each bishop gets a chance to speak on the *Ordnung* and any changes he thinks are necessary. We begin with the [bishops] longest in office first, then go to the senior minister and end up with the last ordained deacon." After everyone has had a chance to speak, a second round of conversation seeks discernment and direction. "We start with the senior bishop. He gives his opinion and then the other bishops give theirs." On many issues the senior bishop tries to discern the majority opinion and states it as a direction, in the hopes his fellow bishops and ministers will endorse it. "Sometimes," said one leader, "we have a question-and-answer time after the bishops give their opinion." A formal vote is not taken, but often, "the senior bishop proposes a solution and his authority brings the argument to an end. This is harder to do today with so many bishops." Binding conference decisions require the bishops' unanimous support.

Despite their personal convictions and divergent views in their local districts, the leaders seek solutions that reflect the sentiment of all the ministers and serve the welfare of the church as a whole. Individual bishops may disagree with a decision, yet they are obliged to support all the decisions of the conference. As noted above, one bishop would have preferred to accept computers without modems rather than to ban them completely, as the conference ruled, but he complied with the collective wisdom of the conference.

The senior bishop carries enormous authority in the conference meetings. Conference leaders will not consider meeting outside Lancaster County as long as a retired senior bishop, sidelined by old age, is still living. Why does the church defer so much to an elderly retired bishop? "He just has a way about him," explained a lay member. "He is self-confident, but always humble. He never makes enemies by being blunt; he is really a great statesman."[14]

After the ministers' conference decides the direction for all the issues, the rules and counsels are read by each bishop at the local preparatory services prior to communion. This is the moment when the rank-and-file members learn the outcome of the discussions that have been floating around the community for weeks before the conference. The power and authority to regulate social change rests with the ordained leaders, especially the bishops gathered in conference. Lay members do not vote to ratify the proposed actions of the ministers' conference. There is no congregational autonomy or local business meetings to discern moral direction.

Although members can voice concerns to the ministry in the counsel meeting and at other times, final decisions rest on the shoulders of the ordained leaders meeting in conference. Moreover, authority lies in the collective action of the conference, not in an individual bishop. If a bishop refuses to enforce an action of the conference, local ministers and lay members can bypass their bishop and appeal directly to the conference leaders. Contrary to conference action, one bishop, for example, wanted to forbid the use of tobacco and belting wheels on tractors. The ministers and members of his church, resisting his strict interpretation, appealed directly to the conference leaders, who supported them. Again, despite a bishop's personal view, he is obligated to uphold the rules of the conference.

The actions of the ministers' conference, year after year, make sense in light of Wenger history and the pressures of the moment. Yet some decisions may look odd to outsiders who do not understand the larger stream of Wenger history. Aware of this, a farmer explained that the regulations of the church are similar to a story he read about "an old shop building that was made up of additions that were tacked on as needs arose over the years. That's not how we would build a new shop today if we started from scratch. But that's like the *Ordnung* of our church. We've made little adaptations along the way to protect it from harm and different things and this is how it ended up."

A Wenger-owned hardware store. Involvement in retail stores and other nonfarm work leads to more frequent interactions with the larger world.

✣ STEPPING TOWARD THE WORLD

Ordained officials worry that too much change, too fast, will send them down the tracks of assimilation. "The train starts off ever so gradually," said one bishop, "and it gains speed slowly until it picks up more speed and then it gains and gains and gains." The list of forbidden amusements grows as new forms of entertainment bring ever more temptations. Referring to the customary reading of the *Ordnung* at the preparatory service, one leader said, "It takes twice as long to read the *Ordnung* in church today as when I was young."

Changes in the larger society and new patterns of interaction with the outside world continually require the church to reassess its relation to the dominant culture. Will changes help safeguard the church, or will they lead to new forms of worldliness that will undermine separation from the world and bring the demise of the church? Some things are nonnegotiable, in the mind of one farmer: "We might allow rubber tires on a tractor some time in the future, or a cell phone, but something like divorce and remarriage, they're never negotiable. We want our children to have a happy childhood, and to

✤ TABLE 10 The drift from Old Order ways to mainstream Christianity

There is a way that seemeth right unto a man, but the end thereof is the way of death.
—*Proverbs 14:12*

From Old Order		To mainstream
	Teaching	
Emphasis on humility		Emphasis on self-esteem
Emphasis on the fruits of faith		Emphasis on faith alone
Accountability to the church		Accountability to God alone
Outward appearance		Inner experience
God of judgment		God of mercy
Obedience		Tolerance
Separation		Reaching out
	Attitude	
Self-denial		Self-acceptance
Accountability		Independence
Humility		Self-esteem
Submission		Self-exaltation
	Physical appearance	
Tradition		Fashion
Modesty		Adornment
Formal		Casual
Concealing		Revealing

SOURCE: Abbreviated version of a diagram developed by a Wenger member.

learn to work hard." For this member, family and hard work are two fixed, nonnegotiable values.

One member diagrammed a twenty-five-step process that leads away from Old Order traditions toward "mainstream Christianity."[15] The steps of this transformation, in the mind of this Old Order writer, appear in Table 10. The first twelve steps ascend toward a pinnacle of "evangelism and missions," and then turn sharply downward in a twelve-step decline that ends in the mainstream of Protestantism—the bottom of the slippery slope in Wenger eyes. Proverbs 14:12, "There is a way that seemeth right unto a man, but the end thereof is the way of death," heads the table. The basic argument is that although mission activities may appear to be a desirable and tempting goal, they lead to a downward path that ends in mainstream Protestantism.

The small steps toward missions, in the Old Order mind, include an emphasis on individual experience, self-esteem, greater use of English, assurance of salvation, moving off the farm, automobiles, Bible school, Sunday school, and revival meetings. These activities culminate in aggressive evangelism and mission activities, which then lead downward to educated ministers, higher education, entertaining worship, fashionable dress, sports, worldly activities, worldly jobs, larger businesses, an emphasis on "free grace," television, small families, and less time in prayer—the final step on the slippery slope to mainstream religion. The author suggests that the changes occur in three areas: teaching (theological content), attitude, and physical appearance.

He summarizes the progression this way: "This is a path that many individuals, families, and church groups have taken and continue to take: leaving the Old Order, reaching a spiritual high, and then drifting toward mainstream American society. At first, they embrace teachings on love, mercy, grace, forbearance and independence, but then neglect the teachings on obedience, submission, accountability, humility, self-denial, and separation. This change of emphasis often takes them away from a simple, disciplined lifestyle with close family ties, to the fast, undisciplined lifestyle of modern society where adultery, divorce and remarriage, broken homes, lawsuits, and unwanted and neglected children are commonplace." This succinct statement shows remarkable analytic insight into the process of assimilation from an Old Order perspective.

Whether the issue is a technological or cultural practice, the Wenger Church seeks to manage social change so that it can avoid assimilation into the cultural mainstream and thus preserve the integrity of Old Order life. The complex process requires the wisdom to understand how a particular practice is embedded in a network of issues that may trigger other changes. Ironically, a traditional community such as the Wengers engages in a process of selective modernization—an informal mode of rational, strategic planning—to protect its traditional way of life. This process of selective modernization requires deliberate decision making to discern which aspects of modern life to accept and which ones to spurn. Such discernment is a delicate challenge for Wenger pilgrims in a rapidly changing world.

Is there any place for humility in a postmodern world? How do the Wengers negotiate the surprises of a virtual society? We explore these questions in Chapter 9, after discussing how the Wengers navigate their way through the world of other Plain groups.

Pilgrims in a Postmodern World

Live in humility as strangers and pilgrims . . . separated
from the world.

—WENGER *ORDNUNG*

❖ SOCIAL FIELDS

Wenger pilgrims navigate their journey in two different
social worlds: the world of Old Order religious communities and the emerging world of postmodern society. Group
behavior never occurs in a social vacuum, but in a dynamic
field of crisscrossing social forces—akin to a game of soccer, where behavior, oriented toward the other team, constantly shifts throughout the course of the game.[1] Yet with
multiple teams in the Old Order world, intergroup relations become more complicated than a simple soccer game
ever would be. Intergroup relations invariably change as
social life unfolds.

Wenger leaders monitor the position of their redemptive community vis-à-vis other religious groups as well as

the changing trajectory of the larger world.[2] Social comparisons are always relative and shaped by the ethnocentric perspective of each group, but they produce perceptions that generate meaning and identity. The Wengers play on a religious field where the action focuses on other faith communities, and as we have seen, they also play on the larger, postmodern social field.

The Wengers function in three religious worlds: the Old Order world; the larger Anabaptist world, which includes assimilated Mennonite groups that share the Wengers' theological heritage; and the *Kircheleut* world of High Church Catholics, Lutherans, Presbyterians, and others who worship in sanctuaries with altars, stained-glass windows, and steeples. Because of their memories of persecution in Europe, the Wengers see themselves as more distant from churches in the High Church world. This is not a deep-seated historical grudge, but an awareness that humble people, worshiping in simple churchhouses, have a profoundly different view of the church and its relation to the larger world.

When some scholars write about Old Order groups, they compare them with "mainstream" Anabaptist churches, implying that the culturally as-similated groups represent the authentic version of Anabaptism. The main-stream label sidelines Old Order expressions of Anabaptism, suggesting that they are less important and less relevant than those of the more pro-gressive groups. If mainstream is used in a quantitative sense to refer to size of membership, it may be an appropriate label if the assimilated groups are the numerical majority. Even if the numerical meaning is accurate, however, the implicit bias of word mainstream suggests that larger groups offer a more important, more authentic representation of Anabaptism—one that has most faithfully preserved the historical forms of Swiss Anabaptism, at least as they developed in North America. Things appear quite different from the Old Order perspective, which sees assimilated groups as the ones that have drifted *away* from the Anabaptist mainstream into the whirlpools of worldliness. Out of sensitivity to these issues, we have used the term as-similated, rather than mainstream, to refer to groups actively participating in the larger society.

We begin the comparative analysis by exploring the Wengers' relation-ship with religious communities *within* the Anabaptist world.[3] One Wenger farmer placed the Old Orders on "the bottom rung, the lower end of the ladder." The Wengers might be on the lower end of the religious ladder in Lancaster County, but they are not on the bottom rung. Several other groups espouse more traditional practices than the Wengers. We have fo-cused on five groups that shape Wenger self-understanding: the Stauffers, the Reidenbachs, the Amish, the Hornings, and the Lancaster Conference Mennonites from whom the Old Orders originated in 1893.[4] The first three groups, like the Wengers, speak Pennsylvania German in family and church life. The Hornings and the Lancaster Conference members no longer use the dialect. We begin with the most traditional group: the Stauffers.

⚜ THE STAUFFERS

Nicknamed the "Pikers" for the location of their first churchhouse (along an old turnpike), the Stauffers left the Lancaster Conference in 1845, nearly fifty years before the Old Order division in 1893. Thus, although the Wengers share historical roots with the Pikers, the Wengers have more direct church and family ties with the Reidenbachs and the Hornings. Generalizations about Stauffer practice are complicated by the fact that they have one large group as well as several smaller subgroups. Our description focuses on the larger fellowship, known as the Jacob Stauffer group.[5]

Because of their early departure from the Lancaster Conference, the Stauffers have preserved many of the early nineteenth-century Mennonite ritual practices related to church life. They live among Wengers in Lancaster County, so the Stauffers are a frequent point of comparison. On the one hand, the Stauffers provide convenient examples of conservative rigidity that make the Wenger approach to social change appear more pliable and, in Wenger eyes, more reasonable. The comparison can be turned on its head, of course, to show how worldly the Wengers have become in contrast to the tenacious traditionalism of the Stauffers.

The general design of Stauffer churchhouses is similar to that of Wenger churchhouses, but Stauffer men sit on the left and the women on the right, facing the preachers' bench. The Stauffers sing from the same German songbook as the Wengers, but at a somewhat slower pace and using a smaller repertoire of tunes. At their ordination, Stauffer ministers and deacons kneel to receive their charge, whereas among the Wengers, only bishops kneel. And the Stauffers have more formal and firmer practices of shunning excommunicated members. Stauffer youth have traditionally engaged in more rowdy behavior and join the church after marriage. In recent years, though, most have become baptized at a younger age.

The Stauffers dress more plainly than the Wengers. In addition to larger bonnets and head coverings, Stauffer girls wear black tie strings on their coverings; Wenger women have white tie strings until a few years after they are married. Stauffer women also tie the strings much more tightly, closer to the chin. Women wear an older-style, more pointed cape over their stark plain dresses, which are made either from solid color fabrics or those with very small prints. Compared with the Wengers, Stauffer men wear hats with wider brims and have longer hair, which is combed front and parted in the middle.

Unlike the Wengers, the Stauffers shun electricity and telephones in their homes, but they do use propane gas for heating, cooking, and refrigeration. On the farm, instead of tractors for fieldwork, Stauffers use motorized horse-drawn machinery. They use air- and hydraulic-powered tools in their shops. Using and raising tobacco is not frowned upon by the Stauffer Church. Cars, of course, are completely banned. Stauffer carriages are more traditional than those driven by Wengers. They have no windows, no battery-powered headlights, no rubber tires, and no flashing red lights on the back like the Wenger carriages.

Despite their differences, some Stauffer children attend one-room schools operated by the Wengers or Amish. Living side by side in Lancaster County, the Stauffers provide a ready and convenient point of comparison by which the Wengers chart their speed of cultural change.

❖ THE REIDENBACHS

The Reidenbachs, who broke off from the Wengers in 1946, are similar to them in some practices.[6] During World War II, the Wengers debated whether their young men should participate in Civilian Public Service (CPS)—an alternative to military service for conscientious objectors. The most traditional-minded Wengers opposed sending their young men to CPS projects, which were administered by more assimilated Mennonite groups, because the youth would be exposed not only to the larger society but to more progressive Mennonite youth as well.[7] These and other issues led some traditionalist Wengers to form the Reidenbach Church in 1946.[8] In addition to their objections to CPS, the Reidenbachs opposed participation in the food rationing program during the war and also thought the Wenger Church had adopted too much modern technology.

Nicknamed the "Thirty-fivers,"[9] the Reidenbachs have now splintered into numerous subgroups, some of which are small family clans. Reidenbach groups have four churchhouses in Pennsylvania. In Kentucky, Missouri, and Pennsylvania, a number of extended family groups meet in homes for ser-

Stauffer Mennonites prepare their fields for planting. Horses in the field and a windmill indicate that this is a Stauffer farm.

vices. Numbering only about three hundred members, the Reidenbachs are much more exclusive theologically than the Wengers. The Reidenbachs see their church as the only true church of God and, unlike the Wengers, they practice a strict form of shunning.

As Wenger practices changed during the last half of the twentieth century, the Reidenbachs continued a very traditional lifestyle. In their homes, they prohibit telephones and public utility electricity, although most of them do have water under pressure and flush toilets. Some, but not all, of them use propane gas for refrigeration, cooking, and heating.

On the farm, the Reidenbachs use horse-drawn equipment to harvest crops. Field corn is husked by hand, for example, and many farmers bring dry hay to the barn in loose piles rather than baling it. The Reidenbachs do not have large dairy herds but operate small family farms with a few cows, some steers, and chickens. Some families grow produce for sale at roadside stands and public produce auctions, and a few own small woodworking shops.

Reidenbach buggies are similar to Wenger buggies, except that they do not have rubber tires. Reidenbach clothing styles are similar to Wenger styles and are even less restrictive in several areas. The Reidenbachs severely limit formal interaction with outsiders, prohibiting hunting and fishing licenses, for example. In all of these ways and others, the Reidenbachs lag conspicuously behind the Wengers. Despite these differences, however, the Reidenbachs, like the Stauffers, cooperate with the Wengers on schooling.

✣ THE AMISH

Unlike the Stauffers and Reidenbachs, who are clearly behind the Wengers on the Old Order playing field, the Amish provide a complicated point of comparison with the Wengers—ahead of them in some areas, behind them in others. Because Amish practices developed separately after 1693, they do not correspond as directly with Wenger practices as do those of other Old Order Mennonite groups. Still, the Amish and the Wengers share some practices and they certainly share an Old Order worldview.

Surface Distinctions
A long-standing springtime tradition at farm auctions is corner ball. This barnyard game, played by two teams of six players, provides hours of free entertainment for the hundreds of spectators who flock to auctions. In Lancaster County, where Wengers and Amish mingle, the game often pits Wenger teams against Amish teams. This playful ritual reminds players and spectators alike of the two larger teams—Wenger and Amish—that play on the contested cultural fields of Lancaster County.

Wengers do not have a direct historical connection to the Amish apart from their European Anabaptist lineage prior to 1693, when the Amish and Mennonites parted ways. Outsiders often confuse the Wengers and the Amish, because at first blush, they look similar. There are many commonalities, but on the Old Order playing field, many differences flourish as well.

The Wengers and the Lancaster Amish both drive horse-drawn carriages, send their children to one-room private schools, speak the Pennsylvania German dialect, and follow the 1632 Dordrecht Confession. They also share an Old Order Anabaptist worldview and select lay ministers from within their congregations. Apart from their church directories and the education publications of Schoolaid, the Wengers do not print any periodicals of their own, but many subscribe to Amish publications—*Die Botschaft, Family Life, Young Companion,* and *Blackboard Bulletin*—and also contribute letters and essays to them. The Wengers and Amish cooperate in the areas of schooling, government relations, and other projects such as Whispering Hope, an Old Order home for emotionally disturbed people. All of these commonalities create a shared consciousness of kindred kind—an Old Order Anabaptist kinship—even though the Wengers and the Amish have no formal organizational ties.

Despite their historical religious lineage, many differences mark the two communities. Wengers wear shirts and dresses with fine prints in contrast to the more distinctive solid-color fabrics of the Amish, which create a sharper "ethnic profile" for that group, according to one Wenger man. Unlike Amish men, Wenger men do not wear beards. Wenger carriages are black with small side windows, while Amish carriages are gray. This difference identifies Amish and Wengers on public roadways in the Lancaster area. Wengers gather to worship in churchhouses, whereas the Amish meet in their homes. Unlike the Amish, the Wengers have electricity and telephones in their homes, barns, and shops, and they use tractors in their fields. Finally, the Wengers ride bicycles, which are not typical among the Amish of Lancaster County.

Church Structure

Deeper differences, not obvious on first sight, also abound. A major one is church polity. The Wenger ministers' conference creates a more uniform *Ordnung* and more centralized authority than is the case among the loosely networked Amish congregations. The small Amish districts, with twenty-five to thirty-five families each, have more autonomy than the larger Wenger congregations. Each Amish bishop, overseeing one or two districts, has some flexibility to interpret the Amish *Ordnung*. With some 150 congregations, the Lancaster-area Amish have approximately seventy-five bishops, in marked contrast to the two Wenger bishops who preside over ten large Wenger congregations in Lancaster County.[9]

The entire Wenger Church has only thirteen active bishops for forty-nine church districts in nine states. Moreover, the rules of the Wenger *Ordnung*, crafted at the ministers' conference, cover all Wenger churches in every state, a uniformity unparalleled among the Amish. Among the Wengers, clothing style, churchhouse design, and use of technology is virtually identical from Missouri to New York. Indeed, it is the uniform *Ordnung* and central conference structure that, in the eyes of one Wenger leader, have prevented any new Wenger settlements from failing since 1927. Among the Wengers, regional differences are carried to the conference where "they get settled," according to one member. On rare occasions, a local Amish congregation

Wenger and Amish parents interact at an end-of-the-year school picnic. Dress styles identify their church affiliations.

facing severe internal dissension might postpone communion until the issue is resolved. "That could never happen among us," explained one Wenger. "Our whole church, every single congregation, would have to postpone it because peace must be reached as a whole; postponing communion is simply unheard of." The difference in communion practice underscores the stronger autonomy of individual Amish congregations.

The conference structure reflects a theological worldview that is more centralized and formal than the more organic and flexible Amish approach. "The Amish," said one Wenger, "use the rules of their church differently than we do. They try to work around them to get something. An Amish shop owner might sell the majority (51 percent) share of his company to an English person to get a truck or computer. We [Wengers] can be in partnership but can't use forbidden equipment. We strive harder [than the Amish] to have the rules make sense and to follow them consistently."

The more informal, decentralized Amish style, with more leaders interpreting the *Ordnung*, leads to greater variation among Amish congregations—a variation that appears inconsistent to some Wengers. A Wenger woman pointed out with annoyance that some Amish women "just wear a bandanna on their heads when they work outside and don't always wear their capes or aprons when they work around the house. Some put up Christmas lights," and others reportedly "even have electric in their house." "Some of us call them 'hickory Amish,'" said one member, "because they bend like a hickory stick." Another Wenger retorted, "We have some 'hickory people' in our church too and when we point our finger at others we are just being self-righteous and holding ourselves higher than others, which is wrong."

Although the Wengers readily admit that inconsistencies abound among their people as well, they do emphasize a more literal and formal approach to Scripture. Some Wenger ministers use an electronic dictionary/translator to search for the English meaning of a German Bible verse. Both groups discourage small-group Bible study, because such study could promote new interpretations that might challenge long-standing beliefs. The centralized structure of the Wenger Church makes it easier to promote uniformity of belief and practice than is the case among the Amish.

Business

Another difference marks the contours separating the Amish and Wenger cultures. The Amish have entered the world of business more aggressively than the Wengers, who are more committed to farming. Many Wengers have moved out of Lancaster County to buy cheaper farmland in other states, unlike the Amish, who developed hundreds of businesses when squeezed out of good farmland.[10] The Wengers have developed some enterprises as described in Chapter 7, but not nearly on the scale of the Amish. Wenger and Amish businesses compete as well as cooperate. Because Wengers are permitted to use computer-operated manufacturing equipment, they sometimes sell computer-designed parts to Amish shops, which are not permitted to use computerized equipment.

The conference structure is one factor that partially explains the Wenger pursuit of farming. From the 1970s through the 1990s, when the Amish were rapidly abandoning their plows to enter business, the senior Wenger bishop consistently urged his people to search for land beyond Lancaster County so that they could raise their children on the farm. Strong fears of the city, concerns that separation from the world might be jeopardized with too many commercial involvements, and the repeated endorsement by the senior bishop's authoritative voice encouraged people to migrate as far away as Iowa and Missouri for land and rural isolation.

Youth

Another difference frequently mentioned by some observers is the rowdiness of Amish youth. Wenger youth, in the eyes of their elders, are less likely to wander into serious mischief—drugs, alcohol, boisterous parties, cars, and worldly entertainment. In all fairness to the Amish, a few rambunctious Amish youth may mar the reputation of the many teens who embody Amish virtues even during *Rumspringa*. And, of course, some Wenger youth stray into temptation, unbeknownst to their elders. "We have our own problems with our youth having radios, tape players, and some drinking," said one mother.

Several factors help account for the differences between Wenger and Amish youth. In large Amish settlements, the presence of many groups with a hundred members or more leads to wide variations in behavior, because teens select which group they will join. A few youth groups may be rowdy, while others may have a reputation for good behavior. By contrast, Lancaster Wengers encourage their youth to meet in "open crowd" gatherings that encompass all the youth, which may number nearly five hundred. The smaller size of Wenger settlements makes it possible to keep all the youth together rather than forming numerous subgroups, which in the Amish case makes deviance more difficult to control.

Several other Wenger practices bolster their efforts to stifle youthful mischief. The relatively young age of baptism (seventeen to eighteen years old) brings Wenger youth, especially young men, under the supervision of the church more quickly than Amish young men, who often wait to join the church until just before marriage. Related to this custom is the strong Wenger encouragement for youth to be baptized before they begin dating. These patterns narrow the window of freedom for Wenger youth more than for some Amish, who may stretch *Rumspringa* from sixteen to twenty-two years of age or older, depending on when they get baptized and married. Despite the different practices, the vast majority of both Amish and Wenger youth eventually join their respective churches.

Ritual

Patterns of worship and ritual also vary between the two groups. The singers' table in the Wenger churchhouse is unheard of among the Amish, who gather in homes and sing from a different songbook (the *Ausbund*). Formal shunning of excommunicated persons is not practiced by the Wengers, despite the fact that both groups subscribe to the Dordrecht Confession. The two churches interpret Article XVII on shunning somewhat differently. The social avoidance of ex-members was a major wedge of contention between the Amish and Swiss Mennonites in 1693.[11] The Wengers shun ex-members from the Lord's Table, the communion service, and also informally in social relations, depending on the situation. The Lancaster Amish apply shunning more formally and broadly to some other activities such as eating, exchanging money, and engaging in business. In the words of a Wenger bishop, "We just shun the sin, not the sinner."[12]

After attending a Wenger church service, an Amishman reflected on the differences between the two groups.

> So different, yet in many ways our thoughts and problems are the same. In this Mennonite and Amish religion, the carriages are different, but still [have] four wheels and [are] horse drawn. The simple [Wenger] meetinghouse, with hat racks and the singing table, where our worship service may be in shops, tobacco sheds, house or barn, chicken house, or at times in stores or warehouses. With their [Wenger] three ministers per 600 to 800 souls, where we install four per 140 to 200 souls. There could be many questions. No doubt it started the same in the old country. Now today many differences and we [Amish] have service every two weeks for three hours and a meal afterwards. Thus, about four to five hours of fellowship while the Mennonites have two hours of worship every Sunday. Then after the service, everyone visits for a spell, then home for the *Mittag* [noon meal].[13]

Despite the many differences, this Amishman clearly feels a sense of kinship between the two communities.

In addition to the Stauffers, Reidenbachs, and Amish, the Wengers monitor the "progress" of the Hornings and the Lancaster Conference Mennonites who are surely ahead of them on the road to worldliness. The Wengers take a keen interest in both groups because they branched off from them.

✥ THE HORNINGS

The Horning Church provides the Wengers with the most interesting and complicated relationship that they have with another church. On the one hand, given their common history between 1893 and 1927, they share many practices even today. On the other hand, the Hornings embody specific examples of worldliness that the Wengers seek to avoid. Given their duty to carry the conservative banner since 1927, the Wengers, for their own collective integrity, must lag somewhat behind the Hornings, but the gap between the two groups is always tenuous. If the Wengers close the gap too much, members who want a car can easily slip over and join the Hornings. Yet if the Wengers lag too far behind, some progressive-leaning members, frustrated by excessive tradition, may be tempted to join the Hornings. The relationship between the two groups is cordial but delicate, because unhappy Wengers can always threaten to join the Hornings and, in fact, "that is where most of our people who leave go," said one Wenger.

Despite the differences and tensions, what is remarkable and indeed a testimony to their underlying kinship and commitment to Old Order ways is the fact that, in Lancaster County, the groups share five churchhouses on a regular basis.[14] On one Sunday, horses and carriages wheel into the churchyards. On the next Sunday, black cars pull into the same lots. The joint use of churchhouses requires continual negotiation between the two groups.

The Hornings cannot add the amenities that are found in some of their other churchhouses—indoor plumbing, electric lights, and permanent sound systems—to these shared churchhouses. Indeed, the two groups reached a careful compromise on a sound system at the Weaverland churchhouse. When the Hornings use the building, they bring a portable sound system for amplification, but the Wengers have agreed to permit a tiny, nearly hidden, microphone to remain on a hat rack above the preacher's table. The line snaking from the microphone to the ceiling is painted white to conceal its appearance as much as possible.[15] Another issue in some of the shared churchhouses is lights that the Hornings would like to install for evening meetings, but which the Wengers are opposed to. Sharing churchhouses creates an ongoing dilemma of trying to work together gracefully despite different views of appropriate technology for a house of worship.

Both groups affirm the Dordrecht Confession and share similar ritual prescriptions for conducting religious ceremonies, ranging from worship to ordination, from preparatory service to communion.[16] Common religious practices include ordaining lay ministers out of the congregation, singing *a cappella* (without instrumental accompaniment), and forbidding Sunday schools and revival meetings.

There are, in fact, two issues where the Hornings are more traditional than the Wengers: jury duty and their baptismal vows. The Hornings discourage all jury duty and have developed an exemption form to present to civil authorities. The Wengers only forbid jury duty if it might involve capital punishment. And following an older Mennonite practice, the Horning bishop asks baptismal candidates, "Are you willing to submit to the Gospel of Jesus Christ, especially Matthew 18 . . . willing to have this used against you and help use it against others as necessity may demand? Can you answer 'yes'?"[17] The reference to Matthew 18:12–20, which outlines a three-step process of speaking directly to others about offensive actions, was dropped from Wenger vows. This deletion reflects a subtle shift of authority for church accountability from lay members to ministers, which may serve to strengthen the influence of Wenger leaders.

Although most ceremonial practices are similar, there are some minor differences. The Hornings have a benediction following the last song when the congregation is standing, whereas the Wenger benediction comes before the final song. Horning ministers are more likely to say, when giving a brief testimony to another minister's sermon, that they give a "hearty testimony." Such phrases sound overly self-confident to the humility-minded Wengers.[18] To the outsider, these differences would hardly be noticeable and, even to most lay members, they are negligible in comparison to the bigger issues that separate the two communities.

The two big differences that have separated the Wengers and the Hornings are the ownership of cars since 1927 and the later use of English in church services. Apart from these two practices, one Wenger, as noted earlier, declares that *"everything* else is window dressing!" The car was the divisive issue in 1927, when the two groups separated. "If you have a car like the Hornings," said one Wenger, "then it can lead anywhere—to a big farm or into big business. Our steel wheels on tractors and using horse and buggy keep things small."

After the 1927 division, the Horning group gradually began using more English for preaching and singing except for a token German sermon during the annual Thanksgiving service. This significant linguistic transition reflects greater acculturation into American society and a growing distance from their German cultural heritage. Horse-and-buggy transportation and the use of the German dialect for religious discourse keep the Wengers more firmly grounded in Old Order culture.

Many other social and economic practices separate the two groups and signal to the Wengers that the Hornings are drifting dangerously toward the mainstream of American culture. Horning people have more readily left the farm to establish businesses, some of which have hundreds of employees. Even those on the farm face no restrictions on tractor wheels or computerized feeding operations. Horning farms, for the most part, are indistinguish-

A Horning woman (left) stands near a Stauffer woman and boy at a public auction. Again, their dress styles mark their church affiliations.

able from non-Mennonite ones. Except for a taboo on Internet connections, Horning shop owners face no other technological taboos on computers or cell phones like their Wenger neighbors. "The Horning people," said one Wenger farmer, "are into big business and big farms. We are more farm- and family-oriented, not so much in business."

Both groups join hands in banning media technology—radio, television, video, and Internet connections—but the Hornings accept cameras and tape players. In terms of home décor, Horning homes are worldlier in Wenger eyes. According to one Wenger informant, Horning homes have "more landscaping, bigger print on their wallpaper, more colored curtains and drapes, more wall-to-wall carpeting, and some of them don't even have a garden!" Yet home decorations "really vary from family to family," said one Wenger woman, who noted that "some Wengers also have drapes and landscaping."

Some Wenger leaders find evangelical-style expressions of religious life among the Hornings just as troubling, if not more so. The Hornings have a mission interest committee that supports and encourages evangelistic work, which in Wenger eyes is a dramatic departure from Old Order ways. The Hornings have formalized other patterns of church life as well. Their mutual aid programs for fire and storm and car insurance, while operated within the church, are more formally organized along the lines of an insurance company with annual premiums.[19] A retirement home operated by the Hornings provides care for the elderly and houses a historical library with an outstanding collection of Old Order materials.[20] Weddings and social gatherings are often held at a special facility rather than in homes. All of these developments, in Wenger eyes, signal a drift toward mainstream Protestant practices.

In addition to these changing practices, Horning thinking about religious matters tends to be more systematic and formalized than that of the Wengers, who lean on face-to-face communication and more oral, traditional explanations. The Hornings have a church paper, *Home Messenger*, which is mailed to members once a month. The twenty-page black-and-white stapled publication, without advertising, appears plain and modest alongside the four-color glossy magazines of many denominations. *Home Messenger* has a column entitled "Bible Doctrine Briefly Stated" and another called "Seeking Guidance," with questions and answers on topics ranging from courtship to mission work. The essays in these columns provide examples of the systematic nature of Horning discourse.[21]

In Lancaster County, where Wengers and Hornings live side by side and even share churchhouses, they keep a close and usually friendly eye on each other. Leaders in both groups are curious about the long-term outcome of the 1927 division. It would be wrong to blame the automobile for all the changes among the Hornings since then, because car proponents in 1927 represented the progressive-leaning flank of the church that favored other changes as well. Nevertheless, to the Wengers, the accumulation of changes over nearly eight decades of Horning life reveal a worldly direction that, if not driven by the car, certainly accompany it.

As their stories unfold, leaders in both groups are tracking the growth of their two bodies, which began with virtually equal numbers in 1927. "The Wengers began to pull ahead in the 1980s," said one Wenger member. The

Wenger growth, according to this person, results from larger families and a higher rate of retention. "It's true," said a Horning leader. "The more disciplined Old Order groups are, the more they hold their young people." The flow of members between the two groups is virtually a one-way street from Wenger to Horning. Very rarely do members from any group want to step down the Old Order ladder. Thus, despite a trickle of members to the Hornings, Wenger growth has outpaced the Hornings. And speaking of growth, one Horning leader confessed, "The Wengers are healthier than we are today."

✢

✢ LANCASTER CONFERENCE

The Lancaster Mennonite Conference provides the Wengers with a concrete example of what they intend to avoid. For over a hundred years, since the division of 1893, the Old Orders have charted the drift of the Lancaster Conference into the whirlpools of worldliness. In the heart of Wenger country, the brick Weaverland Mennonite Church, affiliated with the Lancaster Conference, sits across the road from the stone Old Order Weaverland churchhouse. These two buildings—symbolizing the humility of Old Order ways and the "worldliness" of more assimilated Mennonites—stand as monuments to the powerful forces of history and century-old decisions that have shaped the practical lives of members in these two communities.

On a typical Sunday morning, the car-driving Lancaster Conference Mennonites zoom past slow-paced Wenger carriages on back country roads. Both are headed for worship services, but in different styles in very different buildings, a short distance from one another. For the most part, there is little interaction and little awareness of the two different cultural worlds inhabited by these people, who were part of the same church family before 1893. And while the Wengers think that the Lancaster Conference Mennonites have drifted into worldliness, some of their Lancaster Conference cousins see the Wengers as simply clinging to archaic nineteenth-century customs. Indeed, many assimilated Mennonites are embarrassed to be associated with Old Order Mennonites who shun cars and drive steel-wheeled tractors.

The Wengers pay more attention to their Lancaster Conference kin than vice versa because the Lancaster Conference, for the Wengers, is a negative reference group on the risky road to worldliness that the Wengers hope to avoid. "Lancaster Conference," said one member, "is an example of exactly where we don't want to go." The Lancaster Conference provides a poignant example to the Wengers that worldly drift can happen in a short time among people, even family, from the same religious stock. Despite their fear of following the Lancaster path, a Wenger member noted a continuing sense of kinship. "If a young family leaves our church and goes to Lancaster Conference, the parents feel bad, but they would feel much worse if they went to the Worship Center," a large, evangelical congregation that includes many ex-members of various Anabaptist churches.

Although the Lancaster Conference is seen as a conservative flank in the national Mennonite world, it has accepted many practices that the Wengers want to shun. Indeed, one member confessed, "We use Lancaster Conference as a scapegoat for the things we don't like." Some Lancaster Conference churches sport contemporary features such as small steeples, air conditioning, carpet, drapes, pianos, small organs, and worship centers with flowers. Such fancy buildings that overflow with pride, in Wenger eyes, are nevertheless quite modest, if not plain, compared with more ornate edifices.

The worship service of some Lancaster Conference churches includes praise teams, worship bands, dramatic presentations, PowerPoint images, vocal and instrumental ensembles, revivalist preachers, and personal testimonies laced with emotion. For Wengers, all of these practices testify to egocentric pride and a performance-based worship designed for spectators, marking a dramatic departure from the lowly paths of humility. Moreover, the professionally trained ministers in some Lancaster Conference congregations attest to credentials and professional achievement driven by individual desire, rather than by simple obedience to a call from God revealed through the casting of lots.

Also troubling to Wenger sensibilities are the many examples of worldly practices that have seeped into the Lancaster Conference. Not only have its members fully adopted English as their mother tongue, but they also drive sporty cars, wear fashionable dress and jewelry, use computers, and surf the Web with little restraint. Televisions are found even in the homes of ministers and the elderly. Some members go to theaters to see the latest Hollywood movie. "Can you imagine," asked a Wenger bishop, "what in the world old Lancaster Conference Bishop J. Paul Graybill (1900–1975) would say if he saw Lancaster Conference today?" Another Wenger leader, lamenting the fact that women in a Lancaster Conference congregation had "cut their hair and wore earrings and jewelry," declared sadly, "There's just not much Mennonite left in them anymore!" Clearly, ethnic identity and religious practice are strands of the same cloth, in this bishop's mind.

Deeply disturbing to many Wengers is the loss of not only an *Ordnung*, with guidelines for ethical behavior, but also any form of church discipline.

This Lancaster Mennonite Conference church is found in the center of the Wenger community.

Persons who are divorced and remarried are accepted as members, and those who file lawsuits are not expelled from the church. Indeed, some Lancaster Conference members make their living as lawyers. A few members hold political office in county and state government, and even military service might be tolerated in some Lancaster Conference congregations. The Wengers wonder whatever happened to the meek and lowly practice of nonresistance. Speaking of lowliness, one Wenger man asked in disbelief, "Do Lancaster Conference members still wash feet?"—referring to the long-standing practice in Mennonite communion services.

The Wengers' litany of lament could go on and on with comments about extravagant weddings, stylish upscale homes, and women abandoning their families for professional work and assuming leadership roles in church. In addition, Lancaster Conference members accept commercial life insurance and Social Security without hesitation. All of these aspects of cultural assimilation provide Wengers with abundant evidence of the seductive power of worldliness that they so desperately hope to avoid.

When asked why they don't become more involved in mission work, one Wenger explained emphatically, "Because Lancaster Conference does missions and just look what happened to them!" Echoing similar sentiments, another member said, "Missionary work is off-limits, because we think we should live our faith and not talk about it. That's half the reason, but the other half is that we don't want to become like the Lancaster Mennonite Conference. Just look what happened to them." "Our greatest mission," said another Wenger, "is right here, letting our light shine and raising our children in the fear and admonition of the Lord."

All these issues can be flipped upside down by members of Mennonite groups who are more engaged with the larger dominant American culture. Such members might ask what virtue lies in social separation and even argue that such separation borders on social irresponsibility in the midst of pressing needs in the larger world. A Wenger woman compared the contributions of assimilated Mennonites with Old Orders: "Lancaster Conference does mission work and that's a valuable contribution to the well-being of society. We have our own contributions. We grow food, have dairies, make furniture, and so on, which contribute to the larger society. They shouldn't look down on us and we [Wengers] shouldn't feel superior to them. The main thing is that we all serve God in whatever capacity we can."

Clearly, the Lancaster Conference and the Hornings are negative reference groups that illustrate how specific steps of change may lead to undesirable outcomes, at least from the Wenger perspective. These two groups, part of the Wengers' own history, have encouraged the Wengers to become more thoughtful and intentional about how they control change in their own community.[22] Despite intramural skirmishes with other Anabaptist teams, the bigger question for the Wengers focuses on the larger playing field—that is, their relationship to modernity or, more realistically, postmodernity.

❖ THE MODERN FIELD

Social scientists sometimes distinguish among *traditional, modern,* and *postmodern* phases in the transformation of human societies. Typical traits of *traditional* societies include a local, rural economy, an extended family structure, oral discourse based on face-to-face relationships, and the use of animal power. With roots in the European Age of Enlightenment, the *modern* era largely mirrors the rise of industrialization that developed in the nineteenth century and flourished in the first part of the twentieth century in Europe and North America. The *postmodern* phase of society, according to some observers, began to emerge in the late twentieth century. The meaning of postmodernity is widely debated, but most analysts would agree that it parallels the decline of the industrial economy and the rise of a global information/ service society. Rather than emphasizing a linear historical narrative and a single source of truth, postmodern proclivities lean toward relative, subjective, and diverse sources of moral perspective. In addition to philosophical differences, technological applications that create digital images of virtual reality on electronic media and the World Wide Web add to the decontextualization of social life that characterizes the emerging postmodern era.

These three broad phases identify gradual transitions in the cultural and social transformation of societies. All three phases can coexist in a particular society and on a global scale, but societies often exhibit the dominant features of one phase more than another. In any event, most analysts would agree that the period from 1850 to 1950, when the Old Order movement emerged and the Wengers were born, was a distinctly modern moment in the larger span of history. The Wengers' relationship to the larger society is entangled with the modern story.

A review of the voluminous literature on the meaning of modernity goes far beyond the scope of this book. Modernity is a broad and deep concept that focuses on culture (worldview and values) as well as on the structures of social organization. We have argued that the Wengers have engaged in selective modernization, rejecting some aspects of modernity while embracing others. How have they been selective? Below, we highlight five dimensions of modernity—technology, separation, abstraction, choice, and individuation— that are especially pertinent to understanding Wenger culture and society.

+ *Technology.* One obvious feature of the modern period is the shift away from human and animal power to various forms of inanimate energy— steam, electricity, and internal combustion, among others. This massive transformation of power involves the application of technology, in the broadest sense, to virtually all aspects of human life from transportation to health care, from contraception to communication.
+ *Separation.* The powerful forces of history in modern times have pulled many social functions—birth, education, work, leisure—away from the home, a process that Anthony Giddens calls the "disembedding" of social life.[23] The extraction of these activities from the home was driven at least in part by occupational specialization in industrial societies, which required advanced and specialized education. These trends pulled activities out of the home and separated them—not only in function but also in location—from the control of the extended family. The specializing and scattering of social functions encouraged mobility made possible by new forms of transportation.

+ *Abstraction.* Shifting the locus of activities away from the home elevates centralized and distant centers of power and control. Many of the forces of modern life are abstract and removed from local communities. Decisions that impact local communities are made in corporate centers in urban areas or in other countries around the globe. Distant centers of power determine fast food menus and designer clothing styles, which, of course, penetrate social life in local areas.[24] Formal written communication and bureaucratic structures reflect a more rationalized style of interaction that replaces face-to-face communication.

+ *Choice.* One of the consequences of modern life is a dazzling array of choices, from occupations to frozen pizzas, from entertainment to family size. Peter Berger has argued that, above all else, *choice* is the distinguishing feature of modernity.[25] Compared to the traditional society, in which fate and custom determine destiny, modern life is open-ended, so to speak, because it offers a huge smorgasbord of choices that enable groups and individuals to sort and select—in essence, to customize—their own world. In Berger's words, the traditional society, driven by fate, "lifts the burden of choice from the shoulders of the individual."

+ *Individuation.* In the traditional society, individual identity is embedded in the collective identity of the tribe, clan, or extended family. With traditional customs torn asunder in the modern world, with the demise of the extended family, with advanced specialization, and with the proliferation of choice, individual identity is separated from collective identity. Facing a panorama of choices and freed from the constraints of custom, individuals have the opportunity to shape their own autobiographies. The individual becomes the primary source of authority, the locus of decision making.

❖ SELECTIVE MODERNIZATION

We have argued throughout this book that in order to protect the viability of their redemptive community, the Wengers have tried to limit their interaction with the larger society, engaging in a process of selective modernization. How does the Wenger story interface with the larger story of societal transitions? Are the Wengers a traditional society that has largely shunned the modern era or a mostly modern group with a few residual trappings of a traditional world? More important, what is unique and distinctive about how the Wengers have engaged modernity?

Five young boys ponder the future of Wenger society.

On the one hand, the Wengers reflect modern traits by making intentional, rational choices about which external influences to accept and which to reject. The Wengers have engaged in a reflexive, deliberate decision-making process to manage their discourse with modernity; it would be an egregious error to see them as a traditional society that yields itself to the dictates of fate. They are neither victims of fatalism nor driven by thoughtless custom. However, one of their choices at the collective level has been to constrain the choices of individual members in order to keep the redemptive community the primary locus of moral authority. The Wengers have bridled choice at the individual level, which at first blush makes them appear quite traditional. Collectively they have *chosen* to retain many aspects of traditional life and have engaged in a vigorous screening of modernity, and for the most part they have boycotted all forms of emergent postmodern life.

Several key Wenger decisions illustrate their dialogue with modernity. As we have seen in Chapter 3, the rejection of the car lies at the very foundation of Wenger identity. The automobile, unlike any other invention, is the chief icon of the modern era. In his analysis of the shift from modernity to postmodernity, David Harvey considers not only the car but also the automated assembly line that produced it the prime embodiments of modernity. This technological system, which he calls "Fordism," entailed the entire economic, corporate, and industrial apparatus that was developed by Henry Ford and other industrialists to produce the car.[26] By rejecting the car, the Wengers were not merely spurning the brightest ornament of modernity; they were also rejecting the industrial system that produced it, as well as many of the secondary consequences that would spin off from it. By clinging to horse-and-buggy transportation, the Wengers were holding on to vestiges of a traditional social order.

In contrast to the car, the Wengers accepted the tractor, another product of automated assembly lines. Tractors were a key step in the transition from traditional to modern societies—and certainly crucial to the shift from labor-intensive agriculture to large-scale corporate farming, which enabled a small percentage of people to feed the entire nation, not to mention export food to other nations. By accepting the tractor, the Wengers cast their lot with modernity, but they did it in a way that supported small family farms and their rural lifestyle. By requiring steel wheels and counseling against large tractors, they strategically used this tool of modernity to maintain their traditional, small-family-farming way of life.[27]

The Wengers' ten-year debate on tractor wheels, described in Chapter 3, was really a debate about border issues between traditional and modern societies. Having accepted the tractor, the dynamo of modern agriculture, would they follow it to the car, which would lead to the main boulevard of modernity? Keeping the horse on the road and the tractor in the field, the Wengers straddled the fence between traditional and modern life. The debate over tractor wheels became contentious because it was a conversation about the fate of their community. Would they remain a traditional society or would they concede to the forces of modernity? The identity and destiny of their community lurked beneath the public discussion of tractor wheels.

The roots of group identity vary among conservative Anabaptist groups. Although they often share similar prohibitions, such as the taboo on television, Old Order groups accent different issues in shaping their identity. The Wengers have emphasized dialect and technology more than dress. Although they strongly encourage certain forms of dress, the guidelines are considered counsels—not rules that, if violated, could result in excommunication. Some of the technology taboos, especially those related to rubber tires, computers, and the Internet, are considered rules, which could bring serious sanction if violated. For other Plain groups that drive cars and use English in their church services, dress plays a more important role in shaping identity and marking boundaries with the outside world than it does with the Wengers.[28]

Without a doubt, the Wengers have absorbed some features of the modern world. Most centrally, they have engaged in strategic decision making about how to chart the future of their community in the larger society. Their use of technology—tractors, farm machinery, household appliances, electricity, telephones, modern medicine, chemical fertilizers, and artificial insemination of cattle—all testify to their acceptance of many things modern. Their growing involvement in the world of commercial business, even under the church's scrutiny, reflects the values of a rational worldview.

Despite these streaks of modernity, Wenger society shows a preponderance of traditionally oriented values and practices, chief of which is the subordination of the individual to the collective order, the redemptive community. *Gelassenheit*, regardless of how it is parsed, opposes the free-floating individualism of modern life. Vows of obedience to the church, collective restrictions on dress, and prohibitions against high school and higher education constrain the self and personal freedom. Sizable nuclear families, large extended families, marriage within the community, and the taboo on divorce all reflect traditional social practices. Moreover, the Wenger economy is based on communal, familial units of production, not on an individualistic consumerism driven by status seeking and conspicuous display.

✥ SEPARATING FROM THE GREAT SEPARATOR

Beneath the Old Order fear of "the world" lies a fear of social disintegration. The advent of the telephone and the car forced Old Order Mennonites to clarify their relationship to the outside social order. The telephone offered instant communication and vast possibilities for long-distance connections. In modern eyes it was a stunning achievement, but for conservative Mennonites, it opened the door to communication with strangers. Moreover, it promised to undermine the patterns of face-to-face visiting that integrated their orally based communities. When television arrived in midcentury, it posed an even greater threat—"channeling" the values and images of a decadent culture directly into rural homes. Without hesitation, all Old Order groups slapped a firm taboo on television, a taboo that continues today.

The car, as we have argued throughout this book, was a symbol of modernity par excellence: automatic mobility, independence, individualism, and power. The product of a highly specialized assembly line, the automobile promised to obliterate geographical boundaries, expand social horizons, and free individuals from local constraints. For progressives, the automobile was a striking achievement of the forces of modernity. The Wengers thought otherwise. In their minds, the car promised to unravel their tightly knit ethnic communities. For them, modernity was the great separator that threatened to pull their corporate life asunder.[29]

Rather than abandon farming as their chief occupation, many Wengers have moved to other states in search of fertile land and rural seclusion. The antiurban sentiments that run deep in their culture betray the Wenger affinity for the traditional world. The city is the base of the great separator. Wengers prefer rural, isolated settings, where face-to-face communication in a special dialect supports their redemptive community. Their taboo on radio, television, and the Internet—their wholesale rejection of mass media, except for local newspapers—excludes them from urban discourse, an exclusion about which the Wengers have few regrets.

The Wengers engage in selective modernization, all the while making collective decisions that keep them rooted in traditional social soil. They look to the past for their moral compass. Ancient sources of authority are prized above contemporary ones. Traditional practice and bygone wisdom carry more influence than scientific arguments. Looking back for moral authority departs from the contemporary quest to find it in human reflection, critical thinking, and scientific findings. If they imbibe these modern values, they worry that they will lose the soul of their redemptive community.

In all of these ways, the Wengers define their very existence over against the modern project, and use religious and biblical imagery to sanction their stance. Sectarians to the core, they pit themselves against the modern enterprise, which they simply call "the world." They can only preserve their redemptive community by separating from the great separator, which threatens to splinter their bonds of ethnic solidarity. In many ways, Old Order history can be read as an attempt to hold the powerful forces of modernity at bay. Wenger resistance to these pervasive forces has been successful for nearly eighty years. How the Wengers will fare in the long term, however, is another story, yet to be told.

❖ A DIFFERENT VIEW OF PROGRESS

The celebrated Age of Enlightenment, in many ways, pointed to the beginning of the modern era. The Enlightenment promised to shatter the traditions that had shackled the human spirit for many centuries. Human reason, technology, and the hope of democracy promised freedom from the bondage of provincial habits as well as liberation from the oppressions of autocracy, racism, and patriarchy, to name a few. A disenchanted world would be a brighter one. Progress, moving forward and upward with industrial efficiency, became the mantra of the new age. The Enlightenment promised greater happiness for those freed from their fettered past. A liberated self, emancipated from religious and social restrictions, would be a more satisfied and fulfilled one.

As others rushed forward, the Wengers not only hesitated—they challenged many of the assumptions undergirding the entire modern project. Proclaiming themselves pilgrims on another road, they doubted that technological progress and personal freedom would really garner greater happiness. In fact, they saw the frenzy, speed, and commotion about them as the handiwork of sinful humans. At its deepest level, their protest was aimed at the spirit of progress itself. The Wengers—as a countercultural community—challenged the Enlightenment venture and all the notions of progress that flowed from it.

The proponents of progress derided the Wengers as backward and primitive, a people lagging behind the times. Some progressives viewed them as hopelessly naive, unwilling to face up to the realities of the modern world. The Wengers, who rejected cars, telephones, and televisions—the ubiquitous symbols of progress—as well as individualism, higher education, and scientific achievement sometimes became objects of scorn in the first half of the century. Even some fellow Anabaptists mocked the conservers for their narrow-minded traditionalism.[30] These stubborn traditionalists, many thought, would surely fade into oblivion as modernity marched forward. Certainly the powerful forces of popular culture would displace them.

Wengers held numerous reservations about the twentieth-century assumptions underlying the effervescent spirit of progress. We have noted their worries about how technology might impair their community. Yet a deeper reservation challenged contemporary notions of moral authority. For Wengers, moral authority was not found in individual experience, but in the counsel of the church. The redemptive community, not the individual, was the chief agent of ethical discernment; the communal wisdom of *Gelassenheit*, in their minds, should supersede individual experience and personal opinion. This granted the church uncontested authority to discern a wide spectrum of moral issues based on Wenger interpretations of biblical Scripture. In all of these ways, the Wengers challenged the fundamental assumptions of modernity.

The Wengers contended that communal choices, at least in some areas of life, were safer than individual ones. Without guidance from the redemptive community, members might otherwise make unwise choices. Social choices greatly expanded throughout the twentieth century, however, as we have noted. The array of choices offered endless possibilities for food, clothing, entertainment, lifestyle, and even faith, confirming Berger's contention that choice is the dominant imprint of modernity. Wenger society contends that constraining choices, at least for individuals, brings happiness and satisfaction for those who yield to the wisdom of the redemptive community. Barry Schwartz, in *The Paradox of Choice*, argues that just because some choice is good does not necessarily mean that more choice is better. Indeed, he suggests that we should ask whether freedom of choice nourishes us or debilitates us. He proposes that too many choices may impair personal freedom and lower satisfaction, leading to feelings of inadequacy and clinical depression.[31] Schwartz's suggestion that excessive choice may shrink human satisfaction and also produce psychological debilitation reinforces Wenger sentiments.

Choices, of course, are somewhat limited in Wenger life. When asked if Wenger women are happy, a health-care professional who works with many of them said, "Some are and some aren't. There's a lot of depression because they don't have many choices. If you are female, married, and a mother, all you can do is bake and make clothes and the only way to have a break from that is to have another baby." In the mind of this outsider, the problem is compounded when Wenger women have several children, because then "they are confined to the home because many of them don't drive teams."[32] This professional's observation gives credence to Schwartz's contention that some, but not too much, choice is essential for human satisfaction and happiness. It also underscores the linkage between gender and choice—more specifically, who controls the range of choice.

For some Wenger women, there is another side to the story.[33] One mother said, "We are not confined to our homes, we love it here. We do have choices, and happiness comes from knowing that we are where God wants us to be. Frankly I don't know of any depressed, unhappy women." In the words of another Wenger woman, "Sometimes depression can come from having children so close and the body becomes run down. But I know a lot of Wenger women who *do* drive horses and *are* happy!" A young Wenger mother asked rhetorically,

Why is Prozac the most prescribed medication in this country? Granted there is some depression among Plain people, but

I think there's a lot less among Plain women for several reasons. First, they don't have to worry that their husbands will run off for a younger, prettier woman. Second, they don't feel like they have to have a career to prove that they are a worthwhile person. Third, Plain women are not as isolated as other American women. Stay-at-home American women may live in a neighborhood where no one else is at home. Their mom may be divorced, remarried or living with someone and because they come from a small family they don't have many siblings for support. Now contrast that with Plain women. Their friends, relatives, and moms are all at home and support them. Finally, some outside women may be depressed because they are always tired, burning the candle at both ends, because they feel they have to have a career and raise children.

Another Wenger woman likely spoke for many of them when she wrote, "To imply that Wenger women are not as happy as women who have mobility does not apply to the majority of us. And if mobility would bring happiness, millions of Americans should be forever happy. I think I speak for hundreds of Wenger women when I say, 'I am happy where I am; in the heart of my home, with my children all around me and with a husband standing by my side, whose heart does safely trust in me.'" She continued with her description of Wenger women:

> And as for choices, in my small circle of buddies, we do many things besides "baking and sewing and having babies for breaks." Besides keeping homes in perfect order, one paints to sell, two raise dogs, one has a retail greenhouse, one manages a food warehouse, one runs a retail clothing and fabric store, one makes and sews clothing. Do you get the drift? I don't feel that just having more choices outside family will bring happiness. I don't know of one Wenger woman who is pining because of her lack of choices. As for myself, I don't recall ever once wishing for a career. Happiness is right here where I love to be.

These Wenger women argue that happiness does not necessarily flow from having more choices and that the confines of traditional family life can nurture deep forms of contentment. We are "freer and happier," claimed one woman, "because we are not exhausted from a job away from home. We can be creative and do fun things and do whatever we want to throughout the day." Many modern folks may beg to differ, but such Wenger voices challenge some of the modern assumptions about the roots of happiness.

⁂ HUMILITY IN A POSTMODERN WORLD

If the horse signifies the animate power of traditional society and the car the machine power of the modern world, surely the Internet signifies the evolutionary shape of the postmodern milieu, a world whose distinguishing traits are still emerging. Some prognosticators see the transition as simply a hyperform of modernity; others consider postmodernity as qualitatively different, even though its contours are still blurred. In any event, the Internet has replaced the factory as the dominant metaphor of social life. Virtual reality, instantaneous global communication, and multiple images of reality—thanks to the splicing of digital images—offer harbingers of the postmodern habitat.

For the moment at least, the Wengers decline citizenship in the postmodern world. Although they permit modest computerization for word processing and manufacturing equipment, they unequivocally oppose the Internet. The cell phone is another postmodern tool that they spurn. Although they employ some modern tools for productive purposes, they do not use them to open portals of cultural influences from the outside world.

Surprisingly, a few features of Wenger life mimic some aspects of postmodernity—collaborative decision making, doubts about the claims of science, and doubts about the virtues of progress—but make no mistake, the Wengers show little sympathy for fundamental postmodern sensitivities. "Call it the 'Heisenberg principle,'" said one Wenger man. "All is relative and subjective, nothing can be known with any degree of certainty, *except the uncertainty of it all!*"[34] The writer continued, "For totally different reasons, we feel that our objections to such views are rational. We think that moral truths are absolute and that postmodernism is irrational!"

Ironically, many of the underlying assumptions of postmodernity are couched in philosophical humility—primarily, the uncertainties of any grand narrative of history and the uncertainty that any truth claims are absolute and universal. But while the spirit of humility may undergird both Wenger ways and postmodern thought, they are different versions of humility. For Wengers, humility before God and others in the church does not extend to a rejection of certainty in moral matters and eternal truths.

The buggy is a stark symbol of humility in a postmodern world.

For one Old Order historian, postmodern simply means "ultra modern." In his mind, "the Old Order community stands in contradiction" to the notion that there are "no givens which are universally true." For Old Orders, the church community is one of the normative anchors of life.

> We have an anchor in life . . . from the fact that we belong to something bigger than ourselves. Most members of the Old Order community delight in the knowledge of belonging to a community, to something that is normative. The beauty of the Old Order community is the lack of loneliness and isolation found among modern— or I guess I should say postmodern—people. I really do believe that the realities of the Old Order and mainstream culture are a world apart . . . there is indeed a huge chasm that stands between the Old Order person and the people of the world.[35]

The Wengers are fans of networking—of face-to-face visiting—in extended families, but their version is quite different from surfing the electronic links that encircle the globe. Any resemblances the Wengers share with postmoderns are shrouded under a sectarian religious canopy that firmly assumes that divine truth, as revealed in the Bible, will shape the course of history. Such notions contradict postmodern sentiments that favor cultural relativity, a multiplicity of moral authorities, and the primacy of individual experience. For Wengers, moral authority is lodged in the redemptive community, a community that holds uncontested authority over a wide spectrum of issues.

Humility, the queen of Wenger virtues, is homeless in a fragile, ephemeral postmodern world overflowing with fleeting images flashing across digital screens. Humility can only flourish when it is nurtured by the repetition of redemptive rituals in a face-to-face community. Wenger pilgrims live on the margins of the postmodern world; they live in an Old Order world where humility still works—where, in fact, it is necessary in order to keep the community intact. Individuals who inhabit a postmodern world face endless choices not only about consumer products and lifestyles but also about personal identities to fit their many different roles. Survival in the midst of overwhelming choices in the postmodern world requires assertive, independent selves, not humility and the yieldedness of *Gelassenheit*.

As we have seen, the Wengers have protested the press of modern progress for nearly eighty years. In many ways, their protest has successfully preserved their community. But a protest against modernity, in which things are concrete, visible, and fixed, is quite different from challenging an ever-shifting virtual world linked by wireless webs around the globe. Whether the Wengers will be able to keep their redemptive community together successfully in the face of a virtual electronic octopus is an entirely different question, one that may require eighty more years to answer.

As cultural conservationists, the Wengers cherish the rhythms of traditional ways, but they also engage in selective modernization, accepting technological advancements that fit their worldview and benefit the well-being and future destiny of their community. Again, Wenger notions about the good life challenge some of the taken-for-granted assumptions of contemporary life: Wenger pilgrims contend that newer, bigger, and faster are not necessarily better; that sacrifice should be esteemed over pleasure; that work is more fulfilling than consumption; that humility and obedience bring order and unity; that participation in a redemptive community brings personal fulfillment; and that the unity of the *Gmay* is the ultimate good.

"We are strange and peculiar people," said an Old Order historian. "We have a strange kind of beauty ... like all real beauty ... it goes deeper than the surface and is always difficult to see and understand. It is the strange beauty of submission of the self to the faith community."[36] These affirmations confirm that the Wengers are, indeed, pilgrims and strangers in the contemporary world. For the most part, their core values have withstood the relentless press of so-called progress. They believe that true progress and deep satisfaction emerge when people yield to the collective wisdom of a redemptive community and that those who surrender to the precepts of providence, embedded in communal wisdom, will receive the blessings of contentment and fulfillment.

❖ APPENDIX A: methods and sources

INTERVIEWS

The information for this study was gathered through a variety of methods: face-to-face interviews, participant observation in church and family activities, a longitudinal (1968–98) study of membership in one church district, and the use of various primary documents and secondary sources, described below. The data-gathering process began in the early 1990s and extended into 2005.

Approximately sixty face-to-face interviews were conducted, mostly in Lancaster County (Pa.) but also in Indiana, Kentucky, New York, and Wisconsin. Several telephone interviews were also conducted with Wengers living in other states. Most of the interviews were held in homes and shops. Some, but not all, were recorded and transcribed. James P. Hurd and Donald B. Kraybill conducted the bulk of the interviews. They were assisted by Florence Horning, who interviewed some people in the summer of 1992. The field notes and transcriptions of interviews provided the primary data sources for the quotations in the text. Out of repeated requests for anonymity, the authors have tried to protect the identity of subjects in the text unless their story was already public information.

DIRECTORIES

National Directories

Laura and Beatrice Shirk from Berks County (Pa.) have published four editions of *Directory of the Groffdale Conference Mennonite Churches* (1987, 1992, 1997, 2002). These large books, which have grown from 600 to 900 pages, provide a rich resource of demographic data for all Wenger settlements. *Di-*

rectory 2002, for example, contains the name of the head of the household, birth date, father's name, address, and telephone number (and, for ministers, date of ordination). If the head of the household is married, the directory lists the marriage date, the name of the wife and her father's name, the name and birth date of each child, and the name of the spouse of each married child.

In 1987, 1,670 households appeared in the Wenger church directory, with an estimated 130 families unlisted. Fifteen years later, in 2002, the number of households had grown to 2,890. For bibliographic detail, see *Directory* in the Selected References.

Local Settlement Maps and Directories
All the settlements have printed their own maps and directories, which identify the location of homes, schools, and churchhouses. The maps include a listing of members with their addresses and phone numbers. The local Wenger maps and directories, combined with the national directories, allowed a statistical analysis of the demography of each settlement. They were also invaluable for contacting informants.

ANNUAL SCHEDULES OF MEETINGS AND OFFICIALS

Schedules of the Groffdale Conference Mennonite Churches, a small booklet published annually, lists all the churchhouses, church officials, and church meetings in Indiana, Iowa, Kentucky, Michigan, Missouri, New York, Ohio, Pennsylvania, and Wisconsin. It also includes the Old Order (horse-and-buggy) Virginia Mennonite Church, a group that is in fellowship with the Groffdale Conference. This list of church services in all the settlements maps the significant rituals, meetings, and special days of the church year.

SOURCE DOCUMENTS AND BOOKS

The Ordnung of the Groffdale Conference
One version of the 1976 Wenger *Ordnung* has been printed as a small twelve-page booklet in German. It does not list an editor, author, publisher, or date of publication. The senior bishop in the 1970s said, however, that he wrote it in 1976. The *Ordnung* is updated periodically and is typically only available to the bishops—not to ministers, deacons, lay members, or the public. The senior bishop takes the lead in updating and revising it as new decisions of the Groffdale Conference evolve. The 1976 version cited in this book was translated by Hedda Durnbaugh, Amos B. Hoover, and Florence Horning. The *Ordnung*

is the most important document for tracking official changes of approved and disapproved practices in the Groffdale Conference.

Conversation on Saving Faith for the Young in Questions and Answers

An important resource of religious writings for the Wengers is *Conversation on Saving Faith for the Young in Questions and Answers* (1984). Its German title is *Christliches Gemüths-Gespräch*. Some of the essays were written by Gerhard Roosen (1612–1711), a prominent Mennonite bishop in Northern Germany, and first published in America in German in 1769. John Baer and Sons published the first English edition in 1857. It was revised and reprinted several times, most recently in 1974 by a committee of Mennonites in Ephrata (Pa.).

The 300-page book contains several sections. The first two sections, in question-and-answer format, cover a wide range of Mennonite beliefs on topics such as baptism, love, revenge, oaths, excommunications, and church practices. The third section contains the Dordrecht Confession of Faith. The final section has essays entitled "True Repentance" and "Saving Faith and Pure Love" as well as a variety of other topics and texts, including the Ten Commandments, the Apostles' Creed, and a Morning Prayer.

Ordination Listing

A compilation of all ordinations is available in *Records of Ordinations of the Old Order Mennonites Groffdale Conference Churches, 1750 to 2004*, compiled by Martin Rissler (Ephrata, Pa.: Grace Press, 2004). This 110-page booklet contains the names of ordained officials, their ages, date of ordination, and, when known, the names of other candidates in the lot. Updates are printed periodically.

Confession of Faith

A key source for church practices is the *Confession of Faith of the Mennonites: Church Forms and Guidelines of the Weaverland Conference*. The first edition was published by the Weaverland (Horning) Conference in 1996.

Although published recently, many of the practices described in this booklet reflect eighteenth- and nineteenth-century Mennonite practices in southeastern Pennsylvania. There are two forms of this 90-page booklet: a ministers' edition, which contains all the Scripture texts that pertain to specific rituals and church services, and a shorter edition, which cites the Scripture references but does not include full texts. The booklet also contains detailed instructions for church ceremonies such as baptism, confession, excommunication, ordination, and communion. These practices emerged among the Lancaster Mennonites in the eighteenth century, and (with minor revisions) they are still followed by the Horning and Wenger Mennonites today.

The Dordrecht Confession of Faith

The text of this document, which contains the eighteen articles of faith affirmed by the Wengers, is printed in *Confession of Faith* (1996).

The Wenger Hymnbook

The Wengers use the *Unpartheyisches Gesangbuch* (Impartial Songbook) for the text of their church hymns. It contains the German words, but only a few musical notations, for nearly four hundred hymns, including many Anabaptist martyr hymns. The *Gesangbuch* was first published in the United States in 1804. Used by various Old Order groups, a recent edition was published by the Amish Book Committee of Lancaster County (Pa.) in 1999.

THE MARTINDALE DISTRICT STUDY (1968–1998)

With the assistance of local informants, detailed data were gathered on 199 individuals in the Martindale District congregation in Lancaster County (Pa.) who were born between 1953 and 1968. The study population included all children fifteen years of age and younger in all households of the district that were listed in the 1968 *Lancaster County Map and Directory of Groffdale Conference Mennonites*. The longitudinal study tracked the cohort of 199 people for thirty years and in 1998 gathered information on age of baptism, church membership, marriage, residence, employment status, and occupation.

❖ APPENDIX B: baptismal and wedding vows

If you are still so minded, you may stand up.

Paul writes in the second chapter of Philippians: Let this mind be in you, which also was in Christ Jesus: Who, being in the form of God, thought it not robbery to be equal with God: but made himself of no reputation, and took upon him the form of a servant, and was made in the likeness of men: and being found in a fashion as a man, he humbled himself, and became obedient unto death, even the death of the cross. Wherefore God also hath highly exalted him, and given him a name which is above every name: that at the name of Jesus every knee should bow, of things in heaven, and things in earth, and things under the earth; and that every tongue should confess that Jesus Christ is Lord, to the glory of God the Father.

So in the name of Jesus you may kneel.

I ask you first of all whether you believe in almighty God and Father, Lord and Creator of heaven and earth, who has created all things visible and invisible, and has taken the lamentable sinful state of man so to heart, that He already in earlier times promised to send His only begotten son as an advocate and redeemer and Savior. And whether you believe that Jesus Christ is the only begotten Son of God, and is our advocate and redeemer and Savior, who in the fullness of time, as had been prophesied, was conceived of the Holy Spirit, became flesh and was born of the Virgin Mary, suffered under Pontius Pilate, was nailed to the cross, and on the cross He died, that He was laid in a new grave, and that on the third day rose victoriously from the dead, and after forty days ascended to heaven to the right hand of God, from whence He will come again with many thousand holy angels to judge the living and the dead. And whether you believe in the Holy Spirit which proceeds from the Father and the Son, and disciplines the world because of sin, because of righteousness, and because of judgment. Whether you believe also that this Holy Spirit is a true guide and helpmeet to all the truly repentant and believing hearts and souls, and that it is through his living power that you have been drawn and made willing to humble yourselves under this scriptural practice. And whether you believe that the Father, Son and Holy Spirit are the one and almighty God in whose name you desire to be baptized with water?

Can you affirm this with "Yes"?

Our Savior says in the sixth chapter of Matthew that no man can serve two masters, for either he will love the one and hate the other, or else he will hold to the one and despise the other. So I ask you whether you are willing to renounce Satan and all his works, the kingdom of darkness and deceitfulness of this world, as well as your own will, lusts and desires; and promise to be true to God, and accept Jesus Christ, and let yourself be led of the good and Holy Spirit to repentance and amendment of life, and to remain faithful in all this unto death?

Can you affirm this with "Yes"?

I ask you also whether you are willing to submit yourselves to the complete scriptural teachings of Jesus Christ, and strive to keep and abide by his commandments, doctrine and bidding unto death. And whether you are willing to submit yourselves to all the scriptural rules of the Church of Jesus Christ and to be obedient to these unto death?

Can you affirm this with "Yes"?

The Lord has heard you. Those who are seated may stand. Let us pray.

Upon repentance and amendment of your life, and the confession of your faith, which you have made before God and these witnesses, I now baptize you with water, in the name of the Father, the Son Jesus Christ, and the Holy Spirit.

In the name of the Lord and in the name of the church I offer you my hand: Stand up to a new beginning and a new walk of life.

May the Lord strengthen and help you to fulfill your newly undertaken work, to be his disciple, to know the truth, and the truth shall make you free.

The baptismal vows were translated by Allen N. Hoover in 2004. A slightly different version of the vows appears in both German and English in *In Meiner Jugend* (2000, 204–8).

WEDDING VOWS

(To both) Do you believe that marriage is an institution of God, renewed and confirmed by Christ? And have you appealed to God in prayer in the hope and confidence that your marriage may be in the Lord? Can you answer this with yes?

And so you as the bridegroom are asked if you are free, single, and disengaged from all other women, as far as marriage is concerned? Can you answer this with yes?

And you as the bride are asked if you are free, single, and disengaged from all other men, as far as marriage is concerned? Can you answer this with yes?

And so you as the bridegroom are asked if you are willing to accept this your bride, our fellow-sister [name], as your wife, to love and to care for her and to stand by her in need, in sickness, or whatever the Lord allows to come upon you, to live with her in a Christian and peaceable manner, to take the heavier responsibility upon yourself, and not to forsake her until death shall separate you. Can you answer this with yes?

So you as the bride are asked if you are willing to accept this your bridegroom, our fellow-brother [name], as your husband, to love and to care for him and to stand by him in need, in sickness, or whatever the Lord allows to come upon you, to live with him in a Christian and peaceable manner, to take the lighter responsibility upon yourself, to be submissive to him and not to forsake him until death shall separate you. Can you answer this with yes?

The wedding vows appear in both German and English in *In Meiner Jugend* (2000, 224–27).

APPENDIX C: two hymns on humility

1.   My God, I bring my heart to Thee,
As an offering and a gift;
Yea, Thou askest this of me,
This I bear in mind.
2.   "Give me, my child, your heart,"
Thou sayest, "It is dear and valuable to me,
You won't find rest otherwise
In heaven and on earth."
3.   Now then, my Father, accept it,
My heart—do not despise it—
I give it as well as I can give it,
Turn Thy face toward me.
4.   Indeed, it is full of sin's rubbish,
And full of vanity,
But the good it is unaware of—
The true godliness.
5.   But now it stands in repentance,
Recognizes its evil condition,
And now has an aversion to that
In which it earlier took delight.

. . . .

16.   Help me to be pure with all my heart
In loving others, and demonstrate
Through works done for Thy glory
That my deeds are not done merely for the appearance.

17.   Help me to be straight-forward with all my heart,
Upright without deceit,
So that my words and works may be right;
Make me wise in simplicity.
18.   Help me with all my heart to feel small,
To exercise humility and meekness,
So that I, pure from all love of the world,
May continually grow in Jesus' love.
19.   Help me to be devout with all my heart,
Without any hypocrisy, that thereby
My whole Christianity may be pleasing to Thee.

.   .   .   .

24.   Away with you, world. Away with you, sin,
I give not my heart to you;
Only Jesus, for Thee is this gift prepared,
Keep it forever and ever.

Author: Johann Casper Schade, 1600s.
Hymnbook: Unpartheyisches Gesangbuch, no. 162, p. 178.
Theme: Proverbs 23:26. (My son, give me thine heart, and let thine eyes observe my ways.)
Summary: The writer offers his heart to God although he realizes it is full of vanity, and he desires to have it cleansed of worldly lusts and pretense.
SOURCE: English translation from *Unpartheyisches Gesangbuch: Translation and Lessons* (1997, 79).

"DEMUT IST DIE SCHÖNSTE TUGEND"

1.   Humility is the most beautiful virtue,
The glory and honor of all Christians,
For it adorns our youth, and the older people much more.
They also do not care to praise those
Who are exalted through good fortune;
It (humility) is more than gold and money
And what is glorious in the world.
2.   Behold, Jesus was humble, He did not exalt himself,
He was friendly, loving, gracious,
As God's word informs us;
In His life one found no boasting or exalting,
Therefore He says to me and you:

"Learn humility from Me."

3.   He who is devoted to humility is loved by everyone;
He who doesn't desire to be great and learned,
He it is to whom God gives honor:
Humility has always pleased God
It is also pleasing to all
Who walk in God's ways
And stand (abide) in Jesus' love.

4.   Humility does not make one contemptible (worthless)
As the proud world cries out (proclaims)
When it boldly and thoughtlessly
Spits at the humble ones:
The proud themselves confess,
When they see devout people around them,
That humility is nobler than a bold, proud Christian.

5.   Humility brings great blessings and finds favor with God,
It (humility) means a great deal,
For he who has this virtue,
Is adorned in his soul,
And blessed in his doings,
He is blissful (happy) in this time,
And saved (blessed) in eternity.

Author: Bishop Christian Herr, in the early days of Pennsylvania history.
Hymnbook: Unpartheyisches Gesangbuch, no. 135, p. 149.
Theme: The merits of humility.
Summary: Humility is the best virtue, adorning every true Christian as it did
Christ, bringing blessings in time and eternity.
SOURCE: English translation from *Unpartheyisches Gesangbuch: Translation and
Lessons* (1997, 65).

✤ APPENDIX D: scripture and hymns for special church services

	HYMNS	SCRIPTURE
Announce counsel	170, 300	Matt. 7:1–14
Counsel service	258, 259, 260, 261	Matt. 18:1–22
Preparatory service	38, 41, 43, 44, 262	Matt. 6:1–24
Communion	104, 113, 113, 115, 117, 457, 476, 468, 482	Luke 22:1–23, 1 Cor. 10:1–24, 1 Cor. 11:16–34, John 13:1–17
Votes for ordination	229, 233	1 Tim. 3, Titus 1, 1 Pet. 5
Ordination service	231 (minor tune), 230, 213, 233, 449, 452	Luke 10:1–21, Matt. 1–16, Rom. 12, Acts 7
New minister's first sermon	449	
Instruction classes	127, 164, 281, 283, 284, 295, 450, 458, 459, 472	
Baptism	98, 102, 450, 460 (vv. 8–14)	Mark 16:11–20
Wedding	324 (morning); 326 (noon)	Col. 3, Eph. 5, 1 Pet. 3
Good Friday	47, 415, 465	Luke 23:27–56
Easter		Mark 15:15–47, Luke 24:1–31
Ascension	58	Acts 1:1–14
Funeral	378 . . . (child), 379, 388, 454, 473, 474, 478	Varies
Thanksgiving	28, 29, 298, 311, 318, 345, 365, 366, 368, 454, 462	Rom. 13
Reinstating penitent sinner	62, 63, 418	Luke 15

SOURCE: Hymn selections from *Ein Gesangbuch Von Deutsche Melodies* (2000, 105). Scripture selections provided by various informants.

❖ APPENDIX E: two essays on the automobile

Preacher John S. Kurtz (1859–1927) was perhaps the most vocal minister to favor a non-fashionable motorcar or truck. In 1918 he once told a young man, "I like your truck." Kurtz wrote a letter in 1920 to Bishop John Dan Wenger in Virginia arguing that other changes have come and that the motor vehicle must come also. Preacher Kurtz died in the spring of 1927, several weeks before the division over the car.

Ephrata, Pennsylvania
September 14th, 1920
Dear Brother and Sister in [the] Faith:

First a greeting of love and well wishing in our Master's name, who was willing to bear our sins and shortcomings so that we can have a free access to the throne of grace and finally be numbered with those in white raiment. We are [as] usual well, hoping and wishing [that] you are the same. I truly feel glad that you had paid us a visit, as it is more natural and creates more love when we see the brethren face-to-face and [it enables us] to build up each other in the holy faith.

But to our sorrow, two or three got autos, and that [is] yet just as the world; but I also heard that one talked of putting it away again. I told you several times that you don't know the position here [that] we are in. So I will try and inform you and give my view. I preached at funerals and otherwise against the auto and other extravagancies and took the apostles for [an] example, who had only a staff, no special clothing to preach in, etc., and stated, in regard to getting around filling appointments, (and) that we had no right to go further than the Word. For all offering not brought in the right way is an abomination and not a blessing, and obedience is more than sacrifice; and that we would better go to heaven with a staff only than by using other means of getting around. . . .

Now in regard to material things, we read of leprosy; it came on the body in the houses and clothing and so it is yet today. It represents sin. It appears on the body like [the] mustache, hair cutting, combing, etc., and in the clothing and in the houses—too much after the world which they have not learned of Christ. Shall we condemn all [of this]? Was not all that we have [at] one time gotten up by worldly people and highly esteemed among men? We must consider leprosy—when it had covered the whole body they were pronounced clean; so in material things when it is [found] all over or common, it is clean for us or else we would condemn our forefathers and ourselves.

Over or about 100 years ago when the first man came to Weaverland church on a cart with a chair on because of him [being] too weighty to ride on a horse, [but] some were very much opposed but could not pronounce it leprosy or sin. Then later they got one with wooden springs—but at first only the puffed-up and "high heads" had them. But soon they were common for our people. And about 70 years ago the steel springs came; those were considered wrong. And in a few years the same people got them and said they are more common now. When my father was single he got a buggy without [a] top and had it a long time that I know of and rode in; the rock-away came later, and when I came to the ministry I got one that a Presbyterian had got for his use but [they] were out of date so much that there were few in our church. And about 10 years before or when they came up [first came into being], some thought they should not be allowed and when the fallen top buggies came, some thought [Bishop] George Weaver should positively not allow them, but did not. But they had their troubles in all these things—so also in clothing. Men and women have changed even in our—what we call "plain [churches]." We need not go far back when it was the soldier's coat, but now they are common so that we can hardly get our ministers [not] to wear them. So in all changes there is also trouble. So it also was in [the] line of machinery. When the sewing machine came, a woman [said] to an old deacon that this devil machine should not be allowed. But he said it is not the machine but those that use it for ruffling, etc.—that is, in the people. And so with all farm machinery and tractions [tractional] engines: some would not allow [them] and others rejoiced, as this would now take off or release the horses. And so it is now with the tractors. And when the railroad was first built, some were so in favor and even Bishop George Weaver took stock and so helped to build [it] because it relieved the horses, although it had its dark and worldly side. So with the trolley: many supported them in building and now most—if not all [brethren] support them by using [them] which is all in one chain. . . .

Now in regard to the machine [auto] or all [things] in the auto line—as some want to have it carried out, or condemned [but]—what does the word say? That we shall not condemn so that we are not condemned. This auto decision is the "shackiest"* I ever saw; when a winds blows or a fox runs against [it], it shatters. Just think of it, even the bishops—some when [away] from home—hire autos to get around, and another had chosen the auto because it was warmer than the carriage. Another talked hard against [it] and before midnight or about midnight was an auto victim. But we can see with Peter how it is if men build on themselves though they say they stand at the pain of death. Just consider the bishops as well as the members and ministers: when they get in a "ditch," then they go for the auto and [the] members that talked so hard against it and want to have put back [expel] such that have [a] truck or even run [drive] a truck. Then they [anti-auto critics] take trips with those very machines and men who[m] they put back [from communion], or consented [upheld]. Now this includes nearly [all], if not all, that supported one way or the other, and got the full benefit.

He that is joined to a harlot is one body at home or abroad. The word makes no difference, and no circumstances or such doctrine would soon make such things necessary. When the spies came to Jericho, a harlot took them in, but not to lust; for she was converted. Her confession and works proved it. And David did not eat idols' meat. What did Christ and the apostles say in regard to such things? By the fruit ye shall know the tree! Now as stated above, that the fruit is so sweet and good in time of need, will we condemn ourselves by condemning a good tree? Some might say that they [autos] are too stylish. Then they must be converted and made common [plain] to suit our confession—not to cut members off and let others have or get the fruit [the auto].

Others may say it gives too much chance to go to forbidden places. The chances are here for the trolley goes to all those places, and with horse and buggy [one can get there as well]—and others can walk. Or did Christ mean when he said, Cut off [your] hand, foot, and pluck [out your] eye, that we should do so, [so] that they could not enjoy or get to such places? Or did he preach true repentance and conversion? No one believes that a converted heart will use its members to go to any illfame[d] (or) place contrary to the word.

The reason I think that a plain truck should be allowed, or that line [of machinery] is because they are in general use in our churches. This was, yes, done [it] as hypocrisy-connected: members [were] put back, and [yet] the auto stays.

A great part of the tobacco was hauled by truck and [by] many of such that stand back from the church and such other things.

Who[m] shall we take for our counselors, the old or the young? The old had it 40 years ago: if some or any get proud or vain, they should be visited and pointed to humility—that is, to Christ. Our bishop never was in favor to make it or have it the way it is. Two years ago he was so pressed and loaded down and got sick and taken to the hospital in an auto and there in prayer and waited for the end of his journey. Then an angel appeared to him and [he] also heard a voice that there would be nothing for such that trust in their own—not that I believe in worshipping angels, but if an angel tells us and points us to Christ alone, then I think we should consider it.

Now if you want my full view, you press in your mind in reading these lines that I don't want to know anything else but Jesus Christ and him crucified. And keep this in your mind as if it were written in between every line. And also consider Matt. 7:17–18, Luke 6:44, James 3:11–12, Matt. 7:1, Luke 6:37, Rom. 2:1, Rom. 14:22–23, Col. 2:8, 18 & 20, [and] Rev. 22:18. The above references point to Christ, and that God requires from us what we require, or the bishop[s] from the members, and that the bishop[s] have clean hands and not be entangled in the things they judge, or they pronounce it against themselves.

I must do my part, but each one has to give an account [of] himself to God. So I can easily bear with them and will do like Paul: keep my body under, so that when I preach [to] others I am not cast away.

If a bishop in our day would have the true love of God and use His word only and set back all that have the appearance of pride, covetousness, selfwill, [and] would search the houses, conveyances, clothing, and their way of dealing, etc., he would have a small flock; but I also feel [one has] to have forbearing.

If you get [too] tired to read it all, [I hope] you can get so much out [of it so that you know] that I am satisfied with Christ['s] word. [May] all come to conference and work that we get things in shape, [and] that we all can live up to [Christ's word] and not only [be] a stumbling block for all to stumble at and fall.

All in love,

J. S. & Maria Kurtz

SOURCE: *Mennonite Historical Bulletin*, no. 4 (October 1976): 5–6. Two paragraphs not directly related to Kurtz's argument are not included here.
*In this context, *shackiest* in the Wenger usage of Pennsylvania German means "binding us to a church rule that does not make sense."

"A CONFESSION OF FAITH" BY J. D. WENGER (C. 1921)

Bishop John Dan Wenger in Virginia, an ally of Bishop Jonas Martin, was a forceful opponent of the automobile. In 1921, possibly in response to J. S. Kurtz's letter and likely encouraged by Jonas Martin, he wrote the following treatise against the car. The essay was printed and widely circulated among Old Order people.

A confession of the faith, in material things; or a reason of our practice in the peaceable principles and true. I have believed, and therefore have I spoken, "We also believe and therefore speak." 2nd Cor. 4:13.

Now to perform our duty in this, we need to be pure and clear in wisdom, strong and powerful in truth, simple and desirable in righteousness; for happy is he that possesses this. His heart rejoices in the Lord; his mouth also speaketh that which is right concerning the things of the Spirit; his labors abound abundantly in the upbuilding of one another and the Church's edification. Indeed, he spends all his mind and strength setting his house in order and holding forth that one pearl of great price, and to keep the vineyard of the Lord in a clean and healthy condition. The hedge must be kept in repair; if any part is broken down, it must be propped up; if any gaps appear it must be closed, lest things come in the Church that will be its certain downfall. If we begin to yield to this and that, we are letting the bars down, and once they are down, we cannot close them again, except something marvelous takes place.

We know that the pure blossom of virginity, once it is lost, is never restored. So it is with the Church. To get it back to where it was fifty years ago in simplicity, humility, and separation from the world, is a thing many are unwilling to do, but would rather tear the Church to pieces and make a scatterment [*sic*] of the flock.

But if every generation would have held her own, and not yielded to seducing things, the Mennonite Church today would not be divided in so many branches. Surely then we ought not to allow things questionable, or that have the appearance of evil. It is true we are sometimes driven to some things, that we cannot help ourselves in material things; but this is not generally so, and if we are faithful, God will make a way for us. For God will surely visit, and sin will find its victim.

But someone will say we have the same worship that our fathers had fifty years ago. In keeping the ordinances this may be true. It is just as true that Israel kept God's ordinances and statutes with marvelous zeal. But because they desired and did do in material things as the world did, they began to be at ease in Zion, put far away the evil day and caused the seat of violence to come near. Lying upon their beds of ivory, and stretching themselves upon their couches, was not suffering affliction with the people of God, but enjoying the pleasure of the world.

But the Church must not be condemned with the world, but rather reprove the world, that the world may be judged by the Church. But if we observe the ordinances, never so strict, and yet desire the highly esteemed things of the world. Luke 16:15. We are no better than rejected Israel, which is written for an example to us.

There are many ways by which men may be led away. Some are led away by adding to the word and making ordinances of their own. Some have idols in their hearts, and others by setting the stumbling block of their iniquity before their face, to enjoy the pleasures of this world. And there are lords many and gods many in the enjoyment of this world, and the world shall rejoice but ye shall have sorrow. But the sorrowful pilgrims and strangers of this earth that rejoice in tribulation and necessity are few indeed. Oh I pray for them that they may magnify the name of the Lord on earth.

There never was a time like now—the inducements so great, the temptations so many, and the appearance so good to lead man astray. But our mother, Eve, was also tempted with so much good; yet there was evil in it, to the sorrow of mankind. We should take warning from such serious, yet apparently little things.

It has been the case that at conference such things have been danced upon until the line of demarcation was erased. And, once it is erased, where will it stop? Indeed, man may know the beginning of sin, but who bounds the issue thereof? I feel that it is important that these things be preached more, and the ministers be in union and speak the same thing, that the trumpet give a certain sound in all things, as well as in material things that are so highly esteemed and more money spent for than almost anything else.

Now the question confronts us about the automobile. Shall we open the door for it? We say "No," because it opens the door for anything; and "the chariots of thy glory shall be the shame of thy Lord's house." Isaiah 22:18. This is begun by coveting after fashionable conveyances as the inhabitants of Lachish, who bound the chariots to the swift beast. It is the beginning of sin to the daughter of Zion, for the transgressions of Israel were found in thee. Micah 1:13.

Let everyone awake. This solemn truth is calling us to the cross, that those luxuries are not the ordained way to Heaven. And it is continually also calling for something else. Besides this, it calls for expensive roads. It is now dangerous for the men of low estate, Romans 12:16, to travel on the highways; and many of our roads are narrow, which make it difficult to pass. We cannot give our consent, not even to the truck or cheap auto, for soon it would be said that the high priced are cheapest. In considering mankind in general, those people who want the auto are a people inclined to popularity, though there may be some exception.

If we do not deny ourselves of those highly esteemed things which are more for pleasure than anything else, why need we deny ourselves of anything? But it is positive that we must deny ourselves, take up the cross, and suffer hardship. There are too many things in the Church already that take the minds of the people; like running the auto, the mind must be there, or it goes to the ditch. But our affections should be above. Well may the prophets declare woe to such things, besides the offenses it causes. And for such, Christ says, "Better that a mill stone were hung to the neck, and he be drowned in the sea. Oh how much better to eat no flesh or leave such things alone while the world standeth rather than offend one of those little ones that believe in Christ." Matthew 18:6, I Cor. 8:13.

If we open the door for the auto, we are in line with the fast element, and the language of the Prophet Amos 6:1–6 will be disregarded, and the Prophet Nahum, second chapter, will apply to us. Let us take warning from such scriptural texts and not follow after such popularity and magnificence.

How vast the difference when Jesus Christ, the Lowly Lamb of God, was here in person and rode to Jerusalem upon an ass to fulfill that prophecy. "Behold thy King cometh unto thee, meek," Matthew 21:5, etc. And again if horses were too gay for the meek and lowly in the day of Pharaoh, how much more should we hold back. It is true not everyone was upright who has ridden a mule, but let us remember that David and Solomon were both up-right when they rode the mule. Should we not go back to the old ways more than to push popularity? Jeremiah 6:16. Would it not be sad if some would leave the Church rather than to deny themselves of such popular things? But where is faith in such people?

Besides this, when people begin to lust after evil things there is no knowing where they stop. No doubt our Lord suffers things to come upon us to try our faith. When the auto first came around, most common people were opposed to it. But many have left their first love and a seared conscience is the result.

But how about other improvements that are in daily use? Shall we do away with them too? It would indeed be better if all would help dig the earth, but as it is, it is an evil case and we are driven to things that we sometimes would rather not. But it is bad enough without pushing popularity with that kind of heaver [in this way]. For the auto is the downfall of many, especially the young that love running about. Nothing better to induce them to taking the spin; they get in the habit, like going to so-called innocent pleasure which results in the heart of a fool in the house of mirth. Eccles. 7:4. Not in vain does the Word say evil communications corrupt good manners.

But some say there is too much ado about material things, for it does not affect the worship of God. Well some materials things do not, and we must also have forbearance in some things. But the mustache we cannot, though some think [it's] the mark of leprosy [by God]. [There's] is no Scripture against it, as the covering was put on. Women wearing hats we cannot tolerate, though some think her hat is different from men's to evade Deuteronomy 22:5. But the hidden wisdom which God ordained for our glory teaches us that the mustache, women wearing hats, and the auto are next things to points of doctrine in our spiritual worship; and upon points of doctrine we cannot, if true, deviate from upon pain of death.

Many years ago when the Mennonite Church was together yet with us, [Old Orders] and they had not yet yielded to this and that, I remember a Harrisonburg merchant came in the first auto to our services, and what an impression it made upon all our minds. All thought that was very worldly. Now such impressions should be cherished as it leads to convictions, and that leads to conversions. I know that many had impressions just similar, and many of them preachers too, that did not have backbone to stand [up] to their real conscience. Is that serving God or men? If some golden wedge is in the camp, God is not there to help, no matter what number they have. But if two agree in His name, there is the promise.

But must we have the auto to fulfill our appointments, the question comes. Must we situate ourselves that we cannot reach them without it? God never intended that we must have a flying machine so that we could reach our appointments. We have Bible characters to teach us in this. Besides, if we preach Christ, and Him crucified, and keep our house [church life] accordingly, we realize that Christ came to his own and his own received him not. Indeed, to do away with the auto, the musical instrument and similitudes, yet all material things seem to many a hard saying, too hard to hear. And possibly the preacher could easily walk to his place of worship betimes.

Do we have need to be afflicted and mourn, to let our laughter be turned to mourning, and our joy to heaviness? Let us place ourselves in the balance of the Word and see if we are found wanting. I do not write these things to set up controversy, which ends in endless genealogies, but simply for such that seek the truth with pleasure. And if any desires to hear more, let him do what is herein contained that it may prove that he wants more, and God will open the door for further consideration. My heart's desire and prayer to God is that all men might be saved. I remain the well-wisher of all who read this little treatise written by an unworthy servant; but do feel yet to say that I was moved by the Spirit to put hand to pen, not for honor, but for the truth. Neither have I fished in other men's waters for this, but it is my own honest convictions; neither would I boast in another man's line of things made ready to my hands, II Cor. 10:16, but being illiterate, unlearned, and having no schooling, I can see through the Spirit that to oppose some material things in the Church until it becomes common and then sanction it will not do. May all the world be set to wondering and searching this solemn truth is my prayer.

The above treatise was written for the *Gospel Herald*, and was rejected as a thing not good to place before the reading public, however it has not been more than twelve months since similar articles were published in it.

This paper is published by a Mennonite fraternity and its editor charges that this treatise lays the burden of guilt upon the lawful users of the auto.

Now the question comes, what is lawful and expedient use? The Mennonite fraternity opposes such material things as wearing of mustache, women wearing hats, the taking of similitudes [photos], having musical instruments, fancy conveyances, automobiles, etc., as well as those scholastic attainments that lead to ill fame, pomp, blare, pride, and exaltation. These things were all denounced by, I dare say, all Mennonites one day, but where are many today? Where is self-denial; where are the cross bearers as in the days of yore? Alas! They are fled and gone indeed, and things have all turned around since twenty years ago.

Now the question confronts us, as I once read in a tract on simplicity, will we remain a self-denying, world ignoring, God honoring people, cleave to the truth and bar the evil out, standing on that rock Christ Jesus, that is higher than I, and withstand a stormy sea. My prayer is that we bestir ourselves and strive to enter at the strait gate, for it is a place of danger. Now let us beware that we lose not our first love.

But someone will say "Let love rule in the church and not compulsion," and so not lose members of the church. Now this is Catholic doctrine and a great error. It might also be said we do not cast out our children from home when disobedient. Now this is very true in natural things, but in the things divine it is not so. Love does rule indeed in the church, and love does many things. Love lays judgment to the line and righteousness to the plummet. Love will sometimes chastise, even our children. Love hates sin. Love has no fellowship with the unfruitful works of darkness. Love has no concord with Belial. Love marks them which cause divisions and offense contrary to the doctrine which we have learned. Love will not bid God-speed to evil, no not to costly array, autos, etc., not even to the appearance of evil, and especially not to presumptuous and heretical doctrine.

Now if some do leave the church after love is applied, it is not more than Christ's word being fulfilled. But as for us to protest against the things herein named until they become common and then open the door [for them] is a thing that is foreign to me. Such doctrine will soon make things common. Things go too fast if we do what we can, without us paving the way. Let us be consistent in all walk of life. It is true we are sometimes picked up, and we cannot help it. But such has been in all ages of the world. The lawyer may be of use. The harlot Rahab was of service to God's people. David and those who were with him ate the shrewbread, a thing not lawful under ordinary circumstances, yet Christ said he was blameless in this. God will never leave his people, but will, with the temptation, make a way for their escape. And as for the auto, we can easily do without it. A Brother said to me this winter, "The auto is only for luxury, for now the auto cannot be used because of the conditions of the roads." Yet the people could go and get to their places of worship even in those short days on good time.

I am writing this for the benefit of the rising generation and all God-fearing people, that we do not change from one thing to another more than we can help. "Jesus Christ, the same yesterday, today, and forever." Yea, in him is no variableness, neither shadow of turning, and the less we have to contend with of the things of this world, material things, the better off we are.

When I consider how much many people are involved in the material things of this world and yet claim to be non-resistant, especially in war times, and coming to our President pleading for protection from military service under the pretence of being the true non-resistant and self-denying people, as were our forefathers that came to America because of their faith. And when the Revolutionary war broke out our fathers came before Parliament! And their very looks, their simplicity and self-denial, their enduring of hardship, and their peculiarity harmonized with their humble plea and confession (of which plea I have a sample copy), and was so touching that it reached the heart, so that there was provision made in the law for such.

But with many professors today, they are as different from them as is light from darkness. I fear such people are no better than the Gibeonites, who by craft obtained a league with Israel, Joshua 9, and so escaped the edge of the sword. I feel that I should expose such things, for it is not right that people pretend a thing, and yet possess it not. I fear there are but few people that deserve such a good government [that grants] exemption from military service.

I believe in letting my light shine, even though I should be tried like Sampson. God, I hope, will give me grace that I could, if need be, like Sampson say, "Let me die with these uncircumcised Philistines, rather than to keep my light under the bushel." To God be glory forever. Amen.

SOURCE: Printed as a pamphlet without date, author, or publisher. Reprinted in Hoover 1982, 813–18.

❖ APPENDIX F: german word usage

USE IN TEXT	FORM	REFERENCE	ENGLISH TRANSLATION
Bede	PG	S:333	prayer
Buss	PG	S:343	repentance
Deitsch	PG	S:37; M:2	Dutch
Demut	SG	S:287	humility
Diener	SG	S:38	servant
Faschtdaag	PG	S:266	fasting day
Fuhr	PG	S:60; M:25	team
Fuhreleit	PG	S:60	team Mennonites
Funkeleit	W	WI	Funk people
Gelassenheit	SG	C:184	yieldedness
Gemeinde	SG	C:184	community
Gmay	W	WI	church/community
Gmayhaus	W	WI	churchhouse
hergewwe	W	WI	yield/give up
Hochmut	PG	S:87	pride
Kircheleit	W	WI	High Church people
Kuchen	PG	S:245	cookies
Leedabuch	W	WI	songbook
Mittag	SG	C:322	noon meal
Nayva sitzah	W	WI	wedding attendants
Ordnung	SG	S:127	Church rules

USE IN TEXT	FORM	REFERENCE	ENGLISH TRANSLATION
Outsida	W	WI	outsider
Pennsilvaanisch	PG	M:2	Pennsylvania
Rumspringa	W	WI	running around
Schtadt	PG	S:383	town/city
Schtedler	PG	S:383	town people
Schtupp	PG	S:346	room
uffgewwe	PG	S:171; M:65	give up/submit
Unpartheyisches Gesangbuch	W	WI	Impartial Songbook
Unsrerleit	PG	S:322	our people
untergeben	SG	C:503	place under
untertanig	SG	C:504	submit to authority
Weberthal	W	WI	Weaverland Valley
Wei	PG	S:399	wine
Weltleit	PG	S:196	worldly people
ya	PG	S:402	yes

Key: PG = Pennsylvania German; SG = standard German; W = Wenger;
C = Cassell 1965; M = Miller 2001; S = Stine 1996; WI = Wenger usage via
informants.

❖ notes

1. This fascinating story has been retold by filmmaker Ken Burns in "Horatio's Drive: America's First Road Trip," shown on many PBS stations in the fall of 2003, at the centennial of the coast-to-coast trip.

2. Some historians estimate that as many as 2,200 different makes of cars were manufactured in the early years of the auto industry in the United States, as entrepreneurs scrambled to produce cars for the huge national market (Clymer 1950, 205).

3. U.S. Department of Transportation statistics, as reported in an Associated Press release written by Leslie Miller, 30 August 2003.

4. Indeed, as late as 1968, one scholar of folk societies predicted that groups such as the Amish and Old Order Mennonites "will eventually be overcome by the greater society" (Glassie 1968, 4).

5. Anthropologists have long focused on worldview as a key concept to understanding the core dispositions and values that shape a culture's perception of and response to its physical and social world. Toelken (1979) devotes chapter 7 of his book to the relationship between folk culture and worldview. In two essays, Dundes (1972, 1980) describes and demonstrates the efficacy of the concept of worldview. In the 1972 essay he shows how folk ideas—proverbs, folktales, and folksongs—are basic units of a culture's worldview. In a penetrating analysis of American folklore, Dundes (1980) pinpoints the dominance of the future orientation in the American worldview. Not surprisingly, the concept of worldview has been vigorously debated in anthropological circles. For a sample of the debate see Hill and Mannheim (1992).

6. Stine's (1996) dictionary of the dialect provides a standard treatment of many common words but does not include all the words that are used by the Wengers. Likewise, S. D. Miller's (2001) dictionary primarily reflects usage in

the Old Order Amish community of Pennsylvania. Beam and Brown (2004) are compiling an extensive dictionary that will include many of the expressions used by the Wengers.

CHAPTER I

1. Martha Shirk, Janet Zimmerman, and Eli Hoover are common—but here, fictitious—names for the people described in the first three paragraphs. We occasionally use other fictitious but typical names throughout the text. The Old Order Mennonites in Indiana are not known as Wenger Mennonites because they affiliated with the Wenger Mennonites in 1973, forty-six years after the Wengers began. The Indiana members are simply known as Old Order Mennonites who are affiliated with the Groffdale Conference. Sometimes they are referred to as the "John Martin people," recalling the name of an Old Order Indiana bishop, John W. Martin (1852–1940). For a concise overview of the Indiana Old Order Mennonites, see Meyers and Nolt (2005).

2. The word "team" does not refer to two horses pulling a carriage, but to the combination of the horse and the carriage. The Wenger people are often called "team Mennonites" because they formed in 1927 over a division related to owning cars. The Wengers wanted to keep the "team" (horse and carriage) in lieu of accepting the car. According to a personal communication from historian Amos B. Hoover, although other Old Order Mennonite groups drive teams, only the Wengers are known as *the* team Mennonites.

3. In Chapter 9, we provide a more detailed description of contemporary Amish and Mennonite differences.

4. The exact number of Wenger members in 1927 is not known. Old Order historians agree that about 200 families affiliated with the Wengers and estimate that the total Wenger population was 1,000 (500 baptized members and 500 children). The 1927 division roughly split the Old Order Mennonite Church in Lancaster County in half, yielding a similar estimate of 500 members in the car-driving Horning Church. In 2005, the national adult membership of the Horning Church was 6,500, whereas the national baptized Wenger membership was about 8,500. According to one Old Order historian, the Horning Church grew faster after the 1927 division, but the adult membership of the two groups was about equivalent by 1984. Since then, the Wenger group has grown faster.

5. This estimate is based on James P. Hurd's and Allen N. Hoover's Martindale District Study (see Appendix A) in Lancaster County; 79 of 177 people emigrated to other states. Residence information was missing for 22 of the 199 subjects.

6. Amish carriage styles and colors vary somewhat by settlement and affiliation. Thus, depending on the settlement, the carriages driven by the Wengers' Amish neighbors may not always be black or gray.

7. For introductions to Anabaptist history and thought, consult Dyck (1993), Klaassen (2001), Loewen and Nolt (1996), Snyder (1995), J. D. Weaver (2005), and G. H. Williams (2000). The *Mennonite Encyclopedia* (1955–59, 1990) includes many articles related to Anabaptist history, beliefs, and practices.

8. Amos B. Hoover (1982, 7), an esteemed Old Order Mennonite historian, makes this statement.

9. *Mennonite Encyclopedia* 2:675–76, s.v. "Hans Haslibacher."

10. The most comprehensive history of Mennonites in Lancaster County is John Ruth's (2001) 1,400-page narrative. Sections of MacMaster's (1985) work also detail the early Mennonite settlement in the Lancaster area. The quarterly journal of the Lancaster Mennonite Historical Society, *Pennsylvania Mennonite Heritage*, provides many essays on the history of Mennonites in Lancaster County.

11. The story of the Mennonite settlement in the Groffdale area and the growth of its Mennonite congregation is told by A. G. Wenger (1992).

12. Two manuscripts of the Lancaster Conference bishop and moderator Jacob Hochstetter (1774–1865) offer some of the best evidence of the practices and beliefs of the Lancaster Conference prior to the printing of the first discipline of the conference in 1881. Hochstetter's two manuscripts appear in Ruth (2001, 1188–213). Amos B. Hoover (1982, 683–86) provides an English translation of the rules and discipline of the Lancaster Conference approved in 1881. See S. M. Nolt (1992) for an analysis of the development and change of the rules and discipline of the Lancaster Conference. *Statement* (1968) provides the wording of the Lancaster Conference rules and discipline that had developed by the mid-twentieth century.

13. We have used the term churchhouse to refer to the buildings where Wengers gather for worship, because this is the English translation that the Wenger Mennonites consistently use. In the Pennsylvania German dialect, the Wengers say *Gmayhaus*. Literally this translates as "community house," because *Gmay* is the dialect's shortcut for the German word *Gemeinde* (community). In the Wenger mind, *Gmay* means both community and church, so they translate the name of the building as churchhouse, not meetinghouse. The word churchhouse also derives from the fact that Mennonite immigrants met in their homes for worship for decades after their arrival in Lancaster County. Some houses were enlarged to accommodate worship services. Indeed, the design of present-day Wenger churchhouses reflects the interior structure of the houses that were used for early church gatherings. Thus, the term churchhouse is a natural label for their church buildings.

14. Although this group of dissidents emerged in the 1780s, they did not organize their church until 1812. For discussions of the formation of the Reformed or so-called New Mennonites, see Ruth (2001, 355–57) and Scott (1996, 105–19).

15. See Ruth (2001, 518–26), Scott (1996, 88–104), and Ulle (1986) for historical overviews of the Stauffer division and the offspring groups. An English translation of Jacob W. Stauffer's views of the Mennonite Church, originally written in 1855, was published in 1992.

16. We use the word "progressive" here and elsewhere in the text to refer to people and ideas related to innovations that move away from traditional practices. Contrary to popular notions, we do not impute a value judgment that progress is beneficial; indeed, some changes labeled as progressive have proven detrimental and regressive to human communities.

17. The first Old Order Mennonite group formed in Indiana and Ohio in 1872; the last one in York County, Pa., in 1913. Compared with the massive amount of literature on the Old Order Amish, the Old Order Mennonites have received little attention from the media and scholars. Scott (1996) provides an excellent introduction to the many varieties of Old Order and conservative Mennonite groups living in the United States and Canada. There are few basic sociological studies or full-length histories of Old Order Mennonites. Hoover, Miller, and Freeman (1978) offer an overview of Old Order history from an Old Order Mennonite perspective. The most comprehensive collection of source documents related to the Old Order movement was compiled by Amos B. Hoover (1982). Entitled *The Jonas Martin Era (1875–1925)*, it contains some 1,100 pages of original letters, source documents, and interpretive essays.

In an insightful essay, Beulah Stauffer Hostetler (1992) compares the formation of several Old Order groups between 1850 and 1900. The best historical introduction to the Old Order Mennonites and Amish in nineteenth century America is Chapter 8, "Keeping the Old Order," in Schlabach (1988, 201–29). Cronk's (1977) study of *Gelassenheit* in Old Order Mennonite and Amish communities provides an excellent analysis of Old Order ritual in both congregational and daily life. A condensed version of her study appeared in Cronk (1981). *The Mennonite Encyclopedia* offers overview essays on the Old Order Mennonites in 4:47–49 and 5:654–55. Lloyd Weiler (1993, 1995) wrote an overview of the history of the Old Order Mennonites from a Horning Mennonite perspective. Scott discusses Old Order Mennonite attire (1986) and also a wedding and baptism (1988).

The Canadian Old Order Mennonites have received much more popular and scholarly attention than the Old Order Mennonites in the United States. This may be partly due to a smaller, less visible Amish community in Ontario. The most prolific Old Order Mennonite writer is Canadian Isaac Horst. His numerous booklets on Mennonite ways and beliefs appear in the references of this book. His most important description of Old Order practices in Ontario is found in *Separate and Peculiar* (1983), *Close Ups of the Great Awakening* (1985), and *A Separate People* (2000).

In recent years, many of Horst's essays have been published in the *Mennonite Reporter*, a newspaper that served Mennonite groups in Canada, and in *Family Life*, an Amish publication. Old Order Mennonite Donald Martin (2003), in a book on the Old Order Mennonites of Ontario, focuses on the themes of *Gelassenheit*, discipleship, and brotherhood. This in-depth history of Old Order Mennonites also covers groups and topics outside Ontario.

Helpful sociological analyses of Canadian Old Order Mennonites are found in essays by John F. Peters (1987, 1994, 2000) as well as in a popular introduction to the horse-and-buggy Mennonites of Canada in *The Plain People* (2003). In a similar fashion, Mary Ann Horst (1992) describes her Old Order Mennonite heritage in Ontario. J. Winfield Fretz (1989) includes the Old Order Mennonites in his sociological study of the Mennonite groups in the Waterloo, Ontario, area. For his master's thesis, Brubacher (1984) studied patterns of social interaction among Old Order Canadian Mennonites.

18. Our discussion of the rise of the Old Order movement and the flash points of contention leans heavily, sometimes verbatim, on the work of Kraybill and Bowman (2001, 61–64). Kern's (1983) work on the changing perceptions of space and time (1880–1918) is especially pertinent to understanding the rise of the Old Order movement.

19. Kniss (1997, 21–39) uses a cultural resources model to analyze the conflicts created by the innovations that led to the Old Order movement.

20. Schlabach (1988, 201–3) as well as Loewen and Nolt (1996, 186–88) see the formation of Old Order identities as an alternative renewal movement.

21. I. R. Horst (1989, 9).

22. Old Order Mennonites cite various New Testament passages to support their understandings of gender roles.

23. Weiler (1993).

24. Bishop Jonas Martin was the major Lancaster leader of the Old Order movement. Amos B. Hoover (1982, 23–40) provides a biographical sketch of Martin as well as this quote from one of Martin's letters (1982, 663). Martin's promises on his knees likely referred to his baptismal promises, but possibly also to his bishop ordination vows "to keep up the watch for souls and keep the church on the old faith" (Hoover 1982, 27). For a succinct and insightful glimpse into the life and times of Martin, see A. B. Hoover (1984). For a book that traces the life and genealogy of Bishop Martin, see Martin and Martin (1985). The 1893–1993 centennial of the Old Order division in Lancaster County brought several historical reflections on the Old Orders. For examples, see Benowitz (1993a and 1993b) and Weiler (1993).

25. Martin and Martin (1985).

26. Weiler (1993).

27. Article XI of the Dordrecht Confession in I. B. Horst (1988).

28. Weiler (1993, 4).

29. A. B. Hoover (1982, 22).

30. Ibid., 33.

31. Weiler (1993, 8).

32. A. B. Hoover (1982, 796–97). Ruth (2001, 657–701) tells the story of the issues and discussions that led to the 1893 division. For an account of the 1893 division from the Old Order perspective, see *Home Messenger*, April 1978, 7–8. (*Home Messenger* is a monthly publication of the Weaverland Mennonite Conference.)

33. Source materials related to this event can be found in A. B. Hoover (1982, 796–806).

34. Amos B. Hoover, citing eyewitness accounts, says they likely rode on horseback rather than in carriages. Amos B. Hoover, interview by Donald B. Kraybill, 10 January 2005.

35. A. B. Hoover (1990, 6).

36. The churchhouses built by the Old Orders after 1893 were Weaverland in 1894, Groffdale in 1895, Pequea in 1896, Churchtown in 1910, and Bowmansville in 1902. Other churchhouses were built later. For a description of the construction of these and other churchhouses, see A. B. Hoover (1990, 5–29).

37. A number of variants of Jonas (*Yoney, Joney, Yonie, Jonie*) appear in the Old Order literature. We have used *Yonie* for consistency. Because of Yonie Martin's influence, Old Order Mennonites in the Lancaster area are often called *Yonies* by both insiders and outsiders. The term is often broadly applied as a blanket term to various Old Order Mennonite groups in the region. For more details, see A. B. Hoover (1982, 21).

38. Ruth (2001, 704). Graber (1979, 175–77) calculated that the average age of the ordained officials in the Weaverland area who joined the Martinites was forty-six, whereas the average age of those who remained with the Lancaster Conference was sixty-three.

39. R. Burkholder (1997) tells the story of the Lancaster Conference Mennonites in the Weaverland area with special focus on the Weaverland congregation which stood across the road from the Old Order (Martinite) churchhouse after the 1893 division.

40. Letter of 12 March 2004 from the board of bishops of Lancaster Mennonite Conference to the Weaverland Mennonite Conference and the Groffdale Mennonite Conference. The Weaverland Mennonite Conference bishops, in a letter dated 8 June 2004, responded to the Lancaster Conference bishops. The Groffdale Conference leadership was involved in verbal discussions but did not respond with a formal letter.

41. See Umble (1996) for a thorough study of the resistance of Old Order communities to the telephone.

42. A. B. Hoover (1982, 29, 689).

43. Although earlier versions of steam automobiles appeared before 1893, the Smithsonian Institute considers the 1893 Duryea the first marketable automobile in America (Clymer 1950 and McShane 1994, 107).

44. A. B. Hoover (1982, 34).

45. Ibid., 812; *Home Messenger*, April 1978, 9.

46. Because they are based in an oral culture, the Wengers have not written much about their own history or the division of 1927. Non-Wenger Mennonite scholars have shown more interest in the initial Old Order division of 1893, which in some cases connected more directly to their own denominational affiliation. For example, Schlabach (1988, 229) devotes a sentence to the 1927 division and Ruth (2001, 704, 899) grants it only a few lines. In his study of Old Order groups, Scott (1996, 31) includes a paragraph on the 1927 schism. The written accounts of the Horning–Wenger division come from several Old Order historians including Amos B. Hoover (1978, 9–10), Michael Horning (1996, 2–5), and Emma Hurst (1960) writing from a Horning perspective, and from Noah Leid (1991, 26–28, 42) and I. N. Shirk (2002) writing from a Wenger view.

Church divisions illustrate a paradox. The conflict reduces the solidarity of the mother group, but often results in increased solidarity in the newly formed groups. For a church that does not try to tolerate wide diversity within its membership, division sometimes provides the only way to keep the peace and maintain the bonds of community.

47. In the fall of 1942, about sixty Wenger members refused to take communion because Wenger Church leaders did not censure young members who entered Civilian Public Service (cps) camps operated by more liberal Mennonite groups. Church leaders let families decide if they wanted their draft-age sons to go to prison or to cps camps. Eventually in 1946, about thirty-three former Wengers established the Reidenbach Church, which later fragmented into several small family-based groups. The nickname "Thirty-fivers" emerged when Deacon Benjamin Hoover reported that "about thirty-five people" refused to take communion at the first two communion services in the fall of 1942. In fact, a total of about sixty people refused to participate in all the communions that fall. Albertson (1996, 36–63) provides a detailed account of the Thirty-fivers who came from the ultra-conservative wing of the Wenger Church. Some of the dissenters joined the Stauffer Mennonites, the conservative group that split off from the Lancaster Conference in 1845. The Stauffers asked the ex-Wengers to eliminate the small windows in the back of their carriages. To comply, some of the ex-Wenger people painted their windows black, earning them the name "blind Joe Wenger people."

48. See Kraybill and Hostetter (2001) for an overview of all the Old Order Anabaptist groups in the United States.

49. Examples in the Lancaster area include Anabaptist-related churches such as the Nationwide Fellowship, Pilgrim Fellowship, MidAtlantic, Keystone, and Charity Christian Fellowship.

50. Funk encouraged church leaders to accept Sunday schools, the use of English, and other new practices that often reflected Protestant customs. His progressive views were one reason for the 1872 Old Order movement in Indiana.

51. Snyder (1995, 351–64).

52. Martin (2003, 315).

53. We are indebted to Cronk (1977) for identifying the importance of *Gelassenheit* and ritual in the redemptive process in Old Order communities. She was the first scholar to highlight the importance of *Gelassenheit* in her dissertation entitled, "*Gelassenheit*: The Rites of the Redemptive Process in Old Order Amish and Old Order Mennonite Communities." Cronk's foundational study spanned both Old Order Amish and Old Order Mennonite communities. Although she used the term redemptive community only occasionally, John A. Hostetler (1980, 1993) began using it frequently after 1980 to interpret the Old Order Amish.

54. This quote comes from Old Order Mennonite historian Donald Martin's (2003, 313) book, *Old Order Mennonites of Ontario: Gelassenheit, Discipleship, Brotherhood*. Martin argues that *Gelassenheit* is the deepest and most central of all Old Order values. Although the term *Gelassenheit* is not used in common parlance by Old Order laypeople or historians, Martin uses it explicitly and extensively as the primary organizing concept of his book. John A. Hostetler was aware of Cronk's (1977) work but he did not use the concept of *Gelassenheit* in the third and fourth editions of *Amish Society* (1980, 1993). Kraybill employed *Gelassenheit* as a key analytical tool in *The Riddle of Amish Culture* (2001).

Social scientists often make a sharp distinction between cultural values and behavior, between the attitudes of individuals and their actions. *Gelassenheit* is a deep and fundamental reality from which values, sentiments, and actions arise, at both individual and group levels—a deep disposition that Bourdieu would call *habitus* (Bourdieu and Wacquant, 1992). See R. Williams (1995) for a general introduction to the sociology of culture.

55. Amos B. Hoover in J. S. Miller (2004, 227).

56. Ronald Grimes (2002) and Randall Collins (2004) provide substantive introductions to contemporary studies in ritual theory.

57. Cronk (1977) separated rituals into social and ecclesiastical forms, whereas Hostetler (1980) labeled them social and ceremonial. Because all rituals are in fact social, we have classified them as formal and informal. These labels and distinctions

refer primarily to the difference between rituals that are performed at a religious site such as a churchhouse and those that are performed in the routines of daily life.

58. This classic distinction between acculturation and assimilation was articulated in 1964 by Milton Gordon (1997). On a conceptual level, acculturation focuses on values, whereas assimilation involves social structures and organizations, but in reality it is often difficult, if not impossible, to disentangle these two processes.

59. A variety of labels have been used for the process that we call selective modernization. In a study of the Hutterites, Eaton (1952) called their process of managing social change "controlled acculturation." Siegal (1970) used the phrase "defensive structuring" to describe how a small group develops structures to defend itself against the forces of assimilation. Stein (2003) speaks of communities of dissent. In his study of social change among the Amish, Kraybill (2001) described the process as one of "negotiating with modernity." We have used the term selective modernization to underscore the fact that the Wengers make intentional choices about what they accept and what they reject from the modern world. Selective modernization demonstrates that the Wengers are not a separatist folk society that is immune to modernization, but in fact are part of that larger society, but have chosen to limit their involvement in it.

60. The literature on modernization is voluminous. For seminal readings on this topic, consult P. Berger (1977), Berger, Berger, and Kellner (1973), Brown (1976), Durkheim (1984), Giddens (1991), and Madsen et al. (2002).

CHAPTER 2

1. *Conversation* (1984).

2. Aaron Z. Sensenig, interview by James P. Hurd, 11 October 1996.

3. Snyder (1995, 351–64) argues that most of the sixteenth-century Anabaptists rejected the sacramental mediation of grace (transubstantiation) through the bread and wine of communion, a belief held by Catholics and some Protestant reformers. Instead, the Anabaptists viewed the gathering of members for worship and moral discernment as a sacrament, a visible sign of invisible grace.

4. The Wengers do not practice shunning in the same way as some Amish groups do, although both the Wengers and the Amish use the Dordrecht Confession, which has an article (xvii) explicitly on shunning. Some Amish groups practice a "strict" shunning, which means that if members are excommunicated, they are shunned until they confess their error and return to the church that shunned them. Other Amish groups and some Mennonite groups practice a milder form of shunning, which is discontinued if the excommunicated member joins another nonresistant Anabaptist church and becomes a member in good standing. See Stoll (1990) for a careful description of these two types of shunning.

Evidence of historical Mennonite teaching on shunning can be found in the *Ordnung* of a ministers' conference in Indiana in 1864, eight years before the Old Order movement first began in that area. The 14 October 1864 conference proceedings were reported in *Herold der Wahrheit* in November 1864. Article IV states that members who have transgressed the *Ordnung* of the church or committed "other gross sins have been expelled from the brotherhood." The counsel was upheld that "such a person so expelled should be shunned. Members shall not seek their companionship and, as much as possible, shall avoid all business and intercourse with them, according to 1 Corinthians 5:11." The *Ordnung* concludes that members may eat with shunned persons, "if they are brought together in unavoidable circumstances," and it urges members "in love to seek to admonish the erring one" (translation by Amos B. Hoover).

In addition to this written account, Amos B. Hoover (interview by Donald B. Kraybill, 10 January 2005) provides persuasive anecdotal evidence that Mennonite groups practiced various forms of shunning. Bishop Abraham Martin frequently admonished members to shun wayward members "decently." In essence, Martin suggested, "If you are sitting at a table and an excommunicated member sits with you, remain seated, but don't take the initiative to sit with an erring member." Hoover contends that the practice of shunning in the Old Order Mennonite churches became privatized in the twentieth century. Members were advised to do it privately in a decent, orderly, and understanding manner. But members who did not shun an excommunicated member were not disciplined by the church for their negligence. Shunning thus became a more private, informal social sanction, which is how it is practiced today among the Wengers.

5. Kraybill and Bowman (2001, 15–16, 206–12) discuss these and other characteristics of the Old Order moral code in their comparative analysis of four Old Order groups.

6. Three documents provide important primary sources for insights into the moral order of Old Order Mennonite communities. The first is the Dordrecht Confession. The second is *Confession of Faith* (1996), a booklet that contains the 1632 Dordrecht Confession as well as procedures for important ceremonies in Old Order congregations—ordinations, communions, marriages, and funerals. Based on an English translation of Benjamin Eby's "Church Regulations," which was written in 1841 and revised several times by various Old Order Mennonite groups, *Confession of Faith* is a revised edition produced by the Weaverland Conference. According to one Old Order Mennonite historian, it reflects the ritual procedures of most Old Order Mennonite groups. The third document is the Groffdale Conference *Ordnung*, a twelve-page typed paper written in German in 1976 that describes beliefs and behavioral expectations—the rules and the counsels—for Wenger mem-

bers. We have used an English translation by Amos B. Hoover (assisted by Florence Horning and Hedda Durnbaugh) as a primary source for this chapter. The word *Ordnung*, as used by the Wengers, carries two meanings: a broad general description of the church's lifestyle expectations (rules and counsels) for members, and a more literal, restricted focus on the specific rules (taboos) established by the ministers' conference.

The Groffdale Conference *Ordnung* was written in 1976 to promote uniformity when new Wenger settlements were established outside Pennsylvania. The senior bishop who wrote it has some regrets about writing it, because some leaders cling to a literal interpretation of the document instead of the more flexible and organic oral tradition. He also "does not want to add or take away from the Gospel." Written copies are revised periodically by ordained leaders for reference but are not circulated to members. One bishop does not want printed copies of the *Ordnung* circulated to members for fear this would lead to trusting in one's own lifestyle, rather than in the grace of God, for salvation.

A printed copy of a 1938 Groffdale Conference *Ordnung* (in German) appears in Amos B. Hoover (1982, 698–99) and in Albertsen (1996, 40), who also provides an English translation. This document will be designated Groffdale Conference *Ordnung* 1938 in future references in this book.

7. Groffdale Conference *Ordnung* 1976.

8. Powwowing—using various mysterious objects and ceremonies for healing—was a widespread practice in rural communities in the nineteenth and early twentieth centuries, before the rise of modern medicine. One Wenger informant reports that powwowing "was used a lot" by Wengers in the first half of the twentieth century. The senior bishop worked to eliminate the practice by linking it to illicit drugs, yoga, and oriental mysticism, all of which were considered objectionable. Because of the senior bishop's efforts against these practices and his affirmation of the use of standard medical procedures, the use of powwowing has declined, according to most informants.

9. Groffdale Conference *Ordnung* 1976.

10. This settlement had no ordained bishop. When bishops from Lancaster County visited to celebrate communion, they did not read the standard *Ordnung* because of the disagreement. Later, a visiting bishop read the revised *Ordnung* written by the local minister. At that communion service, the ministers in attendance and about twenty-five other members did not partake because they did not accept the revised *Ordnung*.

11. The Wengers sometimes speak of "high" and "fast" churches, referring to more culturally assimilated groups. More traditional and restrictive churches are considered "lower" or "slower," that is, "holding back" the process of social change.

The "high" and "fast" designations are used more frequently among the Amish than among the Wengers.

12. Five words in the Pennsylvania German dialect reflect some of the specific meanings of *Gelassenheit*: *Demut* (humility); *uffgewwe* (to give yourself up, to submit); *untertanig* (to place yourself under an authority); *hergewwe* (to give up); and *untergeben* (to submit to). The last two are rarely heard in daily conversation. *Demut*, *uffgewwe*, and *untertanig* are used more frequently in Wenger discourse to capture the meanings of *Gelassenheit*. Old Order historian Amos B. Hoover says that although "the word *Gelassenheit* is in our hymnbook and used in every sermon by the Hutterites, it is not well-known by the average Old Order Mennonite . . . my preference would be the word I learned from my grandfather: *hergewwe* (verb), *Hergewwheit* (noun). This word derives from the High German *hergeben* (1. to hand over, to give up; 2. to yield). I would prefer *Hergewwheit* in the Old Order Mennonite setting. Having said all this . . . I would tend to resort to the word *Demut*, translated normally as humility, but it [*Hergewwheit*] is a broader based word than humility" (in correspondence to Donald B. Kraybill, 24 April 1996). A common word on Wenger tongues is *uffgewwe*. "It means," said one mother, "to totally submit to a rule, to give yourself up to the church when you join the church, make a confession, or are selected minister at an ordination."

13. Groffdale Conference *Ordnung* 1976.

14. Ibid.

15. "Mein Gott! Das Herz Ich Bringe Dir," song number 162 in *Unpartheyisches Gesangbuch*. See Appendix C for an English translation of selected verses.

16. "Demut Ist die Schönste Tugend," song number 135 in *Unpartheyisches Gesangbuch*. See Appendix C for an English translation of selected verses.

17. These disapproved behaviors are all explicitly counseled against in the Groffdale Conference *Ordnung* 1976.

18. The historic Anabaptist tradition embraced a two-kingdom theology that emphasized a strict separation between the kingdom of God (embodied by the local church) and the kingdom of this world (represented by the city, the government, questionable entertainment, the secular marketplace, and outsiders in general). The Schleitheim Confession of Brotherly Union in 1527 is one of the earliest statements of this two-kingdom theology. See Driedger and Kraybill (1994, 22, 54).

19. Anthropologists typically describe acculturation as the process of one culture absorbing the values and the ways of another (usually larger) culture. Sociologists speak of minority groups assimilating into the organizations of the larger society. These terms constitute academic equivalents of the theological concept of worldliness. See Gordon (1997) for the classic distinction between acculturation and assimilation.

20. Wengers would probably agree with Jacques Ellul's (1997) critique of the humanly constructed city as symbolic of the ungodly world. With the technological developments of the twentieth century, urbanism penetrates the rural countryside as well as the city. Without moving there, contemporary rural dwellers seek the technology of the city, its comforts, styles, entertainment, and ideas, confirming in Wenger minds that the city is "of the world." Some Wengers point out that in the Old Testament biblical story, "God was displeased when Lot moved to the city Gomorrah."

21. *Lancaster Intelligencer Journal*, October 2003.

22. Wenger writer I. N. Shirk (2002) concludes his brief history of the Wengers by saying, "Thus we continue in our endeavor to keep the doctrine of nonresistance and nonconformity that was passed down from the forefathers," suggesting that, at least in his mind, these are the two key tenets of faith (in that order of importance).

23. For an overview of the historic tenets of nonresistance, see chapter 1 of Driedger and Kraybill (1994). An interesting and intriguing comparison of Old Order Mennonite and assimilated Mennonite views of nonresistance is provided by Gopin (2000).

24. Original copy in the Muddy Creek Farm Library, Ephrata, Pa.

25. The names of the fourteen Wengers who refused to enter Civilian Public Service and the story of their penitentiary experience are told in Horning et al. (2004, 349–52). (Other Wengers were also arrested, but a judge assigned them to a CPS camp at Sideling Hill, Pennsylvania, rather than to prison.) The fourteen were not eligible for farm deferments. Along with six Stauffer Church youth, they were imprisoned in the Lewisburg Federal Penitentiary in central Pennsylvania from 1942 to 1946. This prison is located near the Wenger settlement in Union County, Pennsylvania. Although they did not begin their Union County settlement until 1960, the Wengers became aware of the fertile Buffalo Valley in Union County through visits to their imprisoned members during World War II.

26. One reason the Wengers gave for not participating in the Mennonite-operated CPS camps was rooted in their Old Order memory. Some Wenger people argued against going to CPS camps during World War II because, as they saw it, "We left the *Funkeleit* twice [in the divisions of 1893 and 1927] already, why should we go back and work with them in CPS?" Eli M. Reiff, interview by Donald B. Kraybill, 12 January 2005. To them, prison was safer than associating with progressive Mennonites!

27. Albertsen (1996) tells the story of the formation of the Reidenbachs.

28. The man was Levi N. Martin, later ordained a bishop in the Wenger Church. His story is recounted in a letter to Donald B. Kraybill by his son-in-law, Eli M. Reiff, 13 January 2005.

29. Gopin (2000, 234–39).

30. Martin (2003, 123).

31. We are grateful to Kyle Kopko for gathering and tabulating the voting data for the 2004 presidential election. The Wenger baptized membership of 2,840 in Lancaster County was used as the base for eligible voters. A total of 286 Wengers were listed as registered and 151 actually voted, but whom they voted for is not known.

32. Scriptures that support these Wenger views include Romans 13:1–7, 1 Timothy 2:2, Acts 4:14, Matthew 6:24, and John 18:36.

33. Ferrara (2003) recounts the story of the Old Order exemption from Social Security.

34. We use the term "Old German" to refer to the unstandardized form of pre-twentieth-century German that was written in a Gothic-style script. Standard German refers to modern High German. Pennsylvania German is a largely oral dialect that is not highly standardized. Although some dictionaries have attempted to standardize it (Beam and Brown 2004, S. D. Miller 2001, and Stine 1996), many variations persist. The variations typically reflect the cultural and religious practices of different social subgroups. No one has developed a dictionary that reflects Wenger usage of Pennsylvania German. See Appendix F for a listing of German words used in this book.

35. The school typically meets on Saturday afternoons from 1:00 to 4:15 P.M. Students and teachers read poetry and stories in the Old German script and children's stories in standard German. Materials include a German story and poem book with questions, a companion yellow book with questions and exercises, a listing of Old German script characters, a question sheet with pictures, a picture book with text, and a notebook of printed hymns with the music notes.

36. Vocal emphasis by the original speaker. There are two major points of distinction (i.e., dialect and automobile) separating the Horning Church from the Wenger Church. Thus, in the Wengers' mind, the Hornings are not an authentic Old Order church because they own automobiles and conduct religious services in English.

37. Although specific patterns of attire are expected by members, dress standards have not been an explicit test of membership in the *Ordnung*. They are enforced by the power of tradition and social participation. For a detailed description of Old Order Mennonite dress practices in various church groups, consult Scott (1986).

38. Dress practices are similar but not identical across the Wenger settlements. The general dress customs described in this section vary somewhat from community to community. The amount of clothing sewed by a mother for her family also

varies; more sewing is increasingly done by seamstresses in the community. More non-fashionable clothing is also being bought in stores.

39. In the New York settlement, white colors are seen as more liberal. For example, on Sunday, older and more conservative men wear muted blue shirts and ministers wear gray ones. Boys wear white suspenders and shift to black ones with age. Those "crowding the fence" may wear "fireman style" suspenders during the week.

40. This exact age "depends on their physical development," explained one mother. "Some begin wearing one when they turn fifteen but others earlier if necessary."

41. This statement comes from the written comments sent to the authors by a Wenger woman when she responded to a draft of the manuscript.

42. Klaassen (2001) provides a discussion of the early Anabaptist rejection of sacred places and objects.

43. The interior structure of Mennonite churchhouses evolved from the interior designs of their colonial-period homes. The simple homes of that era had a loft where children slept and three basic rooms on the first floor—a working kitchen, a large all-purpose room (Schtupp), and a parents' bedroom. The large room, used for eating, socializing, and other daily activities, was also used for church services in the eighteenth century. When the first churchhouses were built, the large living room area was expanded for worship services, and a sexton's family lived in the area equivalent to the kitchen in the colonial-style home. When the Weaverland churchhouse was built in 1882 (prior to the 1893 church division), a small sexton's house was built outside the main churchhouse. The rooms occupied by the sexton in the old-style structures became the women's vestibule and the minister's counsel room in the 1882 building. The design of the 1882 Weaverland churchhouse became the standard pattern for all churchhouses affiliated with the Old Order movement that began in Lancaster in 1893. Amos B. Hoover, interview by Donald B. Kraybill, 10 January 2005.

44. A Wenger deacon suggested that a church district should have about fifty to sixty families and should build a new churchhouse if the district grows larger. Wenger churchhouses built before 1994, however, average 77 households per churchhouse. Of all the churchhouses in Lancaster County, the Groffdale churchhouse has the most households—about 150.

45. For a detailed and illustrated description of Old Order Mennonite churchhouses in Lancaster County, see Kaylor (1987). Wenger churchhouses, painted white with wood or aluminum siding and raised-seam galvanized roofs, range in size from 1,200 to 5,600 square feet. A tall white cement block or red brick chimney rises above the roof to vent exhaust from a coal, propane, or oil stove in the basement. Churchhouses were formerly built of stone. Today they are built of wood,

while many more assimilated Mennonite groups build with brick. The Old Order Martindale stone building, constructed in 1886, stands across the fields from a newer Lancaster Conference brick structure. These two buildings reflect the bitter division of 1893.

Old Order Mennonite churchhouses in Indiana have several distinctive features that do not appear in other Wenger churches. The differences exist because the older Indiana congregations developed their patterns before the Groffdale Conference began in 1927. Indiana churchhouses and affiliated ones in other states have blue walls and ceilings, unlike the white walls and ceilings of other Wenger churchhouses. Indiana benches, painted battleship gray, are permanently screwed to the floor. A low rail runs down the center of the long benches, dividing the women from the men. The ministers sit on a preachers' bench built on top of a one-foot elevated platform. In front of the bench stands a fifteen-foot-long preaching rail or pulpit, one foot wide and three feet high. No other Wenger churchhouses have a platform, pulpit, or dividing rail. The Virginia Old Order Mennonites, who are in fellowship with the Groffdale Conference, also have a pulpit on a low platform and a dividing rail in their churchhouses, but the pulpit stands at one end of the main room, not along the side wall. The larger pulpits in Old Order churchhouses in Virginia, Indiana, and Ontario trace their origins to those of the Franconia Mennonite Conference (Pa.), which reflected Mennonite patterns in Holland.

46. The older churchhouses, following the color schemes of homes, had blue ceilings and cream-colored walls. The Springville churchhouse, constructed in 1938 near Ephrata, Pennsylvania, was the first to use all white paint (on the walls and ceiling) to improve lighting on cloudy days. All the other churchhouses soon followed this pattern, which is the standard today. Springville was also the first (1948) to add a men's cloakroom, which was adopted by many other churchhouses. For more detail, see J. D. Hoover (1990, 11–12).

47. In some settlements, a number of Wenger churchhouses have recently installed gas or oil furnaces.

CHAPTER 3 .

1. Amos B. Hoover (1984, 90) divides Old Order Mennonite history in the Lancaster area into four stages. The first stage was the rise of the Old Order movement (1871–93). He considers the period from 1894 to 1915 "the Golden Age," because leadership and identity of the movement had solidified. The third stage (1916–27) was a time of decline and dissension. The fourth stage, beginning after the 1927 division, was a time of realignment and revitalization for both the Weaverland and Groffdale conferences.

2. Amos B. Hoover (1982, 22). Ibid., 23–54, provides an excellent overview of many issues related to the car controversy in his introduction to the life of Bishop Martin.

3. Ibid., 34.

4. Ibid., 812; *Home Messenger*, April 1978, 9.

5. The ordination record shows two strokes for Moses Horning, suggesting that Bishop Martin did not record Deacon Burkholder's vote but apparently accepted it verbally as a legitimate vote. This story was corroborated by John Dan Wenger in an interview with Amos B. Hoover, as well as by other eyewitness accounts. The booklet in which Jonas Martin recorded the number of votes each nominee received is in the possession of Preacher James H. Reiff. The strokes recorded in the booklet show the following votes for each candidate: Moses G. Horning = 2, Menno S. Zimmerman = 3, John S. Kurtz = 5, Joseph O. Wenger = 6, and Frank Hurst = 10.

6. Horning (1996, 3) and Hurst (1960). For a similar account of this unusual ordination, see R. Burkholder (1997, 77–78).

7. A. B. Hoover (1982, 29, 813). In a letter to Canadian Thomas Ressor, dated 22 December 1920, describing the fall conference, Old Order preacher Frank W. Hurst states, "They [ministers and bishops] all seemed to be well satisfied with our ruling," (A. B. Hoover 2005). Amos B. Hoover thinks the ruling refers to the decision to no longer expel members for having an auto but to only suspend them from communion. According to Hoover, "Some hailed this as a measure of reconciliation, while others felt it was not proper to put someone 'half back' from communion." Members traditionally could miss three communions before being excommunicated. Thus, after the "half-expelled" ruling, members who bought a car were actually not effectively "half-expelled" for nearly a year and a half. Amos B. Hoover, interview by Donald B. Kraybill, 10 January 2005.

8. "A Confession of Faith" by J. D. Wenger, c. 1921, privately printed. The tract is reprinted in A. B. Hoover (1982, 813–19), who suggests that it was likely written about New Year's Day 1921. The text appears in Appendix E.

9. Frank Hurst, letter of 29 September 1926 to Thomas Ressor, in A. B. Hoover (2005).

10. A. B. Hoover (1982, 584–85). For two brief biographical sketches of Wenger, see ibid., 584–85, and A. B. Hoover (1990, 33). An unpublished paper, "Who Are the Wenger Mennonites and Who Founded Them?" written by Amos B. Hoover (ca. 1987) provides additional anecdotal information about Wenger. The paper is in the Muddy Creek Farm Library.

11. The quotations in this paragraph and the next two come from Kurtz's letter, which appears in full in Appendix E.

12. Frank Hurst, letter to Thomas Reesor and family, 2 January 1927, in A. B. Hoover (2005). In an earlier letter to Reesor of 29 September 1926, Hurst noted that "Our trouble is mostly the Auto and language, but Auto the most."

13. Bishop Aaron Z. Sensenig confirmed this fact as well as other examples of Wenger's strong opposition to the use of English because he feared that it would encourage pride. Aaron Z. Sensenig, interview by Donald B. Kraybill, 8 April 2005.

14. Hurst, letter of 2 January 1927 to Reesor, in A. B. Hoover (2005). In a 29 September 1926 letter to Reesor in ibid., Hurst notes that "We had no communion last spring."

15. Menno B. Weaver's essay, written in March 1927, appears in full in Hoover (1982, 831–42).

16. The story of this customized car that resembled a carriage was told by Amos B. Hoover. Amos B. Hoover, interview by Donald B. Kraybill, 31 August 2004. For additional detail, see Amos Hoover's (2005) notes to Frank Hurst's letter written on 11 December 1935. In an engaging and well-written text, Romaine Stauffer (2003) tells the story of her paternal grandmother, Anna Mary (Martin) Burkholder (1884–1950). Stauffer's book, *Annie's Day of Light*, provides helpful insights into Old Order life and the car debate at the time of the 1927 division.

17. Various sources suggest that Moses Horning's mild and meek disposition averted a bitter confrontation, but because of stress over the car, he suffered emotional distress, loss of sleep, and other illnesses (*Home Messenger*, April 1976, 10; Horning 1996, 4; Hurst 1960, 9).

18. Who convened the conference in Bishop Horning's absence? Bishop Aaron Z. Sensenig suggested that perhaps Bishop John Dan Wenger of Virginia convened it (interview by Donald B. Kraybill, 8 April 2005). Another possibility is Preacher Menno Zimmerman, the longest ordained (in 1884) leader at the time. Second in ordination tenure was Joseph O. Wenger, ordained in 1896, but he likely deferred to Zimmerman. Preacher John S. Kurtz had died in March 1927, leaving pro-car preacher Frank Hurst third in line. He had the most votes from lay members when he was nominated for bishop in 1914, when Moses Horning was ordained. Hurst was an influential preacher. Some members at the time said the Horning Church should have been called the "Hurst" church, because Frank Hurst was an outstanding preacher, in marked contrast to Horning's modest skills. According to historian Amos B. Hoover, people repeated many of the sayings that Hurst presented in his sermons.

19. Even though Virginia bishop John Dan Wenger was technically not a member of the Weaverland Conference, Amos B. Hoover has oral evidence that Wenger attended the 8 April 1927 conference. Bishop Aaron Z. Sensenig (interview by Donald B. Kraybill, 8 April 2005) concurred that Wenger attended the Groffdale

ministers' conferences until 1953. The fact that the Weaverland Conference had supported the Old Order division in Virginia in 1901, that Wenger was ordained by Jonas Martin, and that Wenger was a close confidant of Martin gave him a special relationship with the Weaverland Conference and then with the Groffdale Conference after 1927.

20. Bishop John Dan Wenger's view of the division was provided by Amos B. Hoover (interviews with Donald Kraybill, 31 August 2004 and 10 January 2005). Hoover's sources included eyewitness accounts and a lengthy personal interview with Wenger before his death.

21. Some accounts of the 1927 division suggest that it took place on Easter Sunday, 17 April 1927. That is the day that the first communion should have occurred, but it was postponed because of the stalemate in the spring ministers' conference. Amos B. Hoover has conclusively determined that the aborted communion that sealed the division occurred on 1 May 1927. No communions were held on April 17 (Easter) and April 24 because of the stalemate. Amos B. Hoover, interview by Donald B. Kraybill, 31 August 2004.

22. After the May 1927 division, the Wengers had no bishop for four months. Virginia bishop John Dan Wenger was deeply disappointed that the Wenger leaders did not ask him to ordain a new bishop promptly after the division because he, of course, supported their opposition to the automobile. One of the reasons that Wenger leaders did not ask John Dan Wenger to ordain the new bishop was because he would have used English in the ordination service since he was not fluent in Pennsylvania German (Aaron Z. Sensenig, interview by Donald B. Kraybill, 8 April 2005). The Old Order Mennonites in Virginia had formed in 1901 after English was common among most Virginia Mennonites and thus the Old Orders there no longer spoke Pennsylvania German.

Wenger leaders turned to Bishop John W. Martin of Indiana to conduct the bishop ordination for at least two reasons. The Indiana Old Order community had been established much earlier than the one in Lancaster County. Lancaster leaders paid deference to that tenure and also knew that Martin would conduct the service in German. One problem, however, was that the Indiana Old Orders strictly forbid telephones and electricity. In 1907, the Weaverland Conference had accepted telephones for lay members but not for ministers. According to one Wenger minister, oral tradition says that John W. Martin of Indiana at first would not assist the Wengers because Indiana forbade telephones and electricity. He eventually agreed to assist them with the ordination with the understanding that Wenger leaders would continue to forbid electricity and telephones for ministers and admonish against this technology for lay members, even though the two items would not be a test of membership.

23. Wenger bishop Aaron Z. Sensenig (interview by Donald B. Kraybill, 8 April 2005) remembers going with his father to Horning Church services on a Sunday soon after the division. After just one Sunday, Sensenig's father decided to go with the Wenger group—possibly because Mrs. Sensenig was strongly opposed to the automobile.

24. Wenger historian Allen N. Hoover makes this estimate based on his research. There is not an exact accounting of the number of members who affiliated with the two groups. Graber (1979, 196–207) shows that the ages of ordained leaders in both groups (Wengers and Hornings) were similar but provides evidence that the average wealth (based on farmland values) may have been higher among Wenger officials.

25. Amos B. Hoover, interview by Donald B. Kraybill, 10 January 2005.

26. The ownership of automobiles was also an issue in schisms within Old Order communities in Indiana and Ontario. In each case, the more progressive group eventually permitted cars and the more traditional group continued to travel by horse and buggy.

27. Although the Horning Church has accepted the car, it seeks to regulate the size and power of vehicles that are permitted by the church and eligible for insurance coverage through a church aid program. Acceptable cars are listed on a handout that is periodically revised and distributed to members. Titus B. Hoover (1998) offers a severe critique of the car from a very conservative Mennonite perspective.

28. R. Stauffer (2003, 248–61) describes the impact of the car controversy on one family.

29. The Wengers were not oblivious to these developments in mobility. Their 1938 *Ordnung* prohibited automobiles, automobile trucks, motor cycles, travel in airplanes, and rubber-tired tractors. (Albertsen 1996, 40). See M. Berger (1979) for the story of rural resistance to the car in American society and Holtz (1997) and McShane (1994) for critical analyses of the impact of the car on society.

30. Groffdale Conference *Ordnung* 1976.

31. Horse-and-buggy travel poses many dangers on high-speed roads. In 1996, seven children returning from a fishing trip along the Susquehanna River were traveling in a spring wagon when the hub of their wagon scraped the guardrail. The noise spooked the horse, which jumped in front of a truck going seventy-five miles an hour. The tragic accident killed three children and the horse. In 2002, across all the Wenger settlements in the United States, there was one fatality related to a bicycle accident and one involving a buggy accident. In addition, a total of nineteen transportation-related injuries were reported: eight involving bicycles, seven involving buggies, and four involving hired motor vehicles. These fatalities and injuries were reported by the Old Order Farm Injury Project at Purdue University, directed

by Professor William Field. The incidents were gathered from reports in several national Old Order newspapers and magazines throughout 2002.

32. The rule against rubber on carriage wheels was actually lifted in 1938, as part of a compromise at a ministers' conference. The conference proposed making a rule against rubber-tired tractors. A minister who objected to the taboo on rubber tractor tires agreed to accept it if the conference agreed to permit rubber on buggy wheels. Lifting the rubber ban on buggy wheels was never announced publicly and it took more than forty years to make the transition, according to a senior bishop. Aaron Z. Sensenig, interview by Donald B. Kraybill, 8 April 2005.

33. In 1938, the Groffdale Conference *Ordnung* prohibited rubber-tired tractors.

34. The Virginia Old Order Mennonite Conference, which cooperates closely with the Wengers, allows pneumatic tires on tractors. Ontario Old Order Mennonites also permit rubber pneumatic tires on tractors, but regulate them in other ways, by forbidding: 1) tractors with more than 100 horsepower, 2) cabs and rollover bars on tractors, 3) the use of tractors for road transportation, and 4) tractor speeds over ten miles per hour. These restrictions keep the tractor under the scrutiny of the church and reduce the chance that it will give birth to the car. Out of respect to the Groffdale Conference and mindful of setting high standards, ministers in the Ontario Conference install steel wheels on their tractors, at considerable expense.

35. The New Order Amish have fewer technological restrictions than the Old Order Amish. Some of the New Orders use tractors for local transportation on the road. The Beachy Amish permit electricity and car ownership. For more information on these groups, see Kraybill and Hostetter (2001).

36. The *Ephrata Review* reported on 12 May 1916 the story of a "wide awake and progressive" Lancaster County farmer who was one of the first to use a tractor to plow his fields. Farm magazines began proclaiming the virtues of rubber-tired tractors in the mid-1930s. For examples, see *The Pennsylvania Farmer*, 19 August 1933, 12 May 1934, 15 September 1934, 12 February 1938, and 12 March 1938. R. C. Williams (1987) describes the introduction of the tractor in American agriculture.

37. "Hacker" is not a Wenger word. We use it here to describe the creative energy and imagination of Wenger mechanics in circumventing the formal church restrictions related to rubber tires.

38. One minister urged his members to remove all rubber on their tires, including rubber blocks. Since the conference accepts belting wheels, however, he cannot excommunicate members for having them unless he withdraws from the Groffdale Conference. A minister can only discipline members within the *Ordnung* of the conference. He cannot impose a stricter discipline of his own.

39. Nolt died in 1975 from injuries in a bicycle accident with a car. Some of his writings and poetry appear in H. H. Nolt (1999).

40. Now critical of the Wengers, Weaver argues that while Lancaster bishops prohibit people from driving trucks and owning trucks, some people actually own trucks and let other people drive them! "Ask the Lancaster bishop about it," he says. "They force people to be hypocritical. They need the innovations but can't use them openly because of restraining church rules."

41. Abrahams (1977, 63). We are grateful to Judson Reid, Cornell Cooperative Extension agent in Yates County, New York, for this cogent observation.

42. We thank Simon Bronner for alerting us to this important essay on mobility and for reminding us of the many metaphors of mobility that permeate American culture.

CHAPTER 4

1. There is an abundance of scholarly literature and discussion of the concept of community, beginning with Tönnies' (1957) classic sociological treatise *Community and Society*, written in 1887. For other sample selections of the literature on community, consult Baltzell (1968), Bellah et al. (1986), Bender (1978), and Etzioni (1993). On human-sized communities, see Barth (1974), Sale (1982), and Schumacher (1973).

2. For example, in the Elkhart, Indiana, settlement, services are held each Sunday in two of the three churchhouses. In Union County, Pa., both churchhouses are open for three Sundays in a row; then only one churchhouse is open the fourth Sunday. In Lancaster County, six of the ten districts meet only every other week (Groffdale, Martindale, Churchtown, Weaverland, Bowmansville, and Millway). Except for Millway, the car-driving Hornings use the churchhouses on the off Sundays.

3. The Groffdale Conference discourages ministers from setting up new settlements because such a practice might encourage opinionated ministers to gather like-minded families and form new settlements at odds with the teaching and practice of the ministers' conference. The conference encourages clusters of lay members to form a new community and then ordain leaders from within their group.

4. See Barth (1978) for a discussion of this process of "social replication."

5. The roles of and selection criteria for ordained leaders are described in Article IX of the Dordrecht Confession. A discussion on "Leaders in the Church," appears on pp. 87–96 of the ministers' edition of *Confession of Faith*, 1996. This section of the manual describes the protocol for an ordination, as well as the various vows that leaders are expected to make at their ordination. These "Church Forms and Guidelines," published by the Weaverland Conference, also pertain, with a few exceptions, to the Groffdale Conference as well.

6. *Confession of Faith* (1996, 96).

7. These data come from *Schedules of the Groffdale Conference Mennonite Churches*, a listing of meetings and officials, published annually.

8. Based on an estimated 3,310 households in spring 2005, which include those in the 2002 directory as well as new ones started after the 2002 directory was published.

9. This is Donald Martin's (2003, 282) summary of the ethos of the conference. He provides a detailed description of a conference meeting on pp. 281–82. See also *Confession of Faith* (1996, 7).

10. In the spring, the cycle of preparatory services starts on Good Friday.

11. In the Indiana settlement, each family pays the first $700 of their medical bill and the church pays three quarters of the balance, unless the bill grows very large, in which case the church pays more. Two deacons in the community announce how much is needed, and then collect money from the members. The church makes no demands—people put in whatever they can. If the deacons do not collect enough, they simply take another collection, but usually the first collection exceeds the needed amount.

12. These age-based data from the 1997 directory likely reflect the current age distribution as well.

13. The phrase "average number of children" refers to what demographers call the total fertility rate, the best single measure of a group's fertility at a single point in time. This is a synthetic figure based on the number of children produced by women in different age categories over the course of a single year. In 1966, the total fertility rate for the Wengers was 10.3, and in 1976 it was 8.6. In 1986 it was 9.19, and in 1996 it was 8.3. These findings are based on James P. Hurd's (2005) statistical analysis of fertility data from the 1997 Groffdale church directory.

14. During the twentieth century, only 1.21 percent of all first births were conceived before marriage. After 1980, the rate dropped to 0.83 percent. Calculations are based on James P. Hurd's analysis of data from the 1997 directory.

15. The average age of 252 young people baptized in 1997 was 18.1 years, with males just slightly older than females. None were baptized before age seventeen, and only sixteen were baptized at over nineteen years of age. Wenger youth are typically baptized at a younger age than the more conservative Stauffer ("Pike") Mennonites. The Pikers maintain stricter standards for adult members, but these rules encourage many young people to delay joining church until later in life. Stauffer youth are sometimes called "the wild Pikers." The Wengers do not allow their young people as much freedom as the Stauffers.

16. The Martindale district study (Appendix A) traced children who were fifteen years of age and under in 1968 for thirty years. In the study of 199 children under fifteen

years of age in 1968, only ten were not baptized in the Wenger Church by 1998. One of the ten was baptized in the Horning Church, one in the Holdeman Church, one in the small William Weaver break-off church in Indiana, three in a Lancaster Conference Mennonite church, one in an Eastern Mennonite church, and one in the Church of the Brethren. All these churches have Anabaptist roots. Two of these Wenger-born people remained unbaptized in any church. Some Lancaster County defectors join Charity Fellowship, an independent church started by a former Amishman that attracts some defectors from more conservative Anabaptist-related churches.

17. Some adults leave the community after baptism and marriage, but exact numbers across all settlements are not known. Some members estimate that as many, if not more, leave after baptism as before. If in fact that is the case, the gross retention rate may be closer to 85 percent than 90 percent. Participants in the Martindale study ranged from thirty to forty-five years of age by 1998. Very few people leave the church after age forty. For comparative retention rates among the Old Order Amish, consult Meyers (1991 and 1994).

18. In the past, youth gave their wages to their parents until they were twenty-one. More recently, the typical age is twenty. Most parents give their children a small spending allowance, though. If parents permit their sons to keep their outside wages, then the parents require them to buy their own horses, carriage, horse blankets, and so on, according to one informant.

19. Based on records maintained and provided by Lucy Martin, one of the first settlers in Yates County.

20. The Holdeman Church (Church of God in Christ Mennonite) began in 1859. Strongly exclusivist, they sometimes seek new members from among more traditional Mennonites.

21. One minister joined the Elmo Stoll church (now extinct) in Tennessee, a small church composed of people from different Old Order backgrounds who shunned much of the technology that the Wengers allowed. One minister in Kentucky has distanced himself from the Wengers and seeks a cooperative relationship with an Old Order group in Canada. Another minister in Kentucky and two in Missouri grew dissatisfied with the Wengers and sought to form a coalition with the followers of a Lancaster County Wenger deacon, John Martin, who left the Wenger Church in 1993.

22. A settlement is considered established when it has constructed a churchhouse. A new settlement that formed in Missouri in 2005 was not included in our count of settlements, because it had not yet ordained its own ministry or constructed a churchhouse.

23. We are grateful to Allen N. Hoover for assistance in gathering the demographic data across all settlements for Table 6.

24. As shown in Table 5, in 1998, only forty-one of them (21 percent) resided in the Martindale District, thirty-seven (18 percent) resided in greater Lancaster County, twenty (10 percent) in other counties in Pennsylvania, and seventy-nine (40 percent) had moved to other states. The residences of twenty-two (11 percent) were unknown.

25. The average age of ministers in Iowa, for example, is thirty-two. It is thirty-seven in Michigan, and thirty-nine in Indiana.

26. This quote comes from a member who lives in a more conservative settlement outside of Pennsylvania. A Lancaster member said that she only knew of one girl who wore a tube skirt with a slit on the side. Another mother, living in another Pennsylvania county, said, "Lancaster has both kinds, plain and liberal."

27. For a listing and description of extinct Amish settlements, see Luthy (1986).

28. A comprehensive 360-page history (1960–2004) of the Wenger settlement in Union County, Pa., has been compiled by Horning et al. (2004).

29. John B. Shirk (1998, v) notes the bishop's concern. The story of the Wenger migration to Morgan County, Missouri, and their subsequent growth is told by Shirk in a 130-page book.

30. This story was reported by Jan Horgen in *The Iowa Farmer Today*, 3 March 2004.

31. Lucy Martin, the unofficial historian of the Yates County settlement, has kept an annual record of all its significant developments since its beginning.

32. The best introduction to the Old Order Mennonite community in Indiana is found in Chapter 9 of Meyers and Nolt (2005). This excellent overview describes the history and culture of the Old Order Mennonite Church in northern Indiana and its connection to the Groffdale Conference (2005, 154–58). The incorporation of the Indiana churches into the Groffdale Conference came through a careful compromise that gives Indiana full conference status but allows for small deviations in practice.

33. One Wenger historian estimates that 140 families were missing from the 1987 directory and about fifteen from the 1992 directory, but thinks that the 1997 and 2002 directories are essentially complete. See Appendix A for a complete description of the directories.

CHAPTER 5

1. *Schedules* (2005) is an annual booklet that lists the dates of all church services for all the settlements. It also identifies the dates for counsel meetings, preparatory services, communions, and instruction meetings. The booklet includes the names and addresses of all ordained leaders. Descriptions of the ritual formula for

more than a dozen church ceremonies appear in *Confession of Faith* (1996). Many of these ceremonies are also discussed by Martin (2003). Although both of these publications reflect Weaverland Conference practices, with minor exceptions, they also describe Groffdale Conference ritual.

2. Wenger people exchange some Christmas cards and gifts, especially among the young folks. Leaders advise moderation, however, so that the true meaning of Christmas is not lost in material things.

3. See Martin (2003, 277–79) for a discussion of Old Order holidays.

4. This description of church services and rituals follows the practices of the Pennsylvania congregations for the most part. The routines vary slightly among Indiana Old Order Mennonites who joined the Wengers in 1973. Ministers typically follow the formulas for special services—baptism, communion, ordination—outlined in *Confession of Faith* (1996). The structure and symbolism of the worship service reinforce central Wenger values and draw the community together in common belief, experience, and purpose. Various Old Order rituals are described in *Confession of Faith* (1996) and by I. R. Horst (1983) and Scott (1988, 1996). Specific discussions of the Sunday service appear in *Confession of Faith* (1996, 62–65) and in Martin (2003, 261–62).

5. Other biblical references to the holy kiss include Rom. 16:16, II Cor. 13:12, I Thess. 5:26, and I Pet. 5:14. Wengers never exchange a holy kiss with a member of a different religious denomination, although Wenger men sometimes use it to greet a man from a different Old Order affiliation who lives far away. It is typical for lay members to greet Wenger visitors at church services from distant settlements with a kiss, but they rarely greet each other with a kiss at regular services in their home congregation. (Lay members do, however, exchange a holy kiss after the footwashing part of the communion service.) The meaning and use of the ritual kiss and its demise in many groups deserves deeper study and analysis.

6. The seating pattern is reversed (men on left, women on right, facing the preachers' bench) in the Bowmansville churchhouse in Lancaster County and in the churchhouses in Indiana that had established their customs before affiliating with the Groffdale Conference in 1973.

7. Although a few tunes appear in the hymnbook, officially entitled *Unpartheyisches Gesangbuch,* most hymns only have the words. A thorough treatment of the history and content of *Unpartheyisches Gesangbuch* is provided by Weiler et al. (2004). For a discussion of the importance of Old Order singing, see Martin (2003, 264–68). David Rempel Smucker (2004) presents an excellent discussion of the changes in hymnody in Mennonite churches in the nineteenth century.

8. Amos B. Hoover (interview by Donald B. Kraybill, 31 August 2004) reports that the "worship service" begins with the opening sermon and concludes with the benediction. Thus, the singing occurs before and after the service, not within it. This

older pattern was dropped by the Weaverland Conference in 1946, when it began to pronounce the benediction after singing two final hymns.

9. Amos B. Hoover (1982, 32–33) suggests that Bishop Jonas Martin was responsible for introducing the practice of lining a hymn before it was sung into Old Order Mennonite worship. Martin likely did this in 1881 and 1882 during the early years of his role as bishop. This argument is supported by the fact that the Wisler Old Order Mennonites in other states (who did not descend from the Martinites), the Stauffers, and the Amish do not practice lining.

10. The testimonies by the other ministers provide communal restraints for screening and reinforcing the biblical interpretation of the preachers. Lay members never give testimonies in church meetings because such expressions are viewed as too individualistic and subjective.

11. These are shortened versions of the three questions. The complete questions appear in Appendix B. The vows in Appendix B were translated by Allen N. Hoover. They vary slightly from an earlier translation printed in *In Meiner Jugend* (2000, 204–8) in both German and English. The ritual procedures for the baptism service are available in *Confession of Faith* (1996, 71–76). The Wenger baptismal questions differ slightly from the ones used by the Hornings. Older forms of the baptismal vows, still being used by the Horning Church, include a reference to Matthew 18. They ask the candidates in the third vow, "Are you willing to have this [Matt. 18] used against you and to help to use it against others as necessity may demand?" (*Confession of Faith* 1996, 50). Most Wenger bishops no longer include this phrase in the vows; however, at least one still does. The change occurred when the senior Wenger bishop in the 1980s thought that the first four verses of Matthew 18, which emphasize the importance of humility, were being overlooked; too much emphasis on verses 15 to 17 gave an unbalanced view. In his opinion, it was important to be obedient to the whole Gospel (Aaron Z. Sensenig, interview by Donald B. Kraybill, 8 April 2005). Amos B. Hoover thinks that Matthew 18:15–17 appeared in the Lancaster Conference baptism vows after the Stauffer division of 1846.

Another change in Wenger vows in recent years also involves the third vow, where applicants are now asked, "Are you willing to submit yourselves to all the scriptural rules of the church of Jesus Christ and to be obedient to these unto death?" Previously, applicants were asked to be obedient, unto death, "to all the scriptural rules of *this* church." The earlier wording focused explicitly on obedience to all of the scriptural rules of the Wenger Church. The newer language, with its use of the "rules of the church of Jesus Christ," is less exclusive and lightens the burden of guilt if a member leaves the Wenger Church for another one.

12. In the early 2000s, the Wenger ministers' conference discussed the appropriateness of removing the woman's head covering for baptism. Some people

thought it was more appropriate to pour the water directly on the covering and let it drip through the mesh onto the head. The ministers' conference agreed to continue the traditional practice of removing the covering, at least for the time being. The custom of removing the covering for baptism "is being challenged in many Old Order groups," according to Amos B. Hoover, who wrote an essay on the topic for the November 2004 *Home Messenger*.

13. In Pennsylvania German, this sometimes is called *Buss, Bede, und Faschtdaag* (repentance, prayer, and fasting day). For a discussion of this service, consult *Confession of Faith* (1996, 70–71) and Martin (2003, 282–84).

14. In the spring, the cycle of fasting days usually begins on Good Friday for the first round of congregations that have communion on Easter; it occurs on subsequent Saturdays for the remaining congregations.

15. One member explained, "The bishop normally stands to read Scripture and preach, but otherwise sits for everything else, including reading the rules, but he stands to excommunicate someone."

16. Wallace (1966). See *Confession of Faith* (1996, 77–79) and Martin (2003, 120–21) on Old Order communion beliefs and practices.

17. If they are starting a new community, members may live far from an established churchhouse. The Grant County, Wisconsin, settlement began in 1997 with just a few families. The nearest Wenger churchhouse was several hours away. The families traveled to a distant churchhouse at least twice a year for communion until they built their own building.

18. One member noted that on Communion Sunday, the ministers typically do not open the Bible when they preach but simply retell Old Testament stories. The first preacher traces the biblical story from Genesis to the Tower of Babel, to the Red Sea crossing, and to the brazen serpent. The stories in the first two sermons are often called the types and figures. In the third sermon, the bishop focuses on New Testament stories and does read the text on footwashing from the Bible. During regular Sunday services, the preachers open the Bible and may read a verse as they are preaching.

19. Typically, on the fourth verse of the hymn, the bishop will begin lining the remainder of the hymn because he has finished washing feet.

20. This only occurs when churchhouses are located close to a major highway. Some churchhouses are in more quiet and isolated rural areas.

21. Very infrequently, a bishop may refuse to give someone communion if the member has transgressed the *Ordnung*, refused to confess his or her wrongdoing, and yet tries to participate in communion. Informants agree that these issues should be settled before the communion service. "The time to clean house," said one woman, "is before this moment."

22. For an Old Order description of the footwashing service, consult *Confession of Faith* (1996, 79–80).

23. Some Mennonite groups call their exclusive communion services "close" communion, meaning that it is open to members in close fellowship with each other. The Wengers, however, typically speak of it as "closed" communion, meaning that the sacred ritual is closed to people who are not members of the Wenger Church. Max Weber (1958) observed that closed communion serves a useful economic function by increasing the creditworthiness of the communicants. This worthiness arose not so much by adhering to a set of doctrines as by following the church's moral guidelines and being in harmony with other members. Excommunication from communion lowered a person's credit rating! Among the Wengers, communion signals a time when members should make any needed moral or economic adjustments before the service. Members should not partake unless they have settled their moral accounts with others in the community.

24. The fact that a member may miss communion three times before he or she is excommunicated means that, in some cases, church leaders may try to solve a problem with a wayward member over an eighteen-month period of time. This underscores the fact that excommunication is not a quick decision but is usually the result of numerous efforts, over many months, to amend the situation. On the other hand, if a member decides to leave the church, little can be done, and excommunication may happen more quickly.

25. The Wengers do not formally practice shunning, although Article XVII of the Dordrecht Confession explicitly calls for shunning the excommunicated. The Swiss Mennonites to whom the Wengers trace their roots never adopted the Dordrecht Confession. The Amish accepted the Dordrecht Confession during their formation in the 1690s and emphasized the practice of shunning.

26. For descriptions of the ordination procedure and the charges given to the newly ordained, consult *Confession of Faith* (1996, 88–97) and Martin (2003, 122–23).

27. In some cases, two congregations may hold a single ordination; nominees can come from both congregations. In new communities, the supervising bishop may urge people to nominate candidates who have lived in the community for a year or more.

28. Although the Wengers continue to use the word "candidate," the Horning Church prefers to use "nominee" to avoid the political overtones suggested by "candidate." See *Confession of Faith* (1996, 63–67).

29. *Records* (2004) provides a full listing of all the ordinations in the history of the Groffdale Conference, from 1750 to 2004, including the name and birth date of each ordained man, the date and location of the ordination, and the names of all the candidates who were in the lot.

30. The following description is based on the observations of Donald B. Kraybill at an ordination service in Lancaster County (Pa.) on 12 December 1995, and the observations of James P. Hurd at an ordination service on 19 November 1996 in the Shippensburg churchhouse in Cumberland County (Pa.).

31. The hymn, number 209 on page 231 in *Gesangbuch*, is in a minor key. One member explained it has a mournful sound that reflects the heavy and somber significance of the day. The theme of the text emphasizes comfort in suffering.

32. The word *uffgawwe* was used by this member to underscore the deep yieldedness to God's will that is required of a minister.

CHAPTER 6

1. According to a non-Wenger midwife, the church discourages artificial contraceptives but accepts natural forms of family planning. She estimates that no more than 5 percent use some form of contraceptives and knows of only one woman who received a contraceptive injection. One Wenger woman thinks the use of contraceptives is higher than 5 percent. Wenger women are very hesitant to use IUDs, and very few have tubal ligations. A few women may agree to a tubal ligation if they deliver their children by cesarean section. The midwife knows of no men who had a vasectomy.

A Wenger woman said, "Outside people may think we are too uneducated, unenlightened, and backward to limit our families to two children. The problem is that the outside society has a growing disrespect for large families and stay-at-home moms. Too many women want fulfillment in jobs and careers and put their children in day care, and to safeguard their jobs and careers, contraception has become a must."

2. One Wenger leader said, "The Amish tend to favor natural remedies, but we favor standard medicine." He estimated that perhaps 20 percent of the Wengers might favor natural remedies, but the overwhelming majority favors standard medical practices. This preference developed, according to this informant, because Aaron Z. Sensenig, the senior bishop for many years, encouraged the use of standard medicine.

3. One of the controversies involved the use of the so-called Rife Ray Machine, first developed in 1934 and purported to cure cancer. Some members claimed that a new version of the machine provided cures for cancer and other diseases. Others charged that the machine involved New Age medicine, mysticism, and Eastern religion. In an attempt to clarify some of the confusion swirling around the controversy, Allen N. Hoover wrote a detailed and unbiased assessment of the Rife Ray Machine and concluded, "So far I have not seen any conclusive evidence that the Rife Ray Machine has helped anyone." See p. 3 of Hoover, "A 1934 Cancer Cure?" (unpublished four-page paper).

4. The Clinic for Special Children is located at 535 Bunker Hill Road, Strasburg, Pennsylvania (phone: 717-687-9407; Web site: www.clinicforspecialchildren.org). One example of the clinic's services involves a newborn who was unable to swallow. Her parents took her to a Lancaster hospital, thinking that it was a problem with her esophagus. She did not respond and was sent to Hershey Medical Center, where blood tests suggested a metabolic problem. Overnight, the baby developed seizures and was rushed to Dr. Morton, who used a protein formula to correct a deficiency caused by maple syrup urine disease. These events occurred during the first week of the infant's life. She recovered and lives a normal life today.

5. Dr. Erik Puffenberger, laboratory director at the clinic, has calculated the degree of inbreeding among the families of Hirschsprung's disease victims, based on genealogies twelve generations deep. His calculations estimate that 1 in 170 children in the families carrying Hirschsprung's disease are at risk. Puffenberger has published the findings of his genetic research in various scientific journals. For an overview of the diseases that are prevalent among Old Order Mennonites, see Puffenberger (2003). Puffenberger also summarized his findings in a lecture entitled "Plain Genetics: How Old Order Communities Advance Genetic Disease Research," which was given at the Young Center of Elizabethtown College, 27 January 2005.

6. For stories of Wenger children with various genetic disorders and special needs, see God's Golden Children (2002) and Recipes (2003).

7. Puffenberger (2003, 26).

8. Religious practices in the home "vary greatly among families," according to one mother. Some people are more devout and conscientious than others in their daily religious observances. In the early twentieth century, it was common to have a second silent prayer, called "returning thanks," at the end of the meal. Gradually the practice declined, but the most conservative families and ministers have continued to observe this silent end-of-the-meal prayer. Upon ordination, ministers' families observe both prayers, and if a minister is present for a meal with other families, the end-of-the-meal prayer is typically observed.

9. From a sermon preached in English by a Virginia Mennonite minister at Yellow Creek churchhouse in Indiana, 1996.

10. These words describing childhood rites of passage were written by a Wenger member for the authors in 2001. Interestingly, the author uses the technical term "rites of passage," which demonstrates familiarity with the concept—although the transitions described here do not have the sharp steps of separation, liminality, and reincorporation as given in Arnold van Gennep's classic formulation.

11. Some families—perhaps 10 percent, according to one informant—receive local daily newspapers. One member noted, however, that subscriptions to local

papers declined during the extensive coverage of President Clinton's sexual indiscretions while he was in office in the 1990s.

12. Exact initials, parental lineage, and residence are necessary to separate the otherwise entangled genealogical maze. These data and tabulations come from the 2002 directory.

13. Based on an enumeration of household heads in the 2002 directory.

14. Mary Ann Horst was raised in an Ontario Old Order community (M. Horst 1992, 19–21).

15. The quotations in these two paragraphs come from Canadian Old Order Mennonite Isaac Horst (1990).

16. The four-day series, entitled "Silenced by Shame," appeared in the *Lancaster Intelligencer Journal*, July 12–15, 2004. One Wenger man living outside Pennsylvania said, "This biased, slanted series of trash enraged me. The newspaper refused to publish or greatly censored letters that I sent in response." Furthermore, he noted, "Every Wenger case mentioned in this series was prosecuted."

Because no systematic research has been conducted, it is unknown whether sexual and physical abuse rates among Wengers are higher or lower than in the general population. One Wenger woman contends that domestic abuse among Plain people is "overwhelmingly due to mental illness." An outside health-care worker who has spoken to many Wenger women thinks that the rate of sexual abuse, based on her observations, may be similar to other populations, but she estimates that the rate of physical abuse is lower. Young women may be sexually abused by a father, uncle, cousin, or other male authority figure. In one settlement, a minister was "silenced," taken out of the ministry, for sexually molesting his daughters. When cases of abuse are reported within the community, the ministers try to handle the transgressions within the confines of the church, much like other offenses. Such sanctions, however, may not be effective with habitual offenders. Whether or not sexual or physical abuse incidents are reported to health-care or law-enforcement officials depends on the situation, the family, and the responsible church leaders.

17. More children attended public schools in the 1970s and 1980s than in 2005. Homeschooling is discouraged because homeschool instruction materials are filled with religious content developed by outside religious groups. Wenger schools will not accept homeschool credits, but a few families do homeschool their children. Most parents want their children to interact with other children so that they will learn to cooperate and to respect the authority of teachers. The literature on Wenger schools is very sparse. Much more has been written about Amish schools. See, for example, Kraybill (2001), Lapp (1991), and Meyers (2003). Dewalt and Troxell (1989) and Troxell (2002) provide an ethnographic description of an Old Order Mennonite school. The most thorough study of Old Order Mennonite schooling

was conducted by Karen Johnson-Weiner (forthcoming). Her book-length manuscript, which compares Mennonite schools with various Amish schools, is in the process of being published. One chapter is largely devoted to Old Order Mennonite schools in Lancaster County.

18. In Lancaster County, the Old Order Mennonites and Amish stubbornly resisted sending their children to consolidated public schools in the 1940s and 1950s. The confrontation with public officials peaked from 1950 to 1955, when some parents were arrested and jailed for a brief period of time. See Kraybill (2001, 161–87) for an overview of this conflict and the rise of Old Order private schools. Lapp (1991) provides an extensive history, newspaper clippings, and source documents of the school conflict from an Amish perspective.

19. *Blackboard Bulletin* provides an annual enumeration of Old Order schools across the country. The numbers reported here come from the January 2005 issue for the 2004–5 school year.

20. Horning schools go through the twelfth grade. Because of their more conservative convictions, Stauffers will not serve on a school board with other Mennonites, nor will they allow non-Stauffer trustees to serve on the board of a Stauffer school. They will occasionally send their children to Wenger schools, however.

21. In New York, the State Department of Education requires a second language and the Wenger schools teach German, of course. Some of the adults in the New York settlement who were raised in Pennsylvania report that their children know German much better than they do.

22. This example comes from the field observations of anthropologist Karen Johnson-Weiner (forthcoming).

23. Minutes of the Old Order Mennonite State School Directors' meeting at Hillside School, July 23, 2003.

24. *Mankind* (2001, 95–96).

25. Dedication in both *Mankind* (2001) and *Body's* (1999).

26. This exemption was supported by the United States Supreme Court in 1972 in the case of Wisconsin v. Yoder.

27. Along with the Amish, the Wengers developed a so-called vocational school in the mid-1950s. The weekly three-hour vocational school only meets in Pennsylvania out of respect to an agreement that Old Order groups negotiated with the Pennsylvania Department of Instruction in 1955. Wenger youth in other states terminate formal schooling at the end of eighth grade or whenever they turn fourteen years old. The Wenger view of education differs drastically from mainstream American assumptions about the purpose of public education. See Reich (2002) for a scathing critique of Old Order schools that do not seek to develop autonomous individuals for participation in civic life.

28. Minutes of the Old Order Mennonite State School directors' meeting at Hillside School, July 23, 2003.

29. Carrie Bender is the pen name used by a Wenger woman. The majority of her books were published by Herald Press from 1993 to 2003 in three different series—the Dora's Diary, Miriam's Journal, and Whispering Brook series. Herald Press discontinued publishing new titles by Bender in 2004. See an announcement of this decision in *The Mennonite Weekly Review*, 2 February 2004, 11. Masthof Press currently publishes books by Carrie Bender (including the Joy's Journal series, the most recent volume of which was released in January 2005). Zimmerman writes for *The Herald*, Morrisons Cove, Pennsylvania. Another Wenger writer, Mabel Burkholder (2003), wrote a history of early Mennonite settlers in Lancaster County.

30. Although seventeen is the typical age, it varies somewhat from family to family, depending on parental preferences.

31. Quoits, a colonial game similar to throwing horseshoes, has persisted in Pennsylvania German settlements in the Lancaster area. Unlike a horseshoe, a quoit is a complete circle that weighs about four pounds.

32. Informal comments by Canadian Old Order Mennonite Isaac Horst to Donald B. Kraybill.

33. Other topics are detailed in the Dordrecht Confession of 1632. The first five instruction meetings are public ones, open to youth who not baptismal candidates as well as to interested adults. The sixth one, held in the home district of the applicants, is a private one attended only by the applicants, the ministry of their home district, and one or two local song leaders. The wives of the ministers typically do not attend. This "let's get serious" meeting is a time when the bishop clarifies the *Ordnung* expectations for members and it is also the penultimate step to baptism. It offers applicants the last opportunity to drop out of the process without public embarrassment.

34. John F. Peters, in several publications (1987, 2000, 2003), provides a sociological description of socialization and family life stages that lead to church membership among the Old Order Mennonites of Ontario.

35. This percentage is based on the decision of 199 youth who were under the age of fifteen in the Martindale District Study (Lancaster County) in 1968.

36. These estimates are based on the Martindale District Study and thoughtful estimates of various leaders. Some Mennonite informants estimate retention rates higher than 90 percent in their congregations. Some couples leave after they are married; thus the long-term overall (pre- and post-baptism) retention rate may be closer to 85 percent.

37. According to one Wenger informant, the senior bishop decided to preach against the practice when a young woman came to him to confess her involvement

in fornication and told him, "I was never taught it was wrong." After hearing her comment, he resolved that no young person would ever say that again. If a woman discovers that she is pregnant before marriage, "the couple typically goes to the bishop and confesses the situation and he excommunicates them," according to one member, "and then they are married by a justice of the peace or a minister in another church." The couple typically is "set back" from one communion. They can then be reinstated into full fellowship in the church if they make a public confession of sorrow for their sin.

38. These numbers are based on a random sample of one hundred youth (fifty married couples) selected by Allen N. Hoover. Only one person was nineteen years of age and only five were over twenty-six years of age.

39. Hurd (2005).

40. For various descriptions of Wenger weddings, see J. D. Hoover (1990), I. R. Horst (2000), Scott (1988, 36–38), Shively (2004, 353–59), and E. Zimmerman (1987). The description in the text reflects observations by James P. Hurd at a Wenger wedding in November 1996 near Leola, Pennsylvania. Hurd and his wife received privileged seats next to the ministers, directly in front of where the bride and groom sat. On rare occasions, a short wedding ceremony may be held before a Sunday morning church service in the anteroom of a churchhouse for the second marriage of a widow or widower, or if the bride's home is very small.

41. The exact wording of the wedding vows appears in Appendix B.

42. The patterns of seating and participation vary somewhat across settlements. One woman notes that in her community, women sit in the living room and participate in the singing.

43. In the early years of the Wenger Church, this was also the time when Bishop Joseph Wenger left the room because people would never sing English in his presence due to his strong preference for German. Bishop Aaron Z. Sensenig, out of respect for Wenger, also followed the practice of leaving the room after singing German songs. His departure signaled that the English singing could begin.

44. Other colors may be worn by the bridal party. Bow ties are worn in some settlements but not in others. Sometimes the bow tie color matches the dress color of the women in the bridal party.

45. Ibid. Emphasis added to quoted material in the text.

46. According to a farm injury study of Old Order communities conducted by William Field at Purdue University, among the Wengers there were forty-one reported injuries, but no fatalities, related to agriculture in 2002.

47. *Confession of Faith* (1996, 102–12) and Martin (2003, 287–90) provide information on the customs and biblical references used for funeral sermons and burials. The description in the text is based on a funeral attended by James P. Hurd in Berks County (Pa.) on 7 December 1996 at the Center churchhouse.

48. There is no religious significance to the pine box. At one time walnut wood was used. The primary concern for the coffin is simplicity and plainness. The same principles apply to gravestones. These are purchased from a commercial company that makes memorial stones. There are no religious guidelines for gravestones, but a large, ornate stone would be considered ostentatious.

49. Unlike many mainline religious groups that have a public viewing of the deceased at a funeral home or in a church, the Wengers have kept their viewings at home and outside the churchhouse, symbolic of their resistance to modern trends that remove key social functions from the home.

50. Horning men, by contrast, usually remove their hats in the viewing line before the graveside service, even when attending a Wenger burial. A Wenger minister conducts the graveside service, not the bishop, who speaks in the churchhouse at the funeral.

51. In the case of suicide, the body is buried in the cemetery "in line," according to one member, "not on the edge or outside, but we may not call the person 'our dear brother' or 'our dear sister.'"

CHAPTER 7

1. Confirming that estimate, the Martindale District. Study revealed that 74 percent of the men were farmers, as shown in Table 8.

2. The most detailed analysis of Old Order Mennonite work and economics was conducted by Peters (1994) among Ontario Mennonites. He found that 38 percent of Mennonites over twenty-four years of age were involved in some type of nonfarm work, but many of these were also involved in farming.

3. Ed Klimuska (1993) describes the different responses to the decline of farmland in Lancaster County in a series of six articles, entitled "Old Order Lancaster County," that appeared in the *Lancaster New Era* and were subsequently published as a tabloid reprint.

4. The 1968 *Lancaster County Map and Directory* provides identification of 199 children fifteen years of age or younger who lived in the Martindale district in 1968. In 1998, these individuals were between thirty and forty-five years old. The data in Table 8 reflect their occupational pursuits.

5. These estimates are based on a farmland ownership project directed by sociologist Conrad Kanagy at Elizabethtown College. Heads of households in the 1995 Wenger map and directory were matched with those that appeared on the tax rolls in 1996, according to the 1996 Lancaster County tax assessor's data. The acreage lies in fourteen eastern Lancaster County townships: Brecknock, Caernarvon, Clay, East Cocalico, West Cocalico, Earl, East Earl, West Earl, Elizabeth, Ephrata, Upper Leacock, Manheim, Salisbury, and Warwick. The three Earl townships have

the highest concentration of Wenger farms: Earl (3,816 acres), East Earl (4,030 acres), and West Earl (3,849 acres). The next highest concentrations are found in the townships of Caernarvon (2,903 acres) and Brecknock (2,646 acres). Seventy-nine percent of the total Wenger acreage lies in Caernarvon, Brecknock, and the three Earl townships. Lancaster County claimed some 6,156 farms larger than 25 acres near the turn of the twenty-first century; 409 of these (6.6 percent) belonged to Wenger people.

The most land owned by any one person is 170 acres (two plots of 75 and 95 acres, respectively). Three hundred fifty-eight Wengers own only one plot, twenty-four own two plots, and four members own three plots.

6. The trend data (1984–2002) were calculated by Conrad Kanagy and his students, using Lancaster County land sales information that was matched with Wenger directories.

7. Letter from Judson Reid, Cornell Cooperative Extension agent in Yates County, New York, to Donald B. Kraybill, 16 July 2004.

8. Many of the Wenger dairy farmers in Yates County practice rotational grazing rather than using land for cash crops harvested for extra income.

9. An Old Order Mennonite man in Elkhart County, Indiana, bought 18,000 chickens to raise. When they got sick, he spent thousands of dollars on medicine, and he finally had to sell them cheaply as "Bs" because there was no market for them. That loss forced him to mortgage his farm.

10. This is a very rough estimate. One Wenger leader said, "I would be surprised if more than 5 percent of Wengers farmed tobacco today. And some day, I expect tobacco to become a test of membership." The percent of Wengers who raise tobacco varies enormously, depending on whether one considers Wenger farmers in Lancaster County or Wenger farmers in all settlements.

11. Reid (2004, 12).

12. Judson Reid, Cornell Cooperative Extension agent in Yates County, New York, interview by Donald B. Kraybill, 12 August 2004.

13. One hundred eight small businesses are listed in the histories of two settlements: the one in Union County, Pennsylvania (Horning et al. 2004), and the one in Morgan County, Missouri (J. B. Shirk 1998).

14. The programmable computer numeric controlled (CNC) machines do high-precision drilling and milling of aluminum and metal.

15. A news story describing this shop, "Talent of the Hands," written by Michele Carlton, appeared in the *Kentucky New Era* on 19 January 2002.

16. The history of and reasons for these federal and state exemptions for Old Order communities can be found in Kraybill (2001; 2003).

17. This observation by Marc Olshan (1994, 139) of Amish businesses applies to the Wenger Mennonites as well. Although such signs are a graphic denial of separation from the world in an economic sense, there are, of course, various dimensions and levels of separation from the world.

18. The Web site can be found at www.weaverviewfarms.com.

19. Kraybill and Nolt (2004) report this level in their study of some 1,600 Amish enterprises in Lancaster County (Pa.).

20. For an introduction to the social science literature on the impact of size and scale on social organizations, consult Barth (1978) and Sale (1982).

CHAPTER 8

1. Some informants indicate that the fall conference and communions begin on eastern standard time out of deference to the retired senior bishop, who objected to daylight saving time for many years. The standard time for the fall conference and communions is clearly marked on the *Schedules* (2005), pages 1 and 8. Outside Lancaster County, the communions typically follow daylight saving time.

2. Sale (1995) tells the story of the Luddites who, in his mind, were "rebels against the future." Tenner (1997) describes some of the negative and unexpected consequences of technology. See Brende (2004) for a firsthand description of an Old Order Amish and Mennonite community that restricts technology much more severely than the Wengers.

3. Rejecting electricity and telephones was the norm for many years, although it was never an official test of membership. According to one member, after the 1927 division Isaac Nolt, a lay member, tore out his telephone, as did Deacon Ben Hoover. In the late 1930s, a lay member bought a farm from an English neighbor and took out the electricity and the telephone.

4. This is the opinion of Old Order historian Amos B. Hoover (interview by Donald B. Kraybill, 10 January 2005).

5. Deacon John Martin and his followers formed what became known as the John Martin group of Old Order Mennonites. As of 2005, about thirty-eight families are affiliated with the group in Kentucky (12 families), Missouri (21), and Pennsylvania (5). Although John Martin attends the services of his namesake group, he has been excommunicated by them for a number of reasons.

6. These numbers are based on telephone numbers printed in the *Lancaster County Map and Directory of Groffdale Conference Mennonites*, 1995 and 2003 editions.

7. This decision was driven primarily by Lancaster County members, some of whom serve as volunteer firemen. The ruling to permit voice beepers was not

greeted warmly by ministers in some other settlements, where members are less involved in local fire companies.

8. Although word processors with both small, built-in screens and large monitors are acceptable, they are difficult to buy; according to one man, most companies have stopped making them. Some Wengers are following the attempts of several Amish technicians to develop a small "Amish" word processor with a small flip screen. The Wengers and Amish ask different questions about word processors, according to one Wenger leader: "The Amish ask, 'Does it look like a computer or a television?' We ask 'What does it do?' We want our rules to make sense."

9. The acceptance of CNC machines occurred at the time the ministers' conference made a decision to reject personal computers and the Internet. Although many ministers would not have understood these technical distinctions, they were persuaded by a paper written by a lay member that argued that computer-controlled machines did not represent a moral danger like personal computers and the Internet. The acceptance of CNC machines gives Wenger shop owners who use them a commercial advantage over Amish shop owners, whose church prohibits CNC usage.

10. Groffdale Conference *Ordnung* 1976.

11. This portable meat canner, operated by MCC, travels to rural Mennonite and Amish communities where volunteers process and can meat to ship overseas to victims of famine, war, and social displacement.

12. This is not an inevitable transition. Some groups, such as the Old Order River Brethren and the Old German Baptist Brethren, blend the warm subjective language of personal faith with explicit standards for dress and behavior.

13. The Wengers are beginning to exhibit what Max Weber (1958) called rationalization, the shift from informal tradition-directed behavior to practices based on more formal, rational calculations. Some signs of this trend in the Wenger church include (1) writing down the *Ordnung* and distributing it to the ministers in distant settlements, (2) printing the church calendar (*Schedules*) a year ahead of time and organizing it into columns and rows, with each special meeting indicated by a different symbol, and (3) making church decisions based upon pragmatic reasoning rather than tradition (for example, using some English in church services when visitors are present). At first glance, decisions about technology may appear to be formal judgments based on economic considerations, but in the Wenger context, as we have seen, some technological decisions are driven by religious values regarding the community's welfare, not just by economic criteria. One member contends, "Our traditions are based on practical reasoning from our religious values."

14. Even though an older bishop may not be able to carry the duties of his office, he will typically attend the ministers' conference as long as he is physically able. The retired senior bishop described in this paragraph said he has no objection to

the ministers' conference meeting outside Lancaster County despite the other leaders' willingness to keep the conference in Lancaster in deference to him (Aaron Z. Sensenig, interview by Donald B. Kraybill, 8 April 2005).

15. An Amishman originally prepared the list of steps that lead, in his mind, from Old Order life toward mainstream society. The Amishman's steps were revised by a Wenger member to reflect the steps toward the world from a Wenger perspective.

CHAPTER 9

1. The conceptualization of group behavior in the context of fields of social forces is not new. Kurt Lewin (1951) pioneered the concept, which Bourdieu (1977) later expanded as central to his theoretical understanding of society (Bourdieu and Wacquant 1992; Swartz 1997).

2. The process of social comparison is one of the most fundamental social processes at both the individual and group level. The social position of an individual or a group only becomes meaningful in the context of its relationship to other social entities. A sub-theme of lateral social comparison places the comparisons on a vertical scale of hierarchy. The power dynamics of social relationships focus on domination—who is up and who is down in terms of influence, power, and status. Whether horizontal or vertical, social comparison is the deep underlying process that infuses social behavior with meaning.

3. We are grateful to Stephen Scott for helping us identify some of the cultural differences among the Old Order groups in Lancaster County.

4. We have selected these five groups for comparison because the four Mennonite groups are directly related to Wenger history. The Amish are an important contrast because of their many similarities and differences with the Wengers and because of their cooperation on numerous projects. Many other conservative groups, such as the Old Order River Brethren, the Beachy Amish, the New Order Amish, and the Old German Baptist Brethren, would provide interesting points of comparison, but to do so would require a description of each group's historical context, which goes beyond the scope of this work.

5. The Jacob Stauffer group has a total of about twelve hundred members. Some two hundred of these live in Lancaster County. There is a sizable Stauffer community in Snyder County (Pa.), and other settlements have been established in Illinois, Kentucky, Maryland, New York, Missouri, Minnesota, and Ohio.

6. Apart from Albertsen's book (1996), very little has been written about the Reidenbachs. Scott (1996, 68) and Leid (1991, 43–44) provide brief descriptions of this small group.

7. Horning et al. (2004, 349–52) briefly describe some of the challenges faced by the Wengers during World War II.

8. The origin and name of this group are described in Chapter 1. The name Reidenbach comes not from a leader but from an area in Lancaster County where the group formed. The area was known as Reidenbach because of the name of a nearby store (Leid 1991, 43).

9. There are actually three bishops in Lancaster County, but the oldest one is retired, leaving two active bishops to preside over ten congregations.

10. The story of the rapid development of Amish enterprises is told by Kraybill and Nolt (2004). Some Amish families have moved out of Lancaster County and established settlements in Indiana, Kentucky, and Wisconsin, among other states, but the rate at which the Lancaster Amish migrate to other states has been substantially lower than that of the Wengers.

11. Article XVII, "The Shunning of Those Who Are Expelled," in the Dordrecht Confession was the result of a Dutch theological interpretation of the Scripture, one that the Amish accepted. Many Swiss Anabaptists (Mennonites) did not accept shunning; it was a key issue in the division of 1693.

12. As noted in Chapter 2, the distinction between Wenger and Amish shunning varies somewhat by degree and formality. Wengers largely leave it up to individual members and families, and if a member does not shun an ex-member, there are no church sanctions as there are with the Amish. Both the Stauffers and the Amish have a ritual excommunication that invokes 1 Corinthians 5:5 and turns the person over to Satan. Among the Wengers, said one member, "We wish the excommunicated person the Lord's blessing but no longer consider him a brother or sister in the church."

13. The Amishman is Sam Stoltzfus, writing in *Die Botschaft*, 29 January 1998, 25.

14. The five shared churchhouses are Groffdale, Martindale, Churchtown, Weaverland, and Bowmansville.

15. Installing the microphone was a "point of tension" between the two groups, according to one Wenger man. The Hornings, according to this person, wanted to install the sound system but the Wengers wouldn't allow it, so "one night, the Horning people just installed it and it raised quite a stir."

16. Although the basic ritual practices are similar because they go back to a common root in the eighteenth century, there are some differences. The Hornings' procedures are clearly spelled out in the booklet *Confession of Faith of the Mennonites: Church Forms and Guidelines of the Weaverland Conference*, ministers' edition, which was revised and printed in 1996. Many of the Groffdale rituals are similar, but their ministers and bishops use forms developed by Jonas Martin and later revised by Wenger Bishop Aaron Z. Sensenig.

17. The wording for this baptismal question comes from the ministers' edition of *Confession of Faith* (1996, 50). See Chapter 5, note 11, for an elaboration of this point.

18. The Wenger ministers who give testimony to the preacher typically say, *"Von Hatzen yo und Amen"* ("Yes and amen from the heart").

19. The Horning car insurance program has annually stipulated premiums. Their aid program for fire and storm damage has no annual premiums, but collections are gathered as needed. Hospital and medical aid among the Hornings are similar to those of the Wengers, with collections taken as needed and disbursements reported to the church.

20. Fairmount Home near Ephrata (Pa.) provides care for Hornings as well as for residents from other church backgrounds. Many elderly Hornings spend their retirement years in more traditional settings near their children. The Muddy Creek Farm Library is located adjacent to Fairmount Home.

21. Although some sections of *Home Messenger* reflect a more systematic and rational approach to theology in contrast with the more informal, oral, and organic Wenger approach, one Horning leader said, "Not all of our members are impressed with the *Home Messenger*," reflecting some discomfort over the shift toward a more reflective and deliberate articulation of faith. Nevertheless, *Home Messenger* has considerable influence among the Hornings even though it is not an official publication of the church.

22. The Wengers as well as the Hornings lose some of their members to other Mennonite groups, such as the Eastern Mennonite Church, the Mid-Atlantic Mennonite Church, and the Keystone Mennonite Church. These three groups are more conservative than the Lancaster Conference.

23. Giddens (1991, 21–29).

24. Examples of this process include the centralization of government power in urban capitals as well as the ubiquitous golden arches of McDonald's, which symbolize the application of rationality and uniformity to many dimensions of life to improve efficiency and productivity.

25. P. Berger (1974, 19–20). Giddens (1991, 82–88) also underscores the centrality of choice as a consequence of modernity.

26. Harvey (1990, 125–97) devotes four chapters to the rise and significance of Fordism and the subsequent postmodern shift to more flexible forms of social organization.

27. Examples of these groups would include the Weaverland (Horning) Church, the Beachy Amish, and the Old Order River Brethren.

28. One Old Order historian noted that the tractor was more readily accepted because steam engines, which powered threshing machines, had been used by Men-

nonite farmers before the 1893 division. The Old Orders continued to use them into the twentieth century.

29. Kraybill (1994, 32–33) provides an elaboration of this key point that the social forces of modernity—specialization, discontinuity, mobility, and individualism—threatened to fragment the solidarity of closely knit Old Order communities. It was in this sense that modernity (alias "the world") was seen as a "great separator."

30. Jokes and stories in the more "progressive" Mennonite communities, for example, sometimes belittled the perceived provincialism and naiveté of the Wenger Mennonites.

31. Schwartz (2004) provides a cogent exploration of how too many choices can debilitate human satisfaction and happiness, and he offers some suggestions for how moderns can limit choice and increase satisfaction.

32. These observations are not based on any systematic research but are the impressions of a professional woman who has worked closely with many Wenger women. She also contends that, in general, Wenger men are happier than Wenger women because "they have more control over their lives, have more choices." Likewise, she thinks that Horning women tend to be happier than Wenger women, because Horning women have more mobility because they can drive cars.

33. The comments by Wenger women quoted in the following paragraphs in this section come from women who read an early draft of the manuscript. The readers wrote comments in response to the suggestion that depression among Wenger women relates to restricted choices. The quotations derive from correspondence sent to the authors of this book in January 2005.

34. Emphasis is in the original correspondence to the authors, in January 2005, from a Wenger reader of a draft of the manuscript. The writer refers to the founder of quantum theory in physics, Werner Heisenberg (1901–1976). The reference to Heisenberg illustrates the breadth of reading materials available to some Wengers, although this is not typical.

35. Amos B. Hoover, Old Order Horning historian, speaking to Joseph Miller (2004, 226–27). For a description of contemporary urban life that differs dramatically from Wenger society, see Watters (2003).

36. J. S. Miller (2004, 227).

❖ selected references

This reference list includes works cited in the notes as well as other selected entries related to Old Order Mennonites that may be of interest to readers and scholars. Bibliographic information for some sources—interviews, newsletters, local newspapers—not appearing in this list are provided in the notes for each chapter.

Abrahams, Roger D. 1977. "Moving in America." *Prospects: An Annual Journal of American Cultural Studies* (Hampstead, N.Y.) 3:63–82.

Albertsen, Karsten-Gerhard. 1996. *The History and Life of the Reidenbach Mennonites (Thirty-fivers).* Morgantown, Pa.: Masthof Press.

Baltzell, E. Digby, ed. 1968. *The Search for Community in Modern America.* New York: Harper and Row.

Barth, Fredrik. 1974. "Analyzing Dimensions in the Comparison of Social Organizations." *American Anthropologist* 74 (1–2): 207–20.

———, ed. 1978. *Scale and Social Organization.* Oslo: Universitetsforlaget.

Beam, C. Richard, and Joshua R. Brown. 2004. *The Comprehensive Pennsylvania German Dictionary: Vol. 1: A.* Millersville, Pa.: Center for Pennsylvania German Studies.

Bellah, Robert N., et al. 1986. *Habits of the Heart: Individualism and Government in American Life.* New York: Harper.

Bender, Thomas. 1978. *Community and Social Change in America.* New Brunswick, N.J.: Rutgers University Press.

Benowitz, Jean-Paul. 1993a. "The Old Order Mennonite Division of 1893: An Interpretation." *Pennsylvania Mennonite Heritage* 16 (4): 14–17.

———. 1993b. "One Hundred Years of Old Order Mennonite Church Community." *Mennonite Historical Bulletin* 3:8–11.

Berger, Michael L. 1979. *The Devil Wagon in God's Country: The Automobile and Social Change in Rural America, 1893–1929.* Hamden, Conn.: Archon Books.

Berger, Peter L. 1974. *Pyramids of Sacrifice: Political Ethics and Social Change.* New York: Basic Books.

———. 1977. *Facing Up to Modernity.* New York: Basic Books.

Berger, Peter, Brigitte Berger, and Hansfried Kellner. 1973. *The Homeless Mind: Modernization and Consciousness.* New York: Random House.

Bickel, Paul J. 1962. "Sunday at the Old Order Mennonite Meeting-House." *Mennonite Historical Bulletin* (October): 4–5.

Blackboard Bulletin. 1957–. Aylmer, Ont.: Pathway Publishers. [Monthly periodical published for Old Order Amish and Mennonite teachers.]

The Body's Building Blocks. 1999. Churchtown, Pa.: Schoolaid.

Bourdieu, Pierre. 1977. *Outline of a Theory of Practice.* Cambridge: Cambridge University Press.

Bourdieu, Pierre, and Loic J. D. Wacquant. 1992. *An Invitation to Reflexive Sociology.* Chicago: University of Chicago Press.

Braght, Thieleman J. van, comp. 1985. *The Bloody Theatre; or, Martyrs Mirror.* 14th ed. Scottdale, Pa.: Herald Press. [Originally published in Dutch (Dordrecht, 1660).]

Brende, Eric. 2004. *Better Off: Flipping the Switch on Technology.* New York: Harper Collins.

Brown, Richard D. 1976. *Modernization: The Transformation of American Life, 1600–1865.* Toronto: McGraw-Hill Ryerson.

Brubacher, Paul H. 1984. "Dimensions of Social Interaction Between Old Order Mennonites and Non-Mennonites in the Mount Forest Area." Master's thesis, University of Guelph.

Burkholder, Mabel. 2003. *The Herrs and Lancaster County's Other First Mennonite Pioneers.* Morgantown, Pa.: Masthof Press.

Burkholder, Roy S. 1997. *Be Not Conformed to This World.* Morgantown, Pa.: Masthof Press.

Burridege, Kate. 2002. "Steel Tyres or Rubber Tyres—Maintenance or Loss: Pennsylvania German in the 'Horse and Buggy' Communities of Ontario." In *Language Endangerment and Language Maintenance,* ed. David Bradley and Maya Bradley, 203–29. London: Routledge Curzon.

Carlson, Stephanie M., Marjorie Taylor, and Gerald R. Levin. 1998. "The Influence of Culture on Pretend Play: The Case of Mennonite Children." *Merrill-Palmer Quarterly* 44 (4): 538.

Clymer, Floyd. 1950. *Treasury of Early American Automobiles*. New York: Bonanza Books.

Collection of Psalms and Hymns Suited to Various Occasions. 1977. Philadelphia: National Publishing Company. [Compiled by a committee of Mennonites.]

Collins, Randall. 2004. *Interaction Ritual Chains*. Princeton: Princeton University Press.

Confession of Faith of the Mennonites: Church Forms and Guidelines of the Weaverland Conference. 1996. Ministers' edition. Lancaster County, Pa.: Weaverland Conference.

Conversation on Saving Faith for the Young in Questions and Answers. 1984. Adamstown, Pa.: Martin M. Rissler. [Some essays were written by Gerhard Roosen (1612–1711), a Mennonite bishop in Northern Germany. A committee of Mennonites in Ephrata (Pa.) revised it several times, most recently in 1974.]

Cronk, Sandra L. 1977. "Gelassenheit: The Rites of the Redemptive Process in Old Order Amish and Old Order Mennonite Communities." Ph.D. diss., University of Chicago.

———. 1981. "Gelassenheit: The Rites of the Redemptive Process in Old Order Amish and Old Order Mennonite Communities." *Mennonite Quarterly Review* (January): 5–44.

Dewalt, Mark W., and Bonnie K. Troxell. 1989. "Old Order Mennonite One-Room School: A Case Study." *Anthropology and Education Quarterly* 20:308–25.

Directory of the Groffdale Conference Mennonite Churches. 1987. Kutztown, Pa.: Laura N. Shirk.

———. 1992. 2nd ed. Kutztown, Pa.: Laura N. Shirk and Beatrice N. Shirk.

———. 1997. 3rd ed. Kutztown, Pa.: Laura N. Shirk and Beatrice N. Shirk.

———. 2002. 4th ed. Kutztown, Pa.: Laura N. Shirk and Beatrice N. Shirk.

Driedger, Leo, and Donald B. Kraybill. 1994. *Mennonite Peacemaking: From Quietism to Activism*. Scottdale, Pa.: Herald Press.

Dundes, Alan. 1972. "Folk Ideas as Units of World View." In *Toward New Perspectives in Folklore*, ed. Américo Paredes and Richard Bauman. Austin: The University of Texas Press.

———. 1980. *Interpreting Folklore*. Bloomington: Indiana University Press.

Durkheim, Emile. 1984. *The Division of Labor in Society*. Trans. George Simpson. Glencoe, Ill.: Free Press. (Orig. pub. 1893, in French; first English trans., 1933.)

Dyck, Cornelius J. 1993. *An Introduction to Mennonite History: A Popular History of the Anabaptists and the Mennonites*. 3rd ed. Scottdale, Pa.: Herald Press.

Eaton, Joseph W. 1952. "Controlled Acculturation: A Survival Technique of the Hutterites." *American Sociological Review* 17:331–40.

Ein Gesangbuch Von Deutsche Melodies: Groffdale Conference. 2000. Hillsboro, Ohio: Philip A. Weaver.

Ellul, Jacques. 1997. *The Meaning of the City.* Carlisle, U.K.: Paternoster Publishing. (Orig. pub. 1912.)

Epp, Frank H. 1974. *Mennonites in Canada, 1786–1920: The History of a Separate People.* Toronto: Macmillan of Canada.

Etzioni, Amitai. 1993. *The Spirit of Community: Rights, Responsibilities, and the Communitarian Agenda.* New York: Crown Publishers.

Ferrara, Peter J. 2003. "Social Security and Taxes." In *The Amish and the State,* 2nd ed., ed. Donald B. Kraybill, 125–43. Baltimore: Johns Hopkins University Press.

Fretz, J. Winfield. 1989. *The Waterloo Mennonites: A Community in Paradox.* Waterloo, Ont.: Wilfrid Laurier University Press.

Giddens, Anthony. 1991. *Modernity and Self-Identity: Self and Society in the Late Modern Age.* Stanford, Calif.: Stanford University Press.

Glassie, Henry. 1968. *Pattern in the Material Folk Culture of the Eastern United States.* Philadelphia: University of Pennsylvania Press.

God's Golden Children. 2002. Comp. Floyd and Katie Martin. Millersburg, Pa.: Brookside Printing.

Good, Elijah. 1976. "I See Beauty in All These Old Timbers." Told by Phares Hurst to Diana Cohen, et al., in *I Wish I Could Give My Son a Wild Raccoon,* ed. Eliot Wigginton, 178–95. New York: Anchor Books.

Good, Gary. 1996. *Glaube, Hoffnung, und Liebe: Faith, Hope, and Love.* Morgantown, Pa.: Masthof Press.

Gopin, Marc. 2000. "The Religious Component of Mennonite Peacemaking and Its Global Implications." In *From the Ground Up: Mennonite Contributions to International Peacemaking,* ed. Cynthia Sampson and John P. Lederach, 233–55. New York: Oxford University Press.

Gordon, Milton M. 1997. *Assimilation in American Life: The Role of Race, Religion, and National Origins.* Toronto: Oxford University Press.

Graber, Robert Bates. 1979. "The Sociological Differentiation of a Religious Sect: Schisms Among the Pennsylvania German Mennonites." Ph.D. diss., University of Wisconsin-Milwaukee.

Grimes, Ronald L. 2002. *Deeply Into the Bone: Re-inventing Rites of Passage.* New York: University of California Press.

Harvey, David. 1990. *The Condition of Postmodernity: An Enquiry into the Origins of Cultural Change.* Oxford: Basil Blackwell.

Hess, Thomas I. 1978. "The Present Day Migration of the Old Order Mennonites." Unpublished seminar paper, Goshen College Library, Goshen, Indiana.

Hill, Jane H., and Bruce Mannheim. 1992. "Language and Worldview." In *Annual Review of Anthropology*, ed. Bernard J. Siegel, 381–406. Palo Alto: Annual Reviews.

Historic Schaefferstown Record. July and April 1987. Ed. C. Richard Beam. Schaefferstown, Pa.: Historic Schaefferstown.

Holtz Kay, Jane. 1997. *Asphalt Nation: How the Automobile Took Over America and How We Can Take It Back*. New York: Crown Publishers.

Home Messenger. [A monthly publication of the Weaverland (Horning) Mennonite Conference.]

Hoover, Amos B. 1978. "A History of the Martindale Church." *Home Messenger* (April): 10–11; (May): 7–10.

———, trans., ed., and comp. 1982. *The Jonas Martin Era (1875–1925)*. Denver, Pa.: Muddy Creek Farm Library.

———. 1984. "A Tear for Jonas Martin: Old Order Mennonite Origins in Lancaster County." *Pennsylvania Folklife* 33 (2): 90.

———. 1990. "Historical Sketches of the Weaverland Conference Mennonite Congregations." In *Directory of the Weaverland Conference*, comp. Lucille H. Martin, appendix, 1–43. Lititz, Pa.: Lucille H. Martin.

———, comp. 2005. *Whether by Word or Epistle: The Letters of Frank W. Hurst, 1920–1940*. Ephrata, Pa.: Muddy Creek Farm Library.

Hoover, Amos B., with David L. Miller and Leonard Freeman. 1978. "The Old Order Mennonites." In *Mennonite World Handbook*, ed. Paul N. Kraybill, 374–81. Carol Stream, Ill.: Mennonite World Conference.

Hoover, John David. 1990. "An Old Order Mennonite Wedding Ceremony in Pennsylvania." *Pennsylvania Mennonite Heritage* 13 (3): 11.

Hoover, Titus B. 1998. *Unpleasant Questions About the Car: From 1920 to 1998*. Port Trevorton, Pa.: T. B. Hoover.

Horning, Alice M., Adin N. Zimmerman, Eli M. Reiff, and Luke H. Weaver, eds. 2004. *Buffalo Valley History: History of the Groffdale Conference Mennonites in Union County, Pennsylvania, 1960–2004*. Morgantown, Pa.: Masthof Press.

Horning, Michael Z. 1996. *Collection of Old Letters Written by or to Mennonite Bishop Moses G. Horning, 1889–1996*. Newmanstown, Pa.: Michael Z. Horning.

Horst, Irvin B., ed. and trans. 1988. *Mennonite Confession of Faith*. Lancaster, Pa.: Lancaster Mennonite Historical Society. [The Dordrecht Confession of Faith was adopted by the Mennonites in Dordrecht, Holland, 1 April 1632.]

Horst, Isaac R. 1979. *Up the Conestoga.* Mount Forest, Ont.: Isaac R. Horst.

———. 1983. *Separate and Peculiar.* Mount Forest, Ont.: Isaac R. Horst.

———. 1985. *Close Ups of the Great Awakening.* Mount Forest, Ont.: Isaac R. Horst.

———. 1989. "Introducing the Old Order Mennonites." *Mennonite Reporter,* 9 January.

———. 1990. "Our Deprived Children." *Family Life* (April): 22.

———. 1991. "Old Order Youth Prepare to Join the Church." *Mennonite Reporter,* 18 February.

———. 1993. "The Role of Women." *Family Life* (November): 27–29.

———. 2000. *A Separate People.* Scottdale, Pa.: Herald Press.

Horst, Mary Ann. 1992. *My Old Order Mennonite Heritage.* Kitchener, Ont.: Pennsylvania Dutch Crafts and Local Books.

———. 1996. *Reminiscings of Mennonite Life in Waterloo County: Reflections on the Journey from the Old Order Mennonite World to Modern Times.* Kitchener, Ont.: M. A. Horst.

Hostetler, Beulah Stauffer. 1992. "The Formation of the Old Orders." *Mennonite Quarterly Review* 66 (1): 5–25.

Hostetler, John A. 1980. *Amish Society.* 3rd ed. Baltimore: Johns Hopkins University Press.

———. 1993. *Amish Society.* 4th ed. Baltimore: Johns Hopkins University Press.

Hostetler, John A., and Gertrude E. Huntington. 1992. *Amish Children.* Orlando, Fla.: Harcourt College Publishers.

Hurd, James P. 1983a. "Comparison of Isonymy and Pedigree Analysis Measures in Estimating Relationships Between Three 'Nebraska' Amish Churches in Central Pennsylvania." *Human Biology* 55 (2): 349–55.

———. 1983b. "Kin Relatedness and Church Fissioning Among the 'Nebraska' Amish of Pennsylvania." *Social Biology* 30 (1–2): 59–66.

———. 1985a. "Kissing Cousins: Frequencies of Cousin Types in 'Nebraska' Amish Marriages." *Social Biology* 32 (1–2): 82–89.

———. 1985b. "Sex Differences in Mate Choice in the 'Nebraska' Amish of Central Pennsylvania." *Ethnology and Sociobiology* 6:49–57.

———. 1997. "Marriage Practices Among the 'Nebraska' Amish of Mifflin County, Pennsylvania." *Pennsylvania Mennonite Heritage* 20 (2): 20–24.

———. 2005. "The Shape of High Fertility in a Traditional Mennonite Population." Unpublished manuscript.

Hurst, Emma. 1960. "Moses G. Horning and the Old Order Divisions in Pennsylvania." *Mennonite Historical Bulletin* (April): 1–3. [Also appeared as a twelve-page pamphlet printed by the author.]

In Meiner Jugend: A Devotional Reader in German and English. 2000. Aylmer, Ont.: Pathway Publishers.

Johnson-Weiner, Karen. Forthcoming. *Train Up a Child: Old Order Amish and Mennonite Schools.* Baltimore: Johns Hopkins University Press.

Juhnke, James C. 1989. *Vision, Doctrine, War: Mennonite Identity and Organization in America, 1890–1930.* The Mennonite Experience in America, vol. 3. Scottdale, Pa.: Herald Press.

Kaylor, Steven L. 1987. "The Old Order Mennonite Meetinghouses of Lancaster County, Pennsylvania." *Historic Schaefferstown Record* 21 (3): 47–68.

Keim, Albert N., ed. 1975. *Compulsory Education and the Amish: The Right Not to Be Modern.* Boston: Beacon Press.

Kern, Stephen. 1983. *The Culture of Time and Space: 1880–1918.* Cambridge: Harvard University Press.

Klaassen, Walter. 2001. *Anabaptism: Neither Catholic Nor Protestant.* 3rd ed. Kitchner, Ont.: Pandora Press.

Klimuska, Edward. 1993. "Old Order Lancaster County." Lancaster, Pa.: Lancaster Newspapers. [Tabloid reprint of a series of six articles in the *Lancaster New Era*.]

Kniss, Fred. 1997. *Disquiet in the Land: Cultural Conflict in American Mennonite Communities.* New Brunswick, N.J.: Rutgers University Press.

Kraybill, Donald B. 1994. "The Amish Encounter with Modernity." In *The Amish Struggle with Modernity,* ed. Donald B. Kraybill and Marc A. Olshan, 21–33. Hanover, N.H.: University Press of New England.

———. 2001. *The Riddle of Amish Culture.* Rev. ed. Baltimore: Johns Hopkins University Press.

———, ed. 2003. *The Amish and the State.* Rev. ed. Baltimore: Johns Hopkins University Press.

Kraybill, Donald B., and Carl F. Bowman. 2001. *On the Backroad to Heaven: Old Order Hutterites, Mennonites, Amish, and Brethren.* Baltimore: Johns Hopkins University Press.

Kraybill, Donald B., and C. Nelson Hostetter. 2001. *Anabaptist World USA.* Scottdale, Pa.: Herald Press.

Kraybill, Donald B., and Steven M. Nolt. 2004. *Amish Enterprise: From Plows to Profits.* 2nd ed. Baltimore: Johns Hopkins University Press.

Kraybill, Donald B., and Marc A. Olshan, eds. 1994. *The Amish Struggle with Modernity.* Hanover, N.H.: University Press of New England.

Lancaster County Map and Directory of Groffdale Conference Mennonites. 2003. Ephrata, Pa.: Allen Hoover. [Updated and published periodically.]

Lancaster (Pa.) Intelligencer Journal. Lancaster, Pa.: Lancaster Newspapers.

Lancaster (Pa.) New Era. Lancaster, Pa.: Lancaster Newspapers.

Lapp, Christ S. 1991. *Pennsylvania School History, 1690–1990.* Elverson, Pa.: Mennonite Family History.

Lee, Daniel Blair. 1995. "Black Hats and White Bonnets: Religious Ritual and Belief Among Weaverland Conference Mennonites." Ph.D. diss., Syracuse University.

———. 2000. *Old Order Mennonites: Rituals, Beliefs, and Community.* Chicago: Burnham.

Leid, Noah W. 1991. *History of the Bowmansville Mennonites and Related Congregations, Old Order Groups.* East Earl, Pa.: Noah W. Leid.

Lewin, Kurt. 1951. *Field Theory in Social Science.* New York: Harper.

Loewen, Harry, and Steven M. Nolt. 1996. *Through Fire and Water: An Overview of Mennonite History.* Scottdale, Pa.: Herald Press.

Luthy, David. 1986. *The Amish in America: Settlements that Failed, 1840–1960.* Aylmer, Ont.: Pathway Publishers.

MacMaster, Richard K. 1985. *Land, Piety, Peoplehood: The Establishment of Mennonite Communities in America, 1683–1790.* Scottdale, Pa.: Herald Press.

Madsen, Richard, et al., eds. 2002. *Meaning and Modernity: Religion, Polity, and Self.* Berkeley and Los Angeles: University of California Press.

Mankind Marvelously Made. 2001. Churchtown, Pa.: Schoolaid.

Martin, Donald. 2003. *Old Order Mennonites of Ontario: Gelassenheit, Discipleship, Brotherhood.* Kitchener, Ont.: Pandora Press.

Martin, Raymond S., and Elizabeth S. Martin. 1985. *Bishop Jonas H. Martin: His Life and Genealogy.* Baltimore: Gateway Press.

McShane, Clay. 1994. *Down the Asphalt Path: The Automobile and the American City.* New York: Columbia University Press.

The Mennonite Encyclopedia: A Comprehensive Reference Work on the Anabaptist-Mennonite Movement. 1955–90. Vols. 1–4, 1955–59. Hillsboro, Kans.: Mennonite Brethren Publishing House; Newton, Kans.: Mennonite Publication Office; Scottdale, Pa.: Mennonite Publishing House. Vol. 5, 1990. Scottdale, Pa.: Herald Press.

Meyers, Thomas J. 1991. "Population Growth and Its Consequences in the Elkhart-LaGrange Old Order Amish Settlement." *Mennonite Quarterly Review* 65 (3): 308–21.

———. 1994. "The Old Order Amish: To Remain in the Faith or to Leave." *Mennonite Quarterly Review* 68 (3): 378–95.

———. 2003. "Education and Schooling." In *The Amish and the State,* ed. Donald B. Kraybill, 87–106. Baltimore: Johns Hopkins University Press.

Meyers, Thomas J., and Steven M. Nolt. 2005. *An Amish Patchwork: Indiana's Old Orders in the Modern World*. Bloomington, Ind.: Quarry Books.

Miller, Joseph S. 2004. "The Peculiar Beauty of *Gelassenheit*: An Interview with Amos B. Hoover." In *The Measure of My Days*, ed. Reuben Z. Miller and Joseph S. Miller, 201–27. Telford, Pa.: Cascadia Publishing House.

Miller, Stephen D., comp. 2001. *Em Schteffi Miller Sei Waddebuch*. Millersville, Pa.: The Center for German Studies.

Nolt, Harvey H. 1999. *Gedichte: Poems and Writing of Harvey H. Nolt, 1919–1975*. Comp. Luke Nolt. Sugar Creek, Ohio: Carlisle Printing.

Nolt, Steven M. 1992. "Church Discipline in the Lancaster Mennonite Conference: The Printed Rules and Discipline, 1881–1968." *Pennsylvania Mennonite Heritage* 15 (4): 2–16.

Oberlin, Sarah B., and Esther R. Ayers. 1997. *A Heritage That Money Can't Buy: My Growing Up Years as an Old Order Mennonite*. New York: Cas-Ananda Publishing.

Olshan, Marc A. 1994. "Amish Cottage Industries as Trojan Horse." In *The Amish Struggle with Modernity*, ed. Donald B. Kraybill and Marc A. Olshan, 133–46. Hanover, N.H.: University Press of New England.

Overholser, J. Spenser. 1978. "The Terre Hill Oberholtzer Family." *Pennsylvania Mennonite Heritage* 1 (2): 2–8.

Pennsylvania Mennonite Heritage. Lancaster, Pa.: Lancaster Mennonite Historical Society. [Quarterly.]

Peters, John F. 1987. "Socialization Among the Old Order Mennonites." *International Journal of Comparative Sociology* 28 (3–4): 211–23.

———. 1994. "Old Order Mennonite Economics." In *Anabaptist/Mennonite Faith and Economics*, ed. C. Redekop, V. Krahn, and S. Steiner, 153–75. New York: University Press of America.

———. 2000. "The Old Order Mennonites: Application of Family Life Cycle Stages." In *Maintaining Our Differences: Minority Families Within Multicultural Societies*, ed. C. Harvey, 1–16. London: Ashgate Publishing.

———. 2003. *The Plain People: A Glimpse at Life Among the Old Order Mennonites of Ontario*. Kitchener, Ont.: Pandora Press.

Puffenberger, E. G. 2003. "Genetic Heritage of the Old Order Mennonites of Southeastern Pennsylvania." *American Journal of Medical Genetics* 121 (1): 18–31.

Puffenberger, E. G., K. Hosada, S. S. Washington, K. Nakao, D. de Wit, M. Yanagisawa, and A. Chakravarti. 1994. "A Missense Mutation of the Endothelin-B Receptor Gene in Multigenic Hirschsprung's Disease." *Cell* 79 (7): 1257–66.

Recipes from the Heart of Union County: Our Children's Special Needs. 2003. Kearney, Neb.: Morris Press Cookbooks.

Redekop, Calvin. 1989. *Mennonite Society.* Baltimore: Johns Hopkins University Press.

Reich, Rob. 2002. *Bridging Liberalism and Multiculturalism in American Education.* Chicago: University of Chicago Press.

Reid, Judson. 2004. "Oomycetes and Anabaptists in the Finger Lakes: Biological Management of Pythium in Greenhouse Grown Vegetables." Master's thesis, Cornell University.

Rissler, Martin, comp. 2004. *Records of Ordinations of the Old Order Mennonites Groffdale Conference Churches, 1750 to 2004.* Recorded by Israel S. Martin and updated by Earl Z. Weaver. Ephrata, Pa.: Grace Press.

Ruth, John Landis. 2001. *The Earth Is the Lord's: A Narrative History of the Lancaster Mennonite Conference.* Scottdale, Pa.: Herald Press; Telford, Pa.: Cascadia Publishing House.

Sale, Kirkpatrick. 1982. *Human Scale.* New York: Putnam.

———. 1995. *Rebels Against the Future: The Luddites and Their War on the Industrial Revolution.* Reading, Mass.: Addison-Wesley.

Schedules of the Groffdale Conference Mennonite Churches. 2005. New Holland, Pa.: Groffdale Conference. [Includes churches in Indiana, Iowa, Kentucky, Michigan, Missouri, New York, Ohio, Pennsylvania, and Wisconsin. Also includes Old Order Virginia Conference Mennonite Churches.]

Schlabach, Theron F. 1977. "Reveille for *Die Stillen im Lande:* A Stir Among Mennonites in the Late Nineteenth Century." *Mennonite Quarterly Review* 51 (July): 213–26.

———. 1980. *Gospel Versus Gospel: Mission and the Mennonite Church, 1863–1944.* Scottdale, Pa.: Herald Press.

———. 1988. *Peace, Faith, Nation: Mennonites and Amish in Nineteenth-Century America.* Scottdale, Pa.: Herald Press.

Schumacher, E. F. 1973. *Small Is Beautiful: Economics as if People Mattered.* New York: Harper and Row.

Schwartz, Barry. 2004. *The Paradox of Choice.* New York: Harper Collins.

Scott, Stephen E. 1986. *Why Do They Dress That Way?* Intercourse, Pa.: Good Books.

———. 1988. *The Amish Wedding and Other Special Occasions of the Old Order Communities.* Intercourse, Pa.: Good Books.

———. 1996. *Old Order and Conservative Mennonite Groups.* Intercourse, Pa.: Good Books.

Shirk, I. N. 2002. "A Brief History of the Old Order Mennonites, Groffdale Conference." In *Directory of the Groffdale Conference Mennonite Churches*, 4th ed.,
985–90. Kutztown, Pa.: Laura N. Shirk and Beatrice N. Shirk.

Shirk, John B. 1998. *History of the Groffdale Conference in Missouri, 1970–1998*. Morgantown, Pa.: Masthof Press.

Shively, Tony. 2004. "The Marriage of Aaron and Rachel." In *Buffalo Valley History:
History of the Groffdale Conference Mennonites in Union County, Pennsylvania, 1960–2004*, ed. Alice M. Horning, Adin N. Zimmerman, Eli M. Reiff,
and Luke H. Weaver, 353–59. Morgantown, Pa.: Masthof Press.

Shoemaker, Alfred L. 1956–57. "'Team' Mennonites." *The Pennsylvania Dutchman*
8 (2).

———. 1960. "'Horse-and-Buggy' Mennonites." *The Pennsylvania Dutchman* 2 (supplement).

Siegal, Bernard J. 1970. "Defensive Structuring and Environmental Stress." *American Journal of Sociology* 76 (July): 11–32.

Smith, Elmer L. 1997. *Meet the Mennonites in Pennsylvania Dutchland*. Lebanon, Pa.:
Applied Arts Publishers.

Smucker, David Rempel. 2004. "Lifting the Joists with Music: The Hymnological
Transition from German to English for North American Mennonites,
1840–1940." In *Singing the Lord's Song in a Strange Land: Hymnody in
the History of North American Protestantism*, ed. Edith L. Blumhofer and
Mark A. Noll, 140–70. Tuscaloosa, Ala.: University of Alabama Press.

Snyder, C. Arnold. 1995. *Anabaptist History and Theology: An Introduction*. Kitchener, Ont.: Pandora Press.

*Statement of Christian Doctrine and Rules and Discipline of the Lancaster Conference
of the Mennonite Church*. 1968. Salunga, Pa.: Lancaster Mennonite Conference.

Stauffer, Jacob W. 1992. *A Chronicle or History Booklet About the So-Called Mennonite Church*, trans. Amos B. Hoover. Lancaster, Pa.: Lancaster Mennonite
Historical Society. (Orig. pub. 1855.)

Stauffer, Romaine. 2003. *Annie's Day of Light*. Morgantown, Pa.: Masthof Press.

Stein, Stephen J. 2003. *Communities of Dissent: A History of Alternative Religions in
America*. New York: Oxford University Press.

Stine, Eugene S. 1996. *Pennsylvania German Dictionary*. Birdsboro, Pa.: The Pennsylvania German Society.

Stoll, Elmo. 1990. "Discipline in the Church." *Family Life* (January): 7–11.

Swartz, David. 1997. *Culture and Power: The Sociology of Pierre Bourdieu*. Chicago:
University of Chicago Press.

Tenner, Edward. 1997. *Why Things Bite Back: Technology and the Revenge of Unintended Consequences.* New York: Alfred A. Knopf.

Toelken, Barre. 1979. *The Dynamics of Folklore.* Boston: Houghton Mifflin.

Tönnies, Ferdinand. 1957. *Community and Society.* New York: Harper and Row. (Orig. pub. 1887.)

Troxell, Bonita Kline. 2002. "An Old Order Mennonite School: Religious and Cultural Mores in an Old Order Mennonite School." Ph.D. diss., Columbia University.

Ulle, Robert F. 1986. "Origins of the Stauffer (Pike) Mennonite Church." *Pennsylvania Mennonite Heritage* 27 (3): 18–21.

Umble, Diane Z. 1996. *Holding the Line: The Telephone in Old Order Mennonite and Amish Life.* Baltimore: Johns Hopkins University Press.

Unpartheyisches Gesangbuch. 1999. 43rd ed. Lancaster County, Pa.: The Amish Book Committee. [The first Mennonite edition was published in 1804. The first Amish edition was published in 1913 by the Lancaster New Era Printing Company.]

Unpartheyisches Gesangbuch: Translation and Lessons. 1997. East Earl, Pa.: Schoolaid.

Wallace, Anthony F. C. 1956. "Revitalization Movements." *American Anthropologist* 58:264–81.

———. 1966. *Religion: An Anthropological View.* New York: McGraw-Hill.

Watters, Ethan. 2003. *Urban Tribes: A Generation Redefines Friendship, Family, and Commitment.* New York: Bloomsbury.

Weaver, J. Denny. 2005. *Becoming Anabaptist: The Origin and Significance of Sixteenth-Century Anabaptism.* 2d edition. Scottdale, Pa.: Herald Press.

Weaver, Martin G. 1931. *Mennonites of the Lancaster Conference.* Scottdale, Pa.: Mennonite Publishing House.

Weber, Max. 1958. *From Max Weber: Essays in Sociology.* Trans. and ed. H. H. Gerth and C. Wright Mills. New York: Oxford University Press.

———. 1992. *The Protestant Ethic and the Spirit of Capitalism.* London: Routledge. (Orig. pub. 1930.)

Weiler, Lloyd M. 1993. "An Introduction to Old Order Mennonite Origins in Lancaster County, Pennsylvania: 1893 to 1993." *Pennsylvania Mennonite Heritage* 16 (4): 2–13.

———. 1995. "Historical Overview of Weaverland Conference Origins." In *Directory of the Weaverland Conference Mennonite Churches,* appendix, 1–34. Lititz, Pa.: Lucille H. Martin.

Weiler, Lloyd M., John B. Martin, James K. Nolt, and Amos B. Hoover. 1995. "Historical Overview of Weaverland Conference Origins." In *Directory of the*

Weaverland Conference Mennonite Churches, 3rd ed. Womelsdorf, Pa.: Ruth Ann Wise.

———. 2004. "The *Unpartheyisches Gesangbuch*: Two Hundred Years of a Mennonite Hymnal." *Pennsylvania Mennonite Heritage* 27 (4): 20–29.

Wenger, A. Grace. 1992. *Frontiers of Faithfulness: The Story of the Groffdale Mennonite Church*. Leola, Pa.: Groffdale Mennonite Church.

Wenger, J. C. 1966. *The Mennonite Church in America*. Scottdale, Pa.: Herald Press.

———. 1978. "Anecdotes from Mennonite History: A Tragic Error in Discipline." *Mennonite Reporter*, 15 May.

———. 1985. *The Yellow Creek Mennonites: The Original Mennonite Congregations of Western Elkhart County*. Napanee, Ind.: Evangel Press.

Williams, George H. 2000. *The Radical Reformation*. 3rd ed. Kirksville, Mo.: Truman State University Press.

Williams, Raymond. 1995. *The Sociology of Culture*. Chicago: University of Chicago Press.

Williams, Robert C. 1987. *Fordson, Farmall, and Poppin' Johnny*. Chicago: University of Illinois Press.

Zimmerman, Eli Z. 1982. *Precious Memories*. Gordonville, Pa.: Pequea Publishers.

Zimmerman, Elise. 1987. "Old Order Mennonite Wedding." *Historic Schaefferstown Record* 21 (2): 19–42.

❖ photo credits

Jonathan Charles, pp. 104, 216, 225; Dennis Hughes, pp. 3, 22, 48, 61, 81, 126, 132, 136, 248, 264; James P. Hurd, p. 11; Mennonite Historical Library/Dottie Kauffmann, p. 120; Donald B. Kraybill, pp. 6, 118, 162, 197, 232, 256; Judson Reid, pp. 29, 159, 205, 212; Daniel Rodriguez, pp. 10, 40, 72, 81, 82, 85, 86, 98, 130, 145, 166, 189, 192, 200, 203, 239, 242, 252; Blair Seitz, pp. 104, 177; John B. Shirk, p. 115; Robert Wyble, pp. 45, 57, 171, 174.

⟡ index